The Valuation of Green Commercial Real Estate

Readers of this text may be interested in the following publications from the Appraisal Institute:

- *The Appraisal of Real Estate*
- *The Dictionary of Real Estate Appraisal*
- *Residential Green Valuation Tools*

The Valuation of Green Commercial Real Estate

by Timothy P. Runde, MAI, LEED AP, and Stacey L. Thoyre, WELL AP

Appraisal Institute • 200 W. Madison • Suite 1500 • Chicago, IL 60606 • www.appraisalinstitute.org

The Appraisal Institute advances global standards, methodologies, and practices through the professional development of property economics worldwide.

Reviewers: Sandra K. Adomatis, SRA, LEED Green Associate
Norman G. Miller, PhD
Gary R. Papke, MAI, CRE
John A. Schwartz, MAI

Chief Executive Officer: Frederick H. Grubbe, MBA, CAE
Director of Professional Services and Resources: Evan R. Williams, CAE, IOM
Senior Manager, Publications: Stephanie Shea-Joyce
Senior Book Editor/Technical Writer: Michael McKinley
Senior Technical Book Editor: Emily Ruzich
Manager, Book Design/ Production: Michael Landis

For Educational Purposes Only

The materials presented in this text represent the opinions and views of the author. Although these materials may have been reviewed by members of the Appraisal Institute, the views and opinions expressed herein are not endorsed or approved by the Appraisal Institute as policy unless adopted by the Board of Directors pursuant to the Bylaws of the Appraisal Institute. While substantial care has been taken to provide accurate and current data and information, the Appraisal Institute does not warrant the accuracy or timeliness of the data and information contained herein. Further, any principles and conclusions presented in this publication are subject to court decisions and to local, state and federal laws and regulations and any revisions of such laws and regulations.

This book is sold for educational and informational purposes only with the understanding that the Appraisal Institute is not engaged in rendering legal, accounting or other professional advice or services. Nothing in these materials is to be construed as the offering of such advice or services. If expert advice or services are required, readers are responsible for obtaining such advice or services from appropriate professionals.

Nondiscrimination Policy

The Appraisal Institute advocates equal opportunity and nondiscrimination in the appraisal profession and conducts its activities in accordance with applicable federal, state, and local laws.

21 20 19 18 17 1 2 3 4 5

Library of Congress Cataloging-in-Publication Data

Names: Runde, Timothy P., 1962- author. | Thoyre, Stacey L., author.
Title: The valuation of green commercial real estate / by Timothy P. Runde, MAI, LEED AP, and Stacey L. Thoyre, LEED Green Associate.
Description: Chicago, IL : Appraisal Institute, [2017] | Includes index.
Identifiers: LCCN 2017017808 | ISBN 9781935328704
Subjects: LCSH: Sustainable buildings--Valuation--United States. | Commercial real estate--Valuation--United States.
Classification: LCC HD1393.58.U6 R86 2017 | DDC 333.33/87230973--dc23 LC record available at https://lccn.loc.gov/2017017808

Table of Contents

About the Authors

Timothy P. Runde, MAI, LEED AP, is a nationally recognized expert in green building valuation. Tim has a long-standing interest in the nexus between the built and natural environments. The combination of his undergraduate studies in zoology and a graduate degree in real estate appraisal and investment analysis from the University of Wisconsin-Madison allows him a unique perspective into the interplay of the environmental, social, and financial factors that sustainability introduces to real estate.

Tim is a sought-after speaker on the effects of green building and sustainability on the valuation of real estate. He has published numerous articles on the valuation of green buildings and is an approved instructor and course reviewer for the Appraisal Institute. He is also a co-developer of an Appraisal Institute course on the valuation of green commercial real estate based on this textbook.

Besides expertise in green building, he maintains an active general appraisal practice with a focus on complex and special-purpose properties. He frequently testifies as an expert witness on a wide range of topics, including diminution in value, eminent domain, bankruptcy, estate, and ad valorem tax assessment.

Stacey L. Thoyre, WELL AP, LEED Green Associate, combines a risk management perspective and an occupant health focus in her approach to the valuation of green real estate. While completing her undergraduate degree in finance and risk management at the University of Wisconsin-Madison, she had the opportunity to learn the fundamentals of real estate valuation theory from renowned real estate professor Dr. James A. Graaskamp.

After working in the risk management field, Stacey later earned a master's degree in writing and is a published author of both fiction and non-fiction. She has co-authored several articles on green building valuation and is the co-developer of an upcoming course on the valuation of green commercial buildings for the Appraisal Institute.

Most recently, she has completed the Appraisal Institute's Valuation of Sustainable Buildings Professional Development Program and is listed in its online registries of residential and commercial appraisers. She also holds both the WELL AP and LEED Green Associate credentials. The WELL AP credential builds on her prior experience as an ACSM Certified Exercise Physiologist and signifies particular knowledge and expertise regarding the health effects of the built environment.

Tim and Stacey are the co-founders of Runde & Partners, Inc., a commercial real estate appraisal and consultancy firm based in San Francisco. They grew up in Wisconsin, where they met and married, and have resided in San Francisco for nearly 30 years.

Acknowledgments

Writing a book is a humbling experience. It is, as Stacey's father might say, "a real character builder." The amount of effort required by a great number of people could make one wonder how any book realizes publication. In the process, one learns much about a subject, but it also becomes clear how much there is to learn and how much others have done to advance the state of knowledge. This book could not have been possible without the work of the green building thought pioneers and researchers, many of whom continue to contribute to the body of knowledge.

We are also grateful for the generosity of the green building owners and occupiers who shared their experience, including Denis Hayes and the Bullitt Foundation, the David and Lucile Packard Foundation, Byron Benton and the JATC, and developer Kevin Bates, as well as the many architects, designers, and engineers who patiently answered our questions and accompanied us on countless green building tours.

Sandra K. Adomatis, SRA, LEED Green Associate, deserves special mention for her pioneering leadership in green building valuation and her early support and encouragement. We deeply value her professional contributions to green building valuation and cherish her friendship.

The diligent efforts of the reviewers, particularly Gary R. Papke, MAI, CRE, and the editorial team in the Appraisal Institute Publications Department were essential to realizing this text. Thank you especially to Stephanie Shea-Joyce and Emily Ruzich for their countless hours of painstaking work and patience with our need to get it "just right."

We are also thankful for the support of the Appraisal Institute and particularly for the support of Frederick H. Grubbe, MBA, CAE, Scott Robinson, MAI, SRA, AI-GRS, M. Lance Coyle, MAI, SRA, Jim Amorin, MAI, SRA, AI-GRS, Richard L. Borges II, MAI, SRA, AI-GRS, AI-RRS, and Stephen S. Wagner, MAI, SRA, AI-GRS. We appreciate the opportunity to help the Appraisal Institute lead the way in green building valuation and education.

Thanks as well to the late Professor James A. Graaskamp for providing the inspiration to pursue a career in real estate and for the multi-disciplined approach that set the Wisconsin real estate program apart. In writing this book, we often wondered what "Chief" might think about the effects of green building and sustainability on the valuation of real estate. All we know for sure is that he would not have hesitated to tackle the subject and we doubt he would have been surprised by the current evolution of the built environment.

A final thanks to Arlene and Howard Thoyre, whose unflagging support helped us navigate writing a book while simultaneously starting a new appraisal and consulting practice.

Foreword

Green building practices are being widely adopted in commercial real estate, and valuation professionals must master a new set of terminology and concepts to identify and understand green property characteristics and recognize their effects on market demand and value.

The Valuation of Green Commercial Real Estate explains how valuation professionals can incorporate the effect of green building into current appraisal methodology. Chapter 1 begins the discussion by providing a working definition of *green.* Chapters 2 and 3 review green building rating systems and green building design and construction techniques, while Chapters 4 and 6 focus on how to analyze the influence of green building in a particular market. The remaining chapters discuss how to address green building in the appraisal process, including the determination of scope of work, highest and best use analysis, and the application of the approaches to value. Specialized topics such as the valuation of distributed energy generation and the influence of rebates, financing, and tax incentives are discussed in Chapters 10 and 11. Detailed case studies and informative illustrations are provided throughout the text.

The Valuation of Green Commercial Real Estate is a comprehensive guide for practicing appraisers, commercial lenders, investors, developers, brokers, and green building professionals. It is a valuable resource for those who want to keep up and stay ahead of the newest ideas and trends in commercial real estate.

Jim Amorin, MAI, SRA, AI-GRS
2017 President
Appraisal Institute

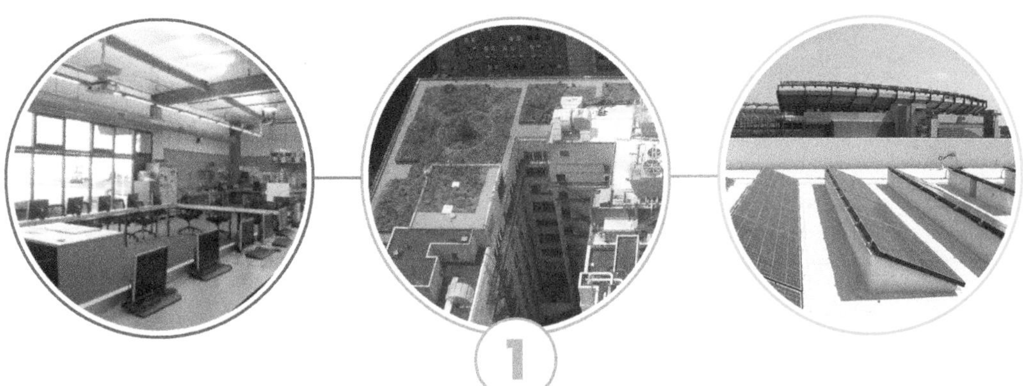

1 What Makes a Building Green?

What is a "green" building? How is a green building different from a "regular" building? Does green building affect the valuation process, and if so, in what ways? Answers to these questions are critical when gauging the value implications of a green building or a conventionally built structure with green features, and when analyzing the effect of changing market demand for green space on non-green properties.

Green building represents a change in the way buildings are designed, constructed, and operated as well as a shift in market demand. These fundamental changes directly affect the valuation process and introduce a new and varied lexicon related to how the built environment is classified. Buildings previously categorized as Class A, B, or C may now also be "green," "high-performing," "sustainable," "net zero," or "regenerative." Concepts such as the resiliency of the structure, site, and surrounding neighborhood, or whether the building's interior environment promotes health and enhances productivity are now entering the discourse. For the valuation professional, many of these terms and concepts are new and often confusing. What is the difference–if any–between a green building and a high-performing building? What does it mean for a building to be "sustainable" or "net zero," or for a site's infrastructure to be "resilient"? And perhaps most importantly, how do these myriad labels influence the valuation process? Does this type of real property require additional data and analysis, and if so, how can these various terms and concepts be parsed so that value effects can be identified and quantified?

Defining Green Building

A single, universally accepted definition of *green building* remains elusive. As will be discussed in Chapter 2, considerable differences may exist even among buildings that are certified as green. While this may at first seem to be unnecessarily confounding, having the flexibility to accommodate customized solutions to achieving green building goals is a key feature of many of the green building rating systems. This flexibility makes the process of identifying and defining a green building more difficult and nuanced for the valuation professional. While it may be tempting to want to reduce green building to a check-box item or a cut-and-dried definition, is it realistic to expect green building to be a homogenous product or attribute? Why should green building be different from any other set of property characteristics that is used as a market differentiator?

Consider the definition of *Class A office space*. The Building Owners and Managers Association (BOMA) International notes that distinguishing between Class A, B, and C space is subjective, relative to a building's peers, and based on numerous factors that may vary between markets or property types.[1] Valuation professionals have witnessed that what is considered Class A office space has evolved over time to include air conditioning, high-speed elevators, and now, in certain central business districts (CBDs) of major markets, LEED certification and Energy Star ratings.[2] Yet in the suburbs of those same markets, *Class A* might be defined differently. It may mean a building must be at least three stories tall or built after 1980. Green certification may or may not be necessary. Therefore, if the definition of *Class A* is not the same today as it was in 1940, may not be the same in the suburbs as in the CBD, and does not have a definite set of standards that apply to all buildings in all markets, why should the definition of *green building* be any different?

What makes a building green will continue to evolve over time at different paces, in different areas, for different property types, and with differing relevance to valuation. Thus, defining "green" in a particular market will require sufficient understanding of green building design and construction to identify the relevant property characteristics and appropriately assess the market's response to them.

1. BOMA International, "Building Class Definitions," accessed May 4, 2017, www.boma.org/research/pages/building-class-definitions.aspx.

2. LEED stands for Leadership in Energy and Environmental Design and is a widely used green building rating system for commercial real estate in the United States. It will be discussed in more depth in Chapter 2.

The Beginnings of Green Building

The concept of sustainability underlies green building.[3] The energy crisis of the 1970s did much to spur interest in energy-efficient buildings, but green buildings are about more than energy efficiency. Sustainability's influence on real estate development is responsible for expanding the focus beyond economic feasibility to include the environmental and societal effects of the built environment. The question, "Is this building cost-effective to build, and can it be operated at a profit to the owner/investor?" expands to include additional questions such as: "How does this property affect the surrounding ecosystem?" and "Does this building enhance occupant productivity and promote occupant health?" This expansion of scope to include non-economic concerns is sometimes referred to as the "triple bottom line," which was coined by John Elkington in the early 1990s to express the concept of sustainability in business terms.

In this respect, green building was not originally conceived as a way to create less expensive buildings with lower operating costs. Rather, its initial objectives addressed the negative effects of the built environment on the natural environment and human health. As is often the case, new technologies and methods may not be cost-effective in the near term.

During the early stages of green building, economic hurdles made market-wide adoption difficult. Green building professionals were very much aware of the need to overcome this economic barrier so that green building could move beyond a niche and into the mainstream. The early green rating systems, such as BREEAM and LEED, provided a common framework that spurred industry growth. In turn, greater experience with green building technologies and practices allowed green building to become more cost-effective.

Green building is still evolving, which contributes to the difficulty in precisely defining what a green building is and is not. For example, some green building advocates have proposed that there should be a distinction between "green buildings" and "sustainable buildings." By focusing on environmental and to a lesser extent, economic outcomes, early rating systems have been criticized for certifying "green" buildings that are not sustainable in the strictest sense. Rating systems have continued to change over time. The LEED rating system, for example, is now at Version 4, with each successive release being more rigorous than the last. Other rating systems, such as the Living Building Challenge, set the bar for what is considered "green" even higher.[4]

---

3. Sustainability, as it applies to real estate valuation, is explored further in Chapter 4.
4. Green building rating systems and the valuation process are discussed in more depth in Chapter 2.

From the perspective of the valuation professional, the distinction between green and sustainable is important to the degree that a given market makes a similar distinction. However, this book uses an inclusive definition of *green building* as it is most commonly expressed at this point in time. Thus, the terms *green* or *green building* as used in this book encompass the full spectrum of high-performing, sustainable, and other similar labels, unless specifically noted otherwise. Buildings that do not conform to the concept of green design and construction are referred to throughout this book as "conventional" buildings or structures.[5]

Key Characteristics of Green Building

While the definition of what a green building looks like or how it performs may remain fluid, a general consensus has emerged about the basic practice of green building. Consider the following definition of *green building*:

> The practice of creating structures and using processes that are environmentally responsible and resource-efficient throughout a building's life cycle from siting to design, construction, operation, maintenance, renovation, and deconstruction. This practice expands and complements the classical building design concerns of economy, utility, durability, and comfort. Green building is also known as *sustainable* or *high-performance building*.[6]

While this definition does not directly address the specific physical characteristics of a green building, it does provide a basis for how a green building differs from a conventional one. Namely, green buildings are designed to use resources efficiently during the entire building life cycle, and to incorporate environmental and societal factors, in addition to economic factors, into the building's design, construction, and operation.

green characteristics

This definition also importantly notes that green building "expands and complements" rather than replaces conventional building construction and operation practices, a theme that will recur throughout this book. Green building represents an evolution in building design and construction practices rather than an "either/or" proposition. Green building practices do not disregard the concept that a building should perform competitively on a net operating income-per-square foot basis; rather, they add other performance metrics to be considered, such as energy use intensity, water use, or occupant comfort and productivity. Larger appraisal concepts such as highest and best use analysis do not presume that green is automatically better but rather that green building expands the set of property characteristics to be analyzed in order to determine a property's highest and best use.

5. The goals and strategies pursued in green building design and construction are discussed and described more fully in Chapter 3.

6. *The Dictionary of Real Estate Appraisal*, 6th ed. (Chicago: Appraisal Institute, 2015), 338.

Efficient Use of Resources

Resource efficiency, particularly energy efficiency, has been one of the most ubiquitous aspects of green building to date, to the extent that energy-efficiency is often incorrectly equated with green building. A major goal of green building is the efficient use of all resources–not just energy– in constructing and operating buildings. Furthermore, green building considers resources and systems as an integrated whole, and strives for a balance between resource efficiency and other aspects of building performance, such as indoor air quality and site impacts.

This focus on resource efficiency may seem new when cloaked in the elaborate building technologies now available, but it actually has a long history. If resource efficiency is viewed as the inevitable result of the perceived scarcity of resources, it can be seen as an expected and necessary refinement in construction practices rather than a technologically driven, newly emerging goal.

The sidebar on the next page details an elaborate rain catchment system built in the 1700s in Old San Juan, Puerto Rico. As an island surrounded by saltwater, Puerto Rico needed drinking water for the troops that occupied Castillo San Felipe del Morro and Castillo San Cristóbal, immense fortresses built by the Spanish for protection against invading armies. Without the technology to transform saltwater to potable water or the ability to easily bring freshwater into Old San Juan, the architects and engineers of the time devised a system to use these massive structures to catch, collect, and retain rainwater. Even now, these cisterns are being used to provide non-potable water for restrooms, maintenance facilities, and other uses at the site, which saves money while reducing dependency on the local water system.

This idea of harvesting and retaining rainwater for future use is still used today. Consider the newly built LEED-certified office building in Madison, Wisconsin, shown here, which incorporates a 10,000-gallon cistern to manage excess rainwater runoff while harvesting water for later use in landscape irrigation. When combined with low-flow fixtures, this results in a building designed to use 70% less water than a comparable code-built building.

This 85,000-sq.-ft., LEED-certified office building was completed in 2013 in Madison, Wisconsin. The improvements include a 10,000-gallon underground tank and gray water system used to capture and retain rainwater for non-potable uses.

While water and energy use are commonly measured resources in both green and conventional buildings, additional resources are considered in green buildings. Siting, materials use, and waste management may be less

A New Old Idea

An early example of resource efficiency in building construction can be seen in San Juan, Puerto Rico. Built primarily in the 1700s, Castillo San Cristóbal and Castillo San Felipe del Morro were constructed by the Spanish to guard against invading armies. Both fortresses feature an elaborate rain catchment system, which provided an essential source of freshwater to the troops who occupied the forts. Because a source of freshwater was not readily available, the architects and engineers designed the structures to catch, collect, and retain rainwater using a system of sloped floors and roofs, drainage ducts, and channels that captured and directed the water into large underground cisterns. The images here show some of the drainage channels on the roof and the above-ground wells that led to the underground cisterns.

The National Park Service now operates the forts and has restored many of the cisterns so that they can be used to provide non-potable water for the restrooms, maintenance facilities, and other non-potable water uses at the site. Restoration of the cisterns was completed in 2011, with current capacity at nearly 250,000 gallons at El Morro and more than 500,000 gallons at San Cristóbal.[7]

The drainage channels on the roof of Castillo San Cristóbal

These above-ground wells at Fort San Cristóbal lead to underground cisterns.

familiar to valuation professionals. Examples of site efficiency may include whether or not the site is proximate to public transit and the potential for solar- or wind-powered energy generation. Materials use concerns the materials used for initial construction (such as whether they are from a renewable source or comprised of recycled content) as well as whether the building is designed in such a way as to make future renovations less material-intensive. The use of an under-floor air distribution (UFAD) system for heating and cooling, for example, can make future tenant improvements less costly while also reducing the need for duct work. Re-using existing materials during construction can reduce landfill waste, as can establishing ongoing operations and maintenance systems for separating recycling, compostables, and landfill-destined trash. This approach can yield cost savings to the building owner by reducing the operating expenses for trash removal.

7. National Park Service, "San Juan National Historic Site, Puerto Rico: Cisterns," November 29, 2011, www.nps.gov/saju/learn/news/inauguration-of-restored-rain-harvesting-systems.htm.

Determining whether or not a building is considered resource-efficient largely depends on comparison to other buildings and on mandated thresholds, neither of which are static reference points. Building codes and legislative mandates may prescribe a certain minimum threshold, but those thresholds change over time. An office building that may have been considered energy-efficient several years ago may not be considered energy-efficient in the future if building codes or comparable properties in the market increase efficiency thresholds. In this respect, resource efficiency, much like green building, is defined relatively, in terms of comparison to a conventional benchmark, and can change over time.

Incorporation of Environmental and Societal Factors

Another distinguishing trait of green building is the broadening of focus from a primarily economic one to include consideration of the building's impact on the natural environment and society. The impact of real estate development on the natural environment is addressed most directly through the previously discussed resource-efficiency goals of green building. While the goal may be to reduce environmental impacts, a building using less energy can also offer discernible economic benefits by directly reducing operating expenses and indirectly reducing the risk of increased energy costs in the future. In this way, the goals of green building can operate synergistically to create environmental benefits as well as a positive impact on net operating income. To the extent that benefits can be expressed economically (for example, higher rent or lower operating expenses) and linked to the underlying real estate asset, value will be affected even if the most likely buyer is not sustainability oriented.

The impact of buildings on occupant health has been increasingly studied. Sick building syndrome, a well-publicized problem first identified in the 1980s, links a building's design and construction to deleterious effects on human health. While indoor air quality is still an important and well-researched issue, additional concerns about how building design can positively affect human health are coming to the fore. Numerous studies are examining the effects of lighting on building occupants, from the positive effects of natural light and views to the outdoors to the potential negative effects of excessive exposure to light at night.[8] Emerging building standards are beginning

8. Harvard Medical School, "Blue Light Has a Dark Side," April 9, 2014, www.health.harvard.edu/staying-healthy/blue-light-has-a-dark-side. The American Medical Association (AMA) has adopted guidance for communities regarding the impact of lighting on human health and the environment, citing specific concerns about the effect of certain types of LED-retrofitted street lights on circadian sleep rhythms. The recommendations cited accumulating medical evidence indicating a correlation between disrupted circadian sleep rhythms and various negative human health outcomes, such as poor sleep quality, impaired daytime functioning, and obesity. (AMA, "AMA Adopts Guidance to Reduce Harm from High Intensity Street Lights," June 14, 2016, www.ama-assn.org/ama-adopts-guidance-reduce-harm-high-intensity-street-lights.)

to address the issue of how lighting in the workplace can support healthy circadian rhythms for its occupants.[9]

The effects of a building's design and construction on occupant productivity are also receiving greater attention. Particularly in high-skill labor markets, buildings that are shown to increase productivity or decrease the number of sick days taken by occupants may have an advantage, due to the high cost of labor relative to the cost of the real estate. From the tenant's perspective, labor costs (i.e., human capital) often dwarf occupancy costs. Identifying and quantifying the connection between productivity enhancement and the underlying real estate remains challenging but is a compelling valuation premise for certain aspects of green building design and construction.

Life-Cycle Focus

Green building encompasses a longer-term perspective of the impacts of a building and expands on the traditional appraisal concept of the building life cycle. *Life-cycle analysis*, which may also be referred to as *life-cycle assessment* or *cradle-to-grave analysis*, examines the various impacts of a building over its expected life, from initial construction ("cradle") to disposal ("grave"). Life-cycle analysis can be applied to the lifetime costs of a building, aggregating the operational costs (repairs and maintenance) and end-of-life costs (demolition, disposal, remediation) with the initial capital cost. When applied in this way, it is referred to as *life-cycle cost analysis*.

Life-cycle analysis also considers the operation and maintenance of a building from an environmental and cost/expense perspective. As one architect quipped, "A building is perfect until it's occupied." This idea that a building's occupants and operators have a profound effect on a building gives rise to many of the green building strategies employed in efficient building operation. Operational efficiency can mitigate adverse environmental impacts, which may or may not have a relevant economic impact. However, the emphasis on operational efficiency can directly affect a building's operating expenses and therefore should be of interest to those financing, purchasing, or valuing the property.

Understanding How "Green" Is Defined

The lack of a single definition of *green building* combined with the heterogeneity of green features and green data adds a layer of complexity to data analysis. Understanding how *green* is defined in a given market or context is important when analyzing or tracking market data.

9. The WELL Building Standard is one set of green standards that addresses this issue and others related to occupant health, wellness, and productivity. Wellness-based green rating systems will be discussed in more detail in the sidebar titled "Wellness-Based Design" in Chapter 2 (page 19).

Even if a particular market clearly defines the basic elements of what constitutes a green building, there can be considerable variation in how organizations collect and report the data. For example, if a comparable data service offers green building search parameters, does "green building" in that context incorporate the previously discussed key characteristics, or does it simply mean that the building has some type of energy-efficiency or green building rating (such as Energy Star or LEED)? If the data service tracks ratings such as LEED, does it allow for differences within that rating system, such as LEED Silver versus LEED Gold, or New Construction versus Operations and Maintenance? Additionally, not all green buildings will be labeled or certified as such, so relying on "green data" may eliminate otherwise relevant comparable data points.

The Effects of Green Building on Conventional Properties

Chapter 3 addresses the ways green buildings differ from conventional buildings. However, this distinction can lead to the misperception that green building characteristics are exclusive to green buildings. On the contrary, green building characteristics, also known as green features, can exist in any type of building. New conventional buildings and renovations may incorporate green features, which may have discrete value impacts. An existing 100-year-old, multifamily apartment building that upgrades to an energy-efficient HVAC system and installs low-flow water fixtures and water-efficient landscaping can create a more energy- and water-efficient building. If these particular upgrades lower the building's operating expenses there will likely be a market value impact, even though the upgrades may not be enough to meet the market threshold definition for a green building.

Obsolescence Risk

Green building can also affect conventional buildings through regulation and market expectations. Local regulations, such as building codes, can raise the standards for new construction and renovations by incorporating energy-efficient, green, or sustainable elements. Since building codes are periodically updated and increasingly include green building requirements, the rising threshold creates the potential for obsolescence in properties that do not conform to the more stringent standards. Market interest in green buildings may also push demand toward green or sustainable properties, resulting in additional obsolescence for older, unrenovated properties that lack the market-preferred characteristics. In this manner, green building features may function similarly to the central air conditioning and high-speed elevators that ushered in the era of the modern high-rise after World War II, or regulations such as those for ADA compliance.

This potential for obsolescence in non-green properties may be, in many markets, a more significant and immediate concern than the potential for a "green premium."[10] The matrix in Exhibit 1.1 provides an overview of how a given property may or may not be in sync with the local market's demand. For example, is the subject property a green building in a market that demands green (also known as a sustainability-oriented (SO) market)? Or is the subject a conventionally built property in that same SO market? The former may have a potential for a value premium (sale or rent), whereas the latter may have some obsolescence exposure. On the other hand, a green property in a market that is not sustainability-oriented (NSO) may face superadequacy, yet another type of obsolescence. These issues related to obsolescence risk are discussed in more depth in subsequent chapters.

Exhibit 1.1 **How Does the Subject Property Compare to Its Local Market?**

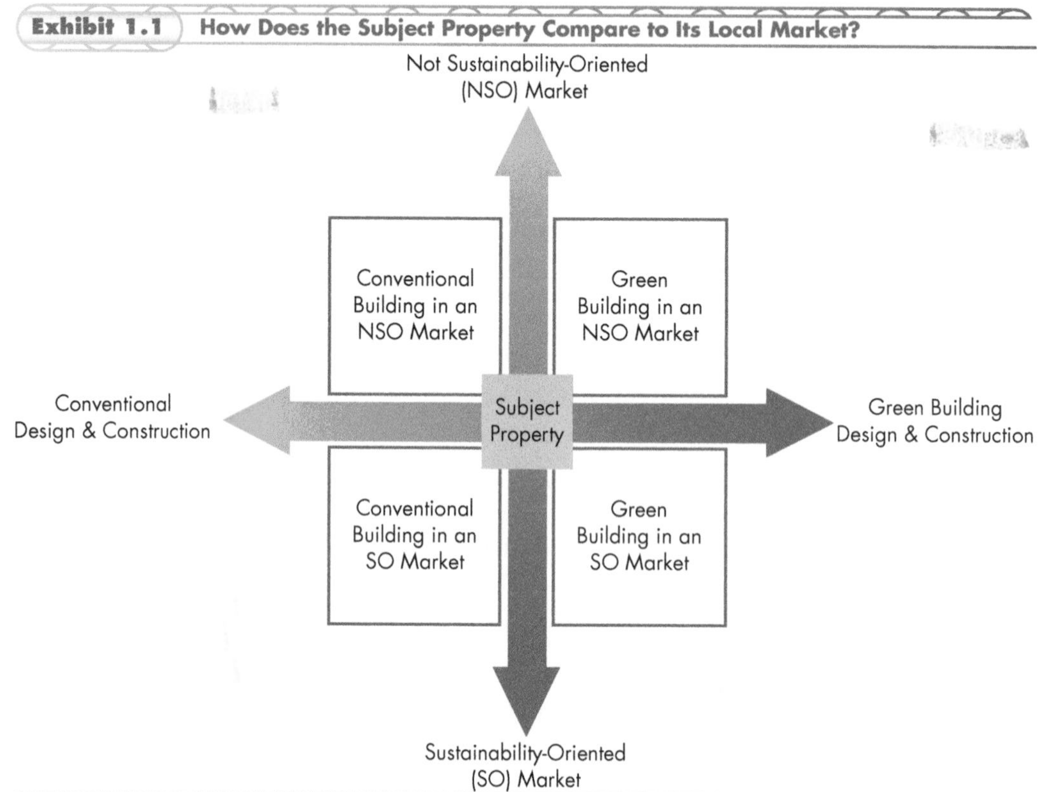

10. The term *green premium*, as noted here, refers to an increase in value (sale or rent) as opposed to a higher cost for building green.

What Does a Green Building Look Like?

Green commercial buildings may be schools, office buildings, retail properties, airports, multifamily developments, industrial buildings, sports facilities, and so on. They may be newly constructed or existing buildings in an urban, suburban, or rural setting. So if a green building can be any type of building in any location, how can the valuation professional tell if the building being observed on paper or in person is green? How can a green building be distinguished from a conventional one?

Identifying green buildings may be one of the biggest challenges facing valuation professionals when integrating green building and sustainability into the valuation process. Green buildings may look very much like conventional buildings. The result of many green building practices may be entirely invisible or difficult to discern from physical observation or a review of operating statements. Third-party certifications, discussed in the next chapter, can be very helpful in this respect. However, a certification alone may not be enough or may not even be necessary.

Verified energy- or water-efficiency performance or on-site energy generation may be more important to certain market participants. In other cases, the occupant experience including the indoor air quality and access to natural light in the workspace may matter most in determining what makes a building green.

Ultimately, green building is largely defined by the relevant market participants–i.e., the owners, operators, occupants, and users of the space. It is therefore likely to vary geographically and over time. However, buildings that more comprehensively address resource efficiency, life cycle focus, and social and environmental impact sensitivity are more likely to meet the green building thresholds in any market and are less likely to fall below the threshold, even if the minimum standards increase over time. The accompanying sidebar takes a closer look at a green office building.

A Closer Look at a Green Building

If no one told you that the 255,000-sq.-ft. office building in this photo was a LEED Gold-certified green building, would you be able to tell that it was?

A LEED Gold-certified office building located in the Bay Area of Northern California

The solar-powered electrical vehicle charging station and the drought-tolerant landscaping may be the first clues that this building is green. One might even notice that the paving is pitched to drain water into the landscaped areas, so that rainwater is managed on site rather than collected in the storm sewer and piped off-site for treatment.

But perhaps more significant to the overall building performance in terms of both energy use and occupant well-being and productivity is something less obvious, the configuration of the floor plates. This building floor plan consists of a "slipped H" design that offsets two, relatively narrow and long floor plates and connects them with a seven-story, glass-enclosed atrium. This design provides extensive glass line on the building exterior and the interior walls of the atrium, allowing natural light in and providing outdoor views to the maximum number of occupants.

The two aerial photographs show how floor plate depth can affect the amount of natural light available to building occupants. The first aerial photo shows this building's floor plate. The two main building sections are each approximately 65 feet wide and are connected by an open atrium. In contrast, the aerial photograph of a comparable conventional building located nearby shows that the building's floor plate has nearly twice the depth, resulting in a significantly lower window line-to-floor area ratio. Despite having a nearly identical floor plate area to the green building, the conventional building offers far fewer opportunities for daylighting. For a single-story building, the lack of window line can be ameliorated by adding skylights. In a multistory building, however, the options are far more limited.

An aerial view of the Bay Area green office building shows that its two main sections are each 65 feet wide and connected by an atrium, providing more opportunity for daylighting. Image obtained via Google Earth.

This aerial view of a nearby conventional Bay Area office building indicates that its floor plate depth is 120 feet, resulting in a lower window line-to-floor area ratio and reduced opportunity for daylighting. Image obtained via Google Earth.

Bringing natural light into a building's interior—a concept known as *daylighting*—not only benefits the building occupants but also reduces energy use for electric lighting. This building's daylighting strategy contributed to a 35% reduction in the building's projected energy use relative to a code-built building. Notice, for example, how far apart the suspended light fixtures in the green building are spaced as shown in the first interior photograph, and compare it to the spacing of the light fixtures in the conventional building shown in the second interior photograph. Less obvious but also important are the daylight sensors that automatically dim the LED lighting when ambient outdoor light is adequate for the task at hand.

While long, narrow floor plates provide certain advantages, trade-offs such as heat gain and glare can negatively impact occupant comfort, satisfaction, and productivity and increase the amount of energy required for cooling the space. Controlling heat and glare in this type of building configuration becomes an important design consideration. The accompanying photograph shows how the green building design incorporates automated blinds, a window film, and perforated vertical fins protruding from the facade to manage heat gain and glare.

This interior view of the green building shows how daylighting can reduce artificial lighting needs. Note the spacing of the suspended light fixtures.

Conventional electric lighting density with typical bay depth at a nearby conventional office building. Note that the ceiling light fixtures are much closer together as compared to the prior photo.

Various strategies can be used to manage glare and solar heat gain associated with narrower floor plates, such as exterior sun shades, window film, and automated window blinds.

Controlling solar heat and glare also contributed to more efficient use of materials for construction, since the daylighting and solar controls allowed work stations to be situated closer to the windows. The resulting increased occupant density meant fewer construction materials used per occupant and less energy used to light and thermally condition the interior.

In addition to increasing the potential for daylighting, the building's seven-story atrium harvests the prevailing westerly winds of the moderate marine climate using two rows of operable, mechanically controlled transom windows that permit natural ventilation of the atrium when outdoor temperatures are between 65°F and 78°F, reducing air conditioning energy use. This strategy is an example of passive design, which is discussed in more detail in the sidebar in Chapter 3 titled "Harnessing 'Free' Energy: Passive Design Basics" (page 58).

Some of the other green features in this building could easily be mistaken for elements that simply reflect current design aesthetics. For example, this building includes design elements that mimic or incorporate nature in the built environment. These are known as *biophilic* elements, which are discussed in detail in the sidebar in Chapter 2 titled "Biophilia: The Human Connection to Nature." (page 40) In this building, the design includes exposed natural wood surfaces, live plants in the atrium, and organic shapes incorporated into the furniture and the design of the carpeting, which is made from recycled fish net.

Occupant health considerations are reflected in the building's prominent central staircase and comparatively obscured elevators, the adjacent fitness center and health clinic, "walking" desks, kitchens located on every floor, and a quiet area that includes circadian pods. Carbon dioxide sensors detect when occupied areas need more fresh air and automatically adjust outdoor air flow based on occupant load to optimize occupant health and productivity. Doors on the copy rooms prevent harmful toner and paper dust from contaminating the work environment, while walk-off mats at the building entrances reduce the amount of contaminants being carried inside.

There are also many additional green elements in this building that might be easy to miss or could not be discerned upon physical observation, such as the following:

- A building management system (BMS) with submeters, digital "smart" controls, and sensors to optimize operational performance
- Water-efficient strategies such as low-flow restroom fixtures, a gray water "purple pipe" plumbing system, and drought-tolerant landscaping
- A green cleaning program to limit occupant and environmental exposure to harmful cleaning agents

Effectively managing glare and heat gain allows for work stations to be situated closer to the window line, as can be seen in this green building's office interior.

The seven-story atrium separates the building's two long and narrow floor plates. It also provides natural light and features operable windows that utilize natural ventilation.

- A dedicated, secure indoor bike parking area with showers to encourage alternative transportation

There are many variations on what a green building looks like as well as the features and strategies used to attain green building goals. What is common to all green buildings is market performance metrics have expanded to include resource efficiency in terms of construction and operation as well as occupant health, well-being, and productivity. This building's green characteristics and design strategies illustrate how a building's use of all resources—energy, water, materials, and site factors—and consideration of occupants and the surrounding community brings a wider perspective to the built environment than what is typically considered in conventional building design and construction.

Incorporating natural elements, such as live plants and exposed natural wood surfaces, in a building's interior is an example of *biophilic* design.

Summary

Green building, both as a process ("building green") and as a product ("a green building"), presents valuation professionals with a series of challenges. Integrating "green" into the valuation process requires the ability to recognize the effects of green building and sustainability on market demand and to identify and understand a new set of property characteristics. Established appraisal methodology can accommodate these changes, but valuation professionals must first master a new set of concepts and terminology.

A universally accepted, single definition of *green building* does not yet exist. There is, however, a general consensus that green building takes a life-cycle approach to building design, construction, and operation, and seeks to create structures that make efficient use of all resources—not just energy—over the entire life of the building. In addition, green buildings address the environmental and societal impacts of the built environment on occupants, the surrounding community, and the natural environment.

This change in how buildings are designed, constructed, and operated directly affects the valuation process. While valuation in the past has been primarily concerned with the economic, social, and environmental impacts *on* the subject property, green building and sustainability expand this process to include the impact *of* the subject property on the surrounding economy, community, and natural environment.

Green features do not exist solely in green buildings. Conventional buildings may also incorporate green building features due to the voluntary actions of property owners or via regulatory mechanisms such as building codes. Conventional buildings may face obsolescence risk due to green building proliferation, particularly in sustainability-oriented markets.

This book focuses on how valuation professionals can integrate green building and sustainability into current appraisal methodology. Chapters 2 and 3 review green building rating systems and the basics of green building design and construction, while Chapters 4 and 6 focus on how to discern and analyze the influence of green building and sustainability in a particular market. The remaining chapters discuss how to address the impact of green building in the various aspects of the appraisal process, including the scope of work, highest and best use analysis, and the approaches to value. Specialized topics such as the valuation of distributed generation and the influence of rebates, financing, and tax incentives are discussed in Chapters 10 and 11.

2 Green Building Rating Systems

A wide variety of labels that certify everything from household products to manufacturing processes to various types of buildings as "green" or "sustainable" has permeated consumer and real estate markets. But with all the labels and claims comes a certain level of natural skepticism: Is the product, process, or property really green, or is it just a product of "greenwashing"? How can valuation professionals assess the credibility of the green claim and know whether or not it may need to be addressed in the valuation process?

"Greenwashing" is any green or environmental claim that is unsubstantiated, unverifiable, or inconsistent with the principle of sustainability.[1] In their role as objective third-party observers of the market, appraisers are acutely attuned to any type of claim that lacks substance as it relates to value. Green building and sustainability claims are no different in this respect. Being able to distinguish between credible and greenwashed claims is important to the valuation professional's role.

Making this distinction is not necessarily an easy or straightforward task, especially in light of the variability related to defining green building. Consider *The Dictionary of Real Estate Appraisal*'s definition of *green building* that was cited in Chapter 1: "The practice of creating structures and using processes that are environmentally responsible and resource-efficient throughout a building's life cycle from siting to design, construction, operation, maintenance, renovation, and deconstruction." While this definition summarizes the key

1. Timothy P. Runde and Stacey L. Thoyre, "Integrating Sustainability and Green Building into the Appraisal Process," *Journal of Sustainable Real Estate* 2, no.1 (2010): 233.

intents behind the practice of green building, it lacks specifics regarding how buildings should be created to achieve those objectives. It is difficult to connect such a broad definition to a particular structure to determine whether or not it meets the definition. For example, what does it mean, in practical terms, to be "environmentally responsible"? How is "resource efficiency" measured?

Green building rating systems, on the other hand, can be both descriptive and prescriptive in terms of how these goals are achieved. They can also stipulate performance metrics. Rating systems help connect the concept of green building to the physical reality of a specific building. In this way, rating systems seek to ensure that the structure created will achieve the desired end result by guiding implementation and assessing conformance. In short, a credible green building rating system can provide an objective measure to the property owner, prospective buyer, tenant, or valuation professional, so that they can assess if a building is actually green or just a product of hype.

Note that the previous statement specified that in order for a rating system to be useful as an objective measure, it must be considered *credible*. Just as with any type of labeling, some labels stipulate more robust or broader-based requirements than others. Furthermore, rating systems for green buildings have evolved over time, with requirements becoming increasingly more stringent as technologies and techniques improve and building codes raise the minimum thresholds for compliance. As discussed in the previous chapter, green building implies a level of comparison to minimum code thresholds and a building's peer group. In a market where building code requirements have become more strict or the dominant rating system has evolved, a building certified as green under a particular rating system five or ten years ago may or may not meet the current market requirements for a green building. It may not even meet the current requirements of the same green rating system.

Various rating systems are emerging that expand upon the initial green building metrics popularized by early rating systems such as BREEAM (Building Research Establishment Environmental Assessment Method) and LEED (Leadership in Energy and Environmental Design). Many of these new systems seek to synergize with and strengthen existing rating systems. For example, the WELL Building Standard, discussed in the accompanying sidebar, focuses on creating buildings that optimize occupant health and well-being. Alternately, the Sustainable SITES Initiative targets landscape factors such as rainwater management, the health of the surrounding ecosystems, and the site's resilience to catastrophic events such as natural disasters.

Since the creation of green building rating systems, there have been varying degrees of market penetration. Federal, state, and local municipalities have often been at the forefront in adopting and codifying green building standards or rating systems.[2] Most recently, the US General Services Administration (GSA) adopted the Sustainable SITES Initiative program and later incorporated it as a reference standard in their 2016 *Facilities Standards for the Public Buildings Service.*[3]

While certain green building rating systems may continue to dominate in a particular market or with a particular property type, it remains unlikely that the numerous systems will coalesce into a single system. Based on the market penetration and regulatory adoption to date, it appears more likely that rating systems will continue to evolve and may even proliferate, at least for the foreseeable future. This presents an unusually challenging situation for valuation professionals who are accustomed to dealing with structures and markets that have generally been much slower to change. Because the basis for obtaining a green certification can shift over time (sometimes rapidly), it is most useful to apply a systemic framework to analyzing a given rating system and discerning the green label's effect on value. The next section of this chapter explores this approach in more depth.

Wellness-Based Design: Can a Building Promote Health and Well-Being?

Emerging health and wellness-based design rating systems consider how the built environment can improve occupant health and well-being. Established in 2014, the WELL Building Standard is administered and managed by the International WELL Building Institute and certified by Green Business Certification Inc. (GBCI), the same organization that certifies LEED buildings for the US Green Building Council (USGBC). While the WELL Building Standard was the first such system, other wellness-based standards are being released such as Fitwel, which was developed by the Centers for Disease Control and Prevention and the GSA.

There are seven categories in the WELL Building Standard: air, water, nourishment, light, fitness, comfort, and mind. These categories, referred to as "concepts," function similarly to the credit categories within the LEED rating system, with the intent to complement LEED and other green building rating systems rather than supplant them.

Unlike other green building rating systems that may or may not require performance assessments, the WELL standard requires that the project meet a base level of performance ("preconditions") for each of the seven concepts. This performance is measured and verified on site by a specifically trained and accredited WELL assessor. This documentation submittal and performance verification process is then repeated every three years, which is a relatively rigorous standard compared to other rating systems.

There are currently two main categories for commercial building certification in the WELL Building Standard: new and existing buildings, and new and existing interiors. Pilot programs are currently in place for additional property types such as retail, educational, and multifamily residential, among others.

The WELL standard employs various strategies within the seven concepts. Some of these strategies are familiar to valuation professionals, such as air quality requirements and lighting standards. Others may be

2. The US General Services Administration (GSA), for example, mandated LEED certification for all of its new building construction projects beginning in 2003. For leased space, Green Globes certification is an allowed option. In January 2011, California enacted CALGreen, which added basic green building practices pertaining to site, water, energy, and indoor air quality to the state-wide building code. At the local level, municipalities in different parts of the country have incorporated green standards or certification requirements for new construction or renovations.

3. GSA, *Facilities Standards for the Public Buildings Service (PBS-P100)*, March 2016, www.gsa.gov/portal/mediaId/127494/fileName/P100_2016.action.

more unfamiliar, such as biophilic design (see the sidebar later in this chapter titled "Biophilia: The Human Connection to Nature" on page 40) and lighting strategies that go well beyond current code requirements to address the built environment's effect on circadian rhythms.

An early case study of the cost and preliminary effect of WELL certification can be seen in CBRE's 48,000-sq.-ft. headquarters building in Los Angeles, the first office building to be WELL certified. The cost of the WELL-certified improvements were reported at $3.60 per square foot, which CBRE noted was a 1.73% cost premium over conventional space build-out. In a study released in 2014, CBRE reported various outcomes of the certification, such as 83% of employees feeling more productive, 93% who felt collaboration was enhanced, and 94% indicating a positive impact on business performance.

Exhibit 2.1 The First WELL-Certified Office

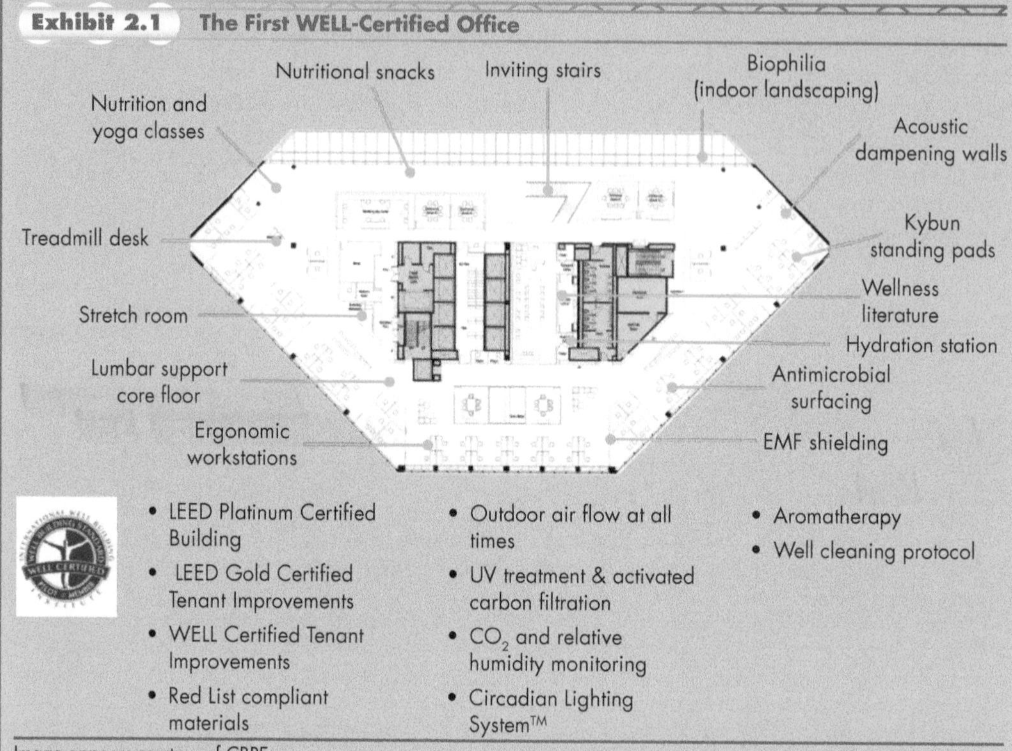

Image appears courtesy of CBRE.

Exhibit 2.1 illustrates the various WELL features incorporated into the CBRE office build-out. The accompanying photographs also illustrate various strategies incorporated in the CBRE space.

Certifications focused on the occupant experience, such as WELL and Fitwel, may impact the valuation process through direct and indirect means. Hard costs may be impacted (as in the CBRE example), and operating expenses may be affected positively or negatively. Indirect impacts may be seen in changes to marketability or vacancy allowance. A valuation professional may also encounter features focused on health and well-being even in buildings that are not formally certified. Just as with other green building features, the key is to recognize them and then assess whether they impact value in the given market. While rating systems such as the WELL Building Standard and Fitwel are relatively new, interest in the built environment's impact on productivity and health is increasing.

The reception area of the CBRE headquarters building includes a variety of biophilic design elements: nature *in* the space (plants and daylighting to bring in natural light), natural analogues (wood flooring), and nature *of* the space (open floor plan providing *prospect*, a biophilic design concept referring to an unimpeded view of space). Photo by Robert Downs Photography.

Floor-to-ceiling glass partition walls allow natural light to penetrate more deeply into interior office spaces and provide occupants views to the outside. This style of interior build-out differs from the traditional hard-walled perimeter office design. The ergonomic desks can also be adjusted for sitting or standing. Photo by Robert Downs Photography.

A prominent, inviting staircase is meant to encourage the use of stairs over elevators. Photo by Robert Downs Photography.

Analyzing Green Building Rating Systems

A green certification, rating, or label may or may not be a requirement for a structure to be considered a green building. A building may be designed, operated, and regarded by the market as green but may lack a formal certification. Conversely, although a building may be purported to be green-certified, the validity and value impact of that green label may not be discernable without further investigation. Regardless of whether a structure is green-rated or -certified, having an understanding of green building rating systems provides the valuation professional with useful knowledge of green features and processes and how they are implemented, documented, measured, and verified.

RSMeans, the cost-estimating service, suggests that a rating system should be science-based (i.e., the results are reproducible), transparent (the requirements for certification are openly available), objective (the certifying body has no conflict of interest), and progressive (the standard goes beyond current minimum requirements).[4] While these are useful criteria, they focus on the merits of the rating system rather than the structure. Valuation professionals need to not only consider the validity of the rating system but need to be able to determine the degree to which the certification or rating impacts value to a specific property at a specific point in time. Thus, valuation requires looking beyond the rating system to the physical reality of the building and its components: How does a particular rating or certification impact the valuation process of the "bricks and sticks"?

Determining whether a green certification or claim has an impact on valuation requires understanding precisely what is being certified and what the certification entails. The following aspects, illustrated in Exhibit 2.2, can serve as a useful framework when analyzing a green building rating system or label through the lens of property valuation:

1. *What* is being rated or certified?
2. *How* is compliance achieved?
3. *Who* is verifying compliance?

What Is Being Rated or Certified?

Identifying what is being rated or certified may seem like an obvious and unnecessary step. The task can quickly become challenging, however, with the wide range of rating systems and green labels currently in use. Therefore, beginning with a solid understanding of exactly *what* is being rated or certified is a crucial part of the analysis.

4. RSMeans, *Green Building: Project Planning and Cost Estimating*, 3rd ed. (Hoboken, NJ: John Wiley & Sons, 2011), Chapter 9.

Exhibit 2.2 Steps in Analyzing a Green Building Rating or Certification

What is being rated or certified?	• Does the rating or certification apply to a building, process, product, individual, community, or organization? • Is it rating single or multiple attributes? Which one(s)? • For real property, does it apply to the entire site and improvements or only a portion of the improvements?
How is compliance achieved?	• Is compliance prescriptive or performance-based? • Is performance based on modeled (predicted) or actual (historical) data?
Who is verifying compliance?	• Is compliance verified by a third-party individual or organization?

Animal, Vegetable, or Mineral?

Green ratings, certifications, and labels can apply to buildings, processes, products, and even individuals, organizations, and communities, as seen in Exhibit 2.3. Within the context of a valuation assignment, it is usually clear when a rating is addressing real property versus products, individuals, or processes. However, because the same or very similar terminology is sometimes used and because much of the green building vocabulary is still new to many valuation professionals and market participants, it is reasonable to begin by considering what is being rated or certified in the broadest sense. Does the LEED label pertain to the building (a LEED-certified building) or an individual on the design team (a LEED-accredited professional)? Does the Energy Star label refer to products contained within the improvements (Energy Star appliances) or a reduced energy use profile relative to its peers (an Energy Star-certified building)? If a property is purported to be "built to LEED standards," is this the same as being LEED-certified? While it is not an exhaustive list of all possible green-related ratings, certifications, or labels, Exhibit 2.3 illustrates the wide range of green labels that may be related to real estate. These items may or may not have concrete or uniform standards or requirements for obtaining the rating, certification, or label.

Even when the terminology does not overlap, it may not be precisely clear what is being rated or certified. For instance, does lumber designated as being "FSC (Forest Stewardship Council)-Certified" apply to the *type* of wood harvested (a product), *how* it was managed or harvested (a process), or both? Alternatively, if a developer states that a project is a "sustainable renovation," what–if any–standards have been met?

While valuers of real property may be most attuned to ratings that apply to buildings, they should also be aware of the other types of green labels. Beyond the issue of not wanting to mistake a product certification as applying to the real property, green product certifications or labels may be relevant when evaluating interior finishes

Exhibit 2.3 Examples of Green Ratings, Certifications, and Labels in Various Categories

Individuals
- LEED AP or Green Associate
- RESNET Green Rater
- Green Globes Professional or Assessor
- HERS Rater
- WELL Assessor

Organizations and Communities
- Certified B Corp
- GRESB score
- Green Lease Leader
- USGBC Member
- STAR Community
- Sustaining Places Recognition

Buildings
- LEED
- Energy Star (for buildings)
- Green Globes
- BREEAM
- HERS
- WELL

Products
- FSC-certified lumber
- Energy Star (appliances)
- Green Seal
- WaterSense
- Greenguard
- Cradle to Cradle Certified
- BuildingGreen Approved

Processes
- FSC Forest Management Certification
- Sustainable renovation or development
- Cradle-to-cradle or regenerative design
- Integrative design process

and tenant build-outs. For example, if a renovation project notes the use of FSC-certified lumber, certain valuation-related questions arise: Does FSC-certified lumber cost more per square foot? Does the local market note any distinction for using this type of lumber? Is there any evidence that this type of lumber is more or less resistant to the elements or to pest damage? The rest of this chapter focuses on ratings and certifications that apply to real property, but real estate professionals could apply a similar approach to analyzing green labels applied to non-real property that may be encountered during the course of a given valuation assignment.

Single- versus Multi-Attribute Rating Systems

Rating systems used to describe green buildings or features may consist of a single performance metric or target multiple facets of building features and performance.[5] Single-attribute rating systems may focus on site characteristics, resource use, or indoor environmental quality, for example, while multi-attribute systems are intended to encompass a comprehensive range of goals and performance

5. Green labels pertaining to the other categories noted in Exhibit 2.3 may also be described as being rated on single or multiple attributes.

standards. Energy Star (for buildings), which primarily focuses on a building's performance on the single attribute of energy use, and LEED, which requires a building to comply with requirements across multiple attributes, are examples of these two categories of systems.

As alluded to in the previous chapter, a building certified or rated as green implies that the structure encompasses multiple aspects of the building's design and construction and considers a variety of building performance metrics including relevant impacts of the development beyond the property line. The design and construction of green buildings are distinctly different from conventional buildings; this will be addressed more fully in Chapter 3. Conventional buildings do not become green buildings simply by "bolting on" a single green feature or attribute. Buildings that achieve a rating from a single category or attribute (such as energy efficiency) but do not address any other elements (such as quality of the interior environment or site impact considerations) would need to be investigated further to determine if other green features exist. Otherwise, the building may be best described as energy-efficient rather than green.

This distinction between single and multiple attributes does not mean that a building rated under a single-attribute system is inherently inferior to a building rated under a multi-attribute system. As with any property characteristic, it is up to the valuation professional to determine how these characteristics affect a building's performance and whether they are valued by the market. For valuation professionals, distinguishing between single- and multi-attribute systems becomes important so that a label such as an "Energy Star-certified building" (a single-attribute system) is not conflated with a "LEED-certified building" (a multi-attribute system) during the valuation process, such as when selecting and analyzing comparable data. Furthermore, the presence of a single-attribute rating system should encourage an examination into whether the building has incorporated other value-affecting green features that may or may not be formally rated or certified.

Part and Parcel?

When considering ratings that apply to real property, it may also be relevant to discern if the entire site and improvements or only a portion of the site or improvements are being evaluated. For example, a newly constructed building may obtain a LEED certification under the Building Design and Construction (BD+C) or Interior Design and Construction (ID+C) tracks (or both). These two tracks vary in terms of what aspects of the improvements are rated and the types of features that are eligible for credits. For rating systems such as the Sustainable SITES Initiative described earlier in this chapter, the property's site factors may be targeted to a greater degree. Depending on the given market, these distinctions may have different effects on the valuation process.

Rating System Checklists, Scorecards, and Worksheets

Rating systems often employ a checklist, scorecard, or worksheet that lists green features, elements, or design strategies that target specific objectives such as resource efficiency or improving the quality of the indoor environment. Often referred to as *credits*, these green building attributes are generally grouped into categories, which differ between rating systems. Typically, baseline prerequisites must be met within each category, with certification levels awarded based on the cumulative total of credits earned. A sample project checklist for the LEED BD+C rating system (Version 4) is shown in Exhibit 2.4. The number of accumulated points required for each level of certification is noted on the bottom right of the checklist. Checklists, scorecards, and worksheets for other rating systems may or may not include this information about certification levels directly on the checklist. Project checklists can be very useful to valuation professionals in highlighting and pinpointing green building features and elements.

Currently, most of the green building rating systems employ a unique checklist or scorecard; there is no universal green building rating scorecard or worksheet. Thus, the precise breakdown of categories, credits, and points required differs between systems. Because certifications are often awarded on a total accumulated point level, two buildings with the same certification level can attain certification with different strategies that could have different effects on value. For example, a building rated under the LEED BD+C New Construction track will earn most of its credits for the design and construction of the building, and any energy credits will be based on predicted energy use. However, it may receive the same certification level as an existing building that is certified under the LEED Operations and Maintenance (O+M) track, where the credits are earned primarily for operational practices and actual, historical energy use. This aspect of the rating systems can complicate the process of assessing value impacts of certifications.

General Categories within Rating Systems

While numerous and distinct green building rating systems are used worldwide, the most commonly used systems for commercial buildings in leading green building markets can be viewed as having common categories upon which the ratings are based.[6] These generalized categories also shape many of the other less-common rating systems.

6. Leading green building markets include the United States (Leadership in Energy and Environmental Design, or LEED), the United Kingdom (Building Research Establishment Assessment Method, or BREEAM), and Japan (Comprehensive Assessment System for Building Environmental Efficiency, or CASBEE).

Exhibit 2.4 Sample LEED Project Checklist

LEED v4 for BD+C: New Construction and Major Renovation
Project Checklist

Project Name:
Date:

Y	?	N	Type	Item	Points
			Credit	Integrative Process	**1**
0	**0**	**0**		**Location and Transportation**	**16**
			Credit	LEED for Neighborhood Development Location	16
			Credit	Sensitive Land Protection	1
			Credit	High Priority Site	2
			Credit	Surrounding Density and Diverse Uses	5
			Credit	Access to Quality Transit	5
			Credit	Bicycle Facilities	1
			Credit	Reduced Parking Footprint	1
			Credit	Green Vehicles	1
0	**0**	**0**		**Sustainable Sites**	**10**
Y			Prereq	Construction Activity Pollution Prevention	Required
			Credit	Site Assessment	1
			Credit	Site Development - Protect or Restore Habitat	2
			Credit	Open Space	1
			Credit	Rainwater Management	3
			Credit	Heat Island Reduction	2
			Credit	Light Pollution Reduction	1
0	**0**	**0**		**Water Efficiency**	**11**
Y			Prereq	Outdoor Water Use Reduction	Required
Y			Prereq	Indoor Water Use Reduction	Required
Y			Prereq	Building-Level Water Metering	Required
			Credit	Outdoor Water Use Reduction	2
			Credit	Indoor Water Use Reduction	6
			Credit	Cooling Tower Water Use	2
			Credit	Water Metering	1
0	**0**	**0**		**Energy and Atmosphere**	**33**
Y			Prereq	Fundamental Commissioning and Verification	Required
Y			Prereq	Minimum Energy Performance	Required
Y			Prereq	Building-Level Energy Metering	Required
Y			Prereq	Fundamental Refrigerant Management	Required
			Credit	Enhanced Commissioning	6
			Credit	Optimize Energy Performance	18
			Credit	Advanced Energy Metering	1
			Credit	Demand Response	2
			Credit	Renewable Energy Production	3
			Credit	Enhanced Refrigerant Management	1
			Credit	Green Power and Carbon Offsets	2

Y	?	N	Type	Item	Points
0	**0**	**0**		**Materials and Resources**	**13**
Y			Prereq	Storage and Collection of Recyclables	Required
Y			Prereq	Construction and Demolition Waste Management Planning	Required
			Credit	Building Life-Cycle Impact Reduction	5
			Credit	Building Product Disclosure and Optimization - Environmental Product Declarations	2
			Credit	Building Product Disclosure and Optimization - Sourcing of Raw Materials	2
			Credit	Building Product Disclosure and Optimization - Material Ingredients	2
			Credit	Construction and Demolition Waste Management	2
0	**0**	**0**		**Indoor Environmental Quality**	**16**
Y			Prereq	Minimum Indoor Air Quality Performance	Required
Y			Prereq	Environmental Tobacco Smoke Control	Required
			Credit	Enhanced Indoor Air Quality Strategies	2
			Credit	Low-Emitting Materials	3
			Credit	Construction Indoor Air Quality Management Plan	1
			Credit	Indoor Air Quality Assessment	2
			Credit	Thermal Comfort	1
			Credit	Interior Lighting	2
			Credit	Daylight	3
			Credit	Quality Views	1
			Credit	Acoustic Performance	1
0	**0**	**0**		**Innovation**	**6**
			Credit	Innovation	5
			Credit	LEED Accredited Professional	1
0	**0**	**0**		**Regional Priority**	**4**
			Credit	Regional Priority: Specific Credit	1
			Credit	Regional Priority: Specific Credit	1
			Credit	Regional Priority: Specific Credit	1
			Credit	Regional Priority: Specific Credit	1
0	0	0		**TOTALS** Possible Points:	**110**

Certified: 40 to 49 points, **Silver:** 50 to 59 points, **Gold:** 60 to 79 points, **Platinum:** 80 to 110

Source: USGBC, "Checklist: LEED v4 for Building Design and Construction," April 5, 2016, www.usgbc.org/resources/leed-v4-building-design-and-construction-checklist.

Becoming familiar with these general categories can be helpful when encountering new rating systems or analyzing green building projects or buildings. These categories can also illuminate areas of disparity between conventional and green properties in a given market. The categories of the most common green building rating systems can be broadly grouped as follows:

- Site and location characteristics
  What is the effect of the development on the surrounding community and environment? What is the nature of the site's linkages to the community in terms of transportation, housing, places of employment, services, and amenities?
- Resource use efficiency
  How much and what kind of resources (energy, water and building materials) are used to construct, renovate, deconstruct, operate, and maintain the building? How is construction and operational waste managed?
- Interior environment and occupant experience
  What is the quality of the occupant experience (health, well-being, safety, comfort, productivity) in the interior space of the building?

These categories are intentionally broad to organize the discussion presented here. In practice, valuation professionals will find that rating systems often have several subcategories within each main category, and may have specialized tracks that focus on specific aspects of the building, such as operations and maintenance. Some less common rating systems, such as the Living Building Challenge system (discussed later in this chapter), may include categories that differ markedly. From a valuation standpoint, however, the nomenclature of the categories or systems is far less important than the intent behind the category. Considering whether the category's goal is focused on resource efficiency, the occupant experience, or the relationship between the building and the surrounding environment can be useful when analyzing the effect of green rating systems on the valuation process.

The following section provides an overview of these categories and their possible effects on the valuation process.

Site and Location Characteristics

Because real estate is intrinsically tied to a specific location, a property's linkages–such as automobile and public transit access and proximity to schools, shopping centers, and recreational amenities–are key factors in establishing site value. However, a property also has the potential to impact the surrounding community and environment beyond its property line. While development can bring needed housing, jobs, health care, and other services and amenities to an area, the construction and operation of real estate is resource-intensive. Real estate development can have unintended adverse effects on the community and environment, such as increased vehicular traffic, noise and light pollution, demands on the public school system, and rainwater runoff that carries chemicals and debris into sewer lines and adjacent waterway and groundwater aquifers.

Site factors in the context of green building ratings and certifications examine how site development affects the surrounding community and environment. Specifically, what can be done to mitigate the adverse effects of a development's impact on the existing infrastructure, such as roadways and sewer lines, surrounding habitats, and adjacent waterways and groundwater aquifers?[7]

For this category, rating systems often award points or credits for such factors as choosing infill sites or sites that are proximate to public transit or daily needs (restaurants, pharmacies, schools, etc.). In addition, credits may be awarded for strategies such as permeable hardscaping and bioswales, which can control, reduce, and treat the rainwater runoff associated with development on a site. The Green Feature Gallery in Appendix A shows examples of bioswales in a shopping center, a university residence hall, and an office building (pages 278-279).

While green building design professionals may be able to articulate a value premise in providing bike racks or reducing single-occupant vehicle trips, these types of green building features may cause some level of value disconnect from those within the commercial real estate profession. Part of the challenge in determining the economic effect of green building is that many of the goals of green building–and therefore the benefits–may not appear to accrue to the property owner, or at least do not accrue solely or directly to the property owner. This may be particularly true for site factors, as the intention is primarily focused on the effects of real estate development on the surrounding community and environment. The valuation question then becomes how to accurately reflect the economic value to the property owner without pricing in benefits that accrue to the community or environment.[8]

may not actually add value

Consider, for example, the effect on acquisition and development costs due to the use of a previously improved site, referred to as an *infill site*, versus an undeveloped site at the suburban fringe. The infill

7. Discussion continues as to whether green building rating systems should go beyond the objective of "doing less bad" to "doing some good." That is, should rating systems reward mitigation of adverse effects or instead seek to design and construct buildings that improve the surrounding ecosystem and community and enhance occupant health and well-being?

8. At the same time, care must be taken not to assume that there are *no* potential value impacts that accrue to a property owner who undertakes practices that may appear to benefit only the property or the environment.

site takes advantage of existing infrastructure like sewers, streets, and transit rather than requiring new infrastructure and services typically needed for the development of an undeveloped site. Furthermore, infill sites also tend to have better access and proximity to multiple transportation modes like walking, biking, public transit, and shared ride services as well as daily needs such as shopping, dining, day care, and schools. This improved access reduces single-occupant automobile trips. This in turn can result in decreased site or construction costs for the property owner due to reduced on-site parking needs, such that a smaller site or less structured parking is required. The reduction in vehicle trips also reduces the load on the existing infrastructure and may obviate the need for special assessments to pay for added lanes on the street or highway or a new freeway interchange. In this case, the green characteristics that benefit the community also positively affect the subject property.

The economic effects of green-oriented site factors are not always readily apparent. For example, transit proximity may affect vacancy and absorption.[9] In addition, green features such as rainwater control or reduction can benefit the property owner or developer via a facilitated entitlement process.[10]

Resource Use Efficiency

Resource use is another major area of focus among green building rating systems. Buildings use a variety of resources for operations and maintenance and during construction, renovation, and deconstruction. Green building rating systems consider the efficiency of the use of all of these resources, including energy, water, and building materials, and consider the waste stream impacts. Use efficiencies and reduction of waste can affect construction budgets as well as net operating income. As a result, this is a particularly relevant category for valuation professionals.

Within various rating systems, these resources are often broken out into the following categories:

- Energy
- Water
- Building materials and waste stream impacts

Energy

In terms of energy efficiency, the focus is usually on reducing the energy use of a building–particularly the energy use derived from

9. See Case Study 5.A in Chapter 5 (page 91).
10. For example, a national developer of a LEED-certified shopping center noted that providing bioswales and similar green benefits expedited entitlements for the development. He added that in another case, their reputation as developers of sustainable shopping centers was a material factor in winning the competitive bid for another site it purchased from a large energy company.

non-renewable energy sources–but can also include the generation or purchase of renewable energy from solar, geothermal, or wind sources.

Green building rating systems typically award credits for reducing energy use below a baseline, which is usually based on the energy use for a code-compliant building. With each tier of improved performance, additional credits may be earned. Most systems award credits for documented design, construction, and mechanical systems that meet the projected use thresholds based on an energy model, which can be thought of as a cash flow model for energy use in a building.

Credits can also be earned for building commissioning. Building commissioning, discussed in the accompanying sidebar, is intended to verify that systems are installed and operating as designed. In some rating systems, a basic level of commissioning is a prerequisite, while more rigorous or comprehensive commissioning earns additional credits. Commissioning is an important step in verifying that construction was completed and systems operate as planned, particularly when rating new or proposed construction. Commissioning can also uncover system conflicts or interoperability faults.

Reducing energy use has obvious bottom-line benefits to the property owner. Reducing or eliminating the energy cost, which is typically the largest controllable operating expense in a building, presents the valuer with a relatively straightforward adjustment.

What Is Building Commissioning?

Green building design and construction, as will be explained in Chapter 3, utilizes integrated systems that are designed to function as a whole. These systems and their interrelated functions may be complex and involve numerous pieces of equipment and technologies. Building commissioning, sometimes abbreviated as Cx, is essentially a verification process to ensure that systems are performing the way they were designed to perform and are free of conflicts or errors.

The Building Commissioning Association (BCA) defines *building commissioning* as "a quality-focused process for enhancing the delivery of a project and includes verifying and documenting that the facility and its systems and assemblies are planned, designed, installed, tested, operated, and maintained to meet the owner's project requirements."[11]

The term *commissioning* has historical origins in shipbuilding. According to the California Commissioning Collaborative, "A commissioned ship is one deemed ready for service. Before being awarded this title, however, a ship must pass several milestones. Equipment is installed and tested, problems are identified and corrected, and the prospective crew is extensively trained. A commissioned ship is one whose materials, systems, and staff have successfully completed a thorough quality assurance process."[12]

Building commissioning applies the same approach to buildings. Building commissioning is a quality assurance process that begins in the design phase and continues through construction, extending to post-occupancy operations. Successful building commissioning provides the owner with two important assurances:

11. BCA, "New Construction Building Commissioning Best Practices," February 2016, www.bcxa.org/wp-content/uploads/2016/03/BCxA.NCCx-BestPractices_031616.pdf.

12. California Commissioning Collective, *California Commissioning Guide: New Buildings* (Sacramento: California Commissioning Collaborative, 2006), 2, www.cacx.org/resources/documents/CA_Commissioning_Guide_New.pdf.

that the building operates as intended, and that the operations staff is trained to successfully operate and maintain the building systems and equipment.

Types of Commissioning

Building commissioning can vary in terms of scope and rigor. Originally focused on the HVAC system, commissioning now typically includes all energy-using systems, on-site energy generation, and water-using systems and fixtures. It may even include commissioning the building envelope.

Commissioning can be performed by the subcontractor or general contractor for the project, but most green building certifications require an independent third party, known as the commissioning agent (CxA) or commissioning provider (CxP), who works for the property owner. The role of the commissioning agent or provider is to ensure that the owner's project requirements (OPRs) for building performance are met. While the bulk of the agent or provider's work occurs after construction is completed, best practices suggest that the commissioning process begin in the design phase for new construction, with the development of the OPR continuing through project completion.

Existing buildings can also be commissioned, a process sometimes referred to as *retrocommissioning*. Ongoing or continuous commissioning is a process of continual measurement and verification as the building is operated to ensure that it continues to perform according to the OPR. This type of commissioning may be necessary to maintain occupant satisfaction, prevent interoperability conflicts, or maintain energy use performance targets for high-performance buildings.

Commissioning Reports

Commissioning reports can be fairly brief or significantly more voluminous depending on the scope of the commissioning assignment. It may or may not follow a third-party standard such as the National Institute of Building Sciences (NIBS) or ASHRAE. The scope of work, the systems commissioned, and the standard of measurement are typically outlined in the commissioning report.

The mere fact that commissioning was completed at any level is important information for the valuation professional, particularly if it was performed by a third-party commissioning authority. Even more helpful is a copy of the commissioning report for a recently completed green building. The commissioning report typically identifies the standards to which the systems were intended to perform, including other basic information such as verification that the equipment was installed, that it was inspected by the building inspector, and that it is operating as intended. This information is helpful in the property description as well as in assessing the contributory value of components and systems. A commissioning report could also be used to assess the risk of the property relative to its potential to perform as designed. Thus, commissioning could be a factor to consider in the overall and yield rate analyses.

Commissioning reports provide third-party verification that the system is functional and that what was intended at the outset was in fact completed. This level of verification is particularly relevant for the more complex systems and integrated design typical of many green and high-performance buildings. It can also be useful in assessing the performance of conventional building systems and individual green building components. For example, retrocommissioning performed on a five-year-old, twin-array solar PV system showed that one was generating 99.5% of its predicted output (considering degradation, shading, soiling, inverter and wire losses, and current mismatch), while the other was generating 103.0% of its predicted output. This information was critical to the contractor and design team as they planned a subsequent renovation of the building as a net zero energy (NZE) facility. For the valuer assigned to estimate the contributory value of this solar PV system, the retrocommissioning was useful in two ways: the production of the existing arrays was independently verified, and the performance of the solar arrays within the design range was confirmed. The retrocommissioning thus served as a check on the solar installers' production projections for future assignments.

Water

Water-efficient building features can encompass more than low-flow fixtures. Various water-efficient landscaping design and features such as drip irrigation or the use of reclaimed or gray water systems may count towards green certification. Credits may also be awarded for reducing indoor water use through low-flow plumbing fixtures, cooling tower water management, submetering, and drought-tolerant landscaping. More advanced levels of water credits include harvesting rainwater for non-potable use on site (toilets and landscape irrigation), treating reclaimed water for potable use, and treating wastewater on site. The use of reclaimed water from a municipal source or an on-site treatment system can yield significant cost savings, as the cost of using reclaimed water is typically less than the cost of potable water.

As with reduced energy use, reduced water use is readily measurable and quantifiable. However, water represents a relatively small component of the operating budget in most areas, so reducing this cost through green building strategies may not yield a significant cost savings. Nonetheless, plumbing upgrades can have a noticeable impact on the net income, particularly in older properties that may not have been upgraded recently or that may have plumbing leaks.[13]

Types of Water

A variety of terms relating to water are used in green building, which can sometimes lead to confusion. Generally, *potable water* is what is commonly referred to as "drinking water" that is deemed safe for domestic use and consumption. Typically, potable water has been treated via mechanical filtration and/or chemical means to remove or kill pathogens. Public health concerns place a high priority on potable water safety. As a result, potable water sources that serve the public, such as municipal systems, are highly regulated. Water that is consumed privately and not available to the public may not be subject to the same restrictions.

Non-potable water refers to most other water sources that are not considered safe to drink. This category includes untreated and untested groundwater, rainwater, and water from lakes, rivers, and streams. Reclaimed or recycled water is a special class of non-potable water that was previously potable but has been used at least once for domestic purposes and treated but is not typically up to potable standards. Because reclaimed and recycled water is usually unfit to drink, its uses are also highly regulated and it may not be permitted even for landscape irrigation in some jurisdictions. In areas where reclaimed or recycled water is permitted for such use, it is typically required to be prominently labeled as unsafe to drink.

The following definitions are taken from the US Environmental Protection Agency's (EPA's) 1994 *Drinking Water Glossary* and the California State Water Resources Board's *Water Words*.[14]

potable water. Water that is safe for drinking and cooking.

non-potable water. Water that may contain objectionable pollution, contamination, minerals, or infective agents and is considered unsafe and/or unpalatable for drinking.

gray water (or grey water) and black water. Definitions of these terms may vary based on jurisdiction. In some cases, *gray water* may be defined broadly as domestic wastewater originating from the kitchen, bathroom, and laundry sinks, tubs, and washers. In other municipalities, wastewater from the kitchen and laundry facilities may be classed as black water. Wastewater from toilets is always considered black water, no matter the jurisdiction.

reclaimed wastewater. Treated wastewater that can be reused for beneficial purposes such as irrigation.

recycled water. Water that is used more than one time before it passes back into the natural hydrologic system and is suitable for a beneficial use.

13. See Case Study 7.A in Chapter 7 (page 132).

14. EPA, *Drinking Water Glossary: A Dictionary of Technical and Legal Terms Related to Drinking Water*, 1994, https://nepis.epa.gov; California Environmental Protection Agency, *Water Words: Glossary and Definitions*, February 16, 2011, www.waterboards.ca.gov/publications_forms/available_documents/water_words.shtml.

Building Materials and Waste Stream Impacts

Buildings use other natural resources besides energy and water for construction, renovation, tenant improvements, operations, and maintenance. Additionally, because waste is generated as a by-product of building construction and operation, waste reduction is considered in this category as well.

The focus of building materials use is on the quantity and type of materials used in construction and operation. The intent is to reduce adverse environmental and occupant health impacts through materials choices and operational decisions over the building's life cycle.

For new construction projects, credits may be earned by reusing an existing structure rather than building new, using recycled or repurposed materials, or implementing design strategies that demonstrate lower resource use over the building life cycle. Credits may be earned for strategies that reduce construction debris, encouraging the recycling of construction materials and building operational waste. The following series of photographs shows examples of the reuse of materials in the renovation of a 1970s-era, concrete building in Northern California.

The stringency and strategies used by the various rating systems vary. The Living Building Challenge, described in more detail at the end of this chapter, maintains a "Red List" (shown in Exhibit 2.5) of materials and chemicals that are forbidden due to their adverse impact on the environment or the health of construction workers and building occupants. In many cases, credits may also be earned for the use of products or building components that include recycled content or contain no or low levels of volatile organic compounds (VOCs).

For operationally focused rating systems like Green Globes Existing Buildings and LEED O+M, the focus is on reducing solid waste

The building before renovation. Note the very limited window line.

This project required cutting 86 windows through six-inch concrete slab walls to improve daylighting and natural ventilation. Some of the waste material was repurposed into the landscaping, shown here under construction.

Some of the concrete removed for the windows was salvaged and used as outdoor seating for the patio. A green screen designed to shield the view of the parking area surrounds the patio. (In this photo, the plant material has not yet grown in.) Note the electric vehicle charging station behind the trellis.

Wood salvaged from the interior demolition was refinished and repurposed as stair treads and railing caps in the renovated project.

The completed renovation

through recycling and composting, using cleaning and maintenance products and practices that are not detrimental to the environment or human health, and reducing the amount of materials used in ongoing renovations.

The amount, type, and cost of materials used in the initial construction or renovation has a direct impact when valuing new construction in the cost approach to value. The sales comparison and income capitalization approaches may also be affected if renovation costs, or costs to complete, are deducted to arrive at an as-is value. As will be discussed more fully in the following chapter, some of the strategies used in green building can result in higher up-front costs that may be offset by lower operational costs or lower renovation costs over time. This cost shift between future operational and initial capital costs can have material implications in the valuation process.[15]

Interior Environment and Occupant Experience

In addition to site factors and resource use categories, green building rating systems focus on various aspects of the building's interior. Here the focus is on the health, safety, comfort, and productivity of the occupants.

15. For further detail, see the cost approach section of Chapter 9 (page 172).

Exhibit 2.5 **The Living Building Challenge "Red List"**

This list specifies chemicals that cannot be used in materials of a project seeking Living Building Challenge certification.

- Alkylphenols
- Asbestos
- Bisphenol A (BPA)
- Cadmium
- Chlorinated polyethylene and chlorosulfonated polyethylene
- Chlorobenzenes
- Chlorofluorocarbons (CFCs) and hydrochlorofluorocarbons (HCFCs)
- Chloroprene (neoprene)
- Chromium VI
- Formaldehyde (added)
- Halogenated flame retardants (HFRs)
- Lead (added)
- Mercury
- Polychlorinated biphenyls (PCBs)
- Perfluorinated compounds (PFCs)
- Phthalates
- Polyvinyl chloride (PVC), chlorinated polyvinyl chloride (CPVC), and polyvinylidene chloride (PVDC)
- Short chain chlorinated paraffins (SCCPs)
- Volatile organic compounds (VOCs) in wet applied products
- Wood treatments containing creosote, arsenic, or pentachlorophenol

Source: International Living Future Institute, "The Red List," accessed June 26, 2017, https://living-future.org/declare/declare-about/red-list/.

Studies have shown that we spend approximately 90% of our time indoors and that pollutant levels are often far greater indoors than out.[16] This has led to an increased focus on the quality of the occupant experience. Is the interior space healthy, safe, comfortable, and productivity-enhancing?

Sick Building Syndrome (SBS) became a well-publicized public health concern in the late twentieth century and was often linked to reduced ventilation resulting from tightened building envelopes aimed at increasing energy efficiency. Before SBS, the potential for buildings and building materials to cause human health problems was already an issue, from the use of lead-based paints (particularly in schools

16. EPA, "Report to Congress on Indoor Air Quality Volume II: Assessment and Control of Indoor Air Pollution," 1989, https://nepis.epa.gov; N. E. Klepeis et al., "The National Human Activity Pattern Survey (NHAPS): A Resource for Assessing Exposure to Environmental Pollutants," *Journal of Exposure Analysis and Environmental Epidemiology* 11 (2001): 231–252; EPA, "The Total Exposure Assessment Methodology (TEAM) Study," 1987, https://nepis.epa.gov; Prashant Kumar et al., "Real-Time Sensors for Indoor Air Monitoring and Challenges Ahead in Deploying Them to Urban Buildings," *Science of the Total Environment* 560–561 (April 2016): 150–159.

Clearing The Air: Why Ventilation Rates Matter

When air quality is discussed, the emphasis is often on the quality of the exterior, or outside, air. Issues such as smog, vehicle emissions, and pollen counts tend to dominate the discussion. But considering that most of us spend the majority of our time indoors, it would seem that we should be at least as focused—if not more so—on the quality of indoor air.

This shift in focus has been gaining momentum over the past few decades. Sick Building Syndrome (SBS), which linked a too-tight building envelope and other indoor air contaminants to occupant illness, provided an initial impetus for paying greater attention to the quality of interior air and its effect on human health, comfort, and productivity.

Researchers have been studying how the presence and concentration of substances such as VOCs and carbon dioxide affect building occupants. The research indicates that not only is the quality of indoor air sometimes worse than that of outdoor air, but that monitoring and improving indoor air quality can have a variety of positive effects.

ASHRAE Standard 62.1

In 1973, the first version of ASHRAE Standard 62.1, *Ventilation for Acceptable Indoor Air Quality*, was published.[17] It was meant to provide guidance and standardization regarding ventilation rates for buildings. Prior to the publication of this standard, a century or more of debate transpired regarding the nature and appropriate response to indoor air contaminants. In the 1930s, for example, a team of researchers conducted experiments based on subjective evaluations of body odor as correlated to various ventilation rates. This idea that the primary objective of ventilation rates was to control human body odor and the effects of human activities persisted through the 1970s.[18]

The stated purpose of ASHRAE 62.1 is to set a minimum standard for "indoor air quality that is acceptable to human occupants and that minimizes adverse health effects."[19] It is worth noting that this standard was not designed to optimize human health but merely to provide a minimum level of compliance that minimizes deleterious health effects related to indoor air quality.

Fast forward through several decades of research and much debate and revision regarding acceptable ventilation rates, and the question still remains: What is the ventilation rate for indoor environments that will optimize human health, comfort, and productivity?[20]

What Happens when Ventilation Rates Increase?

As ASHRAE 62.1 does not specify an optimal ventilation rate, researchers have experimented in past decades in search of more definitive information regarding whether the ASHRAE minimum standard is sufficient or if higher ventilation rates would be healthier for building occupants. A study performed in 2000 examined whether ventilation rates could affect symptoms related to SBS and found that increasing ventilation rates above the minimum standards and guidelines reduces health effects associated with SBS and increases occupant productivity.[21]

---

17. ASHRAE 62.1 pertains to commercial, institutional, and high-rise residential buildings, whereas ASHRAE Standard 62.2 is specific to low-rise residential buildings.

18. "In the era of mechanical ventilation, requirements for outdoor air derive primarily from the need for odor control. The odors arise from human beings and their activities (e.g., smoking)." William S. Cain and Larry G. Berglund, "Role of Odors in Ventilation Requirements for Buildings," *Proceedings of the Human Factors and Ergonomics Society Annual Meeting* 23, no. 1 (1979), http://journals.sagepub.com/doi/pdf/10.1177/107118137902300135.

19. ASHRAE, *Standard 62.1: Ventilation for Acceptable Indoor Air Quality*, 2016, www.ashrae.org/resources--publications/bookstore/standards-62-1--62-2.

20. For discussion of the history of ASHRAE 62.1, see Andrew Persily, "Challenges in Developing Ventilation and Indoor Air Quality Standards: The Story of ASHRAE Standard 62," *Building and Environment* 91 (2015): 61-69.

21. Pawel Wargocki et al., "The Effects of Outdoor Air Supply Rate in an Office on Perceived Air Quality, Sick Building Syndrome (SBS) Symptoms and Productivity," *Indoor Air* 10, no. 4 (2000) 222–236.

More recently, studies have broadened in scope beyond reducing SBS symptoms to assessing whether a reduction of other indoor contaminants could improve human health and productivity. For example, in 2012 researchers examined the effects of indoor carbon dioxide levels on human decision-making and found that higher indoor concentrations of carbon dioxide correlated with impaired decision-marking performance.[22] A 2015 study confirmed these results, showing the negative effects of carbon dioxide as well as a positive correlation between increasing the ventilation rate above the current ASHRAE minimum standards and improved cognitive function.[23]

So Why Not Increase Ventilation Rates?

The research clearly suggests that increasing ventilation rates above the current minimum guidelines promotes the health and productivity of occupants. The question then becomes: If the research is so convincing, why isn't there greater adoption of enhanced ventilation strategies? There are at least two reasons for this. First of all, increasing ventilation rates comes at the expense of energy efficiency. If a property owner wants to maximize the energy efficiency of a building, increasing ventilation rates may be seen as an "energy penalty," or cost offset to potential energy savings. Second of all, it is not yet common for buildings' interior environments to be monitored in real time for indoor air quality characteristics, such as carbon dioxide or VOC levels. Many factors can influence a particular indoor area's air quality, such as the number of occupants, the ambient temperatures, and equipment being used or activities being performed in that space. There is emerging interest and technological advancement in real-time air monitoring equipment that allows for better control and management of indoor air quality.

To address the inherent trade-off between energy use and ventilation rates, a 2015 study examined the economics of increasing air changes per hour.[24] That study indicated that the cost due to increasing ventilation rates could be mitigated or avoided in most cases by making appropriate adjustments or add-ons to HVAC equipment, such as using an energy recovery ventilation system. In addition, ventilation strategies like demand-controlled ventilation systems automatically adjust ventilation rates based on the occupant load and carbon dioxide levels. Separating ventilation from the heating and cooling of the interior air using a dedicated outside air system is another common strategy that facilitates optimal ventilation while reducing fan energy use and minimizing the energy penalty.

How Do Ventilation Rates Affect Property Value?

The potential value impact of increasing productivity for occupants is based on the relationship between wages and building rent, which is often a factor of 10 or more. That is, the cost of the workers is 10 times or more the cost of the rent when measured on a per-square-foot basis. Thus, a relatively minor increase in productivity would be magnified 10 times when measured on a rentable building area basis. If the changes to the building operations such as ventilation rates result in measurable occupant productivity gains, then the value of the real estate should also be affected to some degree. The same argument would hold true for other building design and construction characteristics, such as daylighting and views to the outdoors that can be shown to result in healthier and more productive occupants. The challenge for the building owner is to make that value connection clear enough to the tenant that a rent premium is attained. If this rent premium is attained on a consistent basis, it would establish the connection between building characteristics that enhance productivity and increased property value. This area warrants careful attention, as research develops and landlords and tenants become more aware of the potential property value implications of occupant health and productivity.

22. Usha Satishet et al., "Is CO_2 an Indoor Pollutant? Direct Effects of Low-to-Moderate CO_2 Concentrations on Human Decision-Making Performance," *Environmental Health Perspectives* 120, no. 12 (September 2012): 1671-1677.

23. Joseph G. Allen et al., "Associations of Cognitive Function Scores with Carbon Dioxide, Ventilation, and Volatile Organic Compound Exposures in Office Workers: A Controlled Exposure Study of Green and Conventional Office Environments," *Environmental Health Perspectives* 124, no. 6 (June 2016): 805-812.

24. Piers MacNaughton et al., "Economic, Environmental and Health Implications of Enhanced Ventilation in Office Buildings," *International Journal of Environmental Research and Public Health* 12, no. 11 (2015).

and homes where children may be exposed) to improperly functioning HVAC systems causing outbreaks of Legionnaire's disease. While buildings can cause health problems for the occupants, studies have shown that interior spaces also have the potential to create distinct benefits.[25] For example, the results from a longitudinal study analyzing a variety of metrics at a newly built LEED-certified hospital showed lowered patient mortality rates.[26] Similarly, an early study from the 1980s found a correlation between rooms that had views of nature and facilitated healing after surgical procedures.[27] In office settings, studies have revealed that buildings in which the ventilation rate exceeds the ASHRAE 62.1 minimum standard of 20 cubic feet per minute (cfm) per person decreased SBS symptoms and improved cognitive performance when ventilation rates reached 40 cfm per person.[28]

Within green building rating systems, some examples of how credits may be earned for this category can include achieving stipulated air quality standards, using low-emitting building materials, designing such that natural light and views to the outdoors are available to all occupants, or utilizing green cleaning products and processes. Biophilic design strategies, such as bringing the natural environment into the interior space, are also included in this category. The accompanying sidebar further explores the concept of biophilic design and its impact on human health and productivity.

As with the site factors category, it may be challenging to ascertain the degree to which benefits created by optimizing the occupant experience affect the underlying real estate value. While research may indicate that a higher number of air changes per hour enhances cognitive ability, the economic benefit of higher productivity or happier workers accrues most directly to the tenant. Value accrues to the real estate when market demand for this type of space increases, resulting in faster absorption, greater tenant retention, and/or higher rental rates.

How Is Compliance Achieved?

Compliance checks occur many times during a building's life cycle, regardless of whether it is green or conventional. The entitlement processes and building permits, for instance, ensure that developments

25. Joseph G. Allen et al., "Green Buildings and Health," *Current Environmental Health Reports* 2, no. 3 (September 2015): 250-258. This article, written by researchers at the Harvard T. H. Chan School of Public Health, provides a comprehensive review and analysis of studies related to the occupant health effects of green buildings.

26. Cassandra Lee Thiel et al., "Building Design and Performance: A Comparative Longitudinal Assessment of a Children's Hospital," *Building and Environment* 78 (August 2014): 130-136.

27. Roger S. Ulrich, "View Through a Window May Influence Recovery from Surgery;" *Science* 224 (April 27, 1984).

28. Pawel Wargocki et al., "The Effects of Outdoor Air Supply Rate in an Office on Perceived Air Quality, Sick Building Syndrome (SBS) Symptoms and Productivity," 222-236;
Allen et al., "Associations of Cognitive Function Scores with Carbon Dioxide, Ventilation, and Volatile Organic Compound Exposures in Office Workers."

Biophilia: The Human Connection to Nature

"It therefore results that the enjoyment of scenery employs the mind without fatigue and yet exercises it; tranquilizes it and yet enlivens it; and thus, through the influence of the mind over the body, gives the effect of refreshing rest and reinvigoration to the whole system."

- Frederick Law Olmsted, in his 1865 report to Congress on the management of Yosemite[29]

Biophilia, at its most basic level, is the idea that humans have an innate desire to connect with nature and other living organisms. *Biophilic design* is the incorporation of biophilia into the built environment. William D. Browning, a leading expert in the field, describes biophilic design as taking characteristics of the places we go to relax and restore and bringing them into the built environment.[30]

A substantial body of research demonstrates a range of positive outcomes associated with biophilic design, such as improved health and well-being, increased productivity, and improved cognitive development and learning in children. Studies have also shown a positive effect on purchase behavior in retail environments due to natural surroundings and daylighting.[31]

One of the first studies to show a measurable health benefit from biophilic elements was the previously mentioned 1984 Ulrich study, which examined whether there was any difference in the medical outcomes of hospital patients who were exposed to views of either nature or a brick wall while recovering from surgery. The study showed that those patients who had views of nature during recovery had shorter hospital stays, a reduced need for strong analgesics, and fewer post-surgical complications, and were judged by the nursing staff as being more positive and less stressed.[32] This study is often credited with causing a fundamental change in hospital design such that outdoor spaces and views to nature have become an important part of hospital and assisted-living facilities.

Browning and his team have broken down biophilic design into 14 patterns, grouped into three categories: nature *in* the space (incorporation of plants, water, and animals in the space), natural analogues (use of materials and patterns that represent nature), and nature *of* the space (deriving the spatial configuration from nature).[33]

One can see these patterns implemented in the modern built environment. Providing views to natural settings or using daylighting to bring natural light into a building interior demonstrates nature in the space. Curvilinear work areas or the use of natural materials such as stone and wood are examples of natural analogues, while open floor plans with perimeter work stations or alcoves address the nature of the space by providing prospect and refuge.

It is not necessary to incorporate all 14 biophilic design patterns in a building to yield positive outcomes. Choosing patterns that are most appropriate for the work and activities conducted in the space can be effective. For example, a 2003 study funded by the California Energy Commission examined the effects of various biophilic design changes at a Sacramento Municipal Utility District call center facility. Employees at the call center reported eye strain due to continuous hours spent in front of a computer screen and engaged in stress-inducing work dealing with customer problems and complaints. One aspect of the study sought to measure whether a view to nature affected productivity. Baseline measures of view and productivity levels were recorded and analyzed, and work stations were then adjusted to improve the view to the outdoors. Results indicated a 6%–12% increase in productivity due to the re-orienting of the workstations, the mod-

29. Frederick Law Olmsted, "The Yosemite Valley and the Mariposa Big Tree Grove," in *America's National Park System: The Critical Documents* (New York: Rowman and Littlefield, 1994).
30. "The Art of Biophilic Design: An Interview with Bill Browning," *Planet Experts* (October 1, 2014), www.planetexperts.com/art-biophilic-design-interview-bill-browning/.
31. Kathleen L. Wolf, "Trees in the Small City Retail Business District: Comparing Resident and Visitor Perceptions," *Journal of Forestry* 103, no. 8 (2005): 390–395 and Yannick Joye et al., "The Effects of Urban Retail Greenery on Consumer Experience," *Urban Forestry and Urban Greening* (February 2010): 57-64; California Energy Commission, "Daylight and Retail Sales," October 2003, http://newbuildings.org/wp-content/uploads/2015/11/A-5_Daylgt_Retail_2.3.71.pdf.
32. Ulrich, "View Through a Window May Influence Recovery from Surgery," 420.
33. Terrapin Bright Green, *The Economics of Biophilia: Why Designing with Nature in Mind Makes Financial Sense*, 2012, 8, www.terrapinbrightgreen.com/report/economics-of-biophilia/.

est cost of which was recovered in four months due to productivity gains.[34]

The photograph here was taken inside a renovated 1970s-era office building in the Silicon Valley of Northern California. It shows an example of a living wall. Living walls are interior greenscapes that bring the natural environment into the interior space for the purpose of enhancing occupant physical and mental health by improving indoor air quality and acoustics and providing a source of natural beauty. This particular building was renovated to operate on an NZE basis and thus employs an exposed concrete floor for its thermal mass effect. The concrete floor, however, has the downside of amplifying acoustical problems and can seem visually stark to occupants. The use of a living wall in this space addresses these issues. In addition, it was designed to serve as a type of living art sculpture that can be seen through the lobby entry from the street when lit at night, enhancing the building's visual appeal.

A living wall was added as part of the renovation of this 1970s-era office building in California's Silicon Valley.

The ideas that humans have an innate connection to nature and predictable reactions to certain, desirable elements of the natural world are not new. What is novel about biophilic design is that it takes a scientific approach to understanding why those in the real estate world intuitively "know" that one space is superior to another. Understanding these inherent human preferences can help fine-tune the valuation process by helping to explain, in a rational, evidence-based approach, why a biophilic space might rent for more or lease faster than another similar space lacking biophilic design. It can lead to a fuller understanding of why office space with a view of a park rents for more than space with a view of a parking garage. Biophilic design may also help explain why certain buildings and design elements endure while others become dated more quickly. In this manner, it can point to deficiencies in existing space or highlight areas of existing or potential obsolescence—curable or otherwise—that might otherwise go unnoticed. More examples of biophilic design can be found in the Green Feature Gallery in Appendix A (pages 302-303).

and renovations meet certain local and state standards and regulations. Within a green building rating system, these same concepts apply: the property owner or developer must meet whatever requirements are stipulated within the rating system to obtain the certification. Just as with other building code requirements, green building rating system credits may be prescriptive or performance-based. The integrated and interrelated systems of green buildings make this distinction relevant.

Prescriptive versus Performance-Based Requirements

Compliance paths can be prescriptive or performance-based. This difference may be thought of as a building's components being *designed and constructed* to a certain standard versus a building *performing* to a certain standard. Put another way, requirements can be based on *what* was performed versus *how* the property performs. For

34. California Energy Commission, *Windows and Offices: A Study of Office Worker Performance and the Indoor Environment.* October 2003, http://h-m-g.com/downloads/Daylighting/A-9_Windows_Offices_2.6.10.pdf; Terrapin Bright Green, *The Economics of Biophilia*, 14.

example, if the goal is to optimize the energy use systems in a building, a prescriptive requirement may stipulate the installation of HVAC and other mechanical systems that meet certain minimum efficiency standards. A performance path, in contrast, may stipulate that the building's overall energy use meet a specified goal demonstrated via an energy model or through actual post-occupancy energy use.

From a valuation perspective, this distinction presents somewhat of a false choice in that valuation professionals are focused on both the specifics of the physical result and how that physical reality performs. The construction type, the quality of the materials used, and the condition and functional utility of what is seen during the site visit is used to gauge the overall quality and condition of the subject property relative to the comparable properties. But just as importantly, the operational or performance aspects are also assessed.

Prescriptive requirements typically describe minimum or maximum values for various components of a building, such as minimum R-values for insulation, and may reference a particular building reference standard, such as those listed in Exhibit 2.6. Alternatively, they may specify that components be installed or assembled in a particular

Exhibit 2.6 Green Building Reference Standards

Reference Standard	Description	Application
ASHRAE* Standard 55	Thermal environmental conditions for human occupancy	Indoor air temperature
ASHRAE Standard 62.1	Ventilation for acceptable indoor air quality	Indoor air quality
ASHRAE Standard 90.1	Energy standard for buildings except low-rise residential buildings	Energy efficiency
ANSI†/ASHRAE/USGBC/IES‡ Standard 189.1	Standard for design of high-performance green buildings except low-rise residential buildings	A comprehensive group of standards including site, water, energy, indoor environmental quality, materials, and resources intended to improve the environmental and health performance of buildings
ANSI Standard S12.60	Acoustical performance criteria, design requirements, and guidelines for schools	Classroom acoustics
ANSI/BIFMA§ e3	Furniture sustainability standard	Furniture chemical content

Note. The effective date of the applicable revision will often be cited after the standard, separated by a hyphen, e.g. ASHRAE 90.1-2010. The applicable standard for compliance with the rating system may or may not be the most recent revision available.

* Formerly known as the American Society of Heating, Refrigerating and Air-Conditioning Engineers, the organization now identifies itself simply as ASHRAE.

† American National Standards Institute

‡ Illuminating Engineering Society

§ The trade organization of the Business and Institutional Furniture Manufacturers

manner, such as requiring daylight sensors for all lighting located within a certain number of feet from the window line. Prescriptive compliance credits may also include a requirement to use a certain building material, fixture, or component, such as low-VOC paint, low-flow toilets, or energy-efficient windows.[35] In each case, the performance of the feature is implied, but not directly measured, based on its physical characteristics. For many green building features, prescriptive compliance is an appropriate and reliable indicator of actual, in-the-field performance. In addition, prescriptive requirements clearly delineate acceptable parameters and thus may make the project less complex to design and construct while also making compliance easier to verify.

Performance-based requirements, on the other hand, focus on building performance regarding various metrics, such as air quality or water use. Since green building components and systems are often designed and constructed using a whole building approach, performance requirements may be more relevant for these integrated systems than they might be for a conventionally built structure.[36] For example, something as straightforward as dual-glazed windows may be more meaningfully evaluated via performance measures when part of a green building design meant to reduce the energy use profile of a building. Dual glazing is, all else being equal, more energy-efficient than single glazing. However, just how much more efficient it will be depends on a variety of other factors, including the local climate, the building's orientation, and the framing material used. Evaluating the windows' contribution to the energy efficiency of the building requires assessing its contribution to the larger wall assembly that includes the window frame and wall components.[37] This type of analysis is often done using energy modeling software to predict actual performance based on a series of inputs. Furthermore, some green building characteristics do not fit the prescriptive mold, either because the performance requires field measurement after the product or system is installed or because performance is contingent on occupant behavior.

Performance-based credits hold an intuitive appeal to valuation professionals who are accustomed to reviewing building performance metrics. Most green building rating systems for proposed construction rely on a combination of prescriptive credits and predicted or modeled performance.[38] In contrast, green building rating systems for existing

---

35. In the case of the Living Building Challenge, the requirement may be expressed as a prohibition against the use of a particular material, as shown in Exhibit 2.5.

36. See Chapter 3 for further detail regarding the differences between green building and traditional design and construction.

37. Additionally, the natural light provided by the window may contribute to daylighting. This reduces the amount of energy used for lighting and possibly even heat gain from the lighting, further decreasing the amount of energy used for cooling.

38. A notable exception is the Living Building Challenge, which requires one year of operation to verify energy and water performance.

Examples of Prescriptive versus Performance-Based LEED Credits

While valuation professionals need not understand precisely how to fulfill the requirements of each of the credits within a given rating system, it is helpful to have a general idea of how credits can be earned and whether compliance can be prescriptive, performance-based, or a combination of the two. Understanding this distinction can allow the valuation professional to better assess the potential value impact of the green improvements.

Below are several examples of both types of compliance paths from the LEED BD+C rating system (Version 4). Note that the performance-based examples predict performance based on a computer model rather than actual use. This is due to the nature of the BD+C track, which is applied to buildings that are not yet built and therefore do not yet have data on post-occupancy energy and water use. In contrast, the LEED O+M track requires 12 months of actual energy and water use data with the building occupied, which is then input into the Energy Star Portfolio Manager program to determine the number of points earned for energy efficiency.

Example 1. Outdoor Water Use Reduction Credit

LEED's outdoor water use reduction credit is an example of a credit that can be earned using either a prescriptive or performance-based path. LEED Version 4 offers the following guidelines:

> **Water Efficiency**
>
> Reduce outdoor water use through one of the following options. Nonvegetated surfaces, such as permeable or impermeable pavement, should be excluded from landscape area calculations. Athletic fields and playgrounds (if vegetated) and food gardens may be included or excluded at the project team's discretion.
>
> ***Option 1. No Irrigation Required***
>
> Show that the landscape does not require a permanent irrigation system beyond a maximum two-year establishment period.
>
> OR
>
> ***Option 2. Reduced Irrigation***
>
> Reduce the project's landscape water requirement (LWR) by at least 50% from the calculated baseline for the site's peak watering month. Reductions must first be achieved through plant species selection and irrigation system efficiency as calculated in the Environmental Protection Agency (EPA) WaterSense Water Budget Tool.[39]

Option 1 is a prescriptive path because it explains what must be done. If it is shown that there is no landscaping or that the landscaping does not need water after it is established, then the project gets the point. Prescriptive paths, also known as *compliance paths*, are based on actions the design team takes and do not directly assess the outcome of those actions.

Option 2 is primarily a performance-based path because a calculation of the projected water use is involved and it is compared to a reference standard or baseline. Here, the design team is required to demonstrate that the outcome—in this case, landscaping water use—will meet a minimum 50% reduction from a reference baseline amount established by the EPA WaterSense program. However, this particular performance path includes some prescriptive language regarding priority to species selection and irrigation efficiency.

Example 2. Energy and Atmosphere Prerequisite

The energy and atmosphere (EA) prerequisite provides another example of prescriptive and performance paths being offered. LEED Version 4 offers the following guidelines:

> ***Option 1. Whole-Building Energy Simulation***
>
> Demonstrate an improvement of 5% for new construction, 3% for major renovations, or 2% for core and shell projects in the proposed building performance rating compared with the baseline building performance rating. Calculate the baseline building performance according to ANSI/ASHRAE/IESNA Standard 90.1–2010, Appendix G, with errata (or a USGBC-approved equivalent standard for projects outside the U.S.), using a simulation model.
>
> OR

39. USGBC, "LEED Reference Guide for Building Design and Construction," Version 4, November 18, 2013, www.usgbc.org/resources/leed-reference-guide-building-design-and-construction.

Option 2. Prescriptive Compliance: ASHRAE 50% Advanced Energy Design Guide[40]
Comply with the mandatory and prescriptive provisions of ANSI/ASHRAE/IESNA Standard 90.1–2010, with errata (or a USGBC-approved equivalent standard for projects outside the U.S.).

Comply with the HVAC and service water heating requirements, including equipment efficiency, economizers, ventilation, and ducts and dampers, in Chapter 4, Design Strategies and Recommendations by Climate Zone, for the appropriate ASHRAE 50% Advanced Energy Design Guide and climate zone.[41]

The performance path (Option 1) requires use of a computerized energy simulation model to establish a predicted baseline for a code-compliant building and then demonstrate a specified percentage reduction in energy use due to the project design and construction. In this case, the predicted outcome of the materials and strategies used by the design team is being measured. The path is performance-based, so it does not specify which materials must be used or the characteristics of the materials to be used.

In contrast, Option 2 is the prescriptive path. Here, the design team must use a guideline document, the *ASHRAE 50% Advanced Energy Design Guide,* to choose from a menu of options for the wall assembly, fenestration, roofing, and mechanical components. The credit does not require that the performance of the building be measured directly. Instead, the overall building performance is predicted based on the sum of the various component parts that have been shown via energy modeling to reduce energy use by at least 50% relative to a typical code-compliant building.

buildings, such as LEED O+M, rely on actual, field-measured performance of energy and water. Care should be taken to discern between performance credits earned based on predictive performance using energy modeling software and credits earned for field-measured actual performance, as will be discussed more fully in the following section.

The accompanying sidebar provides prescriptive and performance-based examples of LEED rating system credits.

Modeled versus Actual Performance

Building performance for energy, water, or lighting use can be measured in one of two ways: using a predictive model such as an energy model, or using the utility meter, which is based on actual consumption. In the case of proposed construction, actual measurement must wait until after the project is completed and occupancy is stabilized for the result to be meaningful. For this reason, energy models are widely used in the design world by architects and engineers to predict energy use under different design scenarios. This process is similar to a sensitivity analysis with a discounted cash flow model, in which certain inputs are tweaked to measure the impact of changing the discount rate by 25 basis points or adjusting the inflation rate assumption.

Predictive models for energy or cash flow can be useful tools but are susceptible to a similar weakness: If the inputs are not consistent with actual conditions, the predicted result is unlikely to be realized. Energy models can be very accurate predictors of actual energy use, since energy behaves according to the laws of thermodynamics. However, if the

40. The *ASHRAE 50% Advanced Energy Design Guide* is a reference guide that lists suites of prescriptive building materials and practices that will reduce predicted energy use by at least 50% relative to a baseline code-compliant building built to ASHRAE 90.1-2004.

41. USGBC, "LEED Reference Guide for Building Design and Construction," Version 4.

automated switches malfunction and leave the lights on all day or are overridden by occupants who are working late, the actual energy use will increase. The predictive power of the model is thus susceptible to real-world conditions such as system faults and occupant behavior. Similarly, if energy use is based on an occupant density of one occupant per 200 square feet but the actual density is one occupant per 125 square feet, the energy model is not likely to predict energy use accurately. In this case, the lighting use may not increase but the plug load and the cooling load due to heat from the additional occupants and equipment will likely increase. Water use in the restrooms will also likely increase. In addition to occupant behaviors, the skill and experience of the energy modeler can also influence the reliability of the result.

Recognizing the inherent limitations of predictive models is important when considering how much reliance to place on the results. However, it would be imprudent to dismiss predictive models outright since they can provide important information, particularly when comparing design or operational scenarios for a building, isolating component contributions to energy use, or comparing different buildings using the same assumptions. Energy models can also identify the energy budget of the building, noting where energy is being used and identifying options to change those use patterns. For the valuation process, the key is to identify whether the measured performance is based on a predictive model or actual results and to avoid conflating design (predicted) performance with actual performance.

Who Is Verifying Compliance?

No matter how stringent the requirements of a given rating system are, they are not meaningful (particularly from a valuation standpoint) if there is no assurance that the requirements were in fact met and the building will perform as designed. Verifying that the building has met the certification requirements is critical when analyzing the potential value impact of the green building rating, certification, or features.

Some rating systems require verification by an independent third party. From the point of view of valuation professionals, third-party verification would be relevant to assessing the credibility of any green building rating system. Some rating systems initially permitted self-reporting without an outside reviewer. While most have moved away from this practice, some still allow it. Having a disinterested third party review the submission and assess its merit promotes public trust in the certification.

Even with third-party verification, however, the robustness of the verification can vary. For example, the USGBC performs independent review of the credit submissions for LEED certification, and certification itself is granted by yet another organization, GBCI.[42] While no

42. Formerly known as the Green Building Certification Institute.

third-party, on-site inspection is required, LEED certification does require that the operation of mechanical systems be verified through commissioning (previously discussed in this chapter) performed by a third party.

Green Globes takes a slightly different approach by permitting initial self-reporting, with the claims being subsequently verified during a final on-site inspection by a third party. Similarly, the Living Building Challenge (LBC) certification of the International Living Future Institute (ILFI) requires an on-site audit by a member of the International Living Building Institute (ILBI) prior to certification. The WELL Building Standard requires on-site, third-party verification of various performance objectives at initial certification and every three years thereafter.

A Closer Look at Two Green Building Rating Systems

The focus so far has been on conveying the basic concepts of rating systems and how they affect valuation. This section takes a closer look at LEED, one of the first and currently one of the most common commercial green building rating systems, and the Living Building Challenge, a green building rating system that may be the most rigorous currently in existence.

LEED

LEED is a green building certification system intended to rank buildings according to various sustainability criteria, including location and site factors, water use, energy use and related effects, interior environmental quality, materials use, and waste. The comprehensive program is intended to be applicable to virtually any type of building improvement and is arranged into five general categories or rating system tracks depending on project type:

- New construction/major renovations: Building Design and Construction (BD+C)
- Tenant improvements/fit-out: Interior Design and Construction (ID+C)
- Ongoing operations: Building Operations and Maintenance (O+M)
- Land development (residential/mixed-use): Neighborhood Development (ND)
- Single-family and one- to three-story residential: Homes

There are individual adaptations for specific property types within each of these categories. For example, the current version's BD+C system has eight separate adaptations: new construction, core and shell, data centers, healthcare, hospitality, retail, schools, and warehouses and distribution centers.

LEED's origins date to 1993, when a group of designers, engineers, product manufacturers, and others formed the USGBC and began developing a consensus-based method to codify green building and sustainable best practices for the design and construction industry. They were initially inspired by the BREEAM program that was first launched in the United Kingdom in 1990. USGBC released its initial version of LEED in 2000. The most recent version (Version 4 or v4) was released in 2013. With each new version, the stringency increases and the program nomenclature and credit categories change slightly. In this discussion, we will use the Version 4 program description.

LEED certification is awarded at one of four levels–Certified, Silver, Gold, or Platinum–based on cumulative points or credits earned for meeting certain prescriptive or performance-based criteria in nine separate credit categories. Exhibit 2.4 (page 27) shows a LEED BD+C New Construction and Major Renovation scorecard with the following categories:

- Integrative process
- Location and transportation
- Sustainable sites
- Water efficiency
- Energy and atmosphere
- Materials and resources
- Indoor environmental quality
- Innovation
- Regional priority

Integrative process and location and transit are newly added categories in Version 4.

Certification is awarded based on cumulative credits earned. There are certain prerequisites in each category. Nonetheless, any individual project can achieve the same certification level with a different credit profile that could have very different value implications. For example, a property earning more credits for energy efficiency alters the focus for potential value impact relative to a similarly rated building with fewer energy-efficiency credits and more credits earned in another category. Even so, for buildings reaching the top levels of Gold and especially Platinum, the credit requirements are structured such that properties must achieve relatively high levels of credits in each category to accumulate sufficient credits for certification.

The USGBC administers the LEED program, including the development of the standards and technical materials. A separate entity,

Exhibit 2.7 The LEED Certification Process and Deciphering LEED Terminology

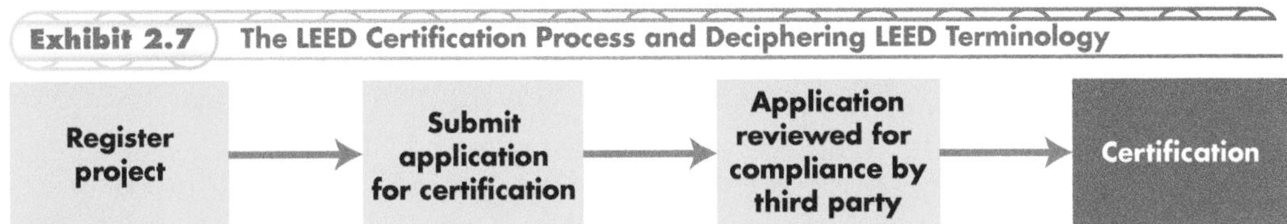

registered. A project that is registered simply means that it has been entered into the system under a specific version and a registration fee has been paid. It does not imply that any further action has been or will be taken. The number of LEED projects registered can be an early indicator of green building uptake in a given market. However, not all projects that are registered become certified. If the valuation assignment or comparable is noted as being registered under the LEED system, this is not the same as a project actually being LEED-certified. The process of moving from registration to certification is depicted above.

Certified versus certified: In contrast, **certified** with a lower-case *c* means that the project has actually met the requirement of any one of LEED's four award levels (Platinum, Gold, Silver, or Certified). Whereas **Certified** with an upper-case *c* is one of the four award levels. For example, a project can be LEED-certified at the Certified level or LEED-certified at the Silver level.

accredited applies to people rather than projects. A LEED AP, for example, is a LEED Accredited Professional.

Note that none of these terms apply to products. There is no such thing as LEED-certified flooring or a LEED-accredited energy system. Labels such as these may indicate either honest mistakes or attempts at greenwashing.

GBCI, provides third-party certification of the buildings, including reviewing the applications and verifying that projects meet the certification level thresholds.

Except for the O+M track, LEED credits and certifications are awarded based on the design of the building and its systems and the specific characteristics of the materials used. This includes credits given for energy efficiency which are based on either a prescriptive standard or a computer model that predicts consumption, but does not measure actual use. For a program focused on new construction and major renovation, this approach is logical in that energy and water use performance cannot be physically measured in a building that does not yet exist and is not yet occupied.

This aspect of LEED highlights the importance of building commissioning. Described in a sidebar earlier in this chapter (page 31), commissioning can be performed at various levels. It may cover only energy-using systems or incorporate water systems and the building envelope, among other components.

The O+M track, in contrast, is designed to be applied to any existing building, whether it is LEED certified under the BD+C track or not, so long as it is substantially occupied and has at least 12 months of operating data. With regards to energy performance, the O+M track uses the Energy Star Portfolio Manager software to compare predicted energy use to actual energy use based on the physical characteristics of the building, its climate, and occupant characteristics relative to comparable buildings.

The Living Building Challenge

The Living Building Challenge (LBC) creator and founder, Jason F. McLennan, has described this rating system as taking the next step beyond the requirements established by LEED towards buildings that are restorative and sustainable.[43] In this way, the LBC and systems such as LEED may be viewed as part of a continuum of green building practices and sustainability in the built environment rather than competitive certifications.

The LBC was first launched in 2006, and Version 3.0 was released in 2014. The LBC is now overseen by the ILFI.

The LBC certification consists of 20 requirements, called "imperatives," that are grouped into seven performance areas, or "petals." The seven petals and corresponding imperatives are summarized and briefly described in Exhibit 2.8.[44]

The LBC differs in several key respects from LEED and many of the other leading rating systems:

- LBC certification for all properties, including proposed construction, is based on actual, measured performance rather than modeled performance.
- LBC certification requires mandatory compliance with 20 criteria, rather than an accumulation of credits across multiple categories.
- Instead of full LBC certification, projects can opt for Petal Certification, which requires certification under at least three of the seven petals, one of which must be water, energy, or materials. Alternatively, projects can pursue NZE building certification, which LBC refers to as *zero energy*.

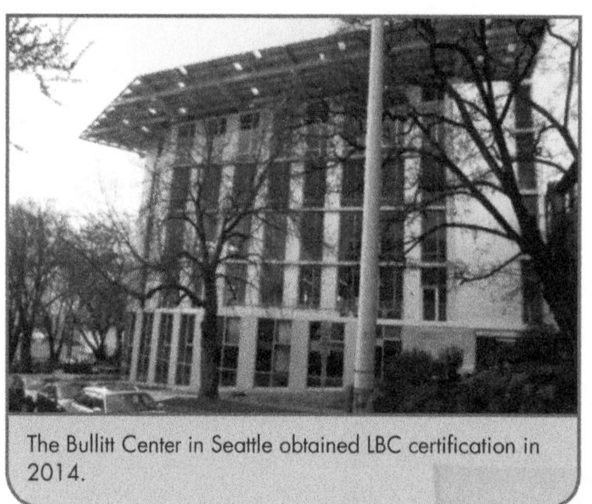

The Bullitt Center in Seattle obtained LBC certification in 2014.

Due to the program's stringency, few buildings have achieved full LBC certification. The Bullitt Center in Seattle is one building that has met these strict standards. This six-story, 44,766-sq.-ft. office building, shown in the accompanying photo, was completed in 2013 and certified under LBC Version 2.0 in 2014. At that time, it was the first multitenant office building and largest building certified under the LBC.

Designed to have a 250-year life span and reflect the Bullitt Foundation's mission of protecting the natural

43. "Beyond LEED: The Living Building Challenge with Jason F. McLennan, Cascadia Green Building Council," *ISSP Insight* (December 2008).

44. For further detail, see the LBC website, http://living-future.org/lbc.

Exhibit 2.8 Petals and Imperatives of the Living Building Challenge

Petal	Imperative	Description
Place	Limits to growth	Only use previously developed land; protect sensitive areas
	Urban agriculture	Dedicate portion of site to food production
	Habitat exchange	Mandatory off-site habitat preservation
	Human-powered living	Emphasize human-powered transportation
Water	Net positive water	100% of water from precipitation, treat on site
Energy	Net positive energy	105% of energy from on-site renewables and battery back-up (mandatory) for resilience
Health & Happiness	Civilized environment	Occupied space must have operable windows
	Healthy interior environment	VOC control; green cleaning; no smoking
	Biophilic environment	Design that enhances connection to nature
Materials	Red list	20 chemicals/groups banned from use*
	Embodied carbon footprint	Carbon footprint must be offset through credits
	Responsible industry sourcing	Use third-party sustainable certified products
	Living economy sourcing	Use locally sourced materials
	Net positive waste	Reduce/eliminate waste during entire life cycle
Equity	Human scale and humane places	Human-scale rather than automobile-scale development
	Universal access to nature and place	Do not block air, water, light, or access of others
	Equitable investment	Mandatory charitable donation of 0.5% of project
	Just organizations	Employment practices disclosure
Beauty	Beauty and spirit	Design for aesthetic enjoyment, public art
	Inspiration and education	Signs, tours, website, brochures, case study

* See Exhibit 2.5 (page 36)

environment and promoting healthy and sustainable ecosystems, the building incorporates a variety of green, high-performance, and sustainable features including the following:

- Very low energy use
  - The site energy use intensity (EUI) of 14.9 kBtus per square foot (2015 actual, 100% occupancy) matches the design EUI of 15.0, and is 75% below a comparable new, code-compliant building in Seattle.
  - The high-efficiency building envelope includes triple glazing and insulation.
  - The HVAC system incorporates passive ventilation with radiant floor heat and a ground-source heat pump.
- On-site energy generation

  A 14,000-sq.-ft., 244 kW rooftop solar array generates 28% more energy than the building used in 2015 (net zero positive), despite a solar-challenged Seattle location.
- Multiple water-efficiency strategies
  - One hundred percent of the building's water use is from on-site rainwater capture, treatment, and storage.
  - One hundred percent of the building's waste water is treated on site using mechanical filtering and a constructed wetland.
  - The building features composting toilets that process solid waste using digesters located in the basement.
- Emphasis on occupant health and well-being
  - The "irresistible staircase" (pictured in the Green Feature Gallery on page 303) encourages occupants to exercise by making the stairs a prominent design feature that is easier to find and more enjoyable to use than the building elevator.
  - Thirteen-foot ceilings with automated exterior blinds and interior shades provide extensive daylighting.
  - The building is designed so that all occupants are situated within 30 feet of natural light and fresh air from operable windows.
- Encourage alternative commuting
  - No automobile parking is allowed.
  - The building has a bike garage with showers on Floors 2-6.
  - The site location has a Walk Score of 99 (out of 100) and a Transit Score of 78 (out of 100).

Summary

Understanding the basic concepts of green building rating systems provides critical and useful information to real estate professionals. Knowing the types of design strategies and construction techniques that can transform the objectives of green building into the physical reality of the built environment gives the valuation professional a greater ability to recognize examples and elements of green building even when there is no green certification or label. Furthermore, rating systems provide guidance as to how these green features or processes can be implemented, documented, measured, and verified.

Credible green building rating systems can provide assurance to market participants that any green claims made have merit. Green building rating systems encompass a wide range of strategies and can be based on single or multiple attributes. Green ratings and certifications vary in terms of the level of rigor required. Evaluating the rating based on what is being rated or certified, how compliance is achieved, and who is verifying compliance can help determine whether the rating system is credible and if the rated features or structure warrant inclusion in the valuation process.

For the valuation professional, green building rating systems can provide a framework for identifying green building features and guidance as to where to look for potential value impacts. The project checklist, or scorecard, can be used to help identify the particular features or design strategies that were employed in earning the certification. Since most multi-attribute certifications are awarded based on cumulative credits earned, specific features can vary widely, even among two buildings of similar type with the same green certification rating. Evaluating the value impact requires identifying and understanding green building features, how those features interact, and the given market's response to these features.

3 Understanding Green Building Design and Construction

Chapter 1 defined green buildings as structures that are resource efficient, address the environmental and societal impacts of real estate development, and focus on the building's entire life cycle. Chapter 2 discussed how a green building rating system can provide a comprehensive strategy and guidance for meeting these objectives. In this chapter, we consider how green objectives are physically realized.

This phase of green building–the physical implementation–is of particular interest to valuation professionals. It is one thing to consider in theory whether a design element or group of elements may or may not have a value impact, but it is only when a building is actually built and occupied that the theories can be tested. Does the building perform better, and if so, on which metrics? Are tenants more likely to occupy and stay in the space? Would investors choose this building over comparable properties?

These questions could and should be asked about any building, green or non-green, by anyone who is evaluating whether a property meets, exceeds, or falls short of market expectations. However, particularly for green buildings, these questions and answers are not always clear. The building technology underlying many of the complex systems in green buildings can be daunting to non-engineers, making the analysis of building performance more difficult. Furthermore, market response can sometimes be challenging to disentangle from other building attributes. For example, did the investor buy the LEED-certified Class A office building because it had superior operational efficiencies due to its energy and water use systems, or because the LEED certification signaled a higher-quality asset independent of its enhanced performance?

This combination of new and often complicated building features with an evolving and not always clear-cut market response can be challenging. As suggested in Chapter 1, breaking down the problem into two parts–identifying and understanding both a new market influence and new building characteristics–can help to clarify the valuation task.

This chapter continues the previous discussion of how the theory and objectives of green building are transformed into a completed project. What are the key concepts of green building design and construction? How does it differ from traditional building design and construction? Subsequent chapters address the market response to these characteristics and how that response can be analyzed within the context of the valuation process.

Key Concepts of Green Building Design and Construction

It makes intuitive sense that if we want to have a different outcome–i.e., an economically feasible building that performs differently than other buildings–the process to get to that outcome will also likely need to be different. Jason McLennan, creator and founder of the Living Building Challenge green building rating system discussed in Chapter 2, puts it this way: "Successful sustainable design requires a shift in status quo thinking about how things are put together, how they are operated and how they are maintained."[1] While stated simply, the ramifications of this type of fundamental change on the design and construction process are far from simple. The following sections examine how the unique philosophical and performance objectives of green building affect the green building design and construction process.

Green Building Design Strategies

Green building pioneers noted early on that there were many obstacles to overcome before green building would gain acceptance and wide application. The cost barrier was often cited as a notable obstruction, as early green buildings were often more expensive to build than conventional buildings due to a variety of factors such as design teams that were inexperienced in green building and higher initial costs of new green technology.[2] Even now, the cost of a green building relative to a conventional one is a source of interest to building designers as well as those tasked with valuing these buildings. Does it cost more to build and operate green buildings? If so, how much more? How much

1. Jason F. McLennan, *The Philosophy of Sustainable Design* (Kansas City, MO: Ecotone Publishing, 2004), 218.
2. Ibid., 196-201.

of any increased cost is captured by increased asset value? This issue of economic feasibility is certainly not the only force affecting green adaptations in the design and construction process, but it may have the most resonance from the perspective of valuation professionals.

As McLennan framed the problem, green buildings require a change in thinking about how buildings and systems are assembled, operated, and maintained. Exhibit 3.1 synthesizes various strategies used by green building proponents and practitioners to address this issue. While there may be some disparity in how these strategies are expressed or prioritized, the core idea is not dissimilar to how risk managers view risk management. The first step is not how to fund the entire spectrum of potential losses. Rather, the process starts with an analysis of the exposures, and then seeks a systematic reduction in those exposures. Risk is avoided when possible and mitigated for unavoidable losses to render a lower risk exposure overall, thereby reducing the amount of risk that has to be funded or transferred via insurance or other means.

Exhibit 3.1 Green Building Design Strategies

Reduce	Harvest	Manage
Reduce Loads to a Minimum • **Analyze** - Identify interrelationships between building, site, systems, and components • **Synergize** - Seek financial and functional efficiencies between systems • **Optimize** - Meet loads as efficiently as possible - Pursue overall building efficiency and performance over the efficiency of isolated systems • **Right-Size** - Taylor systems for expected loads; do not substitute extra capacity for lack of analysis	**Harvest "Free" Resources** • **Replace** - Use passive systems in place of active systems when possible • **Reuse/Regenerate** - Use waste (materials, water, byproducts from other systems) for useful purposes • **Renew** - Harness on-site solar, wind, and/or geothermal resources	**Manage What Remains** • **Mitigate** - Limit loads that cannot be avoided • **Evaluate** - Commission all systems - Document performance for all metrics - Compare documented performance against expected performance and peers (benchmarking) • **Recalibrate** - Fine-tune systems until perfomance goals are met

Harnessing "Free" Energy: Passive Design Basics

Modern technology has acclimated us to the idea that when we want light, we flip a switch, or when we want to heat or cool a space, we engage the HVAC system. But what if the building was designed so that light was naturally available when it was needed and the building synergized with the surrounding environment to provide heating and cooling without mechanical intervention? This is the essence of *passive design*: using the ambient environment of the building in concert with purposeful design and material choices in order to heat, cool, and light the building without active, mechanical systems. Passive strategies include daylighting, natural ventilation, and various passive heating and cooling systems.

Passive design is powered by basic physics, primarily the laws of thermodynamics and fluid dynamics. Thus, passive design informs not only building structural and envelope design but also materials choices. In addition, siting and microclimate factors can be harnessed for passive heating, cooling, and ventilation. Strategies can be simple and straightforward, such as the strategic placement of deciduous trees to provide shade when needed in the summer while allowing for light and direct heat gain in the winter. Passive design can also be quite complex and embedded into an integrated building design.

For example, a passive ventilation strategy may utilize the stack, or chimney, effect. This approach harnesses the inherent physical qualities of gasses like air that have lower densities at higher temperatures in order to replace fan energy that would otherwise be used to mechanically ventilate an interior space. When gases like air absorb heat, the molecules become more energetic and require more volume per molecule, which reduces the density on a volumetric basis. In other words, hot air is lighter than cool air, which is the same physics behind hot air balloons. In buildings, the result is the stack effect. When warm air rises, the denser cool air sinks, creating a pressure differential that can be used to draw cooler outside air indoors and exhaust hot interior air without using fan energy. Passive ventilation can also use prevailing wind patterns to create pressure differentials that replace fan-driven air circulation. This effect can be amplified by building design that leverages fluid dynamics in a manner similar to airplane wing design, creating a negative pressure "lift" that facilitates non-mechanical ventilation.

Thermal mass is the capability of a material to absorb and retain heat energy. It can also be thought of as thermal inertia, or resistance to a change in temperature. Dense materials like concrete and stone are considered to have a high thermal mass, and thus can be used to help modulate building temperature fluctuations due to the diurnal heating and cooling cycles of the environment or occupant and equipment heat load. Thermal mass may also be coupled with insulation to preserve or enhance the thermal mass qualities of a material. Materials with high thermal mass can also be used in conjunction with passive solar design strategies to capture and store heat from sunlight.

In addition to using sunlight to meet heating requirements, passive solar design strategies can be used to bring light deeper into the interior space and reduce daytime lighting needs, a concept known as *daylighting*. These two strategies are often used together. Passive solar design may start with siting the building along an east-west axis to minimize early morning glare and late afternoon heat load. This orientation optimizes natural lighting by exposing the long sides of the building to the southern exposure, which offers the greatest passive solar resource. Since the sun is higher in the sky in the summer, when the solar heat is not typically desired indoors, passive solar design uses exterior overhangs, canopies, light shelves, window treatments, and other strategies to block direct heat gain from the sun. Careful design of these sunlight controls can still permit the sunlight to enter the building indirectly in the summer and directly in the winter. This strategy, particularly when coupled with a high thermal mass flooring material, can allow direct solar heat gain to provide passive heating to the interior in the winter and daylighting all year long.

Passive design strategies are typically sought first in green building design, as they can reduce the energy burden and allow for less reliance on active design strategies such as electric lights and forced-air HVAC systems. However, it is also possible to use a combination of passive and active systems. Hybrid systems—such as energy recovery ventilation systems and ground- or air-source heat pump systems (as shown in the Green Feature Gallery in Appendix A (pages 298-300))—make use of ambient energy with varying levels of mechanical energy.

Passive design strategies are often used as part of an integrated design, as shown in the following photos of a renovated building used as an educational facility. This build-out illustrates several passive design strategies, including daylighting, direct gain solar heating, thermal mass, and natural ventilation. While it may not appear all that different from a conventional build out, the energy and interior environment performance of this net zero energy (NZE) building is superior to that of its conventional peers.

In this example, the concrete slab has been exposed at the perimeter of the building in front of the windows, allowing sunlight to heat the concrete via direct gain. This passive solar strategy uses the concrete's high thermal mass to leverage the benefits of direct solar heat gain and help stabilize and equalize interior temperatures to enhance thermal comfort. The highly polished surface also reflects daylight into the room.

The top portions of some of the windows are operable. Together with the vents in the roof monitors that provide natural light to the interior of the space, this allows for the passive ventilation benefit of the stack effect. In this hybrid or mixed-mode HVAC system, the passive elements consisting of the operable windows and roof monitor vents are mechanically controlled by the building management system, which also controls the variable refrigerant flow air-source heat pump system that supplements the passive components of the system.

The remodel of this building included exposing the concrete slab at the perimeter of the building in front of the windows, allowing sunlight to heat the concrete via direct gain. This passive solar strategy uses the concrete's high thermal mass to leverage the benefits of direct solar heat gain and help stabilize and equalize interior temperatures to enhance thermal comfort. The highly polished surface of the concrete slab reflects daylight into the building. The operable windows together with the roof monitors use the stack effect to provide passive ventilation.

The north-facing roof monitors provide glare-free natural light to the interior as well as facilitate passive ventilation through the automated vents on the side.

The design also eliminates the need for a separate mounting system for the solar PV.

Similarly, green building design does not seek to "fund" all the resources needed (energy, water, materials) to construct and operate the building. As with risk management, the goal instead is to have to fund as little as possible. Interrelationships between the building and its site, systems, and components are identified and analyzed to minimize resource use and optimize performance. "Free" resources unlocked via passive design strategies, regenerative processes such as gray water systems that capture rain and wastewater to use for landscaping, or the reuse of materials then further limit the building's resource use profile. The resource needs that remain are then, at last, "funded" via active, physical systems such as renewable on-site energy or highly efficient, right-sized mechanical systems. Ongoing needs are managed using mitigation strategies (such as low-VOC paints and other building materials that minimize additions to the indoor air filtration burden) and performance evaluation through commissioning, post-occupancy surveys, and ongoing measurement and verification.

Integrated Design

Green building is still evolving as a product (i.e., defining what a green building is) and also as a process (i.e., how to build a green building). As with any process that is still changing, strict guidelines and standards are few and far between. Those who design and construct green buildings are still working on honing techniques and approaches, and the marketplace is still adapting to the availability of new types of buildings, materials, and technologies.

Strictly speaking, there is no hard-and-fast rule that green buildings must depart from a traditional design and construction process. Indeed, green buildings or large-scale green retrofits may still utilize a traditional design and construction process. However, the complexity of high-performing green buildings often requires the input of a larger number of experts and stakeholders, ranging from the property owner or developer to architects, designers, and various engineers and other consultants who specialize in energy, mechanical, and electrical systems. Green buildings may also require a deeper or broader level of expertise in areas such as renewable energy systems, passive design, lighting design, or green infrastructure. Furthermore, a green building's systems are often designed to be interrelated and interdependent. In order to avoid interoperability issues–i.e., "when the gadgets don't talk to one another," as described by one property owner–the experts in charge of those gadgets also have to talk to one another. Without this level of communication and coordination, there may be obstacles to a cohesive integration of the systems that can hinder optimal building performance.

Consider the following example from the *Sustainable Building Technical Manual* about how using a passive solar design strategy affects everything from siting decisions to HVAC requirements:

> Incorporating increased daylighting into a building design, for example, will affect many other factors in the building. This strategy, which takes into account the building's orientation, as well as glazing choices and location, will permit reduction of artificial lighting. The resulting reductions in electricity use and internal heat loads will allow the downsizing of air-conditioning systems. As a result, overall energy usage and energy costs in the building are reduced, and the improved air quality and lighting conditions can result in increased productivity and health of occupants.[3]

The interplay needed between the building systems or elements and the designers of those systems or elements described in the above example can be difficult to achieve using a traditional design process that tends to be incremental and linear, with those involved in the project often working independently of each other. Instead, green building design uses a "whole building" approach to develop integrated building systems that can yield cost, operational, and functional synergies.

"Whole Building" Concept

A "whole building" approach is a type of systems thinking in which the function and operation of the building systems and the site are considered as a whole rather than as individual components. A project team, interacting in an interdisciplinary fashion, seeks to design a structure of interdependent components and systems that work together to create the building. From this point of view, a building is not comprised of discrete parts.

In the book *Natural Capitalism,* coauthors Paul Hawken, Amory Lovins, and L. Hunter Lovins argue the case for a whole building approach to building design as follows:

> Optimizing components in isolation tends to pessimize the whole system – and hence the bottom line. You can actually make a system less efficient while making each of its parts more efficient, simply by not properly linking up those components. If they're not designed to work with one another, they'll tend to work against one another.[4]

In the whole building approach, the relationships between all building elements are considered. How does the microclimate of the site or the building's orientation affect the energy systems? How does the energy system affect ventilation rates, which in turn affect the quality of the interior environment? How do occupant needs such as thermal comfort or daylighting affect the building envelope and the mechanical and electrical systems? The connections can be numerous and involve multiple disciplines, even in regard to a relatively

---

3. Anthony Bernheim and William Reed, *Sustainable Building Technical Manual: Green Building Design, Construction and Operations* (Washington, DC: Public Technology, Inc., 1996), Chapter 3.

4. Paul Hawken, Amory B. Lovins, and L. Hunter Lovins, *Natural Capitalism: Creating the Next Industrial Revolution* (New York: Little, Brown and Company, 1999), 117.

uncomplicated element such as water use. For example, if the goal is to reduce water use, a variety of elements would be impacted, including roofing, rainwater collection, and plumbing fixtures; landscaping choices would also need to be considered.

From a valuation standpoint, the use of the whole building approach over traditional building design is reflected in cost and performance metrics. According to the *Sustainable Building Technical Manual*:

> Integrated building design is a cornerstone for developing sustainable buildings, which are efficiently combined systems of coordinated and environmentally sound products, systems, and design elements. Simply adding or overlaying systems will not result in optimal performance or cost savings. Rather, building designers can obtain the most effective results by designing various building systems and components as interdependent parts of the entire structure.[5]

Noted green building expert and engineer Malcolm Lewis states it even more plainly: "If different elements are designed without regard to the other elements, the result will be less efficient and more expensive."[6]

Synergies and Trade-Offs

The acknowledgement and deliberate analysis of the interrelationships between a building's site, systems, and other components lie at the heart of the difference between green building and traditional design and construction. Interdisciplinary collaboration and the use of whole building analysis yields opportunities for the discovery of synergies between systems and allows for building performance optimization. The use of operable windows in tandem with roof monitors, for example, can use the stack effect to leverage the disparity between hotter-than-desired interior air and a cooler exterior ambient environment.[7] This allows for non-mechanical cooling, which may in turn lead to downsizing the HVAC system and saving up-front costs, while also lowering operating costs through reduced energy use. As roof monitors allow in natural light, they may reduce the need for interior lighting, which would also reduce up-front costs and result in operational savings.

But while there is great potential for cost savings and improved performance, there are also potential tradeoffs. A classic trade-off between building systems is the desire for increased energy efficiency versus optimal indoor air quality for occupants. Sick building syndrome is an example of what happens when building systems

---

5. Bernheim and Reed, *Sustainable Building Technical Manual*, Chapter 3.
6. Malcolm Lewis, "Building for the Future," *ASHRAE Journal* (September 2004): S24.
7. Roof monitors are essentially vertical protrusions through the roof with glazing and possibly air vents. They are often used to provide natural light to areas lacking windows. When used with operable windows, they utilize the stack effect to enhance natural ventilation.

and goals are not balanced. Increasing the tightness of the building envelope to improve energy efficiency led to problems with indoor air quality in many buildings and deleterious impacts on human health. As discussed in Chapter 2, a growing number of studies have shown that increasing air changes per hour (ACH) above the current minimum standard yields cognitive and productivity benefits to occupants. However, increasing the ACH with mechanical systems means more energy is used to move and thermally condition the air, which works against energy-efficiency goals and increases operating costs. Determining how to achieve an acceptable energy-use profile while also optimizing indoor air quality can be challenging. With the increased interest in occupant health and well-being comes an increased interest in how to address the higher costs associated with improving ventilation rates.[8]

The Integrative Process

To address the need for a higher level of communication between systems and systems experts to deliver an optimally functioning and cost-efficient building, the green building design team may utilize an *integrative process* (*IP*), also known as an *integrated design process* (*IDP*). This became a separate credit category as of the most recent release of the LEED green building rating system (Version 4).

Whereas Exhibit 3.1 outlined an overarching strategy for designing green buildings, IP focuses on the tactics that can be used to implement this different way of approaching design and construction. The *Integrative Process (IP) ANSI Consensus National Standard Guide 2.0 for Design and Construction of Sustainable Buildings and Communities* defines it this way:

> The Integrative Process actively seeks to design and construct projects that are cost-effective over both the short and long terms, by engaging all project team members in an intentional process of discovering mutually beneficial interrelationships and synergies between systems and components, in a way that unifies technical and living systems, so that high levels of building performance, human performance, and environmental benefits are achieved.[9]

The integrative process can also be remembered as the "four E's:" *everybody engaging every* issue *early* in the project.[10]

William Reed, a founding member of the US Green Building Council, and John Boecker, founder of the 7group sustainable build-

8. The study by MacNoughton et al. referenced in the sidebar titled "Clearing the Air: Why Ventilation Rates Matter" in Chapter 2 (page 37) discusses the specific cost-benefit tradeoff of increasing ACH and how these costs can be mitigated via energy recovery ventilators.

9. American National Standards Institute (ANSI), *Integrative Process (IP) ANSI Consensus National Standard Guide 2.0 for Design and Construction of Sustainable Buildings and Communities* (Washington, DC: ANSI, 2012), 4, http://webstore.ansi.org/RecordDetail.aspx?-sku=MTS+2012%3a1.

10. Ibid., 7.

ing organization, collaborated on *The Integrative Design Guide to Green Building*, a text that shaped the IP ANSI Standard and serves as a companion guide to it.[11] Reed and Boecker explain the concept of integrative process as follows:

> Almost everything in a building project affects everything else. Consequently, the integrative process examines how to understand in advance how the different systems impact each other and consciously make choices that improve the efficiency of a project.[12]

Exhibit 3.2 outlines some of the key elements that distinguish an integrative process: collaboration, whole-system thinking, and a life-cycle perspective.

Communication among project team members may be one of the most critical elements of this design process.[13] The emphasis on communication and collaboration among a wide variety of experts and building stakeholders may be the most striking feature of an integrative design process.

Communication among the project team also begins from the onset. In the traditional approach, a specific system's expert tends to become involved only when that system is involved. In IP, the design team is assembled and meets collectively from the beginning of the project. These meetings, which those in the design world refer to as "charrettes" or "workshops," center on setting performance objectives, exploring interrelationships between building systems, and proposing design solutions to meet project goals. These sessions then are repeated as needed to fine-tune the building design.

Exhibit 3.2 Key Elements of an Integrative Process

Collaborative Approach

- Inclusive
- Entire project team included at project onset
- Consensus-based decision making
- Interdisciplinary communication
- Iterative process

Whole-System Analysis

- Building viewed as an interrelated "whole" system rather than independently functioning "parts"
- Financial and functional synergies sought between systems

Life-Cycle Perspective

- Economic and functional performance analyzed over the life of the building
- Process continues through completion of construction to post-occupancy

In addition to collaborative, whole-system thinking, an integrative process also emphasizes the need to examine the costs and performance of the project over its life cycle. That is, how does the design of the building affect not just the initial cost to construct, but also the cost to operate and maintain the building? Post-occupancy issues such as

11. Bill Reed and 7group, *The Integrative Design Guide to Green Building: Redefining the Practice of Sustainability* (Hoboken, NJ: Wiley, 2009).
12. John Boecker and Bill Reed, "Understanding Integrative Design in LEED v4," *Lessons Learned* 8 (2012): 35.
13. Malcom Lewis, "Integrated Design for Sustainable Buildings," *ASHRAE Journal* 9, no. 46 (September 2004): S22-S29.

building performance can be monitored and fine-tuned over time using initial and ongoing commissioning and post-occupancy surveys.[14]

Value Implications of the Integrative Process

The financial sector has recognized the potential for an integrative design process to have a financial impact. In 2008, Fireman's Fund issued a risk reduction statement indicating that the use of an integrative design process, specifically the IP ANSI Standard, reduces the operational risk of green buildings as well as the risk surrounding the use of new materials and construction techniques used in green buildings.[15] In addition, the *National Consensus Green Building Investment Underwriting Standards* state the following about the integrative process concept:

> For construction loans, an integrated design approach can have a positive impact on cost overruns, change order reduction, delays and other financial factors that impact budgeted line items and contingency reserves; conversely, not following IP usually has a negative financial impact.[16]

Boecker and Reed recount an example of how the interdisciplinary, whole-building perspective inherent in an integrative design process can yield results that are unlikely to be achieved using a traditional, linear design approach. They describe how during a project team meeting, a query from the lighting and energy consultant regarding the reflectance value of the architect's suggested paint color led to a discovery that by using a slightly lighter paint color with a higher light reflectance value, the number of lighting fixtures could be reduced by 25%. This in turn would reduce the overall heat gain from lamping, thereby reducing cooling costs and allowing the cooling system to be downsized.[17]

However, an integrative design process does not guarantee more desirable cost and performance results. The end result can be highly dependent on the experience and expertise of the project team. A well-seasoned team that has completed similar projects may be able to leverage that experience on subsequent projects, allowing for cost savings and fewer performance glitches. Conversely, a team that is embarking on their first green building project may have learning-curve inefficiencies that result in a higher-than-average cost budget. Having

---

14. Building commissioning is a verification process meant to ensure that systems are performing the way they were designed to perform and are free of conflicts or errors. See the sidebar in Chapter 2 titled "What Is Building Commissioning?" (page 31) for further details.

15. Steve Bushnell, "Risk Reduction Statement: ANSI Integrative Process Standard for Sustainable Buildings and Communities," September 2008, http://mts.sustainableproducts.com/CMP_FFIC_Risk_Reduction_Statement.pdf.

16. Capital Markets Partnership (CMP), *National Consensus Green Building Investment Underwriting Standards: Commercial Buildings*, approved September 2, 2008, and revised July 2012 (Washington, DC: CMP, 2012), 56.

17. Boecker and Reed, "Understanding Integrative Design in LEED v4," 32.

some idea of the project team's experience can aid in gauging the appropriateness of the building cost budget in the cost approach.

Cost Shift

The timing and composition of initial construction and operational costs may shift for green projects as compared to conventional ones. Understanding the potential for shifts in timing and capital cost allocation is critical to properly analyzing cost estimates and construction and operational budgets in a valuation assignment.

The timing shift stems from the life-cycle focus of green building. When the design process incorporates life-cycle costing of the improvements, the design team may make different choices than if the decision were made solely on initial capital cost (also referred to as *first cost*). For example, the green building design team employing a life cycle costing approach considers the higher initial cost of LED lighting in concert with the reduced operations and maintenance costs due to less frequent replacement of LED bulbs compared to the initially less expensive but not as long-lasting fluorescent lamps. In contrast, only the initial capital cost is likely to be considered by a conventional design team that does not use the life-cycle approach.

Shifting costs between the capital and operational budgets is not unique to green building. Property owners routinely consider whether to choose the item with the lower initial cost in exchange for a higher future operational cost, or vice versa. What is different about green building is that the cost shift is often the opposite of the "value engineering" approach of opting for lower-cost items in the construction budget in order to meet a budget threshold or offset cost overruns in other budget areas.

The second cost shift occurs within the construction cost budget itself. As will be discussed in more detail in the cost approach section of Chapter 9, an integrative process often results in higher soft (indirect) costs that may be associated with reduced hard (direct) construction costs. This cost shift is important to keep in mind when analyzing construction cost budgets for green buildings in light of traditional "rules of thumb," particularly for architect and engineering costs that are typically a major component of soft costs. Comparing and adjusting first costs for a green building designed using an integrative design process against a conventionally designed building could result in costs that are stabilized higher or lower than warranted.

Alternatively, the composition of the hard costs themselves may change as compared to a conventional building. As explained in the *Roadmap for the Integrated Design Process,* "Higher capital costs can be redistributed in order to achieve a green building without incremental cost. For example, the higher cost of a combination of high-performance glazing, higher insulation levels, and operable windows can be offset by the related reduction in or elimination of some mechanical components due to reduced heating and cooling loads."[18]

This capital cost allocation or hard cost compositional shift within the construction budget may or may not be cost neutral: Soft costs may be higher without corresponding hard-cost offsets, particularly if the design team chose higher first cost items that have lower operational costs. The experience of the design team is also a factor, as mentioned earlier. Both of these issues are worth considering when assessing the reasonableness of a green building construction cost budget.

Summary

Green building's expanded focus to include resource efficiency and environmental and societal concerns over the building's life cycle necessitates changes to the traditional design and construction process of conventional buildings. To achieve improved performance within a constrained time and monetary budget, green building design uses an interdisciplinary and collaborative holistic analysis of the interrelationships between the building and its site, systems, and components.

A primary goal of this analysis is to minimize resource use via synergies, optimize systems as a whole rather than in isolation, and prudently analyze resource needs so that all building systems can be appropriately sized. Loads may be further reduced by harvesting passive resources of the building and its site and harnessing regenerative and renewable opportunities on site and within the building envelope. Operational resource use is then efficiently managed via mitigation strategies and the evaluation of building performance through commissioning and ongoing measurement and verification.

Green building design and construction affects the valuation process in a number of ways. An integrated, "whole building" design process can affect how costs are viewed and reported within the construction and operational budgets. Appropriately stabilizing these costs in the valuation process requires an understanding of the potential for increased building operational efficiency and the effect on the timing and composition of hard and soft costs.

18. Busby, Perkins, & Will and Stantec Consulting, *Roadmap for the Integrated Design Process*, (Vancouver, BC: BC Green Building Roundtable, 2007), 19.

4 Understanding Green Building Demand

Demand for green building continues to grow. By 2018, one-third of construction companies worldwide are projected to have more green projects than conventional projects underway, doubling the number of companies with more green than conventional projects in just three years.[1] While countries with emerging green markets are expected to see the largest percentage in growth, even mature green building markets such as those in North America and Europe are expected to see substantial growth in green building new construction and retrofits. In the United States, the green construction market is anticipated to grow by over 15% each year between 2015 and 2018, an amount that outperforms growth in non-green construction spending.[2]

The commercial office market has seen particularly strong penetration by green building. Based on floor area, LEED-certified space represented 20% of the total commercial office space in the United States as of the end of 2015, with some markets such as Minneapolis, Chicago, and San Francisco reporting up to 40% of the square footage of office space being LEED-certified.[3] Exhibit 4.1 charts the 10 US cities leading in total certified commercial office space, according to

1. Dodge Data and Analytics, *World Green Building Trends 2016: Developing Markets Accelerate Global Green Growth* (Bedford, MA: Dodge Data and Analytics, 2016) http://fidic.org/sites/default/files/World%20Green%20Building%20Trends%202016%20SmartMarket%20Report%20FINAL.pdf.
2. Booz Allen Hamilton and the US Green Building Council (USGBC), *2015 Green Building Economic Impact Study* (Washington, DC: Booz Allen Hamilton and the USGBC, 2015), 11, http://go.usgbc.org/2015-Green-Building-Economic-Impact-Study.html.
3. If Energy Star-labeled buildings were included, the total amount of certified space nationwide would double to 40%. CBRE and Maastricht University, *National Green Building Adoption Index–2016* (Los Angeles: CBRE, 2016), http://dimension.maps.arcgis.com/apps/MapJournal/index.html?appid=16f3b237348e4128abf30d0fc8651d5a.

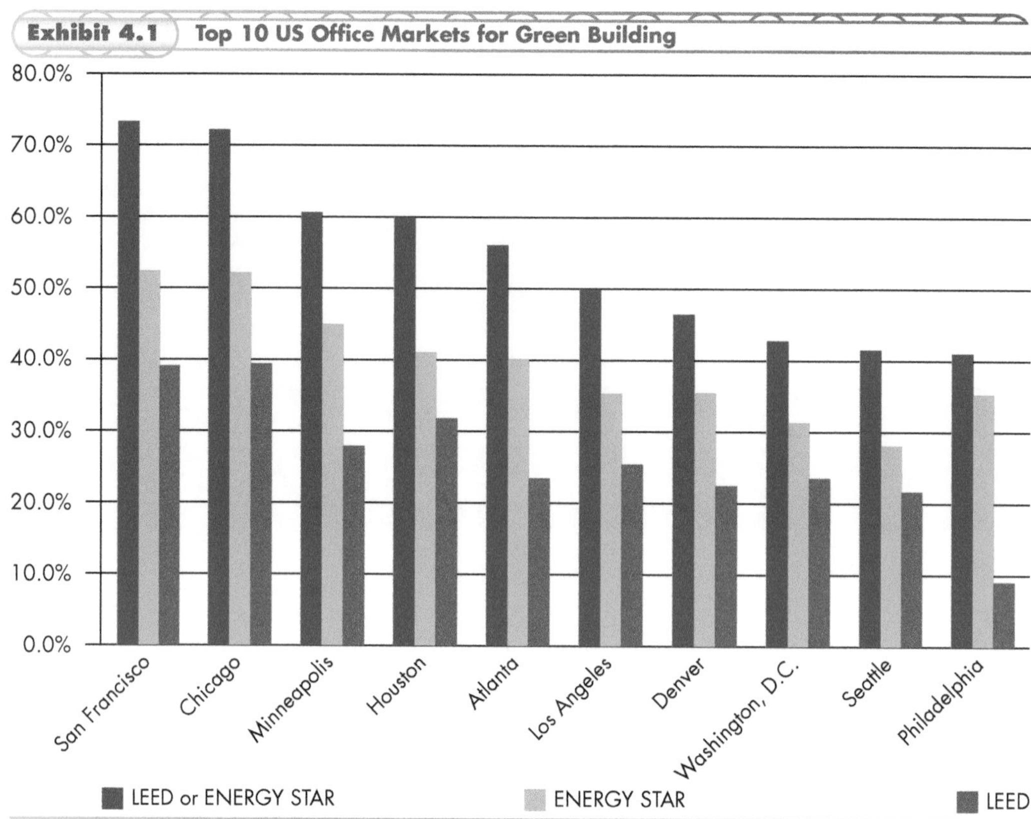

Exhibit 4.1 Top 10 US Office Markets for Green Building

Data compiled from CBRE and Maastricht University, *National Green Building Adoption Index—2016* (Los Angeles: CBRE, 2016), http://dimension.maps.arcgis.com/apps/MapJournal/index.html?appid=16f3b237348e4128abf30d0fc8651d5a.

CBRE's 2016 *National Green Building Adoption Index*. Demand for green institutional and retrofit projects is also increasing.[4]

An unusual aspect of green building is that uptake can be very uneven between markets and even between building types within the same market (e.g., office versus retail versus multifamily). Taking a closer look at the previously quoted statistic of 20% of total office space being LEED-certified, one notes that the top three green markets are performing at nearly double the average rate, while markets such as Kansas City and Detroit have very low percentages (4% and 2%, respectively) of their total commercial office space being LEED-certified.[5] One might conclude that cities with relatively small percentages of LEED certifications are not green or sustainability oriented. However, consider that Kansas City enacted energy and water use reporting requirements in 2015, becoming the fourteenth US city

4. Dodge Data and Analytics, *World Green Building Trends 2016*.
5. CBRE and Maastricht University, *National Green Building Adoption Index–2016*.

to enact benchmarking legislation.[6] Further clouding the picture on exactly what and where "green" is, CBRE and Maastricht University's 2015 *National Green Building Adoption Index* examined building size as it related to LEED certifications and found that 62% of larger buildings (over 500,000 square feet) were LEED-certified versus slightly less than 5% of smaller buildings (under 100,000 square feet).[7]

What does this mean to valuation professionals? How can the effect of green building demand in a particular market be determined? As with any market analysis, it is helpful to begin by looking at who or what is propelling market demand. Broadly speaking, two main factors drive green building growth:

- A change in market demand from property owners, investors, and building occupant end users such as tenants and consumers
- Policy-level goals that generate regulations and incentives

Sustainability as a New Market Influence

In the past few decades, market demand from institutional investors, individual property owners, tenants, and consumers has been shifting in favor of buildings that are more resource efficient and have fewer adverse effects on their surroundings and occupants. Whether the primary objective for pursuing green real estate is to achieve "property operational excellence," as noted by financial services provider TIAA-CREF, or to "do the right thing," as noted by 25% of respondents to the 2016 *World Green Building Trends* study, one can see the effects of sustainability in the real estate sector with the increasing prevalence of green building.[8]

Sustainability was dubbed an "emerging megatrend" by the *Harvard Business Review* in 2010.[9] On par with other megatrends such as globalization and information technology, sustainability is a primary source of the market demand for green building. The influence of sustainability on real estate is both direct and indirect. Direct impacts can be seen in the emphasis on energy efficiency, solar photovoltaic (PV) systems, transit proximity, walkability, and electrical vehicle charging stations. Sustainability also indirectly affects market demand. End users of real estate may have sustainability-related envi-

6. City of Kansas City, Missouri, "Legislation 150299," April 23, 2015, http://cityclerk.kcmo.org/LiveWeb/Documents/Document.aspx?q=N3Zet8doUaC6bG7ssQgYWOXMAwgRm0DSLOVO950ZJpjL15vtkjUygLevztfwWLfh.

7. CBRE and Maastricht University, *National Green Building Adoption Index–2015* (Los Angeles: CBRE, 2015), 4, www.cbre.com/~/media/files/.../green-building-adoption-index-2015.pdf?la=en.

8. TIAA-CREF Life Insurance Company Global Real Estate Strategy and Research (Martha Petyon, Edward F. Pierzak, and Nicholas E. Stolatis), *Sustainable Real Estate Investing: Exploring the Burden of Proof* (New York: TIAA-CREF, 2015), 7, www.tiaa.org/public/pdf/A432020_544403_Sustainable_RE_Investing_White_Paper.pdf. TIAA-CREF manages approximately $89 billion in real estate assets; Dodge Data and Analytics, *World Green Building Trends 2016*, 5.

9. David A. Lubin and Daniel C. Esty, "The Sustainability Imperative," *Harvard Business Review* (May 2010): 1.

ronmental, social, and governance (ESG) reporting requirements.[10] In addition, occupants may find that sustainability efforts are important to employee recruiting and that a green building is tangible evidence of an employer's sustainability commitment.

Sustainability is also prompting changes in land use regulations and policies that have the potential to change highest and best use analysis, as will be discussed in more depth in Chapters 7 and 8. As such, understanding sustainability is crucial to understanding what is driving green building demand and how this affects real estate.

What Is Sustainability?

The study of sustainability has roots in the social and life sciences as well as the inherent tension between the expected carrying capacity of an ecosystem and the social and economic needs and desires of a growing population.[11] The most commonly referenced definition may be the World Commission on Environment and Development (WCED) definition of *sustainable development* as provided in their *1987 Report of the World Commission on Environmental Development*: "development that meets the needs of the present without compromising the ability of future generations to meet their own needs."[12] It is often referred to as the "Brundtland definition" after Gro Harlem Brundtland, who chaired the commission.

While this definition is often cited, it is sometimes mistakenly believed that the "development" in this definition refers primarily to the physical development of the built environment as opposed to the social and economic development of communities and countries. That is, *sustainable development* is misinterpreted as being equivalent to real estate development. It is helpful to bear in mind that in policy statements such as this report, the word "development" has a more expansive connotation than it does within the real estate industry.[13] Indeed, upon a close reading of the report, it becomes clear that sustainable development pertains to a broader issue involving economic and social development rather than real estate development specifically:

---

10. Frameworks such as the Global Reporting Initiative (GRI) and the Sustainability Accounting Standards Boards (SASB) can affect end-users of real estate; institutional investors may also be subject to reporting requirements through organizations such as the Global Real Estate Sustainability Benchmark (GRESB).

11. An ecosystem's *carrying capacity* can be defined as "the maximal population size of a given species that an area can support without reducing its ability to support the same species in the future." G. C. Daily and P. R. Ehrlich, "Population, Sustainability, and Earth's Carrying Capacity: A Framework for Estimating Population Sizes and Lifestyles That Could Be Sustained Without Undermining Future Generations," *BioScience* 42, no. 10 (1992): 761-771.

12. WCED, *Report of the World Commission on Environmental Development: Our Common Future* (New York, Oxford University Press, 1987): 41-42. For an in-depth discussion of the evolution of sustainability prior to this report, see: Pernille Christensen, "Key Strategies of Sustainable Real Estate Decision-Making in the United States: A Delphi Study of the Stakeholders" (PhD dissertation, Clemson University, 2012), 15-27, http://tigerprints.clemson.edu/all_dissertations/1073/.

13. Christensen, "Key Strategies of Sustainable Real Estate Decision-Making in the United States," 14.

> Thus the goals of economic and social development must be defined in terms of sustainability in all countries–developed or developing, market-oriented or centrally planned.... Development involves a progressive transformation of economy and society.... But physical sustainability cannot be secured unless development policies pay attention to such considerations as changes in access to resources and in the distribution of costs and benefits. Even the narrow notion of physical sustainability implies a concern for social equity between generations, a concern that must logically be extended to equity within each generation... Hence sustainable development requires that societies meet human needs both by increasing productive potential and by ensuring equitable opportunities for all.[14]

This distinction is relevant in that understanding sustainability as it relates to real estate valuation cannot begin with the mistaken notion that sustainable development relates primarily to buildings and surrounding infrastructure. Instead, within the context of the WCED definition, sustainable development is not just *what* and *where* we are building ("development" in a real estate sense) but rather *how* buildings and infrastructure are created and in what way buildings contribute to sustainable economic and social development. With this broader concept in mind, it is easier to understand why green building rating systems encompass more than just whether a building is energy-efficient and also consider the larger issues of how the interior environment affects the health and well-being of building occupants as well as how site selection impacts the environment and community.

In an effort to incorporate the principles of sustainability into a business context, sustainability consultant John Elkington developed the concept of the "triple bottom line" in the 1990s. "Sustainability is the principle of ensuring that our actions today do not limit the range of economic, social and environmental options open to future generations," Elkington wrote.[15] Elkington's triple bottom line clearly defines sustainability to include social and environmental aspects while also stipulating economic viability. Elkington argued that companies need to think beyond the traditional bottom line of corporate profit and account for the net effect of their actions on society and the environment. He suggested that only by taking into account all three bottom lines would the true balance sheet of a company be accurately reflected and all costs–and benefits–of conducting business be reconciled. The triple bottom line idea is also sometimes expressed as the 3 Ps: people, planet, and profit.[16]

---

14. WCED, *Report of the World Commission on Environmental Development*, 41-42.
15. John Elkington, *Cannibals with Forks: The Triple Bottom Line of 21st Century Business* (Oxford: Capstone, 1999), 20.
16. There is some debate as to how to reconcile three bottom lines. For example, Goodland and Daly have argued that social, economic, and environmental sustainability are so distinct that they should be disaggregated and analyzed separately, rather than analyzed together under the umbrella term *sustainability*. Robert Goodland and Herman Daly, "Environmental Sustainability: Universal and Non-Negotiable," *Ecological Applications* 6, no. 4 (1996): 1002-1017.

This idea that corporations should be accountable beyond bottom-line profit has led to initiatives such as the Global Reporting Initiative (GRI) and the Sustainability Accounting Standards Board (SASB), both of which require corporations to report performance on a triple bottom line basis. These non-economic performance metrics are generally categorized as corporate social responsibility (CSR) and ESG factors.

But while Elkington's triple bottom line concept may be more specific and applicable to business than the WCED's definition of *sustainable development*, the questions remain: How exactly does one account across three bottom lines? And for those focused on the effect of sustainability on real estate valuation, how do the three Ps factor into real estate development and operation?

Sustainability Applied to Real Estate Valuation

The late professor James Graaskamp, a thought leader in real estate valuation and urban land economics, offered a prescient viewpoint on the ideal use of real estate that was in keeping with the principle of sustainability. He argued that highest and best use obviated relevant aspects that should be considered when determining optimal land use by focusing entirely on maximizing the economic return of real estate. He therefore advocated for a concept he termed "most fitting use" as a way to expand the purely economically driven valuation concept of highest and best use: "The concept of most fitting use is that use of the land which produces the most significant economic surplus while at the same time having the least adverse effect on third parties–economically, environmentally, culturally."[17]

While this idea may not seem like such a radical departure today, sustainability was still in its infancy when Graaskamp posited this view in the mid-1980s. The WCED had yet to convene, and the earliest green building rating systems were still ideas forming in the minds of those who would later pioneer them in the following decade. While the energy crisis of the 1970s led to a great deal of interest in the energy efficiency of real estate, many of the broader environmental and social consequences related to the built environment were not yet being formally addressed.[18]

While Graaskamp's most fitting use concept echoes the Elkington construct of balance beyond an economic bottom line, it also allows

17. James A. Graaskamp, "Real Estate Process" (lecture, University of Wisconsin-Madison, Spring 1987), http://digicoll.library.wisc.edu/cgi-bin/RealEstate/RealEstate-idx?type=turn&entity=-RealEstate.Bus550.p0671&id=RealEstate.Bus550&isize=M.

18. The California Environmental Quality Act signed into law in 1970 by Governor Ronald Reagan is one example of acknowledging and seeking to minimize real estate's environmental impacts. This law requires that any changes to the environment due to a proposed development be considered in the process of granting discretionary entitlements. Projects with environmental impacts that exceed certain thresholds may require mitigation or be prohibited altogether if less impactful alternatives are feasible.

for more specific and concrete interpretations of how sustainability is implemented in a real estate context. While the definition of *most fitting use* clearly implies economic feasibility, the suggestion that the land use should minimize adverse effects seems more in keeping with the reality that buildings and real estate development use resources and affect the surrounding environment and community by their very nature. The goal then becomes one of minimizing those negative impacts.[19] For existing buildings, which account for the vast majority of current building stock, the ability to "green up" in any meaningful way may be constrained due to siting as well as building structural and design factors that are not physically possible or financially feasible to change. For those buildings, the minimization of adverse effects may be the best-case scenario.

The relative immutability of real estate makes it particularly susceptible to changing market demand and changing government regulations. Conventionally constructed buildings are not generally designed to be moved or taken apart like Lego bricks and rebuilt to conform to end-users who may now prefer a very different interior experience. Buildings tend to be constructed with a useful life of decades, if not longer, and so changes in demand for a particular location or construction type (conventional versus green building) can create risks for existing and emerging building stock, especially if the change is relatively abrupt.

Sustainability-Related Risks to Real Estate Value

Corporations have been criticized for being overly focused on short-term results with little regard for entities or individuals outside of the corporation. Whether one believes this to be a fair assessment of most businesses or not, sustainability introduces many new elements that force a longer-term, more expansive scope of concern that encompasses the following:

- Inter-generational equity (concern for future generations)
- Intra-generational equity (social and economic equity within the current generation)
- The balance of social and environmental costs and benefits with economic costs and benefits
- Transparency, disclosure, and stakeholder activism
- Emphasis on the entire supply chain versus the end product only
- Focus on life-cycle cost versus up-front cost
- Resource efficiency and elimination of waste

19. This discussion sets aside for the moment the notion of "regenerative buildings." At this point in time, truly regenerative buildings–structures that do not use any resources in construction or operation outside of what they generate on site–is still a nascent concept.

Professor Dan R. Anderson, risk management and insurance professor and author of *Corporate Survival: The Critical Importance of Sustainability Risk Management,* offers this observation regarding the effect of sustainability in the corporate environment:

> Corporations that take the lead in dealing effectively with sustainability risks will gain competitive advantage, minimize reputation damage, decrease costs and increase long-term profits. Sustainability requires running businesses much differently than before. New production, distribution, manufacturing and marketing systems will all be needed.[20]

The resource-intensive fashion industry is a good example of how sustainability can affect core business practices. Textile and apparel manufacturing produces both pre-consumer and post-consumer waste at nearly every step of production. It has been reported to be the second most-polluting industry in the world next to oil, and the US Environmental Protection Agency (EPA) classifies some types of textile manufacturing facilities as hazardous waste producers.[21] The industry has a complex, global supply chain, complicating efforts to address sustainability goals. Furthermore, much of the notion of modern-day fashion is "disposable," with fashion trends changing long before the garment wears out. This short-term focus runs counter to the longer-range principles of sustainability. In response to the inherent waste of this manufacturing process, some industry leaders have seen an opportunity to broaden their consumer base to millennials and use waste to their advantage.[22] For example, apparel designer Eileen Fisher launched a Green Eileen initiative in 2009 to recycle the clothing line and has worked towards transparency and accountability in textile supply chains. Other apparel manufacturers, such as H&M and Levi's, have also instituted "take back" programs and other waste reduction strategies. Christina Kim, an apparel designer and artist who represents part of a new generation of designers who have embraced a "zero-waste" manufacturing process, began using recycled materials for her garments. For her, changing the process altered the cost breakdown of her products, decreasing the cost of materials while increasing the cost of labor.[23] Minimizing waste is seen by some in the industry as not just a competitive advantage but

20. Dan R. Anderson, *Corporate Survival: The Critical Importance of Sustainability Risk Management* (New York: iUniverse, 2005), 286.

21. Susan Brown and Matilda McQuaid, *Scraps: Fashion, Textiles, and Creative Reuse* (New York: Cooper Hewitt, 2016), 9; EPA, "RCRA in Focus: Textile Manufacturing," accessed April 11, 2017, www.epa.gov/sites/production/files/2015-01/documents/k02028.pdf.

22. Sarah Very, "Can Fast-Fashion Brands Like Zara Go Sustainable?' *Bloomberg Pursuits* (November 29, 2016), www.gbrionline.org/news/can-fast-fashion-brands-like-zara-go-sustainable/.

23. This type of cost shift could be seen as analogous to green building construction cost-shift changes, in which total building cost may be redistributed between up-front and operations/maintenance costs as compared to traditional building construction (as discussed in Chapter 3).

a requirement.[24] The spokesperson for the apparel chain H&M put it plainly: "The consumer interest in sustainability is growing. We believe sustainability is the only way forward if we want to continue to exist as a fashion company."[25]

While the real estate sector may not be as polluting as the apparel industry or rank as high on the EPA's list of hazardous material producers, commercial real estate is very resource-intensive and (like the textile industry) involves a complex supply chain, which can make sustainability risk harder to control. For buildings, there is not only sustainability risk from initial construction as related to worker health and safety, but also a continuous exposure to sustainability risk related to the health and well-being of building occupants.

Sustainability risks to real estate can be broken down into four categories:

- Resource use
- Obsolescence
- Transparency and stakeholder influence
- Externalities

The acronym ROTE can be used as an abbreviation for these four categories.[26]

Resource Use

Real estate is inherently resource-intensive (i.e., building materials, energy, water) to construct and operate. Rising costs for materials, energy, and other resources due to growing global demand and limits on supply affect the feasibility of new construction, the costs of upgrades and renovations to existing buildings, and the operating expenses of all buildings.

Buildings consume 40% of the total energy and over 70% of the total electricity in the United States. Energy use by buildings is projected to grow faster than energy use in any other sector, including transportation and industrial use. Given the high and growing proportion of energy consumed by buildings, energy efficiency will be an increasingly important risk management tool for building owners to address price and volatility risks. The implication when valuing real estate is that the physical characteristics of a property and operational efficiency relative to its peers will require greater attention.

---

24. This sentiment is also echoed in real estate markets where minimizing and controlling resource use, such as energy use, is seen as an issue of "best practices."
25. Very, "Can Fast Fashion Brands like Zara Go Sustainable?"
26. The following section expands upon ideas originally published by the authors in the article "Integrating Sustainability and Green Building into the Appraisal Process," *Journal of Sustainable Real Estate* 2, no. 1 (2010): 228-229.

Obsolescence

Much like the technologies of high-speed elevators and central air conditioning that caused central business district office buildings lacking these features to obsolesce, sustainability has the potential for obsolescence to both existing and future building stock that does not meet sustainability criteria. Properties that cannot readily adapt to increasingly stringent green and energy-efficiency building codes, or to market demand for factors such as green buildings or access to walkable amenities, may face functional and/or economic obsolescence.

The accelerated rate of change or volatility that characterizes many major markets today amplifies the risk of obsolescence to existing properties, especially compared to the past. The increased potential for entire companies to disappear suddenly, industries to contract unexpectedly, or consumer behavior to change abruptly may place greater risk on special-purpose improvements like corporate headquarters, data centers, and even more common land uses such as automobile dealerships, department stores, and shopping centers. Higher re-tenanting costs and unexpected or prolonged vacancies may result, especially for specialized properties with a limited market or limited alternative uses.

Transparency and Stakeholder Influence

Greater requirements for and access to information, such as energy use disclosure laws,[27] facilitate the ability of community groups and legislative bodies to more directly influence the type and location of new development. The ease and low cost of information via the Internet and the connections of social media are increasing transparency and facilitating stakeholder demands.

In the real estate sector, perhaps the most notable repercussion of transparency is the increasing number of cities that have enacted energy disclosure or benchmarking requirements, as shown in Exhibit 4.2. By allowing prospective owners or tenants to more accurately compare energy use (and therefore costs) of building operations, benchmarking requirements not only create an opportunity for buildings that out perform their comparable peers but also pose a risk to those buildings that underperform relative to their peers. For existing buildings that can cost effectively "green up," this type of mandatory disclosure may serve to accelerate building upgrades in markets where investors and tenants demonstrate a preference for higher-performing assets.

In addition, financial stakeholders–such as investors and their shareholders–are increasingly active in directing business decisions in real estate. CalPERS, the largest public pension fund in the US (with $209 billion under management at the time), announced a change in its investment policy in 2010 to prohibit excessive rent in-

27. Energy use disclosure laws are also known as *benchmarking regulations*.

Comparison of U.S. Commercial Building Energy Benchmarking and Transparency Policies

	Legislation	Public Data Available	Policy Impact			Buildings Included	Policy Schedule		Compliance		Additional Elements	
	Jurisdiction	Released	Number of Bldgs	Square Footage	Energy Savings	Types & Sizes	Reporting to Gov't	Transparency	By # of Buildings	By % of Sq. Ft.	Water Tracking	Other Requirements
Cities/Counties	Atlanta	-	2,900	402 million	-	Comm & MF ≥ 50K Comm & MF ≥ 25K	Aug 1, 2015 Jun 1, 2017	(if Energy Star >55) Jan 2017 Sept 2017	-	-	✓	Audits every 10 years
	Austin	-	2,800	113 million	-	Comm ≥ 10K MF ≥ 5 units	Jun 1, Annual	Time of transaction	-	-	-	Audits & mandatory upgrades for high energy use MF buildings
	Berkeley	-	257	13.7 million	-	Comm & MF ≥ 50K Comm & MF ≥ 25K	~Apr 2017 ~Apr 2018	>Apr 2017 >Apr 2018	-	-	✓	Periodic/time of sale energy reports for all buildings (timing based on size)
	Boston	Yes	1,600	250 million	-	Comm ≥ 50K MF ≥ 50K/50 units Comm ≥ 35K MF ≥ 35K/35 units	Sep 15, 2014 May 15, 2015 May 15, 2016 May 15, 2017	Oct 1, 2015 Oct 1, 2015 Oct 1, 2016 Oct 1, 2017	-	84% (2014)	✓	Periodic energy assessments and/or actions
	Boulder	-	475	26 million	-	Comm ≥ 50K New Comm ≥ 10K Comm ≥ 30K Comm ≥ 20K	Aug 1, 2016 Aug 1, 2016 Jun 1, 2018 Jun 1, 2020	>Jun 1, 2019 >Jun 1, 2019 >Jun 1, 2021 >Jun 1, 2023	100% (2016)	100% (2016)	-	Lighting upgrade; audits & RCx every 10 yrs (must invest in RCx measures w/ ≤2yr payback)
	Cambridge	-	1,100	78 million	-	Comm ≥ 50K MF ≥ 50 units Comm ≥ 25K	May 1, 2015 May 1, 2015 May 1, 2016	Sept 1, 2016 Sept 1, 2016 Sept 1, 2017	95% (2015)	93.5% (2014)	✓	-
	Chicago	Yes	3,500	900 million	10% (2010-15)	Comm ≥ 250K MF ≥ 250K Comm ≥ 50K MF ≥ 50K	Jun 1, 2014 Jun 1, 2015 Jun 1, 2015 Jun 1, 2016	December 2015 Jun 1, 2016 Jun 1, 2016 >Jun 1, 2017	84% (2014)	92% (2014)	-	Data verification by licensed professional 1st year & every 3 years
	Denver	-	3,000	360 million	-	Comm & MF ≥ 50K Comm & MF ≥ 25K	Jun 1, 2017 Jun 1, 2018	TBD	-	-	-	-
	District of Columbia	Yes	2,000	357 million	9% (2010-13)	Comm ≥ 50K MF ≥ 50K	Apr 1, Annual	Annually >Apr 1	83% (2013)	-	✓	-
	Evanston, IL	-	557	45.6 million	-	Comm & MF ≥100K Comm & MF ≥ 50K Comm & MF ≥ 20K	Jun 30, 2017 Jun 30, 2018 Jun 30, 2019	TBD	-	-	✓	Data verification by a certified professional 1st year and every 3 years
	Kansas City	-	~1,500	~400 million	-	Comm & MF ≥100K Comm & MF ≥ 50K	May 1, 2017 May 1, 2018	Sept 1, 2018 Sept 1, 2019	-	-	✓	-

Comparison of U.S. Commercial Building Energy Benchmarking and Transparency Policies

	Legislation	Public Data Available	Policy Impact			Buildings Included	Policy Schedule		Compliance		Additional Elements	
	Jurisdiction	Released	Number of Bldgs	Square Footage	Energy Savings	Types & Sizes	Reporting to Gov't	Transparency	By # of Buildings	By % of Sq. Ft.	Water Tracking	Other Requirements
Cities/Counties	Los Angeles	-	14,000	900 million	-	Comm & MF ≥100K Comm & MF ≥ 50K Comm & MF ≥ 20K	Jul 1, 2017 Apr 1, 2018 Apr 1, 2019	TBD	-	-	✓	ASHRAE level II audit and RCx every 5 years
	Minneapolis	Yes	625	110 million	-	Comm ≥100K Comm ≥ 50K	Jun 1, Annual	Aug 31, Annual	87% (2013)	-	✓	-
	Montgomery Co., MD + Rockville, MD	-	~1,000	~110 million	-	Comm ≥ 250K Comm ≥ 50K	June 1, 2016 June 1, 2017	Oct 2017 Oct 2018	~75% (2015)	-	-	Data verification by licensed professional 1st year & every 3 years
	New York City	Yes	33,417	2.8 billion	6-14% (2010-14)	Comm & MF ≥ 50K Comm & MF ≥ 25K	May 1, Annual May 1, 2018	Annually on Sept 1 Anticipated >2018	84% (2012)	84% (2012)	✓	Audits & RCx (LL 87), lighting upgrades & submetering (LL 88)
	Orlando	-	826	125.6 million	-	Comm & MF ≥ 50K	May 1, 2018	Sep 1, 2019	-	-	-	Energy audit or RCx every five years if ENERGY STAR <50. Benchmarking by qualified benchmarker
	Philadelphia	Yes	2,900	390 million	-	Comm ≥ 50K MF ≥ 50K	Jun 30, Annual Jun 30, 2016	Annually >Jun 30 >Jun 30, 2017	91% (2014)	91% (2014)	✓	-
	Pittsburgh	-	861	164 million	-	Comm ≥ 50K	June 1, 2018	Annually >Jun 1	-	-	✓	-
	Portland, ME	-	284	-	-	Comm ≥ 20K MF ≥ 50 units	May 1, 2018	Sept 1, 2019	-	-	✓	-
	Portland, OR	-	1,024	87 million	-	Comm ≥ 50K Comm ≥ 20K	Apr 22, 2016 Apr 22, 2017	Oct 1, 2017 Oct 1, 2018	-	82% (2015)	-	-
	San Francisco	Yes	2,312	203 million	7.9% (2010-14)	Comm ≥ 10K	Apr 1, Annual	Annually >Apr 1	-	82% (2013)	-	ASHRAE level I/II audits or RCx every 5 years
	Seattle	-	3,250	281 million	2.7% (2014-15)	Comm & MF ≥ 20K	Apr 1, Annual	Annually <Dec 31	99.2% (2013)	99.4% (2013)	-	Tune-ups every 5 years for Comm ≥50K
	South Portland, ME	-	-	-	-	Comm ≥ 5K MF ≥ 10 units	May 1, 2018 May 1, 2018	TBD	-	-	✓	Verification every 5 years by professional engineer
	St. Louis	-	900	143 million	-	Comm & MF ≥ 50K	Apr 1, 2018	Aug 1, 2018	-	-	✓	-
States	California	-	20,573	2.4 billion	-	Comm & MF ≥ 50K	TBD	TBD	-	-	-	Mandatory upgrades TBD under AB 758
	Washington State	-	4,600	247 million	-	Comm ≥ 10K	None	Time of transaction	-	-	-	Audits for public buildings with low ratings

Updated 4/10/17

creases and the involuntary displacement of low-income households in their multifamily portfolio. According to CalPERS's then-board president, Rob Feckner, the policy was expected to help "ensure that external managers who deploy CalPERS capital won't inappropriately displace households in rent-regulated units as a result of their investment strategies. Such strategies have exposed CalPERS to risks and have caused adverse impacts to renters that must not happen again." To which investment committee chair George Diehr added, "At the same time, this protection of tenants is consistent with the United Nations Principles for Responsible Investment that are part of our own governance principles, which incorporate environmental, social and governance best practices into our investment decision-making process."[28]

Sustainability demands are also coming from non-financial stakeholders in the form of new legislation and regulation at the local, state, and federal levels. Green building codes, state-level climate change legislation, and the requirement of the US Securities and Exchange Commission that companies disclose climate change risk are examples of government policies that reflect sustainability imperatives. Non-governmental organizations (NGOs)–ranging from national and international organizations like the investor and environmental coalitions CDP and Ceres (both focused on climate change) to neighborhood groups coalescing to fight a proposed development–have a stake in the outcome even though they may not have a direct financial interest in the property or company.

Externalities

Economists use the term *externalities* to describe the effects of activities that are not anticipated or paid for at the time of the economic transaction. Externality risk is the risk that these costs will at some point be charged back, or internalized, to the source.

This concept is not new in real estate, nor is it unique to sustainability. Impact fees charged to new development to pay for community facilities such as schools or infrastructure reflect the internalizing of externalities back to the source. For example, new housing development increases the burden on the local public school system, which may necessitate the construction of new school facilities. In this case, the cost of the new school facility is an externality to the residential development, since neither the developer nor the homebuyer pays directly for the new school. Some communities have internalized this externality by imposing impact fees or exactions, such as those requiring the developer to build the school or donate land for a new school. Transportation management plans required for new office development may require the developer or owner to operate

28. "CalPERS Adopts Tenant-Oriented Rental Policy." *Central Valley Business Times* (April 20, 2010).

a private shuttle service or pay ongoing assessments to an existing public transit system. These costs are another example of externalities being charged back, or internalized, to the source.

Sustainability brings in a new set of potential externalities that could affect real estate, such as greenhouse gas (GHG) emissions due to electrical power generation and commuting, watershed impacts from rainwater runoff, and the health effects of poor indoor air quality on building occupants. One example of the effect of externality risk on real estate is California Senate Bill 375, also known as the Sustainable Communities and Climate Protection Act of 2008, which counts vehicle miles travelled as an environmental impact to be considered in the approval of new real estate development. This legislation is seeking to align the GHG externality associated with motor vehicle trips directly with the source.

Green buildings can be seen as one way to mitigate these types of sustainability-driven externality risks. As noted by the Urban Land Institute, "Some investors are considering climate-change risk as a regulatory risk that can be avoided by owning energy-efficient, low-carbon-emission buildings...In the United Kingdom and Tokyo, Japan, where greenhouse gases associated with buildings are regulated, higher taxes are assessed on buildings that do not use energy efficiently, and, in some cases, such buildings are not allowed to operate without mandatory retrofits."[29]

Policies, Incentives, and Regulations

A wide variety of government programs at various levels influence green building. Public policies, incentives, and regulations affect both the supply of and demand for green building.

Policies tend to be broad and long-range in nature, often consisting of goals and/or performance targets. Public policy serves two important purposes as it relates to green building:

- Provides the framework that guides legislation and government agencies in the implementation of the policy
- Sends clear signals to the private sector regarding the intent of future government actions, including incentives, laws, and regulations

Examples of public policy include energy independence or goals to generate a set percentage of energy from renewable sources by a certain date or reduce greenhouse gases below a certain threshold.

Incentives, as will be discussed in more detail in Chapter 11, are the "carrot" used by the government to encourage market behaviors that are consistent with policy and that otherwise would not occur.

29. Urban Land Institute (Uwe Brandes and Alice LeBlanc), *Risk and Resilience in Coastal Regions: A ULI Global Policy and Practice Forum Report* (Washington, DC: Urban Land Institute, 2013), 15.

The federal energy Investment Tax Credit (ITC) and local utility rebate programs for energy-efficiency programs are two common examples of incentives used to drive market behavior toward renewable energy generation and reduced energy use in buildings.

Incentives can also consist of recognition for hitting certain performance targets. For example, the EPA-operated Energy Star program provides ratings for a wide variety of consumer products and buildings. An Energy Star-certified building is one that performs in the top quartile of its peers based on actual, measured energy use. Buildings that achieve this level receive a rating and a plaque, which may be displayed prominently in the lobby or elsewhere.

Laws and regulations, sometimes referred to as *mandates*, are the "stick" used to enforce minimum performance standards or otherwise control land use and building construction, renovation, and operation decisions. Building codes are an example of a common mandate affecting most real estate. When building codes include green and energy-efficiency requirements, they can play a role in the supply and demand for green building by consistently raising the bar for new construction and renovation. While they are typically enforced locally, building codes may be influenced by state and/or federal laws and regulations.

For example, California has a statewide building code that sets a minimum standard throughout the state, and the 1992 federal Americans with Disabilities Act (ADA) legislation has had an ongoing direct impact on real estate throughout the country.[30] Local building codes are updated periodically and incorporate more stringent standards over time, particularly in relationship to energy efficiency. As a result, buildings built to current codes in most areas are more energy efficient than buildings built as recently as 5 or 10 years ago. A variety of other mandatory measures may also encourage green building practices, such as the energy disclosure or benchmarking requirements that are being enacted in a growing number of areas. As of the end of 2016, 21 municipalities and two states in the United States have passed some type of benchmarking regulation (as shown in Exhibit 4.2). In addition, renewable portfolio standards (RPS) are state-level regulations that require utilities to source specified levels of their energy production from renewable sources. Currently, 29 states plus Washington DC and three territories have some level of RPS requirement, as shown in the map in Exhibit 4.3. RPS can drive the adoption of rooftop solar PV systems in states where utilities can count these systems on homes and businesses towards RPS compliance.

30. The Warren-Alquist Act was passed in California in 1978, after the Arab oil embargo and ensuing energy crisis. This legislation required a periodic review and upgrade of the energy portion of the statewide building code, commonly known as Title 24. This mechanism is expected to play a major role in attaining the net zero energy goals set in motion in 2006 by Assembly Bill 32, the California Global Warming Solutions Act.

Exhibit 4.3 States with Renewable Portfolio Standard Policies

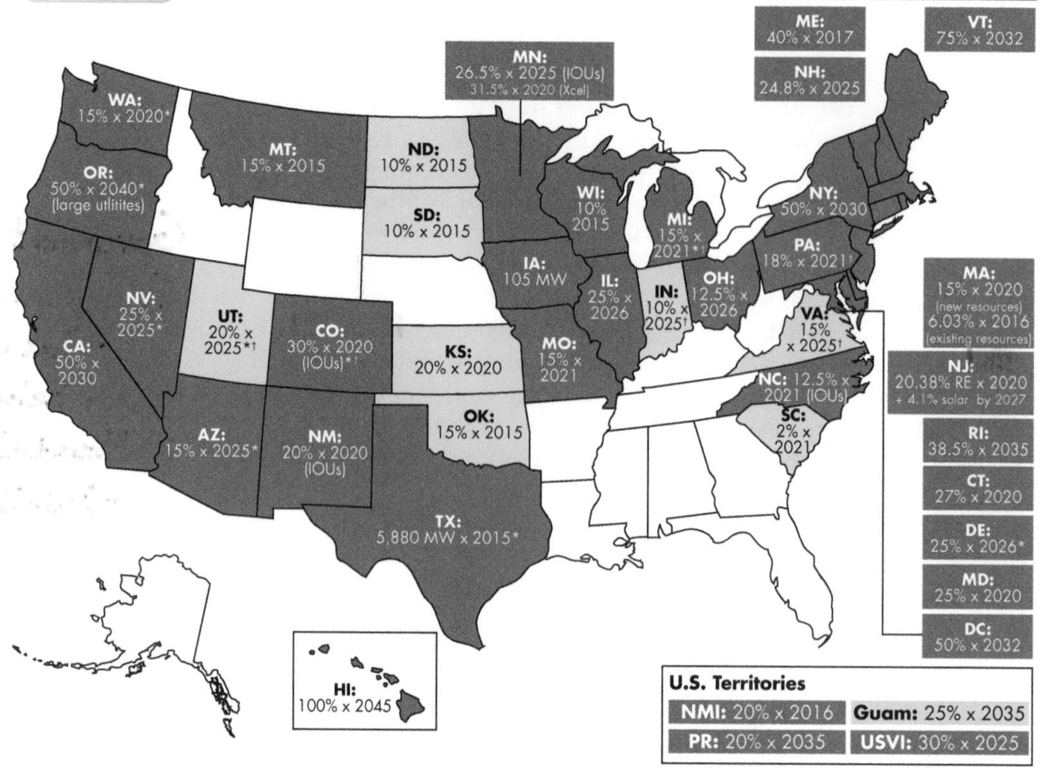

29 States + Washington, DC + 3 territories have a Renewable Portfolio Standard
(8 states and 1 territory have renewable portfolio goals)

* Extra credit for solar or customer-sited renewables

† Includes non-renewable alternative sources

Source: Database of State Incentives for Renewables and Efficiency (DSIRE), "Renewable Portfolio Standards," February 2017, www.dsireusa.org/resources/detailed-summary-maps/.

Direct and Indirect Effects on Market Demand

Policies, incentives, and regulations can affect the market for green building in direct and indirect ways. As the nation's largest civilian landlord, the actions of the US General Services Administration (GSA) affect over 3 billion square feet of space in over 400,000 owned and leased buildings. In January 2007, President George W. Bush issued Executive Order 13423, which instructs federal agencies to "conduct environmental, transportation, and energy-related activities under the law in support of their respective missions in an environmentally, economically, and fiscally sound, integrated, continuously improving, efficient, and sustainable manner."[31] This policy was formalized into law as the Energy Independence and Security Act in December of 2007. The law included specific energy use reduction targets (3% per year, 30% by 2015) and water reduction targets (16% by 2015). In addition, new GSA buildings and major renovations are required to reduce fossil fuel-generated energy consumption by 55% by 2010 and by 100% by 2030. In order to implement these policy goals and meet the legislative requirements, the GSA now requires all new construction and major renovations to meet a minimum of LEED Gold Certification.[32] The law also included nearly $1.5 billion in funding to facilitate the development of commercially viable net zero energy (NZE) commercial and residential buildings in the private sector.[33]

In addition to the direct effect of federally owned and leased buildings on demand for green building products and services, the resulting "greening" of the federal portfolio has had an indirect impact in the private market by stimulating the development of new technologies. It has also increased demand for–and reduced the cost of–green building products and services.

California provides a state-level example of the interrelationship between sustainability policy and green building regulations that affect the real estate market. In 2006, Governor Arnold Schwarzenegger signed Assembly Bill 32, the California Global Warming Solutions Act, into law. This law laid the groundwork for what is now a functioning cap and trade market for carbon emissions, and set the goal of reducing GHGs to 1990 levels by 2020, and by 80% by 2050.[34] This law was followed by the 2007 Integrated Energy Policy Report (IEPR). Recognizing the role of the built environment in reducing greenhouse gas emissions, this IEPR included the goal that all new residential construction be NZE by 2020 and all new commercial construction be NZE by 2030.[35]

The direct and indirect impacts of this California legislation on green building products and the larger real estate market is clear. By combining top-down goals with bottom-up building codes, new buildings will become progressively more energy efficient relative to

---

31. Brookhaven National Laboratory, "Pollution Prevention Program: Executive Order (EO) 13423," accessed April 12, 2017, www.bnl.gov/esh/env/pollutionpreve/EO13423.php.

32. As of 2016, GSA-leased facilities may use either Green Globes or LEED certification systems. New construction and major renovations of owned facilities must meet a minimum of a LEED Gold certification.

33. GSA, "Sustainable Design," February 15, 2017, www.gsa.gov/portal/category/21083.

34. In 2016, these targets were expanded to include a 40% reduction by 2030.

35. NZE buildings require significantly reduced energy use intensity (typically 50%) over current code-compliant building use, such that the remaining energy needs can be met with a renewable, on-site source.

older buildings, independent of market behavior. The implication for valuation is that obsolescence risk increases as buildings age, particularly for unrenovated buildings. Construction and renovation costs may also increase.

Incentives have played a significant role in the expansion of the rooftop solar PV industry. In this case, federal-level incentives coupled with state-level regulations allow for renewable energy at a cost that is competitive with grid-supplied energy. On the federal side, the Energy Policy Act of 2005 created a 30% federal ITC for commercial and residential renewable energy systems. Although the act was originally set to sunset in 2007, it has been extended multiple times–most recently through 2019, after which it will decline in steps.

This federal incentive program has been coupled with a state-level regulation known as net energy metering (NEM), which as of 2016 is mandated in 39 states, Washington DC, and three US territories.[36] This metering and billing system requires rooftop solar owners to be reimbursed for excess electricity generated when it is not needed on site while allowing them to purchase electricity from the grid at night or when demand exceeds generating capacity. Without net metering, the economics of rooftop solar systems deteriorate. As rooftop solar has continued to expand, utilities are seeking to revise net metering laws to permit fixed charges for grid connection and/or reduced reimbursement for net excess generation. Changes to either the federal tax incentive or net metering would likely impact the demand for and the valuation of properties with on-site renewable energy generation, such as solar PV. This is discussed further in Chapter 10.

Sustainability may also drive changes in land use regulations and policy at the local level, either in response to changes in federal or state policy or due to changes in the needs or demands of a given community. For example, there is increasing concern among community leaders and planners about the need for resilience in buildings and infrastructure in response to sustainability imperatives and climate change. In addition, city planners are incorporating sustainability principles into comprehensive plans (also known as *general plans* or *community master plans*) that can affect allowed land uses, development regulations, and highest and best use analysis. Chapter 7 includes more discussion of the effect of resilience risk and planning on the built environment.

Summary

Green building demand continues to increase. This demand varies between markets and property types. Sustainability, the underlying driver of green building, is widely regarded as a market force that

36. DSIRE, "Detailed Summary Maps: Net Metering Policies," April 2017, www.dsireusa.org/resources/detailed-summary-maps/.

has triggered fundamental changes for all business sectors, including real estate. Sustainability as it relates to real estate valuation can be regarded as bringing non-economic factors, such as the environmental and social effects of the built environment, more directly into the valuation process. Understanding the influence of sustainability on real estate valuation and accurately and appropriately accounting for its influence present unique challenges to data-driven professions such as appraisal, in which analysis is rendered quantitatively.

Policies, incentives, and regulations that affect the demand for green building are widespread and may emanate from the federal, state, and local levels. In addition to affecting the demand for green building, changes in policies, incentives, and regulations can affect land use and the built environment in ways that may have a direct bearing on the valuation process. The relevance of any one of these programs will vary depending on the program, locale, property type, and local market characteristics. As regulatory and legislative initiatives vary geographically and change periodically, monitoring these programs for any changes is warranted to appropriately incorporate these factors into the valuation process.

5 Determining the Scope of Work

As discussed in the preceding chapters, green building brings two new aspects to the valuation assignment: changing market demand and altered property characteristics. Both of these aspects have the potential to affect or expand the scope of work of an assignment.

Developing the scope of work in any assignment begins with identifying the valuation problem, a task with which valuation professionals are familiar. Local market experience and knowledge of the built environment are used to ascertain when sufficient information has been gathered about the valuation problem to know what steps are required to solve it. If problem identification is the *who*, *what*, *when*, *where*, and *why* of an assignment, then the scope of work is a description of *how* a valuation problem will be solved.[1]

According to the 14th edition of *The Appraisal of Real Estate*:

> In the valuation process, the identification of the assignment elements leads directly into the determination of the scope of work of an assignment, i.e. the type and extent of research needed to solve an appraisal problem. Professional standards place the responsibility for determining the appropriate scope of work in the appraisal assignment squarely on the shoulders of the appraiser. The scope of work for an assignment is acceptable if it leads to credible assignment results, is consistent with the expectations of parties who are regularly intended users for similar assignments, and is consistent with what the actions of the appraiser's peers would be in the same or a similar assignment.[2]

A credible assignment result hinges on a properly crafted scope of work for which the appraiser bears the ultimate responsibility. In

1. *The Appraisal of Real Estate*, 14th ed. (Chicago: Appraisal Institute, 2013), 89.
2. Ibid., 87.

turn, the scope of work relies on proper identification of the appraisal problem. While this task may vary in difficulty from assignment to assignment, it is doable when appraisal assignments align with the experience and knowledge of the appraiser.

But what happens to this process when the market is changing or there are new property characteristics or processes with which the valuation professional is unfamiliar, such as with green building? How can the problem be properly identified without the backstop of adequate market and building knowledge?

Defining the Assignment

Accurately identifying the valuation problem is the linchpin of any assignment. Green building presents two potential challenges to all parties involved in the valuation process at this point: lack of knowledge and ineffective communication. Lack of knowledge of green building can affect all stages of the valuation process, from the property owner who may not have complete information about the green improvements or know what information should be provided, to the loan officer, appraisal department, and fee appraiser who may also lack a sufficiently robust knowledge base to know how to identify and communicate the green features or processes in a particular property. Effective communication of a property's characteristics relies on the recognition of any green attributes, which in turn relies on sufficient knowledge of green building by all parties involved. The two case studies presented later in this chapter, Case Study 5.B, What Went Wrong? (page 95) and Case Study 5.C,What Went Right? (page 101) illustrate how having (or not having) adequate green building knowledge can make a difference in the appraisal process.

Recognizing Green Building

Even those who are familiar with green building can be hard-pressed to differentiate a green building from a non-green building by visual observation alone. Green buildings often look exactly like non-green buildings, and this chameleon-like quality is only more pronounced for non-green buildings that have green features.

In addition, clients and property owners may have varying degrees of green building knowledge such that valuation assignment inquiries cannot be relied upon to decide whether a building is green. For example, a request for proposal (RFP) may refer to a property as "high-performance" but not provide any further specification. Additional information would be needed to know if this building is performing better than a comparable property or code minimums, and if so, relative to which performance metrics (such as energy, water, waste, or occupant satisfaction). Or is "high-performance" being used as a subjective label without any reference to an objective standard? Alternatively, an RFP may not stipulate anything regarding the performance or greenness of a property, but the lack of green-specific information does not imply that the building is not green or does not have green features, such as a solar photovoltaic (PV) system. Case Study 5.A, Appraiser's Field Notes: LEED Surprise, in which co-author Timothy P. Runde discusses a unique appraisal experience, provides an example of this type of scenario.

So, if the valuation professional cannot rely on a preliminary visual assessment of the property or on the completeness or accuracy of the information provided by the client, what steps can be taken to determine salient facts so that an appropriate scope of work can be determined?

Case Study 5.A Appraiser's Field Notes: LEED Surprise

Timothy P. Runde, MAI, LEED AP

I've often referred to this assignment as the "LEED Surprise" because nothing in the RPF from my lender client suggested that the assignment had anything to do with a green building. I was expecting a garden-variety, 1980s-era suburban office building that had been recently renovated. However, during the site visit, a small sign in the restroom touting the building's waterless urinals piqued my interest enough to ask the property representative whether the building was green certified. As it turned out, the building was LEED Silver certified under Version 2.0.

Signs such as the one I noticed are not uncommon in LEED-certified and other green-rated buildings. These types of informational signs may earn the building LEED credit for educating the occupants and other users about green features, as was the case for this property. In addition, these signs provide a way for the property owner to communicate the building owners' commitment to sustainability. While they may not be intended to alert appraisers to the presence of green features, I have often found such signs to be very valuable in helping to identify green attributes and provide supplemental information.

I requested the LEED scorecard for the building at the end of the site visit. Upon reviewing it, I identified a number of green features that could potentially impact value. The one that surprised me the most was the site credit for transit proximity. How could an office building in a 1980s-era suburban office park earn credit for transit proximity? After examining an online aerial photo, however, it was clear that the subject property was indeed within walking distance–in fact, just across a parking lot–from a mass transit station.

Despite (or perhaps because of) my 20 years of appraisal experience in the market at that time, it hadn't occurred to me that proximity to mass transit–or any transit mode other than a motor vehicle–might matter to the end-user market in a suburban office setting.[3] I was therefore surprised by the response I received

3. This assignment was completed in 2009, when green building adoption was still relatively early in this San Francisco Bay Area market. This market has developed substantially since then. However, it should be noted that in other areas where green building is still in the early stages of adoption, the issue of whether transit proximity matters to property end users may be similar to that of the Bay Area in 2009.

Case Study 5.A *(continued)*

when I asked the tenant whether the LEED certification had any impact on the decision to locate in this building. The tenant replied that while the LEED certification mattered, the real key was the proximity to transit. The tenant went on to explain that in the process of relocating from a more centrally located area with excellent transit, being able to offer employees the opportunity to commute to work via mass transit was a key element in making the locational decision. Subsequent market research, including interviewing local leasing brokers, revealed that transit did indeed matter to the market. In particular, transit access was important for those tenants who were required to report transit proximity and mass transit usage as part of contractual requirements with certain government clients.

Further analysis of the LEED scorecard revealed energy-efficiency improvements including lighting upgrades, daylight and occupancy sensors, and an upgraded HVAC system that were all projected to reduce energy use enough to warrant consideration in the income capitalization approach.

I learned the following lessons from this assignment:

1. As appraisers, we can't rely on our clients to identify all the aspects of what is ultimately our expertise. We have to be vigilant about what we see, and it is our responsibility to ask about whatever unusual aspect we may see in a property, green or otherwise.
2. For property owners and others who want to ensure that any and all green attributes are included in the valuation analysis, it is critical to alert the lender and/or appraiser to the property's green features and provide supporting documentation as needed. In addition, the property owner can request an appraiser with appropriate green building competency at the time of application.
3. While it may sound counterintuitive, professional experience can blind you to new trends and unexpected market behaviors. Even with advanced green building knowledge, I did not immediately recognize the building discussed here as a green building. Furthermore, if not for the LEED scorecard, I might have missed a key element in the market demand for the subject property due to the preconceptions I had regarding the appeal of transit proximity in a suburban, automobile-centric market. The key to overcoming that shortfall was market research– specifically, interviewing the tenant and area brokers. Without a fundamental knowledge of green building, I might not have known to ask about green certification in the first place.

Green Building Education: Addressing the "Unknown Unknowns"

A significant risk for valuation professionals is completely missing green buildings or green features because of an inability to recognize them. It is difficult to identify something with which you are unfamiliar, or as former US Secretary of Defense Donald Rumsfeld put it,

"...we know there are some things we do not know. But there are also unknown unknowns–the ones we don't know we don't know."[4] As sustainability considerations become more prevalent in business and green building practices become more widely adopted in commercial real estate, it is these "unknown unknowns" that pose the greatest risk to the valuation process, to the credibility of the appraiser and the assignment results, and ultimately to the public trust.

Nothing does more to increase the likelihood of credible results for the valuation of green buildings or non-green buildings with green features than all parties having sufficient green building knowledge. Common misconceptions include the belief that green building assignments can easily be avoided if need be or that green building is not affecting a given market and thus appraisers can avoid learning about green building. Unfortunately, these myths only increase the potential for competency lapses.

The building pictured in the accompanying photograph illustrates how green knowledge can help the appraiser make the most out of scant information and more quickly and accurately identify a green building that may not be obviously green. While what appear to be solar panels on the roof are readily visible, indicating that this building has some level of "greenness," the rest of the structure does not look particularly "green." In fact, this building looks decidedly conventional at first glance. But when seen through the eyes of someone knowledgeable about green building, several characteristics suggest there is more here than just a conventional building sporting solar panels:

- The incorporation of a bioswale
- An expanded refuse area that is prominently located and includes multiple waste bins to separate landfill waste from recyclable materials at a point in time when plastic and newspaper recycling are not ubiquitous in the community
- The presence of operable windows in a climate that might ordinarily call for a more tightly regulated building envelope to allow for interior temperature control during hot and humid summers and extremely cold winters

These observations begin to paint a picture of a building that incorporates various green aspects: resource use (energy and waste), quality of the interior environment (operable windows), and site and locational attributes (bioswale to reduce the deleterious effects of rainwater runoff). In this case, a cursory glance from a trained eye yields enough clues to prompt additional questions or research about the property characteristics so that it can be determined if the

4. US Department of Defense, "News Briefing: Secretary Rumsfeld and General Meyers," February 12, 2002, http://archive.defense.gov/transcripts/transcript.aspx?transcriptid=2636.

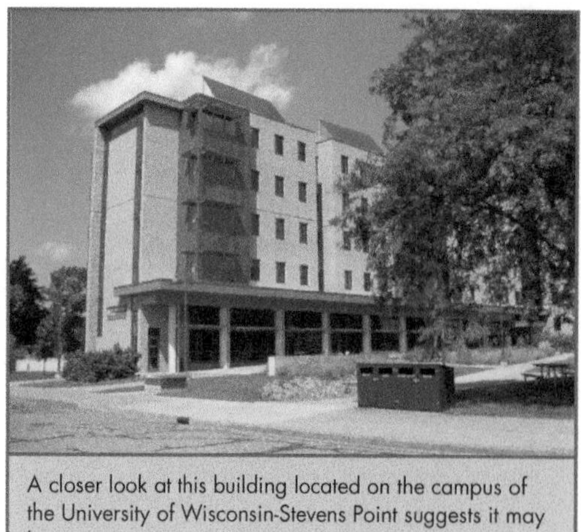

A closer look at this building located on the campus of the University of Wisconsin-Stevens Point suggests it may be green.

building is conventional with an added solar component or if it is a LEED-certified green building. This information is needed so an appropriate scope of work can be developed.[5]

Challenging Green Building Assumptions: Identifying Key Words and Red Flags

If a primary goal is to ensure that salient property characteristics are not missed, shifting the assumption that green building *does not* exist in or affect a given market to the expectation that it *may* be present increases the odds that green features that matter to the market, affect the scope of work, or may possibly affect value are considered in the valuation process. For example, closer scrutiny of requests for valuation assignments with an eye toward the possibility of green building considerations may highlight key words or red flags that might otherwise be overlooked. Couple this changed assumption with basic green building knowledge, and efficient and accurate problem identification becomes much more likely.

Terms such as "high-performance," "green-certified," or "energy-efficient" are obvious prompts that some level of green building may be present and additional follow-up is warranted. But what about an RFP that includes proposed improvements that will make the property have "no reliance on a utility provider"? Without additional clarification as to how grid independence is achieved, the scope of work cannot be properly assessed. If this phrase gets lost among the other property characteristics described in the RFP, the appraiser may become involved in a much more complex valuation assignment than originally envisioned.

Similarly, understanding green building allows valuation professionals to spot red flags that could make a substantive difference in the scope of work, as will be discussed in Case Study 5.B, What Went Wrong?

Casting a Broader Net: Expanding the Search Parameters

A quick Internet search is often one of the first steps a valuation professional takes after receiving an inquiry about a property. Where is it? What does it look like? Who owns it? What type of property is it? Is it for sale or for lease? An initial search may provide a fair bit of

5. In this case, the building was indeed in the process of becoming LEED-certified.

Case Study 5.B What Went Wrong?

A lender issued an RFP for a 40,000-sq.-ft. industrial building via an online bidding system. The RFP included a one-line notation about a proposed $2 million rooftop solar PV installation. No other information regarding the solar installation was noted, nor was any indication given that the lender required an appraiser with expertise in solar valuation or green building. After the bid was awarded and the assigned appraiser began working on the assignment, it became apparent that the required scope of work was different from what was indicated in the RFP and the assignment was far more complex than the appraiser had realized at the time of the bid. The appraiser was forced to turn back the assignment to the lender, who then had to re-bid and re-assign the job. No one–not the appraiser, appraisal department, loan officer, or borrower–was pleased with this result.

How could a more accurate scope of work have been determined? What went wrong in this process?

1. There was lack of detail in the RFP.
   The initial RFP raised a number of immediate questions about the scope of work. Except for a note that the $2 million budget included a new roof, no additional information was provided. Even after deducting an estimate for the cost of the roof, the estimated cost for the solar installation was unusually high based on the current market cost of an installed rooftop solar PV system in this area. More information would be needed to determine if the system was oversized for the industrial use (possible superadequacy), if other costs were included, or if the solar PV installation was priced above market. Whatever the explanation, there would likely be additional work required over and above a simple discounted cash flow analysis to calculate the present value of the avoided electricity cost. However, this complexity would likely go unnoticed by an appraiser who lacks training and experience in solar valuation, such as the appraiser who was first awarded this assignment.
2. There was no stipulation for special expertise in the RFP.
   Valuing solar PV requires additional education and experience on the appraiser's part, particularly for cases such as this that may involve added complexity. For example, in this case, a subsequent review of the installation contract revealed that the $2 million budget was not for a rooftop installation but for more expensive parking lot canopy mounts. The weather protection amenity offered by the carports would not likely translate to higher rents for this industrial user, as might be the case for an office user. And while the solar PV was reportedly sized for the historical use of this high-energy user, it was projected to generate 40% more electricity than comparable industrial properties typically require in the market. Determining whether this relative overproduction affects value requires a working knowledge of local net metering tariffs and regulations as well as consideration of a potential obsolescence adjustment.[6]

6. See Chapter 10 for more information about net metering and its potential impact on the valuation process.

Case Study 5.B *(continued)*

3. The initial appraiser underestimated the need for special expertise. Without a specific requirement in the RFP calling for advanced knowledge or experience in green building or solar valuation, appraisers without such knowledge or experience may not realize they lack the requisite competency to develop an appropriate scope of work. Valuing solar PV, particularly in commercial applications, can vary in terms of complexity from assignment to assignment. Just as with many other areas of expertise in appraisal, experience in solar PV is necessary to know when a more in-depth analysis is required. In this case, a proper scoping of the assignment required:
   - An understanding of the current market price for installed solar PV systems
   - An understanding of how the market views incentives such as tax credits and accelerated depreciation
   - Knowledge of the typical energy production capability (kWh per year) of solar PV based on the rated capacity of the system for this market
   - Knowledge of the typical energy use intensity (EUI) for comparable industrial properties and uses
   - A functional knowledge of electricity tariffs and net-metering arrangements in the local market and the risks potential changes in these arrangements pose to the income-based valuation of solar PV

information about the basics of the property but may not reveal any information about whether it is green without specifically adding this to the search parameters.

Adding search terms such as "Energy Star," "LEED," or "green" to the property address can often be elucidating. The LEED scorecard, which details the specific credits earned, may be available online for LEED-certified buildings.[7] Information such as a project scorecard or worksheet could be very valuable in developing a more precise scope of work. Exhibit 5.1 shows the first-page search results when the search string was amended to include "LEED" along with the property address of the previously mentioned building on the University of Wisconsin-Stevens Point campus. The second search result links to the US Green Building Council (USGBC) website, where a summary of the building's LEED scorecard can be downloaded, as seen in Exhibit 5.2. The summary scorecard provides information on the track of LEED (Building Design and Construction: New Construction), the version (2.2) and the level of certification achieved (Gold), with the number of points

7. Note that not finding a LEED scorecard or similar documentation online does not mean that the property is not certified by LEED or another type of green certification. Property owners may opt out of public disclosure, and some of the earliest LEED-certified buildings may not have detailed project scorecards available online.

Exhibit 5.1 **Expanding the Internet Search String for Green Building Identification**

Google 201 reserve stevens point leed  

All Maps News Shopping Images More ▾ Search tools

About 62,300 results (0.66 seconds)

The Suites@201 Reserve earns LEED gold certification - Portage ... Norton
portagecountybiz.com/the-suites**201-reserve**-earns-**leed**-gold-certification/ ▾
The Suites@**201** residence hall at the University of Wisconsin-**Stevens Point** was awarded a Leadership in Energy and Environmental Design (**LEED**®) Gold ...

UW Stevens Point - New Residence Hall | U.S. Green Building Council Norton
www.usgbc.org/.../uw-**stevens-point**-new-re... ▾ U.S. Green Building Council ▾
LEED BD+C: New Construction v2 - **LEED** 2.2. UW **Stevens Point** - New Residence Hall. **201 Reserve** Street **Stevens Point**, WI 54481. United States Map ...

Suites 201 - Residential Living | UWSP Norton
www.uwsp.edu/.../suites**201**.aspx ▾ University of Wisconsin–Stevens Point ▾
Skip to main content. University of Wisconsin - **Stevens Point** ... Suites @ **201 Reserve** Street (Suites@**201**) ... The Suites@**201** has been certified as **LEED**-Gold.

201 Reserve Street Overview :: Green Building Information Gateway Norton
www.gbig.org › Places › The World › United States › Wisconsin ▾
201 Reserve Street. Building. Building **201 Reserve** Street. University of Wisconsin-**Stevens Point**, **Stevens Point**, WI, USA. UW Stevens ... Gold. **LEED** NC 2.2.

201 Reserve Street Details :: Green Building Information Gateway Norton
www.gbig.org › Places › The World › United States › Wisconsin ▾
201 Reserve Street ... This building has a 5 year timeline with 2 green activities including a **LEED** Gold certification. ... UW **Stevens Point** - New Residence Hall.

earned in each credit category. One can then download the detailed scorecard by clicking where indicated. The detailed scorecard, seen in Exhibit 5.3, provides additional information about which credits were earned in each category. Having this type of detailed information readily available can greatly assist in crafting an appropriate scope of work.

An aerial view of a property can provide additional key information, particularly about the possible presence of roof-mounted solar PV systems. For example, a valuation assignment for the 1960s-era city-owned public library shown in the two accompanying photographs was accepted by an appraiser. No green features were noted

Exhibit 5.2 Summary of LEED Project Scorecard

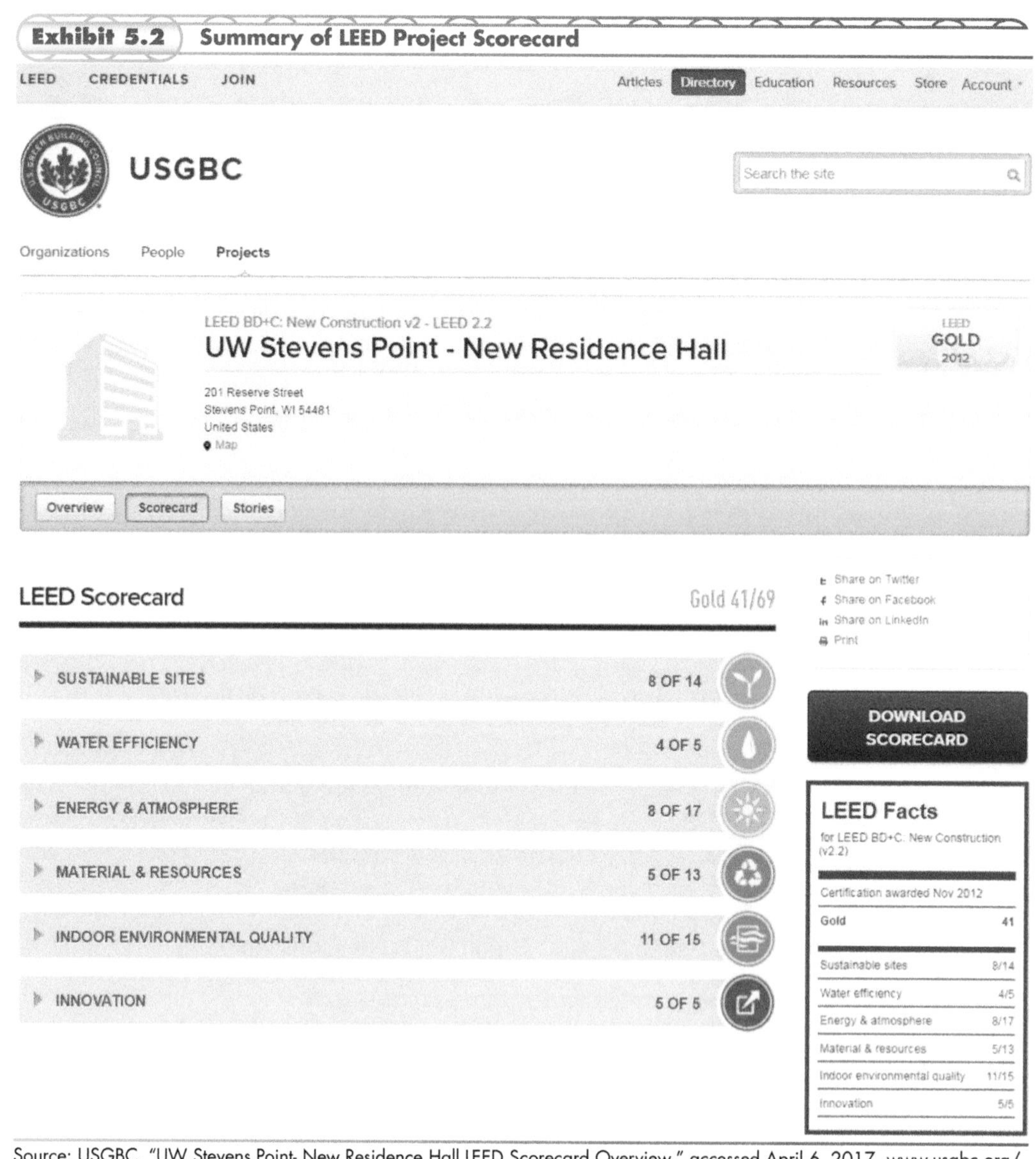

Source: USGBC, "UW Stevens Point- New Residence Hall LEED Scorecard Overview," accessed April 6, 2017, www.usgbc.org/projects/uw-stevens-point-new-residence-hall.

in the process of bidding and awarding the assignment, and no documentation was subsequently provided. However, an aerial view of the property revealed an extensive solar array that could be seen covering most of the roof. The appraiser then requested more information from the property owner on the solar installation, which indicated that the 230 kW DC (kilowatt of direct current) system had been recently installed. Analysis during the valuation process concluded that

Exhibit 5.3 LEED Project Scorecard

0010534781, Stevens Point, WI

UW Stevens Point - New Residence Hall

LEED BD+C: New Construction (v2.2) — GOLD, AWARDED NOV 2012

SUSTAINABLE SITES		AWARDED: 8 / 14
SSc1	Site selection	1 / 1
SSc2	Development density and community connectivity	1 / 1
SSc3	Brownfield redevelopment	1 / 1
SSc4.1	Alternative transportation - public transportation access	1 / 1
SSc4.2	Alternative transportation - bicycle storage and changing rooms	0 / 1
SSc4.3	Alternative transportation - low emitting and fuel efficient vehicles	0 / 1
SSc4.4	Alternative transportation - parking capacity	1 / 1
SSc5.1	Site development - protect or restore habitat	0 / 1
SSc5.2	Site development - maximize open space	1 / 1
SSc6.1	Stormwater design - quantity control	0 / 1
SSc6.2	Stormwater design - quality control	0 / 1
SSc7.1	Heat island effect - non-roof	1 / 1
SSc7.2	Heat island effect - roof	1 / 1
SSc8	Light pollution reduction	0 / 1

WATER EFFICIENCY		AWARDED: 4 / 5
WEc1.1	Water efficient landscaping - reduce by 50%	1 / 1
WEc1.2	Water efficient landscaping - no potable water use or no irrigation	1 / 1
WEc2	Innovative wastewater technologies	0 / 1
WEc3.1	Water use reduction - 20% reduction	1 / 1
WEc3.2	Water use reduction - 30% reduction	1 / 1

ENERGY & ATMOSPHERE		AWARDED: 8 / 17
EAc1	Optimize energy performance	5 / 10
EAc2	On-site renewable energy	1 / 3
EAc3	Enhanced commissioning	0 / 1
EAc4	Enhanced refrigerant Mgmt	1 / 1
EAc5	Measurement and verification	0 / 1
EAc6	Green power	1 / 1

MATERIAL & RESOURCES		AWARDED: 5 / 13
MRc1.1	Building reuse - maintain 75% of existing walls, floors & roof	0 / 1
MRc1.2	Building reuse - maintain 95% of existing walls, floors & roof	0 / 1
MRc1.3	Building reuse - maintain 50% of interior non-structural elements	0 / 1
MRc2.1	Construction waste Mgmt - divert 50% from disposal	1 / 1
MRc2.2	Construction waste Mgmt - divert 75% from disposal	1 / 1
MRc3.1	Materials reuse - 5%	0 / 1

MATERIAL & RESOURCES		CONTINUED
MRc3.2	Materials reuse - 10%	0 / 1
MRc4.1	Recycled content - 10% (post-consumer + 1/2 pre-consumer)	1 / 1
MRc4.2	Recycled content - 20% (post-consumer + 1/2 pre-consumer)	0 / 1
MRc5.1	Regional materials - 10% extracted, processed and manufactured regionally	1 / 1
MRc5.2	Regional materials - 20% extracted, processed and manufactured regionally	1 / 1
MRc6	Rapidly renewable materials	0 / 1
MRc7	Certified wood	0 / 1

INDOOR ENVIRONMENTAL QUALITY		AWARDED: 11 / 15
EQc1	Outdoor air delivery monitoring	1 / 1
EQc2	Increased ventilation	0 / 1
EQc3.1	Construction IAQ Mgmt plan - during construction	1 / 1
EQc3.2	Construction IAQ Mgmt plan - before occupancy	0 / 1
EQc4.1	Low-emitting materials - adhesives and sealants	1 / 1
EQc4.2	Low-emitting materials - paints and coatings	1 / 1
EQc4.3	Low-emitting materials - carpet systems	1 / 1
EQc4.4	Low-emitting materials - composite wood and agrifiber products	0 / 1
EQc5	Indoor chemical and pollutant source control	0 / 1
EQc6.1	Controllability of systems - lighting	1 / 1
EQc6.2	Controllability of systems - thermal comfort	1 / 1
EQc7.1	Thermal comfort - design	1 / 1
EQc7.2	Thermal comfort - verification	1 / 1
EQc8.1	Daylight and views - daylight 75% of spaces	1 / 1
EQc8.2	Daylight and views - views for 90% of spaces	1 / 1

INNOVATION		AWARDED: 5 / 5
IDc1	Innovation in design	4 / 4
IDc2	LEED Accredited Professional	1 / 1

TOTAL		41 / 69

Source: USGBC, "UW Stevens Point- New Residence Hall LEED Scorecard Overview."

Upon first glance, it is not obvious that this public library building has a rooftop solar PV system.

This aerial image of the library building, taken from Google Earth, reveals an extensive solar array covering most of the roof.

the system accounted for a $46,000 annual reduction in energy costs, which was a material factor that required adjustment in both valuation approaches used.

There is a growing body of online resources that seek to coalesce "green data." For example, The Green Building Information Gateway (GBIG) provides comparative data from a variety of programs and sources.[8] While the GBIG is a product of the USGBC, it includes data not only on LEED but also on other types of green certifications (such as Energy Star) and benchmarking data, among other types of data. Checking the subject area on the GBIG site, for example, can quickly show the market prevalence of other green buildings or green-rated properties.

Effective Communication

Effective communication with all parties involved in the valuation process is part of every assignment. However, green building brings to these discussions an unusually broad variability in terminology and knowledge base. As discussed in previous chapters, green building is not a monolithic or static concept. Green building can have different implications and meanings based on the property location or type as well as the intended audience. The integrated nature of green building systems adds additional complexity to property descriptions. Furthermore, what "green" means can change over time. If a property owner describes the building as "green," that could imply that a variety of different features may be present, some of which may affect value and others that may not. Is the building green because the paint does not off-gas, the building uses half the energy of its peers, or because of the combination of the enhanced ventilation, natural daylighting, and biophilic design of the workspace? Contrast this with a conventional building that has readily identifiable and well-defined features such as an elevator that services all floors and recently renovated, ADA-compliant restrooms.

Valuation professionals working on assignments involving green projects or non-green buildings with green features may also find themselves engaging with different types of building professionals than they are accustomed to, such as green building architects and designers, engineers who specialize in energy modeling, or sustainability consultants. All of these varied disciplines have their own terminology, and some of the terms used may have very different meanings than they do in valuation. For example, it is common to hear architects and designers of green buildings speak of "green premiums." While valuation professionals may immediately think of a rent or sale price premium when we hear this term, the architect, designer, or sustainability consultant may actually be referring to

8. www.gbig.org

what valuation professionals would think of as a "cost premium"–that is, the increased cost of the green feature.

Developing the scope of work for a green building (or a non-green building in a sustainability-oriented market) involves the potential for miscommunication arising from the mistaken assumption that all parties define green building in the same way based on a similar level of knowledge. At least at this point in time, it may be prudent to assume that discussions about green buildings, green features, or market demand for green buildings require additional confirmation that all parties indeed mean the same thing when they use a particular green building-related term.

Case Study 5.C, What Went Right? shows how effective communication throughout the valuation process can prevent the problems described in Case Study 5.B, "What Went Wrong?"

Case Study 5.C What Went Right?

The property owner of a 16,000-sq.-ft., 1970s-era wood-frame suburban office building wished to refinance his loan so that he could add solar PV to the property to reduce the energy costs. The owner solicited three solar installation bids, including one for a leased system, and settled on an owned system with a bid price of $325,000 for an 84.5 kW DC system to be mounted on a carport structure in the parking lot.

The lender included the following description in the RFP posted in the online bidding system:

Proposed renovation:	Yes
Renovation description:	Install $350k in solar panels

There were no hiccups in the process of this lender appraisal assignment despite the brevity of the information provided, but the successful result required green building knowledge and the involvement of everyone involved from start to finish.

What went right in this appraisal assignment?

1. The appraiser was qualified for the job.
   The description in the RFP was sufficient for the winning bidder, who was on the Appraisal Institute Green Registry and had the necessary training and experience to know the type of additional work that might be required for this assignment. Given that the $350,000 cost quoted in the RFP was gross cost before incentives, the market value of the system would likely be less. The appraiser assumed that comparable sales would likely be lacking and that a discounted cash flow analysis of the avoided energy cost over the system's economic life would be required. Furthermore, the appraiser knew that the solar installer's bid would need to be reviewed, with specific investigation into the projected energy production of the proposed solar PV system versus

Case Study 5.C (continued)

the expected energy consumption for the property so that any effects of recent changes in net metering regulations in that market could be analyzed. The appraiser was therefore able to develop the appropriate scope of work and bid on the assignment specifying a fee and timing commensurate with the additional work required.

2. The lender was knowledgeable.
   The loan officer provided the appraisal department with the detailed solar bid proposal, including the complete system specifications such as the projected production, module warranty, and inverter details. This experience was a substantive improvement over a previous bid request by the same lender that had not included sufficient information in order to obtain credible bids. (See Case Study 5.B, What Went Wrong?) The appraisal department subsequently selected a qualified appraiser from their panel.
   Finally, the lender placed this assignment with a review appraiser who had knowledge of and experience with green buildings and solar PV. This final step provided further assurance that the value conclusion was credible.
3. The borrower/property owner was cooperative.
   The property owner provided the bank with the complete solar installation proposal, which was provided to the appraiser when the bid was awarded. The proposal included detailed projections of energy production for the system, in addition to the key component metrics. The owner also cooperated with the appraiser's request for competitive bids from other solar installers, contact information for the chosen installer, and permission to access prior energy consumption information for the property from the local utility.

The result of this approach was an assignment that progressed smoothly from start to finish:

- The loan officer requested the proper information.
- The appraisal department recognized the need for special expertise in the process of awarding the bid.
- The appraiser understood how to assess the system size, quantify the reduced energy cost, and adjust the gross cost of the system for the incentives as well as the contributory value of the carport structure.
- The borrower was cooperative in providing supporting information.
- The reviewer understood the nuances of solar PV valuation. The reviewer was also able to understand the appraiser's approach to the contributory value of the solar PV, satisfying both the appraisal requirements and underwriting guidelines.

Competency Considerations

While green building does not change the fact that the valuation professional must determine whether he or she has the knowledge and experience necessary to deliver a credible result once a valuation problem is identified, it can make problem identification more challenging. Furthermore, as illustrated in Case Study 5.B, having insufficient green building experience may lead to a faulty assessment of an assignment's complexity, resulting in a mismatch between a valuation professional's knowledge and the requirements of a specific assignment.

Typically, one thinks of competency as it relates to compliance. However, there are equally important and perhaps more compelling reasons to reconsider it. If *competency* is defined as having the requisite skill and knowledge base for a given assignment, then being *competent* for a particular assignment means that the valuation task will not be overwhelming and that it can be done credibly, making it economically viable in both the short and long term. In short, competency can expand one's scope of services and be a competitive advantage.

In some cases, base competency is defined by the client. A property owner, for example, may stipulate that the lender must choose a valuation professional with appropriate green building knowledge. Alternatively, a lender may independently choose to award green building assignments only to those appraisers who have the requisite experience. For practical purposes, whether competency is deemed adequate is largely determined by the expectations of the users of valuation services and in comparison to professional peers. For example, intended users of valuation services in markets where green building is prevalent may assume a certain level of green building knowledge from valuation professionals whether or not that expectation is supported in practice. Not knowing enough about green building becomes a business and competency risk if potential clients discover that the practitioner has less knowledge about green building than that of typical market participants or other valuation professionals.

Avoiding the Influence of Bias

Appraiser professionalism, competency, and public trust are rooted in the critical role of appraisers as unbiased observers of the market. Even without professional standards specifically cautioning against bias that affects valuation results, common sense and professionalism mandate that every effort be made to deliver an unbiased, credible opinion of value.

Defining *bias* as "A preference or inclination that precludes an appraiser's impartiality, independence, or objectivity in an appraisal assignment,"[9] there are two potential areas of concern specifical-

9. *The Dictionary of Real Estate Appraisal*, 6th ed. (Chicago: Appraisal Institute, 2015), 22.

ly associated with the emergence of green building: bias resulting from personal beliefs ("pro-green" or "anti-green" bias) and bias resulting from lack of experience and/or knowledge. Pro-green bias stems from the preconception that green building has intrinsic value, regardless of whether the green building features are valued by the market. Anti-green bias is a belief, without consideration of market-based evidence, that green building has no discernible value or a negative impact on value. This type of bias can lead to or reinforce a knowledge-gap bias, when the appraiser incorrectly assumes that no additional training or education is required to account for green building's influence in a particular market. While unintended bias due to a lack of experience or knowledge may pose the greatest risk to fulfilling the market's expectation of competent and unbiased professional valuation services, strategies to address this potential problem are relatively straightforward and covered earlier in this chapter. Conversely, belief-based bias can be more difficult to pinpoint and merits closer examination.

Typically, appraisers do not face a substantial hurdle in overcoming personal belief-based bias in most valuation assignments. However, green building seems to incite a higher-than-average "for" or "against" response. For example, it is common to hear opposing viewpoints from peers in the commercial real estate industry such as "I don't believe in all that green building stuff–it's all just industry hype," or "Green building is the right thing to do." This reaction is puzzling, as other property characteristics have not typically prompted a similar belief-oriented reaction, even when those characteristics were novel. For example, people in the industry are not "for" elevators or "against" central heating and air conditioning, despite the fact that elevators and centralized heating and cooling both caused significant fundamental shifts in the design, construction, and operation of real estate similar in scale to the changes prompted by green building.

What is it about green building that tends to elicit a strong personal opinion? One possibility may be green building's roots in the concept of sustainability. Sustainability, as it is expressed in green building, gives credit to projects that tread more lightly on the surrounding infrastructure, interiors that allow natural light to all employees rather than only perimeter offices, and buildings that are most efficient with resources. Land-use goals in the era of sustainability extend beyond the property line and put humans and the impact of their activities under scrutiny. In this light, it becomes understandable that green building may trigger personal opinions and experiences. Awareness of this potential trigger is one of the most powerful ways for the valuation professional to combat this type of bias.

Summary

Identifying the appraisal problem and defining the appropriate scope of work are the foundation of any appraisal. Green building makes problem identification more challenging due largely to the fundamental differences in the way green buildings are designed and constructed. Furthermore, the often seamless incorporation of green building characteristics may mean that green buildings will not necessarily look different from non-green buildings. Without basic knowledge and experience of green building and sustainability influences in the market, it is difficult to identify the valuation problem accurately. As a result, the scope of work may not be appropriate for the appraisal problem.

While professional standards put the ultimate responsibility for developing an appropriate scope of work on the shoulders of the appraiser, this does not mean that it is the *sole* responsibility of the appraiser. Effective communication requires everyone to speak the same language (in this case, share a similar level of knowledge of green features and how to describe them), and to recognize the materiality of the relevant issues. In the critical first step of defining the valuation assignment, everyone involved bears some level of responsibility for identifying key information and ascertaining that the relevant information is effectively communicated to the appraiser. As was clearly demonstrated in Case Study 5.C, What Went Right?, the valuation process is best served when all parties involved are knowledgeable about green building and participate in the process.

Unintentional bias with respect to green building, either due to a knowledge gap or personal beliefs, warrants special attention for valuation professionals. Proactively pursuing green building education before it is required in an assignment is an effective way to address the knowledge gap. Careful attention to market behavior and market participant attitudes pertaining to green building and sustainability is necessary to avoid unintentional personal bias related to this rapidly changing and far-reaching market influence.

6 Market Analysis

Real estate value is inherently contextual: an office building or shopping center in one market is not expected to have an identical value in a different market. Market analysis is the process used to understand this context. In this way, market analysis informs every part of the valuation process. It serves as the foundation for the highest and best use analysis of a property, provides information required to apply the three approaches to value, and gives needed perspective in the final reconciliation of the value indications. The valuation process, therefore, begins with understanding the market–or the context–in which the property operates.

The emergence of green building signals an underlying shift in the market that affects all properties, regardless if they are green or conventional. Green buildings and green building practices reflect a market's incorporation of sustainability principles into its real estate decision matrix. Sustainability broadens the scope of the market analysis to include the effects of the subject property on its occupants and the surrounding community and ecosystem. This shift from focusing primarily on the market's effect on the property to also considering the property's influence on its surroundings can result in material impacts on value. Appropriately addressing any impact of sustainability in an appraisal begins with the market analysis.

Pinpointing the degree to which a market has incorporated green building and sustainability principles to the point that it affects leasing and purchase decisions can seem like a murky, perhaps even daunting, undertaking. The high level of variability among green buildings and green building demand presents a challenge, as does the fact that green building is still in flux. Building technologies and integrated systems are continuing to evolve and be refined, while rating systems are changing and expanding. However, while there is much to green building and green features that may be new to valuation professionals, what remains the same is that the effects on value depend on specific property characteristics and whether that particular market values them.

Assessing the Influence of Sustainability

Identifying the degree to which a given market values green building is relevant for all properties, regardless of whether or not they are green. Chapter 4 discussed how sustainability and policy-level goals are key drivers of green building demand. Identifying and understanding these market influences enhances the valuation professional's ability to assess a property's competitive position in the market. While policy-driven regulations and incentives are readily identifiable, the effect of sustainability on real estate purchase and leasing decisions is often less clear.

Depending on the valuation assignment, how much influence sustainability has on the market may affect the type or quantity of data required and how that data is analyzed. Is the most probable buyer sufficiently influenced by sustainability that it impacts the purchase decision? Which metrics matter most? In this manner, the effect of sustainability on a market becomes another fundamental to consider when examining local market supply and demand.

Sustainability Orientation[1]

A market's sustainability orientation refers to the degree to which that market expresses the principle of sustainability through its behaviors and actions. Sustainability orientation is best viewed as a continuum, as shown in Exhibit 6.1. While there may be markets that exist on either extreme, most markets exist somewhere along the continuum and should be expected to change over time as they continue to react to the influence of sustainability.

The goal of assessing a market's sustainability orientation is to gauge the relative degree of influence sustainability has in that local market. Is this market strongly or weakly influenced by sustainability? Is sustainability a primary factor in the decision-making process? Does sustainability contribute to the decision-making process, but to a lesser degree? Is sustainability peripherally considered, or by only a small segment of the market? Sustainability is not unlike other determinants of market demand in that it assists in gauging the

1. This section expands on the authors' previous work, "Integrating Sustainability and Green Building into the Appraisal Process," *Journal of Sustainable Real Estate* 2, no. 1 (2010): 233-237.

Exhibit 6.1 Market Sustainability Orientation Continuum

Sustainability Orientation	
Weak	**Strong**
• Few regulations or incentives related to green building	• Many green-building related regulations and incentives
• Few green buildings or green features	• Green buildings and green features common
• Green-up* limited to compliance	• Voluntary green-up by property owners
• Limited evidence of sustainability behaviors in community	• Strong evidence of sustainability behaviors in community
• Secondary market data indicates limited green adoption	• Secondary market data indicates widespread green adoption

* The term *green-up* pertains to green building activity such as green upgrades, renovations, or certifications to existing properties.

relative competitive position of a given property within a market and therefore contributes to the assessment of the current and projected demand for that property.

Incorporating the Influence of Sustainability into the Market Analysis

An important part of market analysis is gaining enough understanding of the market to know what questions to ask and what data to collect during the valuation process. While sustainability orientation may be an unfamiliar market characteristic, the approach to analyzing its effect on the market remains the same as for any other market influence: Assess the behaviors of relevant stakeholders, use market surveys and studies when available, and conduct primary research as needed.

Incorporating sustainability orientation into the market analysis may require gathering new or additional sources of data that target the sustainability aspects of market demand. How do green building and sustainability alter the elements of comparison used by market participants in their purchase and leasing decisions? Are additional factors being considered? If so, are they being weighted differently than they would be in a market where sustainability has little influence? The specific sustainability-related data points collected and analyzed will vary based on ownership and property type, as will be discussed in more detail in the following sections of this chapter.

Ownership and End-User Considerations

Market demand for the purchase and leasing of both green and non-green properties can be affected by the influence of sustainability. Examining the sustainability orientation of the most probable buyer and user can be an important part of market analysis.

The sustainability orientation of owner-users and investors, the two main classes of real estate owners, can have a material effect on demand, yet the effect may vary between the two. For example, if the typical buyer of a given property is an institutional investor, the relative demand for green building may be driven by the sustainability goals of institutional investors, even if the sustainability orientation of the local market is low. In these cases, interviewing the representatives who handled the transactions can yield pertinent information that cannot necessarily be gleaned within the local market. Did the purchase fulfill sustainability reporting goals or imperatives? Did the investor filter for green-certified properties, or was the focus instead on property performance metrics such as energy-efficiency regardless of a green label? Was the investor looking for the marketability of a green label to attract potential tenants or to satisfy sustainability reporting requirements? Finding out what drives the decision for that intended market participant can have a discernible effect on the identification and analysis of the comparable properties.

Beyond compliance-related concerns or corporate sustainability goals, investors may be particularly focused on a building's performance, which can affect demand for green or resource-efficient space. Sometimes framed as "best practices," green buildings or conventional buildings with energy- and water-efficiency upgrades can be a way to leverage operating expense efficiencies while acting as a hedge against future obsolescence. In these cases, it may be relevant to collect the Energy Star rating or energy consumption data for the subject and comparable properties to aid the analysis.

Owner-users, in their role as building occupants, may be more interested than investors in the elements of green building that are not directly measured in the income stream, such as indoor environmental quality, productivity, and employee health and well-being. An investor may also care about these issues, but that interest may be limited to the degree that the property generates higher rents, lower tenant turnover, or improved marketability. An owner-user may also be in a better position to match the long-term economic benefits of green building with its costs than an investor with a shorter time horizon, who may be most interested in minimizing a building's first costs rather than its life-cycle costs.

A build-to-suit private school reveals an owner-user who might be particularly interested in the non-income stream benefits of green building. It also illustrates how sustainability can alter and expand the sphere of market participants to be considered in the market analysis. While the building owner is technically the tenant, the students–who are the prime occupants of the space–do not have any economic interest in the property. However, these students–or more specifically, their parents–may be a significant source of demand for a green school.

In the case of certain property types, such as retail, the ultimate driver of the demand for that space may be far distant from the property owner; it may be the tenant's customers who drive the demand for the space similarly to students who occupy a school. And, like a school, the demand for a retail property may be propelled by end users who are neither property owners nor tenants.

For example, a 2016 study released by the World Building Council cites a growing body of evidence linking "green" retail space to higher customer satisfaction and in some cases superior revenue generation.[2] For retail properties in a sustainability-oriented market, this might affect which comparables are used and what questions are asked when confirming comparable data. Do local brokers report that green retail space leases faster than non-green space? Does revenue per square foot or lease-up period of the comparables need to be considered alongside the green characteristics to determine if the green attributes may be contributing to any difference in demand or attainable rents in that market? Given that data such as revenue per square foot might be unavailable for comparable properties, are there other metrics that can be used in that market to tease out the degree to which the green characteristics are affecting value?

The broader influence of sustainability is not limited to schools or retail sectors, however. Office space can also be affected by the concerns and sustainability orientation of its end users. As shown in Case Study 5.A in Chapter 5 (page 91), tenant and broker interviews cited the proximity to public transit of the LEED-certified Class B office building as a key determinant in the decision to lease the space. In this case, transit proximity was an important amenity to the employees of the tenant, which subsequently influenced the leasing decision. Further market research uncovered additional demand in that market arising from tenants whose clients required their vendors to lease office space that is proximate to public transit.

While no single behavior should be construed as evidence of market-wide sustainability orientation, one example of how the observed behavior of consumers could be linked to real estate decisions is found in a 2012 study of price premiums in green-labeled, single-family homes sold between 2007 and 2012 in California. In addition to a price premium for the green label, the researchers identified a positive correlation between price premiums for green-labeled homes and hybrid vehicle registrations, which they identified as a proxy for the property owners' environmental ideology.[3]

---

2. World Green Building Council, *Health, Well-Being and Productivity in Retail: The Impact of Green Building on People and Profit*, February 2016, www.ukgbc.org/sites/default/files/UK-GBC%20Health%20%26%20Wellbeing%20Retail%20Report%202016%20WEB.pdf; E. Conlon and A. Glavas, "The Relationship Between Corporate Sustainability and Firm Financial Performance" 2012, http://business.nd.edu/uploadedFiles/Conlon%20and%20Glavas%202012.pdf.

3. Nils Kok and Matthew E. Kahn, *The Value of Green Labels in the California Housing Market: An Economic Analysis of the Impact of Green Labeling on the Sales Price of a Home*, July 2012, www.pacenation.us/wp-content/uploads/2012/08/KK_Green_Homes_0719121.pdf.

Bearing in mind that the complexity of any given market may make it difficult to ascertain the true motivation behind any observed behavior, the following examples may reflect an underlying sustainability orientation, particularly if the behaviors or actions are not singular or isolated:

- Sustainability-oriented actions of individuals
  - Purchase of hybrid and electric vehicles
  - Solar photovoltaic (PV) installations on residential homes
  - Active commuting (walking, biking)
- Sustainability-oriented marketing by local businesses
  - Signs advertising organic or sustainable products in a discount retail warehouse
  - Leasing brochures that advertise green or sustainable space, transit proximity, bike shower facilities, etc.
- Facilitation of sustainability-oriented behaviors by the community
  - Mandatory electric vehicle charging stations at offices, parking garages, and shopping centers
  - Dedicated car-share parking at offices, shopping centers, and multifamily projects
  - Dedicated bicycle lanes and secure bicycle parking areas
  - Dual- (recycle and landfill) and triple-waste stream (plus composting) receptacles
  - Property Assessed Clean Energy (PACE) financing available for solar PV and energy-efficiency projects

Some examples of observable sustainability-oriented behaviors from these categories are shown in the accompanying photographs.

Property Type Considerations

In addition to ownership and end-user considerations, the property type may affect the type of data collected and analyzed. For example, bike commuting facilities such as showers and secure bicycle storage are likely to be more important for office than for retail or industrial properties. While secure bike storage may be important for multifamily properties, amenities such as changing facilities, showers, and lockers will most likely not be important. Electric vehicle charging may be equally important to office, multifamily, and retail properties, but the ratios and types of charging facilities may differ. Retail may need fast-charging stations, whereas apartments may need a larger quantity of standard chargers suitable for overnight use.

Similarly, land valuation of a transit-oriented site may need to consider the walking distance measured in minutes or tenths of a mile

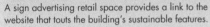

A sign advertising retail space provides a link to the website that touts the building's sustainable features.

An electric vehicle charging station at a LEED-certified shopping center in Dublin, California.

This close-up shows a dedicated space for electric vehicle charging at the same shopping center shown in the prior photo.

A recycling center at Bascom Hall at the University of Wisconsin-Madison, which includes separate receptacles for batteries, media, eye glasses, cell phones, and printer cartridges.

Banners advertising organic products and sustainability in a discount retail warehouse. Organic and sustainable products are often perceived as being more expensive, so seeing this sort of advertising in a discount warehouse may be particularly revealing about this community's sustainability orientation.

Pace Financing

Special financing may be available to you if you are considering energy/water efficiency improvements to your property. Financing known as PACE (Property Assessed Clean Energy) help home and business owners pay the initial cost of improvements, such as solar panel installation, and allows them to pay that cost back over an agreed upon term and rate through the property owner's property tax bill. The City Council has adopted three such programs, all of which serve both residential and commercial properties, allowing them to operate within the City limits. Please contact the program administrators through the websites listed below to determine your eligibility and decide if PACE financing can work for you.

www.heroprogram.com/

www.mpoweradvantage.net/

ygreeneworks.com/

A notice about the availability of PACE financing that was included along with a monthly utility bill. This may be another indicator of a market's sustainability orientation. PACE is a financing vehicle for solar and other energy-efficiency upgrades that is discussed in further detail in Chapter 11.

This sign is prominently displayed at a restaurant in the Burlington, Vermont airport. The photo not only advertises the local sourcing of the food served in the restaurant but informs the customer that eating locally sourced food improves the "local food SCENE (security, community, environment, nutrition, and economy)."

from the local commuter rail station. Which rail station or which lines service the station may also be important. The rail frequency or the schedule of the shuttle bus that services properties that are further than walking distance from the station may also be relevant. In addition, community comprehensive plans and local zoning codes may need closer tracking regarding density bonuses for green-certified buildings or developments located near transit hubs. Automobile parking ratios that may at first seem substandard may need to be reconsidered in light of transit proximity or the proclivity for alternate transport modes such as car sharing, biking, and walking. Bike parking ratios and the type of bike parking available may also need to be considered.[4]

Expanded Market Data Examples

The influence of sustainability in a market can manifest in disparate ways. A variety of information may enhance the analysis of a property's relative advantages and disadvantages within its market due to the influence of sustainability. Below are some examples of data points that may be useful to collect and analyze when assessing the influence of sustainability and green building on market demand. The relevance of these potential elements of comparison depends on the ownership type, property type, and other market characteristics such as relative sustainability orientation.

- Walkability
  Walkability, or the proximity of a specific location to daily needs such

4. For example, San Francisco requires two classes of parking for bicycles: Class 1 long-term storage for employees and residents, and Class 2 for visitors.

that they can be conveniently reached on foot, has emerged as a factor that can affect both purchase and leasing decisions.[5] Walk Score is an online algorithm that ranks proximity to amenities on a scale of 1 to 100 and is available in several countries including the US, Canada, and Australia. The numerical rankings are categorized as "Walker's Paradise," "Very Walkable," "Somewhat Walkable," and "Car Dependent."

- Transit access
  Mobile applications and online mapping programs often show the nearest transit stations and options. In addition, Transit Score, a similar measure as Walk Score but for transit, may be a useful data point. Bike Score is another transit-related rating that may be applicable. It rates an area's "bikeability" based on criteria such as bike lane infrastructure and an area's "hilliness."
- Energy use and energy use intensity (EUI)
  Collecting and maintaining data on energy use and EUI for the subject and comparable properties, much like tracking operating expense information, can be valuable.
- Energy Star rating
  This metric can be used to directly compare building energy efficiency, since the rating is based on a comparison to peers adjusted for size, occupancy, and climate zone.
- Green building certification, including level of certification, date certified, and certification track
  Green building certification scorecards or worksheets can provide important data, such as which specific features or design strategies were employed or which systems or facets of the building were certified.
- Green building market share
  The following two sidebars titled "Green Building Information Gateway Data" and "US Green Building Council Quarterly LEED Updates" provide examples of secondary data that provide useful insight into green building penetration in a specific market. Ascertaining the percentage of a market that is green-certified for a particular property type and determining the dominant green building rating system for a particular market may be helpful.
- Use of green leases or green lease language
  Green leases, or green lease language in conventional leases, reflect clear evidence of a market's sustainability orientation, since they reflect both landlord and tenant behavior.[6]

---

5. Real Capital Analytics, "RCA Trends Alert: Walking to Higher Value," April 2015.
6. More information about green leases can be found in the sidebar titled "What Is a Green Lease?" in Chapter 9, page 213.

- Net energy metering (NEM) policies
  Particularly important for properties that incorporate on-site energy generation, NEM policy and regulatory actions can have a material effect on property value.
- Available incentives and rebates
  The Database of State Incentives for Renewables and Efficiency (DSIRE) (www.dsireusa.org) tracks incentives and policies relating to renewable energy and energy-efficiency within the United States. To the extent that policy can affect market demand, knowing the incentives available in a particular market can be helpful in determining sustainability orientation. It may also help when analyzing the effects of incentives in features such as solar PV installations, as will be discussed in Chapter 11.
- Benchmarking and disclosure requirements:
  Similarly, maps and data regarding benchmarking and renewable portfolio standards (RPS) requirements such as those seen in Exhibits 4.2 and 4.3 in Chapter 4 (pages 79-80 and 84) can provide additional insight into the regulatory influence in a market. In markets that have benchmarking requirements, additional data may be available to the valuation professional when analyzing energy use of the subject and comparable properties.
- Green building code requirements and sustainability-oriented goals within comprehensive general plans
  The influence of sustainability has resulted in changes within building codes and community plans. Chapter 7 discusses these elements in more detail.

Green Building Information Gateway Data

The Green Building Information Gateway (GBIG) provides green building data that is searchable by address. In some cases, the project name is used in lieu of the address. The search can be set to include such factors as green building certifications, green awards, and green-related disclosures. However, it should be noted that it is not all-inclusive for green data. For example, it does not include green building certifications such as BREEAM or Green Globes.

The following screenshots show three different levels of analysis of a market surrounding a LEED-certified, mixed-use building in Grand Rapids, Michigan. As seen in the first photo of the immediate neighborhood, the GBIG data identifies another green building across the street from the subject property. In this case, the comparable is a much-larger LEED Platinum office building that has been certified more recently than the subject property. GBIG data used at this level of analysis can help identify—or eliminate—possible comparable properties for the subject.

Widening the search area, the larger community demonstrates substantial green activity, as seen in the second photo. (The numbers inside each circle indicate how many buildings that have green-related activities are in one area; they are grouped as seen here when individual circles would be overlapping.) This data suggests that the LEED certification of the subject property is not a singular event but indicative of more widespread green building market activity within the community.

The final photo shows the level of green activity statewide. Grand Rapids is second only to Detroit in terms of green building activity in Michigan, but Grand Rapids would top Detroit if green building were analyzed on a per-capita basis.

While this type of analysis alone does not define sustainability orientation, it does provide a strong indicator of overall green uptake in the subject market.

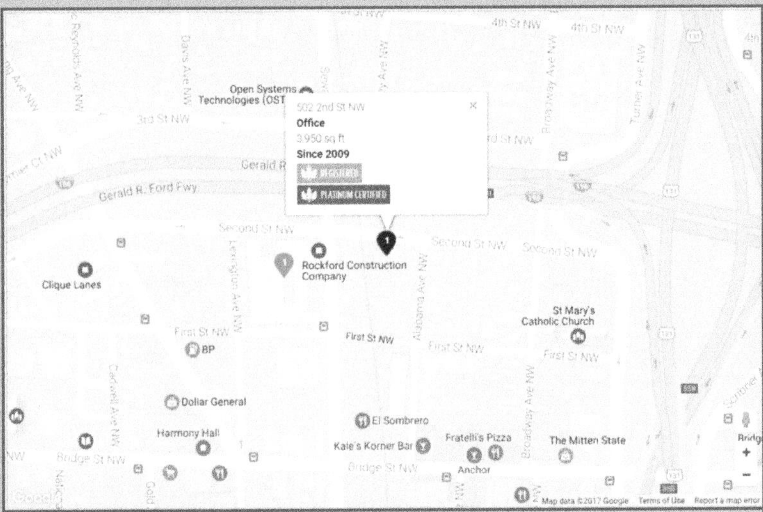

A map of the immediate Grand Rapids neighborhood surrounding the subject property. Another green building is identified across the street from the subject property. Source: www.gbig.org

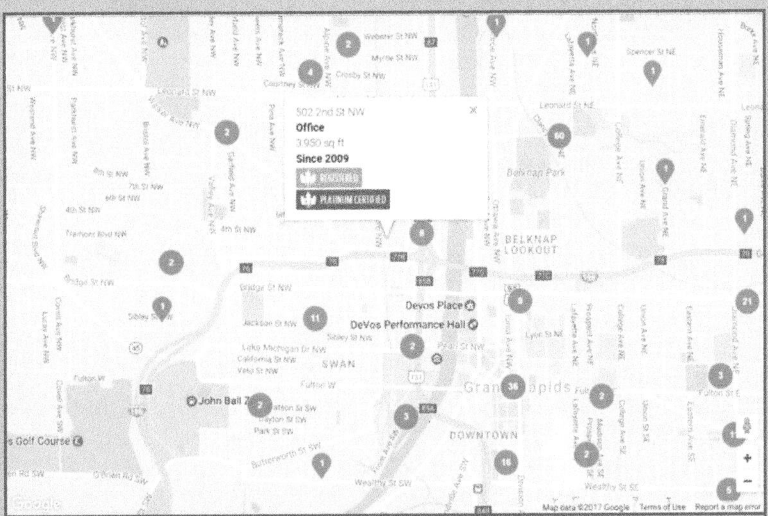

This map of the larger community surrounding the subject property suggests widespread green building activity in the area. Source: www.gbig.org

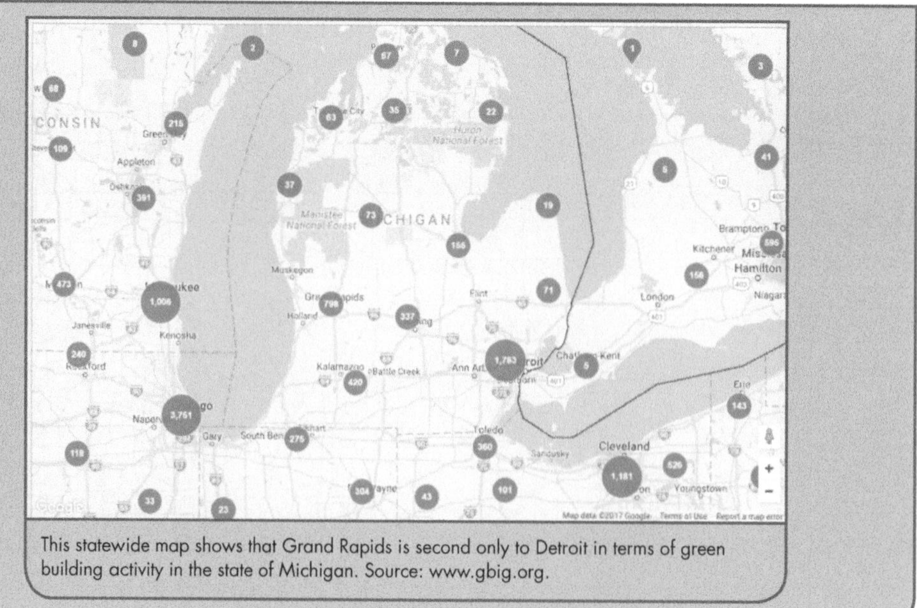

This statewide map shows that Grand Rapids is second only to Detroit in terms of green building activity in the state of Michigan. Source: www.gbig.org.

US Green Building Council Quarterly LEED Updates

The USGBC's quarterly LEED updates can provide a variety of information on market composition and trends related to green building. Exhibit 6.2 shows fourth quarter 2016 LEED project data for the state of Illinois. A similar report is available for each state, the entire US, and internationally on a country-by-country basis.

In the upper left-hand quadrant of Exhibit 6.2, historical registrations and certifications are shown in graphical form. The online version is interactive, permitting an annual analysis of LEED registrations and certifications that could be used for trend analysis. Registrations can be a leading indicator of market direction, while certifications demonstrate market commitment to green building. This information can help clarify if green building interest is growing, stable, or waning in a particular market.

The pie chart below the graph shows the type of rating system used. Although not visually coded in the screenshot, this chart is interactive in the online version: Blue signifies Building Design and Construction (BD+C), green is Operations and Maintenance (O+M), and orange is Interior Design and Construction (ID+C). This information may help answer the question of who is pursuing LEED. Is only new construction (BD+C), which may be mandated by code, getting certified, or are existing buildings (O+M) also part of the green activity? Or is it the tenants that really want the certification (ID+C)?

The horizontal graphic to the right of the pie chart shows the level achieved, which could be used to infer the market maturity. The lower levels are typically pursued early on in a market's implementation of LEED. Higher levels are pursued as LEED penetration increases, design teams gain more experience, and property owners compete for market differentiation.

The middle portions of the graphic titled Space Type and Owner Sector provide data on market composition. This information can also be used to assess overall market sustainability orientation by analyzing how widely dispersed the LEED certifications are by space type and owner type. Early stage markets may be dominated by government, institutional, and other owner-users. The balance can then shift once green

Exhibit 6.2 LEED Certification Update: Fourth Quarter 2016

Select a state
Illinois

LEED project data only includes commercial rating systems. The underlying data does not include LEED ND or LEED for Homes projects.

State Market Brief: Illinois

Cumulative LEED® Registrations

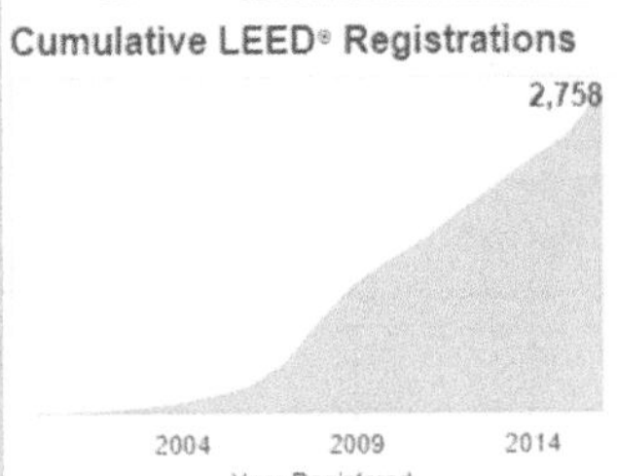

Cumulative LEED® Certifications

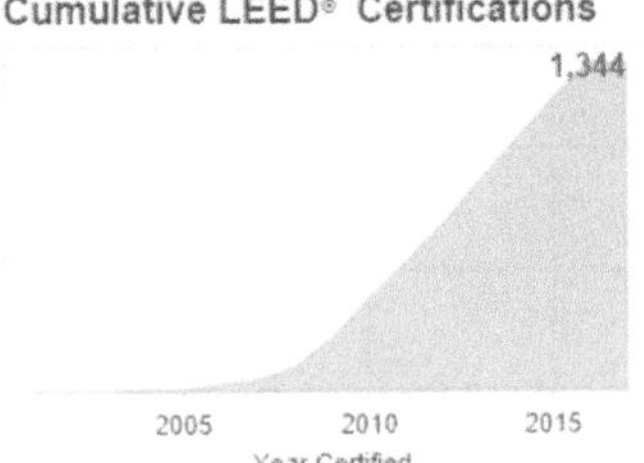

Summary

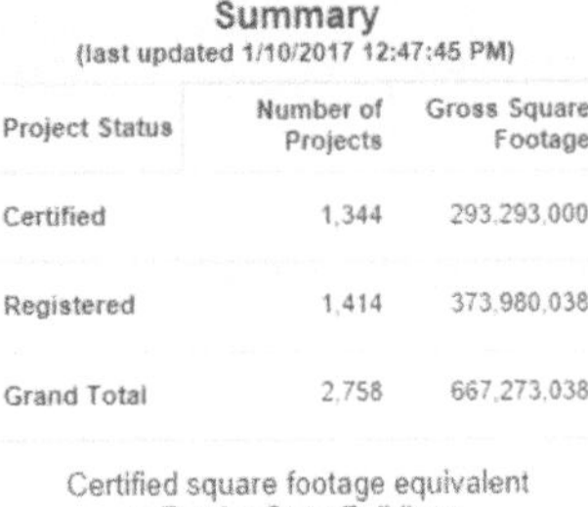

(last updated 1/10/2017 12:47:45 PM)

Project Status	Number of Projects	Gross Square Footage
Certified	1,344	293,293,000
Registered	1,414	373,980,038
Grand Total	2,758	667,273,038

Certified square footage equivalent to Empire State Buildings.

247

LEED® Rating System

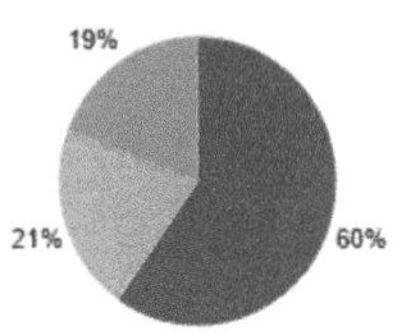

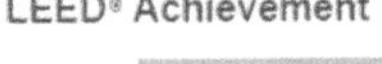

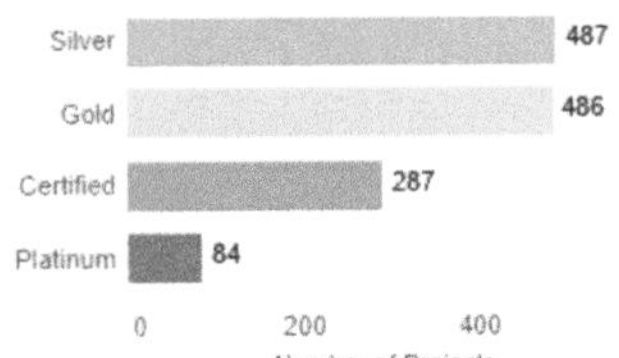

Space Type

Space Type	
Office & Office: Mixed Use	1,013
Education	415
Retail	363
Residential (commercial rating syste..	280
Public Assembly & Religious Worship	180
Health Care	105
Industrial Manufacturing	81
Lodging	60
Public Order and Safety	57
Warehouse and Distribution	57
Other	46
Laboratory	45
Service	30
Datacenter	13
Military Base	13

Owner Sector

Owner Sector	
Corporate & Investor	1,657
Higher Ed	288
Local Government	242
Non-Profit & Religious	228
K-12	155
Federal Government	85
Other	76
State Government	26
Residential	1

USGBC member organizations based in Illinois

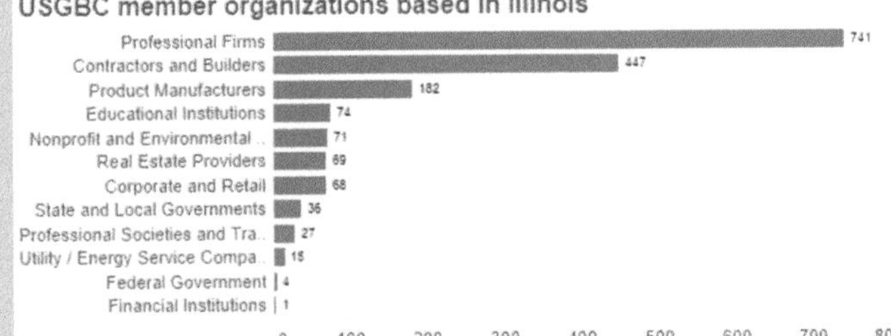

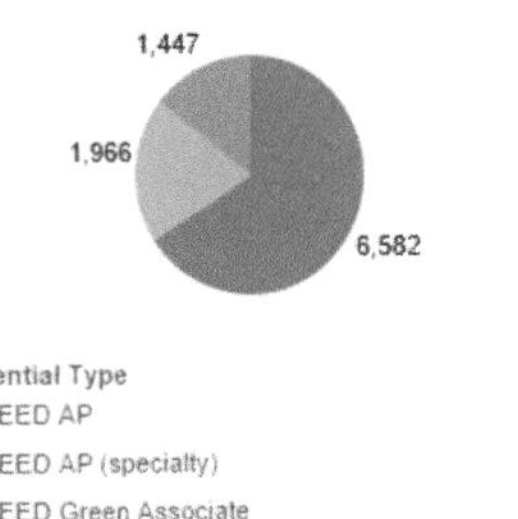

Credential Type
LEED AP
LEED AP (specialty)
LEED Green Associate

Source: USGBC, "LEED Certification Update: Fourth Quarter 2016," January 5, 2017, www.usgbc.org/articles/leed-certification-update-fourth-quarter-2016.

building becomes the best practices standard in the investor market, as it is for many institutional quality office building owners in the US. The relevance of green building and LEED to a particular property sector or owner type could also be inferred from the relative number of certified projects in each category. This could help answer the question of whether green building or certification matters to the subject property's market sector.

The graphics at the bottom of the image relate to membership and credentialing. While not a direct measurement of the green building market, the number of membership firms and credentialed professionals in the green building industry may be another useful indicator of a market's sustainability orientation as well as future green building market activity. Note that while the horizontal graphic reports membership numbers, it understates the number of practicing professionals, since only companies (rather than individuals) can become USGBC members. The pie chart, in contrast, is a better indicator of professional interest, since it reports individuals attaining each credential.

Conducting Primary Research

In addition to collecting secondary data as discussed in the previous section, primary research such as interviewing market participants and observing the neighborhood area surrounding the subject property can help determine the degree to which sustainability affects a given market. Primary data may also provide a level of specificity lacking in secondary market data.

Market Participant Interviews

Interviewing brokers and property owners who are active in the market can be a direct source of information regarding the drivers of market demand for green properties or green space. Sample questions to ask may include the following:

- Are tenants requesting LEED or other green-certified space in this market? Are they government or non-profit tenants? Fortune 500 companies? Local, small businesses?
- Is green space leasing at a rent premium or leasing faster than non-green space?
- Are landlords using green leases? Are tenants asking for them?
- Was the green certification a consideration in the purchase decision? What about Energy Star?
- What is the appeal of the green certification or green features to the purchaser? Is it the label effect ("green the portfolio"), cost savings or operational best practices, or future proofing (delaying obsolescence)?[7]

Neighborhood Observation

A visit to the subject neighborhood can also provide valuable information regarding the sustainability orientation of a local market. For

7. This list is derived from the authors' previous work, "Integrating Sustainability and Green Building into the Appraisal Process," *Journal of Sustainable Real Estate* 2, no. 1 (2010): 236.

example, if the subject property is a green building, what does the surrounding neighborhood look like? Is the subject a brand-new green building surrounded by conventionally built, unrenovated buildings? Or is it one of several green-certified buildings in the same neighborhood, as evidenced by certifications at the front of the building or in lobby areas?[8] When canvassing the neighborhood, noticing features such as transit proximity, bike sharing, or publicly available recycling containers can indicate a degree of sustainability orientation. The following case study discusses the type of information regarding a market's sustainability orientation gleaned when walking the surrounding blocks of an office building in Manhattan's Midtown East neighborhood.

Case Study 6.A Identifying Sustainability-Oriented Signals in the Market

Suppose you have taken on an assignment to provide a market value indication for a high-rise office building in Midtown Manhattan in New York City. When bidding on the assignment, you discovered that the property was LEED-certified in 2011 at the Platinum level under Version 2.2 of the New Construction track.

This is the first green-certified building you have appraised in this market. One of the first questions you have is whether the LEED certification matters to this market, and if so, the degree to which it matters–i.e., the sustainability orientation of the market.

The high-rise office building across the street from the subject property has converted a loading dock to secure bike storage for the building's tenants. The building is also advertising what appears to be a green roof amenity as part of its facade and lobby renovation.

A bike-share service stretches for half a block directly across the street from the subject property.

8. Note that since displaying the plaque indicating green certification is voluntary, lack of a plaque does not necessarily mean that a building is not certified. Similarly, properties that participate in voluntary certifications like Energy Star and LEED may opt out of disclosing their certification(s) in online databases.

Case Study 6.A *(continued)*

The office building next door to the subject has a LEED Gold certification plaque displayed on its front entryway door. This building is a 1920s-era historic building, indicating that the interest in green in this area extends beyond the top-tier, newer properties.

Waste bins dedicated for recycling located in a nearby public park

The subject property features a green roof visible on the main entry canopy and a LEED plaque prominently displayed at the front entry.

On your way to visit the subject property, you observe the neighborhood and surrounding area. You note that a bike-share service is located nearby, there are waste bins dedicated to recycling in a nearby park, the building across the street from the subject converted a loading dock to secure bike storage, and the historic office building next door to the subject is LEED-certified. Upon arriving at the subject, you note that it has a green roof visible on the main entry canopy, a LEED plaque prominently displayed at the front entry, and extensive bike parking adjacent to the main lobby. You take photographs of these features and add notes to your file.

You conclude that based on these observations, there is a high likelihood that this market is sustainability-oriented. Closer analysis and data collection will be required for you to fine-tune the effect of this sustainability orientation on the valuation process.

Bringing It All Together

The process of identifying the drivers of demand for green building will vary over time and by property type, most probable buyer and user, and location. Ultimately, the goal of market analysis is to understand the supply and demand characteristics of a market and communicate a cogent assessment of the relevant market influences. The excerpt in Exhibit 6.3 is an example of the green building portion of the market analysis section of an appraisal report for a LEED-certified suburban office building. It was written at a point in time when green buildings were just beginning to emerge in that market.

Summary

Identifying the degree to which a given market values green building is relevant for all properties, regardless of whether or not they are green. Sustainability, as the underlying driver of green building,

Exhibit 6.3 **Excerpt from the Market Overview Section of an Appraisal Report**

Note. The following excerpt pertains to the property described in Chapter 5, Case Study 5.A, page 91.

The subject property is one of only two LEED-certified office projects in this submarket. The other is a 600,000-sq.-ft., four-building Class A project. The brokers interviewed noted that requests for LEED-certified space are increasing in the area, with one broker estimating that 10%-20% of tenants request LEED space. The broker for a competing project noted that large, credit tenants will only consider LEED-certified space. Another noted that while tenants with LEED requests were still a minor part of the market, sustainability factors like proximity to BART public transit was the decisive issue for a 17,000-sq.-ft. tenant in the subject market, due to the requirements of the US General Services Administration (GSA), which was one of its major clients. Currently, the primary driver is reportedly corporate image, as pressure is increasing for companies to address sustainability, or at least appear to. This includes competition for a young, bright work force. Client and investor requirements are also cited as reasons for seeking LEED space.

There does not yet appear to be evidence of a rent premium for LEED space in this market, which is likely due to the nascent nature of sustainability and green building, as well as the extremely difficult current economic and rental market conditions.* One broker noted that any green or LEED premium is difficult to isolate, since green buildings tend to be the newest product that already garners a premium to older product. However, he did note that "there should be a premium placed on the (green) buildings when comparing apples to apples."

From an investment standpoint, institutional investors are increasingly requiring LEED certifications for the buildings in their portfolios. National property developer/managers are also embracing the program, as it is emerging as a new criterion for Class A space in major markets. Demand is also evident from the tenant side, such as in the GSA sustainability requirement, which specifies LEED certification.

In addition, investors see LEED as a way to satisfy corporate social responsibility (CSR) and responsible property investing (RPI) requirements, as well as "triple bottom line" accounting systems like the Global Reporting Initiative (GRI). The ability to forestall or prevent obsolescence arising from the societal value shift toward sustainability is motivating some owners of existing properties to engage in the LEED certification process.

For a property like the subject, the LEED certification helps it to compete in the Class A market, even though its two-story stature limits it to Class B status in this particular market. The LEED certification may also increase the appeal of the space to more buyers/tenants. Thus, it may reduce lease-up time for vacancy and increase renewal probability. The value impact arising from operational cost savings due to increased HVAC and water efficiency is limited to some extent by the fact that credits earned for modeled efficiency require time to validate with actual performance.

* This property was appraised during the Great Recession.

expands and complements traditional market analysis. Rather than primarily focusing on how the market affects the property, sustainability broadens the analysis to include the effects of the property on its market–including the building's occupants, community, and surrounding physical environment.

A market's sustainability orientation refers to the degree to which that market expresses the principle of sustainability through its behaviors and actions. Sustainability can affect market demand for both conventional and green real properties, but the influence may be uneven across geography and property type. The degree to which sustainability affects a market may also depend on the sustainability orientation of the ownership type (investor versus owner-user) and end user (building occupants, consumers, and the local community).

Assessing the sustainability orientation of a market includes examining the observable sustainability-oriented behaviors of the relevant stakeholders, analyzing secondary market data sources that provide insight into a local market's sustainability-related policies and behaviors, and conducting primary research such as market participant interviews and neighborhood visits. Determining the effect of a market's sustainability orientation on the valuation process requires expanding the existing data collected and analyzed to more fully understand the underlying drivers of market demand for a particular property or property type.

The influence of sustainability and green building in a given market has a "ripple effect" throughout the valuation process. Understanding and appropriately assessing a market's sustainability orientation lays the foundation for data collection, highest and best use analysis, and application of the three approaches to value.

7 Property and Site Analysis

Valuation professionals routinely assess the built environment. They approach a building and start cataloging its physical features. Is it concrete, steel frame, or wood frame construction? How many stories is it? What is its architectural style? How does it compare to other properties in terms of quality? Is the build-out new and functional, or tired and in need of renovation?

Before these questions can be asked, the physical characteristic or condition must first be recognized. To aid in property characteristic identification, valuation professionals may have a written or mental checklist of items they look for during a property and site visit, such as construction type, roofing type, ceiling height, and evidence of deferred maintenance.

For familiar characteristics, identification is generally a straightforward task. But what about characteristics or attributes that may not be on that checklist because they are unfamiliar or not readily noticed, such as green features? As noted in previous chapters, green building elements are often seamlessly integrated into a building's design and construction. If we are not specifically looking for something, do we see it–or more precisely, do we perceive it?

While we may believe that we see "everything" in a particular space, perception is complex and influenced by the experiences and knowledge we have accumulated about similar circumstances. As neuroscientist David Eagleman puts it, "Fixing your gaze on something is no guarantee of seeing it." While our eyes may scan over an object or situation, we are unlikely to register all of the visual details. Instead, what is perceived is a filtered result based on what we expect to see and what is deemed important in that circumstance. "What we experience as seeing," according to Eagleman, "relies less on the light streaming into our eyes, and more on what's already inside our heads."[1]

So what does this filtering phenomenon mean for a valuation professional, for whom being able to quickly and accurately take in the salient physical details of a property is a critical component of the job? Are unfamiliar features or conditions "seen" in a meaningful way, or are they at risk of being filtered out and therefore missed?

Identifying Green Buildings and Green Features

An awareness of the physical characteristics of properties is central to valuation. *The Appraisal of Real Estate* explains,

> Familiarity with the characteristics and attributes of the subject property... enhances the appraiser's ability to identify competitive properties (supply) and to understand the comparative advantages and disadvantages that the subject offers potential buyers or renters (demand.)[2]

Conversely, not having sufficient familiarity to readily identify a property's physical characteristics can create a "blind spot" for valuation professionals. It is one thing to identify a building characteristic and determine that it has no impact on the valuation process, but it is quite another to reach that same value judgement only because the characteristic was missed. This risk is real for any unfamiliar property characteristic, and the newness and pace of change in green building makes this a particularly vulnerable point for valuation professionals.

Green building does not necessarily require valuation professionals to use a different technique to observe and analyze the built environment. It simply requires them to expand the set of features and elements that require that same keen observation. Learning to see a new set of property characteristics is no different than learning how to differentiate between concrete tilt-up, poured-in-place, and concrete masonry construction, for example, or learning to spot potential problems such as signs of structural damage or observe building attributes such as an above-average clearspan. The issue becomes one of acquiring sufficient familiarity with these new property characteristics so that when they are seen, they are truly observed. The following section provides some techniques and tools that can be used to identify green building elements in both green and non-green buildings.

Expand Visual Database

The Green Feature Gallery in Appendix A (page 277) illustrates some of the more common green elements or features that may exist in both

1. David Eagleman, *The Brain: The Story of You* (New York: Pantheon Books, 2015), 51-57.
2. *The Appraisal of Real Estate*, 14th ed. (Chicago: Appraisal Institute, 2013), 300-301.

green and non-green buildings. However, it is far from an exhaustive list, and green characteristics should be assumed to evolve through improvements in technology and experience with green building. While the gallery is a good starting point, valuation professionals may need to seek out other opportunities to gain familiarity with green features. Formal green building-specific coursework is, certainly, an important avenue, but other options can provide many additional learning opportunities. Green building organizations may offer tours, webinars, and lectures, often at little or no cost. Local chapters of green building organizations, such as the US Green Building Council (USGBC), often host educational events that may include tours of local green buildings, often with experts such as architects and engineers present. This presents a prime opportunity for valuation professionals to engage with property attributes first-hand, ask technical questions, or make connections with experts. Additionally, a number of periodicals are devoted to green building and may include case studies of green buildings.[3]

Another useful approach is to focus on green features in general rather than fixate on green buildings. In other words, consider green building features as just another type of property characteristic rather than dividing the world of properties into green and non-green, thereby potentially concluding (erroneously) that green features are only present in green buildings. As discussed in previous chapters, building codes are becoming more stringent and may specify green standards or components such as a minimum green certification or high-efficiency lighting. As a resullt, major renovations subject to these more rigorous codes are causing existing conventional building stock to involuntarily "green up" in many areas. Green upgrades in existing conventional buildings increase the likelihood of missing green elements in a non-green building, particularly if the valuation professional's perspective is that green features are only present in green buildings. Case Study 7.A, Think Green Features, Not Just Green Buildings, which appears later in this chapter (page 132), provides an example of how a few basic green upgrades in a conventional 1920s-era, multifamily apartment building caused a measurable impact on the income stream and value conclusion.

Utilize Green Building Rating System Scorecards, Worksheets, and Checklists

Perhaps one of the most important advantages conferred to the valuation professional by green building rating system scorecards, worksheets, and checklists lies in making the "invisible" green ele-

3. Two particularly noteworthy periodicals are *High Performing Buildings*, published by ASHRAE, and *Building Design and Construction*. These periodicals regularly profile green and high-performing properties and often include specific cost and performance data that would be of particular interest and relevance to valuation professionals.

ments more visible. Some key green features are unlikely to be seen or simply cannot be seen, such as the building management system (BMS) or the insulation between the walls. The BMS can be particularly instrumental in the proper performance of a green building, as described in the Green Feature Gallery in Appendix A (page 294). However, its physical presence may amount to a computer, sensors, and a nondescript control box, or it may be controlled remotely without any discernible physical presence at all.

Case Study 5.A, Appraiser's Field Notes: LEED Surprise, in Chapter 5 (page 91) described how obtaining the LEED scorecard for a valuation assignment revealed sufficient clues so that a value-affecting element (in that case, transit proximity) was noted and incorporated into the valuation process. Having the scorecard or worksheet can also provide an early indication of the primary objectives of the property owner or developer. For example, if the LEED scorecard reveals a large number of credits earned in the energy use category, greater attention should be paid to the mechanical and lighting systems of the property during the site visit since these systems represent a significant portion of the building's energy use. Additionally, if the scorecard or other information provided by the client indicates a complex or atypical HVAC system, this may prompt a request for the engineer to be present during the site visit or otherwise be available to field technical questions.

Exhibit 7.1 breaks down the LEED scorecard of a newly constructed office building in Madison, Wisconsin, by credit category and annotates an appraiser's thought process during an initial review of this scorecard.

The Appraisal Institute's Commercial Green and Energy Efficient Addendum is another tool that can be used to augment the valuation professional's physical or mental checklist. The first page of the Addendum is shown in Exhibit 7.2, and the entire form is included in the back of this book as Appendix B (page 309).

Analyze Operating Data

Changes in operating income and expense patterns in existing buildings can reveal evidence of green building renovations or changes in operating practices that might warrant consideration in the valuation process. Water, energy, and trash collection costs are three areas of resource use that can be directly affected by green building renovations and operating practices. However, the impact of changes in one or more of these expense categories can be difficult if not impossible to assess, since these expenses are often grouped under the generic category of "utilities."

Disaggregating the utility expense category into its components can be surprisingly helpful in uncovering efficiency upgrades or changes in water, energy, or waste systems and can assist in determining the value impact of those improvements. Case Study 7.A illustrates how this process of breaking down total utility expenses into

Exhibit 7.1 Review of a LEED Scorecard from a Newly Constructed Office Building

LEED BD+C: Core and Shell (v2009)

PLATINUM, AWARDED SEP 2014

SUSTAINABLE SITES		AWARDED: 21 / 28
SSc1	Site selection	1 / 1
SSc2	Development density and community connectivity	5 / 5
SSc3	Brownfield redevelopment	0 / 1
SSc4.1	Alternative transportation - public transportation access	6 / 6
SSc4.2	Alternative transportation - bicycle storage and changing rooms	2 / 2
SSc4.3	Alternative transportation - low-emitting and fuel-efficient vehicles	3 / 3
SSc4.4	Alternative transportation - parking capacity	2 / 2
SSc5.1	Site development - protect or restore habitat	0 / 1
SSc5.2	Site development - maximize open space	1 / 1
SSc6.1	Stormwater design - quantity control	1 / 1
SSc6.2	Stormwater design - quality control	0 / 1
SSc7.1	Heat island effect - nonroof	0 / 1
SSc7.2	Heat island effect - roof	0 / 1
SSc8	Light pollution reduction	0 / 1
SSc9	Tenant design and construction guidelines	0 / 1

WATER EFFICIENCY		AWARDED: 10 / 10
WEc1	Water efficient landscaping	4 / 4
WEc2	Innovative wastewater technologies	2 / 2
WEc3	Water use reduction	4 / 4

ENERGY & ATMOSPHERE		AWARDED: 28 / 37
EAc1	Optimize energy performance	20 / 21
EAc2	On-site renewable energy	0 / 4
EAc3	Enhanced commissioning	0 / 2
EAc4	Enhanced refrigerant Mgmt	0 / 2
EAc5.1	Measurement and verification - base building	6 / 3
EAc5.2	Measurement and verification - tenant submetering	0 / 3
EAc6	Green power	2 / 2

MATERIAL & RESOURCES		AWARDED: 7 / 13
MRc1	Building reuse - maintain existing walls, floors and roof	0 / 5
MRc2	Construction waste Mgmt	2 / 2
MRc3	Materials reuse	0 / 1

MATERIAL & RESOURCES		AWARDED: 7 / 13
MRc4	Recycled content	2 / 2
MRc5	Regional materials	2 / 2
MRc6	Certified wood	1 / 1

INDOOR ENVIRONMENTAL QUALITY		AWARDED: 10 / 12
EQc1	Outdoor air delivery monitoring	1 / 1
EQc2	Increased ventilation	0 / 1
EQc3	Construction IAQ Mgmt plan - during construction	1 / 1
EQc4.1	Low-emitting materials - adhesives and sealants	1 / 1
EQc4.2	Low-emitting materials - paints and coatings	1 / 1
EQc4.3	Low-emitting materials - flooring systems	1 / 1
EQc4.4	Low-emitting materials - composite wood and agrifiber products	1 / 1
EQc5	Indoor chemical and pollutant source control	1 / 1
EQc6	Controllability of systems - thermal comfort	1 / 1
EQc7	Thermal comfort - design	1 / 1
EQc8.1	Daylight and views - daylight	0 / 1
EQc8.2	Daylight and views - views	1 / 1

INNOVATION		AWARDED 4 / 6
IDc1	Innovation in design	3 / 5
IDc2	LEED Accredited Professional	1 / 1

REGIONAL PRIORITY		AWARDED: 4 / 4
SSc2	Development density and community connectivity	1 / 1
SSc4.2	Alternative transportation - bicycle storage and changing rooms	1 / 1
SSc4.4	Alternative transportation - parking capacity	1 / 1
SSc6.1	Stormwater design - quantity control	1 / 1
WEc3	Water use reduction	0 / 1

INTEGRATIVE PROCESS CREDITS		AWARDED: 0 / 3
IPpc100	Passive Survivability and Functionality During Emergencies	REQUIRED
IPpc98	Assessment and Planning for Resilience	REQUIRED
IPpc99	Design for Enhanced Resilience	REQUIRED

TOTAL	84 / 110

Detailed Notes

This building is rated under the Building Design and Construction (BD+C) system and awarded platinum level (highest) certification under v2009 (Version 3) in September 2014. It's certified as Core and Shell, which means that building performance for certification was based on modeled projections. Note: Check actual utility consumption to see if the building is meeting the expected performance level. Also: What type of commissioning has been done since the building was completed?

LEED BD+C: Core and Shell (v2009)

PLATINUM, AWARDED SEP 2014

SUSTAINABLE SITES		AWARDED: 21 / 28
SSc1	Site selection	1 / 1
SSc2	Development density and community connectivity	5 / 5
SSc3	Brownfield redevelopment	0 / 1
SSc4.1	Alternative transportation - public transportation access	6 / 6
SSc4.2	Alternative transportation - bicycle storage and changing rooms	2 / 2
SSc4.3	Alternative transportation - low-emitting and fuel-efficient vehicles	3 / 3
SSc4.4	Alternative transportation - parking capacity	2 / 2
SSc5.1	Site development - protect or restore habitat	0 / 1
SSc5.2	Site development - maximize open space	1 / 1
SSc6.1	Stormwater design - quantity control	1 / 1
SSc6.2	Stormwater design - quality control	0 / 1
SSc7.1	Heat island effect - nonroof	0 / 1
SSc7.2	Heat island effect - roof	0 / 1
SSc8	Light pollution reduction	0 / 1
SSc9	Tenant design and construction guidelines	0 / 1

5/5 credits for development density (SSc2), and 6/6 for public alternative transportation access (SSc4.1). Better check Walk Score and Transit Score. Seemed like a typical suburban office location based on Google Earth. What kind of transit options does Google Maps indicate?

Bike storage and showers (SSc4.2): Check out the bike parking and showers/lockers during the site visit. Does secure, dedicated parking for bike commuters matter to this market? What about the employees of these tenants? Note: Inquire about bike commuting when confirming the comparables – especially the leases.

2/2 points earned for parking capacity (SSc4.4). In LEED, that can mean less parking is provided, not more. Is the parking adequate for this market? What exactly is the building parking ratio? The Google Earth aerial view shows a site that doesn't seem to have enough surface parking. Talk to the leasing broker about market parking requirements.

Exhibit 7.1 *(continued)*

Detailed Notes *(continued)*

WATER EFFICIENCY		AWARDED: 10 / 10
WEc1	Water efficient landscaping	4 / 4
WEc2	Innovative wastewater technologies	2 / 2
WEc3	Water use reduction	4 / 4

10/10 - They got every credit possible in the category.

4/4 credits for water-efficient landscaping (WEc1). Yet all that turf? How did they get the credit without drought-tolerant landscaping?

WEc2: What are the innovative wastewater technologies?

WEc3: Water use reduction: what did they do here?

ENERGY & ATMOSPHERE		AWARDED: 28 / 37
EAc1	Optimize energy performance	20 / 21
EAc2	On-site renewable energy	0 / 4
EAc3	Enhanced commissioning	0 / 2
EAc4	Enhanced refrigerant Mgmt	0 / 2
EAc5.1	Measurement and verification - base building	6 / 3
EAc5.2	Measurement and verification - tenant submetering	0 / 3
EAc6	Green power	2 / 2

20/21 for EAc1: Optimize energy performance. Must be some pretty significant energy-efficiency design intent to get 95% credit. Yet, LEED credits under BD&C are awarded for designed performance, not actual historical performance. According to the USGBC website, basic commissioning of energy-using systems is required for certification. However, the scorecard indicates that enhanced commissioning is 0/2, so basic commissioning but nothing above the minimum threshold. Still, any commissioning is better than none. Ask about the commissioning report.

EAc5.1: Measurement and verification (M&V) —base building: 6/3. Talk to LEED consultant about what they did to overachieve at 200% on M&V.

EAc6: 2/2 for green power. Credits earned here are for renewable energy produced elsewhere. Buying credit for someone else's renewable power is not the same as on-site energy generation.

MATERIAL & RESOURCES		AWARDED: 7 / 13
MRc1	Building reuse - maintain existing walls, floors and roof	0 / 5
MRc2	Construction waste Mgmt	2 / 2
MRc3	Materials reuse	0 / 1
MRc4	Recycled content	2 / 2
MRc5	Regional materials	2 / 2
MRc6	Certified wood	1 / 1

Overall, 7/13, so just over 50%. Where did they earn the credits?

MRc4 (2/2) indicates an emphasis on recycled content, while the 2/2 credits earned for regional materials (MRc5) reflects local sourcing. 1/1 for certified wood. Not sure about a market value impact for this credit category.

INDOOR ENVIRONMENTAL QUALITY		AWARDED: 10 / 12
EQc1	Outdoor air delivery monitoring	1 / 1
EQc2	Increased ventilation	0 / 1
EQc3	Construction IAQ Mgmt plan - during construction	1 / 1
EQc4.1	Low-emitting materials - adhesives and sealants	1 / 1
EQc4.2	Low-emitting materials - paints and coatings	1 / 1
EQc4.3	Low-emitting materials - flooring systems	1 / 1
EQc4.4	Low-emitting materials - composite wood and agrifiber products	1 / 1
EQc5	Indoor chemical and pollutant source control	1 / 1
EQc6	Controllability of systems - thermal comfort	1 / 1
EQc7	Thermal comfort - design	1 / 1
EQc8.1	Daylight and views - daylight	0 / 1
EQc8.2	Daylight and views - views	1 / 1

Now we're looking at the occupant experience. 10/12 is pretty significant. What did they do?

Low-emitting materials (EQc4.1- 4.4): If the toxins never enter the interior, how can they harm the occupants? Seems like a good idea and a best practice. What do the prospective tenants think? Is this already required by code?

EQc5, 6, 7: Here we're looking at credits awarded for design decisions— controlling pollutants at the source and designing for and providing tenant control of thermal comfort. Makes sense to incorporate these concerns up front in the design process, but what about a market value impact?

INNOVATION		AWARDED 4 / 6
IDc1	Innovation in design	3 / 5
IDc2	LEED Accredited Professional	1 / 1

Hard to know about market value impact from innovative design without knowing more. Better check what they did to earn 3/5 credits.

REGIONAL PRIORITY		AWARDED: 4 / 4
SSc2	Development density and community connectivity	1 / 1
SSc4.2	Alternative transportation - bicycle storage and changing rooms	1 / 1
SSc4.4	Alternative transportation - parking capacity	1 / 1
SSc6.1	Stormwater design - quantity control	1 / 1
WEc3	Water use reduction	0 / 1

These are bonus points earned in credit categories for locally important green features and practices. Need to follow up to find out what these credits addressed.

INTEGRATIVE PROCESS CREDITS		AWARDED: 0 / 3
IPpc100	Passive Survivability and Functionality During Emergencies	REQUIRED
IPpc98	Assessment and Planning for Resilience	REQUIRED
IPpc99	Design for Enhanced Resilience	REQUIRED

TOTAL	84 / 110

Exhibit 7.2 Appraisal Institute Commercial Green and Energy Efficient Addendum

AI Reports®	Client File #:	Appraisal File #:
	Commercial Green and Energy Efficient Addendum	
	Client:	
	Subject Property:	
Form 821*	City: State:	Zip:

Additional resources to aid in the valuation of green properties and the completion of this form can be found at http://www.appraisalinstitute.org/education/green_energy_addendum.aspx

The appraiser hereby acknowledges that the information provided within this addendum:

- has been considered in the appraiser's development of the appraisal of the subject property only for the client and intended user(s) identified in the appraisal report and only for the intended use stated in the report.
- is not provided by the appraiser for any other purpose and should not be relied upon by parties other than those identified by the appraiser as the client or intended user(s) in the report.
- is the result of the appraiser's routine inspection of and inquiries about the subject property's green and energy efficient features. Extraordinary assumption: Data provided herein is assumed to be accurate and if found to be in error could alter the appraiser's opinions or conclusions.
- is not made as a representation or as a warranty as to the efficiency, quality, function, operability, reliability or cost savings of the reported items or of the subject property in general, and this addendum should not be relied upon for such assessments.
- is not to be construed as a replacement for an appraisal report but is an Addendum to an appraisal report. This Addendum is not designed to assign value to each of the components identified. The Addendum is provided as a part of the description of the properties' special characteristics that have been included in the analysis and value conclusions in the appraisal report. It also serves the client in securing adequate information on the property type to assist in hiring the appraiser with knowledge and experience in this special property type.

Green Building: The practice of creating structures and using processes that are environmentally responsible and resource-efficient throughout a building's lifecycle from siting to design, construction, operation, maintenance, renovation, and deconstruction. This practice expands and complements the classic building design concerns of economy, utility, durability, and comfort.[1] High Performance building and green building are often used interchangeably; however, they do have different definitions.

High Performance Building: A building that integrates and optimizes all major high-performance building attributes, including energy efficiency, durability, life-cycle performance, and occupant productivity.[2]

Six Elements of Green Building: A green building has attributes that fall into the six elements of green building known as (1) site, (2) water, (3) energy, (4) materials, (5) indoor air quality, and (6) maintenance and operation. A Green Building will be energy efficient but an energy efficient building is not synonymous with Green Building.

Property Type

Category of Property: (explain) ____________________________

This Addendum is for property types that include multifamily, all types of commercial, and industrial use properties. The Addendum can be used for proposed or existing structures including retrofits.

Who may complete this Addendum?

The Addendum may be completed by any of the following:

- LEED AP serving on project's charrette
- Green Rater that rated the project
- Developer/builder involved in developing the project
- Investor with sufficient information and documents to support the data
- Appraiser

The appraiser must have sufficient knowledge and experience of the property type to review an Addendum completed by others and comment on any inconsistencies or omissions noted. The person completing the Addendum should complete the "Completed by" Section of this Addendum.

The objective of this Addendum is to standardize the communication of the green and/or high performing features of commercial properties. Identifying the features provides a basis for comparable selection and analysis of the features.

The Addendum will assist the client in extracting the documents necessary to expedite the appraisal process by having a better understanding of the special property features. This will assist the client in securing the appraiser with knowledge and experience in the property type.

The Addendum can be attached to the listing of the property, which will allow the appraiser more detail on sales and listings of similar properties.

The Addendum may be used in its entirety or only the pages that apply.

Intended Users of this Addendum: Lender as part of their scope of work, appraisers as a supplement to the appraisal report, investors as a summary of special green/energy features, and/or real estate agents as a supplement to a listing.

[1] U.S. Environmental Protection Agency at www.epa.gov/greenbuildings/pubs/about.htm

[2] Energy Policy Act of 2005 (Public Law 109-058) at http://www.nibs.org/?page=hpbc

water, energy, and waste revealed a substantive value impact due to the building's water-efficiency upgrades. Without breaking down the utilities into separate components, the year-over-year change in total utilities would likely have been attributed to normal variance. As a result, operating expenses would have been improperly stabilized, which in turn would have negatively affected the value conclusion.

Making a practice of disaggregating utilities also helps develop a useful database of what is typical in the market for energy, water, and waste usage and costs. Without the empirical data to establish a market norm, it is very difficult to identify properties that are either under- or over-performing on those metrics or credibly support an adjustment to the comparable properties.

Case Study 7.A Think Green Features, Not Just Green Buildings

There was nothing particularly green about this 1920s-era, 15-unit apartment building. The three-story, wood-frame building built over garage parking was typical for its San Francisco neighborhood. It had been periodically, although minimally, updated over the years. Several units had renovated kitchens, but the building housed mostly long-term tenants paying below-market rents that were protected by rent control.

In stabilizing the operating expenses, the property owner provided two years of historical operating expenses with all utilities grouped together: common gas and electric, water/sewer, and trash. This practice is typical in the market. The total utilities category showed a fairly significant drop in the most recent year relative to the period two years prior, as shown in the table below. Since it is unusual for utility costs to decline, the initial inclination was to weight the data reported from the earlier year more heavily, stabilizing the expense at $1,600 per unit, or $24,000 per year.

Aggregated Utilities	Year 1	Year 2	Stabilized	per Dwelling Unit (DU)
Total	$25,122	$18,583	$24,000	$1,600

However, the 26% decline in the historical utility expense was unusual enough to prompt a request for a line-item expense breakdown from the property manager. When the utility expenses were disaggregated into component parts (common area electricity and gas, water/sewer, and trash), the results were illuminating, as shown in the table below.

Disaggregated Utilities	Year 1	Year 2	Stabilized	per Dwelling Unit (DU)
Electricity/Gas	$1,213	$1,200	$1,200	$80
Water/Sewer	$15,963	$9,746	$9,750	$650
Trash	$7,946	$7,637	$7,725	$515
Total	$25,122	$18,583	$18,675	$1,245
Difference			$5,325	$355

Case Study 7.A *(continued)*

Disaggregating the utilities revealed that the source of the significant decline in costs was entirely associated with water/sewer, which decreased from nearly $16,000 to less than $10,000, or 39% in one year. The property manager reported that a number of leaks were identified and fixed during a free audit provided by the local water utility, and fixtures were replaced with the help of rebates. According to the property manager, the only reason this issue came to light was the bar graph noting year-over-year water usage that is prominently displayed at the bottom of the monthly bill. Seeing that graphic prompted him to call the utility, and they offered the free audit.

Lessons Learned

This experience taught three lessons. First of all, green features are everywhere, but so are features and practices such as leaks and old fixtures that lead to inefficiencies and non-green performance. The key is to be on the lookout for green features and practices during the site visit, when reviewing the operating statements, and when interviewing the owner or property manager. Of course, the converse is also true. All those unrenovated, vintage components may be signaling more than just deferred maintenance or a tired, neglected property; they may be a sign of obsolescence. In some cases, there may be an opportunity to renovate and upgrade for enhanced operational performance (curable obsolescence). In other cases, incurable obsolescence may be evident when greening up is not financially feasible.

Second, even the water bill, which is usually taken as relatively inconsequential and constant, can have a material impact on the bottom line. In this case, by stabilizing the expenses correctly, the net operating income increased by $5,325 per year, resulting in a value increase of 3.5%.

Finally, this assignment demonstrated how changing the reporting of utility costs could result in a more accurate value conclusion. Instead of aggregating electricity, gas, water/sewer, and trash all in the utility expenses category, these costs may be better analyzed when disaggregated, including separating gas from electricity when possible. This practice can identify changes in the property that affect its operating costs. It can also help identify potential elements of comparison between the subject and comparables, such as electricity use or water use, which may significantly differ from the market and thus warrant an adjustment. Disaggregating utility expenses has the added benefit of helping build a database for energy, water, and waste expenses that can be used in the future when valuing advanced green and high-performance buildings, including NZE and other low-energy buildings.

Consider Site Factors and Linkages

As previously noted, sustainability's effect on the site itself is not just limited to green elements built or designed into the site or structure. Linkages such as transit and proximity to amenities, often referred to as *walkability*, are also important aspects of a green building project. Above-average transit access and proximity to amenities benefit all properties, not just green ones. Conversely, mitigating a transit deficiency by subsidizing public transit or operating private shuttles carries associated ongoing operational costs, as demonstrated in the accompanying sidebar on suburban sustainability.

Suburban Sustainability

After three quarters of a century in which the suburbs dominated growth in the United States, could urban living now be taking over? Has the tide shifted? Consider the following:

- Between 2010 and 2014, 21% of new household formations occurred in urban centers, which is more than double the historic averages.[4]
- Since 2002, job growth in urban centers has exceeded job growth in the suburbs.[5]
- Home values near transit outperformed the overall market by 41.6% during the last recession.[6]
- Between 2004 and 2014, highly walkable commercial properties in central business districts (CBDs) appreciated 125%, versus 43% for highly walkable suburbs. By comparison, commercial properties in car-dependent suburbs appreciated 21%–22%.[7]
- The CEO of one REIT has said, "We used to want modern garden apartment complexes with highway frontage, but now we are only buying high-rise urban assets with great Walk Scores."[8]
- The chief executive of Motorola Solutions, Greg Brown, has stated, "Millennials want the access and vibrancy of downtown. When we post jobs downtown, we get four or five times the response."[9]

The appeal of urban centers includes their vibrant, mixed-use environments that provide live, work, and play options all in one place. Urban centers offer the variety in dining, entertainment, and housing options that is often missing in master-planned suburbs of gated communities, single-purpose business parks, and shopping centers. Walkable amenities, transit, and active commute infrastructure such as walking and biking trails are also part of urban appeal.

Have we reached peak suburbia? Are the suburbs dead? Or, to paraphrase Mark Twain, have the rumors of the suburban demise been greatly exaggerated?

The suburbs continue to offer a compelling business case, particularly for corporate office users, in the form of lower occupancy costs, a lower cost of living that translates to lower labor costs, and proximity to quality, affordable housing options that enhance employee quality of life. Urban living is more expensive, particularly for families, and often public school quality and a yard weigh more heavily than live/work/play when young families decide where to live.

Despite the recent trend toward urbanism, it seems likely that the suburbs will remain a vital part of the built environment for the foreseeable future. As Ed McMahon, chair on sustainable development and environ-

---

4. John Burns and Chris Porter, *Big Shifts Ahead: Demographic Clarity for Businesses* (Charleston, SC: Advantage Media Group, 2016), 221.
5. PwC and the Urban Land Institute (ULI), *Emerging Trends in Real Estate 2016* (Washington, DC: PwC and ULI, 2015), 30.
6. American Public Transportation Association (APTA), National Association of Realtors (NAR), and the Center for Neighborhood Technology (CNT), *The New Real Estate Mantra: Location Near Public Transportation* (Washington, DC: APTA, NAR, and CNT, 2013), 1, www.apta.com/resources/statistics/Documents/NewRealEstateMantra.pdf.
7. Real Capital Analytics, "RCA Trends Alert: Walking to Higher Value," April 2015.
8. PwC and ULI, *Emerging Trends in Real Estate 2016*, 30.
9. Nelson D. Schwartz, "Why Corporate America Is Leaving the Suburbs for the City," *New York Times* (August 1, 2016), www.nytimes.com/2016/08/02/business/economy/why-corporate-america-is-leaving-the-suburbs-for-the-city.html?_r=0.

mental policy at the Urban Land Institute (ULI), foretells, "One of the biggest trends of the next generation is going to be the repurposing of an incredible amount of existing suburban development."[10] Consider the following:

- 64% of US households live in suburban areas.
- 67% of all jobs in the top 50 metropolitan areas are located in the suburbs.
- 79% of household growth will occur in the suburbs between 2015 and 2025.[11]

But not all suburbs are created equal, and it is unclear which ones will survive and thrive to meet future demographic and social needs. The most common strategy among suburbs seeking to meet the needs of the future is to incorporate the best of urban living—mixed uses, walkable amenities, and access to transit—without compromising the appeal of suburban living.

Is it possible to have the best of both worlds? At least one suburban office park owner seems to think so, and is responding to demographic and social changes in ways that incorporate a number of sustainability-oriented behaviors into the development's evolution from a 1980s-era office park to a model of a mixed-use, twenty-first century sustainable suburb.

Background

Bishop Ranch is one of Northern California's top suburban office parks, with over 10 million square feet developed. Of this, 4.2 million square feet remains under the ownership of the original developer, Sunset Development. Carved out of 585 acres of walnut and fruit orchards beginning in 1978, Bishop Ranch rode the wave of suburban corporate relocation to establish itself as one of Northern California's premiere office parks, attracting a tenant roster rich in Fortune 500 companies.

The bucolic location an hour's drive east of San Francisco is scenic, well-served by the regional freeway system, and midway between Walnut Creek and Pleasanton/Dublin. Both of these communities are served by BART, the regional commuter rail network. Designed primarily for automobile access, Bishop Ranch is more than six miles from the nearest regional commuter rail station in nearby Dublin. Despite a county municipal bus system, public transit access is limited. From its early days, the office park provided private commuter shuttles for employees, ultimately expanding to include free transit passes to all tenant employees for the county bus service connections to BART.

The Challenge

Despite adjacent shopping centers and a 375-room, full-service hotel, Bishop Ranch lacked the walkable amenities, transit access, and mixed-use character necessary to compete with the trend toward new urbanism. Bishop Ranch's Walk Score is 44, meaning that the office park is automobile-dependent. The downsizing of AT&T, a 1.8 million-sq.-ft. anchor tenant of the park, also provided additional impetus to update and reposition the park for the future.

The Solution

The solution for Bishop Ranch was to institute a comprehensive sustainability program including LEED certification for the entire park, add walkable amenities, replace several aging office buildings with a new retail and entertainment center, and obtain entitlements for 500 housing units for the remaining vacant and underutilized sites. The repositioning and upgrading of components included the following:

Transit/Transport

- Approximately $2 million was spent annually to provide free transit passes to all park employees.
- Private commuter buses and carpool/vanpool programs were added.
- Electrical vehicle charging stations were added.
- On-site car share and bike share services were added.

10. Robyn A. Friedman, "Companies Trade Suburbs for City Life," *The Wall Street Journal* (April 21, 2015).
11. Burns and Porter, *Big Shifts Ahead*, 221, 236; ULI, *Housing in the Evolving American Suburb* (Washington, DC: ULI, 2016), 2.

Walkable Amenities and Mixed Use

- A portion of the former conference center was converted into a three-restaurant dining hall.
- Several 45-year-old office buildings were demolished to construct a "city center," anchored by a multiplex cinema and an entertainment-focused retail center.
- Entitlements for 500 multifamily housing units were obtained.

Green Building

- LEED certification for all 26 buildings was attained in 2012, and the buildings were recertified in 2016.
- All buildings were certified by Energy Star, with scores ranging from 74 to 95, with an average of 91.
- Five acres of turf were replaced with climate-appropriate plantings, saving 4.5 million gallons of water per year.
- Water used for landscape irrigation was converted from potable to reclaimed.
- A one-acre demonstration farm for flowers, fruits, and vegetables was added.
- A comprehensive recycling program for paper, glass, bottles, cans, and cardboard was instituted.
- A composting program for restroom paper towels and landscaping waste was implemented.

Incorporating Green Building into the Property and Site Analysis

Visiting the site and building improvements provides the primary source of information about a property and its environs. Not only is data collected about the specific physical attributes of the subject property, but the valuation professional is able to see first-hand the context of the property: Is it part of a larger development, or is it isolated? Is the current use consistent with other uses in the neighborhood? What are the nature and condition of the surrounding properties and infrastructure? These contextual observations of the building improvements and site are critically important when evaluating the competitive position of the subject property in the initial market analysis and the highest and best use analysis.

In many cases, a site visit yields more questions than answers, and this may be even more true for a property that has unexpected green features. For example, as was the case with the property described in Case Study 5.A (page 91), the property was not known to be green-certified until the site visit. New information such as this may require modification to other areas of the valuation process, such as the scope of work, the selection of comparable properties, and the nature of the market research. Highest and best use analysis may also be affected. Even for assignments that are properly scoped in the first place, a site visit may indicate a need for more in-depth documentation from the client or property owner, such as energy modeling information, commissioning reports, or specific details about on-site energy generation systems.

Green building and sustainability, however, do not just affect the individual property. As will be discussed later in this chapter, sustainability is fundamentally changing the way communities are planning for infrastructure needs and regulating land uses. As valuation professionals, it is equally important to ascertain the influence of sustainability and green building on individual properties and to understand how sustainability-oriented goals may influence entire neighborhoods and communities in ways that affect real estate values.

Describing the Green Improvements

Green features can exist in both green and non-green buildings and can run the gamut from integrated green building design to discrete elements such as low-flow water fixtures and faucets. The incorporation of green features in a building improvements description can vary widely, depending on the specific characteristics of the property, market, and scope of work. What remains a common denominator, however, is that recognition of the physical characteristics is the critical first step before any meaningful analysis of the property can begin. Exhibit 7.3 provides three different improvements descriptions. Example 1 involves a non-green, historically rated, 100-year-old office building that was re-lamped to provide more energy-efficient lighting. Example 2 discusses the green improvements to a comparable property in a non-green property valuation assignment. This example illustrates how understanding green building may be required even when valuing a conventional property in order to understand

Exhibit 7.3 Sample Improvements Descriptions Involving Green Building or Green Features

Example 1

Description of lighting upgrade in a non-green, historically rated, 100-year-old office building:

> "The building lighting has also been upgraded. The T-12 fluorescent fixtures have been replaced with more efficient T-8 fluorescent fixtures and tubes. Recessed incandescent light bulbs have been replaced with CFLs (compact fluorescent lights). The directional halogen and incandescent lighting has been replaced with LED lighting."

Example 2

Description of a green building used as a comparable for a conventionally built subject property:

> "The comparable's historic two-story improvements are of wood-frame construction and were built in 1914. The property underwent a significant renovation in 2008. The property is LEED Platinum certified (2008) under the new construction (NC v2.2) track. The site includes three 5,000-gallon cisterns for rainwater collection and a permeable parking area for eight vehicles. Sustainable building improvements include operable windows and a rooftop cupola to facilitate natural ventilation. Salvaged materials were used throughout, and large windows facilitate natural light in lieu of artificial light (daylighting). The HVAC system includes a 95%-efficient boiler for heat and a ground source loop for cooling tied to an in-slab radiant floor distribution system. The solar PV cells integrated into the roof tiles reportedly provide sufficient energy to power the building.
>
> The comparable's sustainability-related improvements and LEED Platinum certification indicate a downward adjustment relative to the subject. In addition, the comparable's building-integrated solar PV and energy-efficient mechanical systems and high-performance envelope warrant additional downward adjustment relative to the subject property for the associated lower operating expenses."

Exhibit 7.3 *(continued)*

Example 3

Partial description of a sustainable renovation converting a conventional building to a net zero energy (NZE) building:

"The subject underwent a sustainable renovation. A sustainable renovation differs from a conventional renovation in its focus on reducing its impact on materials use, energy use, and water use, as well as interior environmental quality and ongoing operations and maintenance. In a sustainable renovation, particular emphasis is placed on reusing, rather than demolishing and rebuilding from the ground up.

The proposed renovation entailed demolishing the entire interior and reconstructing a new steel frame second floor supported by perimeter steel columns and a new concrete shear wall near the middle of the building. The second floor consists of a lightweight concrete pour over a corrugated steel pan. The second floor is supported by steel girders that span across the width of the building in a north-south direction. The second floor is accessed via a single hydraulic elevator and two open staircases along the north and south sides of the open atrium that forms the entry lobby of the building. On both levels, the ceilings are open with no suspended ceiling covering. The mechanical equipment is entirely exposed and designed to flow neatly as part of the design aesthetic.

The roof has been re-covered with a foam insulation covering and 10 inches of fiberglass insulation on the underside (interior) of the roof sheathing, providing an R-40 insulation value. The roof was also reinforced and seismically upgraded. The central atrium is lit with a series of skylights that bring daylight into the center of the building. The remainder of the roof is reserved for solar photovoltaic (PV) panels and mechanical equipment, consisting of a total of 44 tons of HVAC cooling capacity in multiple rooftop mounted units, and an exhaust fan used for night-time flushing. Due to the above-standard insulation, passive ventilation, and other design features, the building is expected to consume approximately 30% of the mechanical HVAC energy of a similar conventionally built structure.

The renovation included sawing 86 new window openings into the existing structural concrete tilt-up walls.* The fenestration on the south, west, and east sides of the building consists of low-emissivity (low-e) electro-chromic, dual-pane glazing that changes shading level based on solar exposure by passing an electric current through a thin laminate on the glass. Many of these windows are operable and automated to facilitate passive ventilation. Conventional low-e glass is used on the north side, since there is no direct solar influence. The operable windows are controlled by a building management system to allow for optimal natural ventilation during occupied hours, as well as night flushing.

Originally, the subject's uninsulated six-inch concrete slab walls had an R-2 value. The renovation added 5-5/8" rigid foam insulation to the exterior walls, clad with an elastomeric cement plaster finish with integral color. The walls now have an R-20 value. The concrete walls and floors have been polished and sealed but are otherwise largely uncovered, in order to maximize the thermal mass properties of the concrete and the underlying earth.

The subject has been designed to operate as an NZE building. A typical design strategy for NZE buildings is to seek to minimize requirements for mechanical air movement. In the case of the subject property, duct work is reduced relative to a conventional building. Interior air movement is enhanced in the balance of the space using ceiling fans. The operable windows and skylights are tied to an automated BMS that also controls and integrates the lighting and supplemental HVAC. For example, the BMS opens the windows and skylights in the evening, when the outside air is cooler, allowing the warmer interior air to vent through the skylights using the "stack effect."

Interior lighting consists primarily of pendant LED direct/indirect lighting throughout. The LED lighting includes daylight-sensing dimmers and occupancy sensors. The lighting is also tied to the BMS system and divided into separate zones. Daylight is the primary ambient light source used to illuminate the work areas, with supplemental LED task lighting at the desks. Task lighting and other user loads such as computers and office equipment will be tied to plug controllers that automatically power down the equipment when it is not used. Most of the private offices include interior floor-to-ceiling glass partition walls, allowing natural light in (a strategy referred to as *daylighting*), and views to the outdoors from the interior of the building.

* Concrete tilt-up construction consists of structural reinforced concrete panels that are typically poured on site using forms that are laid horizontally on the ground. Once the concrete has cured, the walls are tilted up into vertical position and tied together with the roof and perpendicular walls.

Example 3 *(continued)*

Water use is reduced relative to conventional buildings utilizing water-efficient landscaping and ultra-low-flow fixtures in the restrooms. Domestic hot water is heated using a roof-mounted solar thermal heater and supplemented by small electric units located near the point of use. The exterior landscaping that previously consisted primarily of turf has been replaced with native, drought-tolerant species, including rosemary.

A living wall (interior vertical landscaping mounted in fabric) has been installed on the main shear wall in the interior. This provides a dramatic visual feature upon entry to the building as well as acoustical dampening. Indoor plants also help to clean the interior air and provide occupants access to views of nature, referred to as *biophilia*.

The renovated space is currently in warm shell condition. Up to 30% of the floor area can be carpeted, focusing on the paths of travel. The remainder will be left as finished, sealed concrete in order to maximize the benefits of thermal massing."

Note. All three examples were excerpted from the workfile of author Timothy P. Runde, MAI, LEED AP, and redacted as needed to preserve confidentiality.

and properly adjust the comparable set. Example 3 is the most complex and at the other end of the spectrum from Example 1. While it is also an older building, the property underwent an extensive sustainable renovation.

The Impact of Sustainability on Local Government Land Use Plans and Regulations

Local municipalities and counties, led by planning organizations such as the American Planning Association (APA), are addressing sustainability in their comprehensive plans, which may also be known as general plans or community master plans. These changing plans for land use and development filter down to requirements for green building elements or other sustainability-related objectives in zoning ordinances, building codes, and other regulations that may affect allowable uses, stipulate construction requirements, and influence other site factors such as density or parking requirements.

Changes to Land Use Goals and Policies

Changing demographics and market preferences, as discussed in Chapter 4, require periodic changes to a community or local jurisdiction's long-range development planning. Comprehensive planning documents often address decade-long periods extending well into the future. This future-oriented thinking whereby planners formulate strategies designed to meet a community's projected needs contrasts with the emphasis on historical trends and recent transactions used by valuation professionals. That is, planners ask, "What will the market value and need in the future?" rather than, "What does the market value today?"

Valuation, and particularly highest and best use analysis under the legally permissible use test, rely on zoning and comprehensive/

general plans to assess how the community's goals and priorities affect the land uses allowed on a particular site, whether it is the subject property or a comparable property. The planning code and zoning ordinances flow directly from the goals and priorities of the community as expressed in the general plan. Since planning by its very nature is forward-looking, it can often be difficult to square the market behavior measured by data points like comparable sales with the intent and goals of the general plan. Data is historical, yet each data point is imbued with the market's expectations of the current and future market and regulatory impacts on the site. Thus, it is not enough to understand what has been allowed on similarly zoned sites in the past. Accurately assessing the development potential of a site in the legally permissible portion of the highest and best use analysis also requires the appraiser to understand the potential for future changes to the zoning code and how the intents and goals of the master plan may affect how that zoning could change, be interpreted, or be applied in the future.

Sustainability is influencing general plans in many areas as planners seek to incorporate this shift in market demand and expectations into guidance that will result in land use patterns that meet the community's future goals. In 2010, the APA introduced the Sustaining Places Initiative at the World Urban Forum in Rio de Janeiro. In the years that followed, the APA worked to define the ways in which local government planning should address the changes and challenges presented by sustainability. They have since issued two reports: *Sustaining Places: The Role of the Comprehensive Plan* (2012) and *Sustaining Places: Best Practices for Comprehensive Plans* (2015). The more recent report is a best practices standards document that details recommended principles and planning practices to address what the APA terms as the "defining challenge of the 21st century."[12]

Exhibit 7.4 lists the six principles contained within the APA's 2015 report and provides examples of the recommended best practices for each of these principles. Looking at the first planning principle, "livable built environment," some of the best practices relate specifically to issues that valuation professionals would find germane to the valuation process. Planning for transit-oriented and infill development or for walkable, bikeable land use patterns may translate to changes in zoning and building codes that have a direct bearing on value. For example, in one city in the Silicon Valley, revision to the general plan changed the zoning of the area within one-half mile of the commuter rail station from business park/light industrial to transit-oriented mixed-use. This, in turn, transformed the highest and best use of a 100,000-sq. ft., single-story office building on an eight-acre site from

12. David R. Godschalk and David C. Rouse, *Sustaining Places: Best Practices for Comprehensive Plans (PAS 578)* (Washington, DC: APA, 2015), 7.

as improved to a high-density, multifamily redevelopment site. That site was subsequently purchased by a multifamily developer on a speculative basis, even before the general plan and zoning code changes were finalized.

The APA's 2015 report also discusses key trends that are predicted to inform and influence comprehensive plans over the next decades. These trends–resilience, systems thinking, community engagement, equity, implantation and adaptation–are listed and described in Exhibit 7.5. They conform to many of the underlying principles of sustainability and green building design that have been discussed in earlier chapters. Community engagement is an example of the type of transparency common in sustainability-oriented practices, as is the concern for social equity. Systems thinking as described here is the same approach that is applied in green building design and referred to commonly in that realm as a "whole building approach." Resilience, which will be described later in this chapter, may be unfamiliar to valuation professionals as a planning goal, but it is a concept garnering an increasing amount of attention from civic leaders, community planners, and property owners. Resilience has important implications for land use decisions, and therefore is pertinent to the valuation process.

For valuation professionals, these efforts to integrate sustainability into communities' comprehensive plans suggest that the effect of green building and sustainability extends beyond an individual property. To the degree that these guidelines are adopted into the periodic revisions of community general plans, these principles of sustainability are increasingly likely to inform the future zoning code changes and interpretations of the existing code. The extent and impact in any particular market will vary, but the need for valuation professionals to be aware of and appropriately consider sustainability-related changes to planning and zoning is only likely to increase with time.

Exhibit 7.6 describes the specific results of this shift in focus by planners to incorporate sustainability into community planning, highlighting some potential areas affecting the valuation process. While the analysis of markets, comparables, and proposed and existing improvements may all be affected by changes in planning-related goals and regulations, it is perhaps the effect on highest and best use analysis that has the potential for the most profound impacts on market value. In the highest and best use analysis, these impacts are most directly addressed in the analysis of legally permissible uses, in which the influence of land use regulations and policies is overtly expressed. The financial feasibility analysis is also likely to be influenced by the permitted uses as well as the cost of incorporating sustainability-related features into the site and improvements.

Exhibit 7.4 **Six Planning Principles and Best Practices of the APA's Standards for Sustaining Places**

Planning Principle	Examples of Best Practices
Livable Built Environment "Ensure that all elements of the built environment, including land use, transportation, housing, energy, and infrastructure, work together to provide sustainable, green places for living, working, and recreation, with a high quality of life."	• Plan for multimodal transportation. • Plan for transit-oriented development. • Plan for mixed land-use patterns that are walkable and bikeable. • Plan for infill development. • Implement green building design and energy conservation. • Discourage development in hazard zones.
Harmony with Nature "Ensure that the contributions of natural resources to human well-being are explicitly recognized and valued and that maintaining their health is a primary objective."	• Restore, connect, and protect natural habitats and sensitive lands. • Plan for the provision and protection of green infrastructure. • Enact policies to reduce carbon footprints. • Provide for renewable energy use. • Encourage water conservation and plan for a lasting water supply. • Protect and manage streams, watersheds, and floodplains.
Resilient Economy "Ensure that the community is prepared to deal with both positive and negative changes in its economic health and to initiate sustainable urban development and redevelopment strategies that foster green business growth and build reliance on local assets."	• Provide the physical capacity for economic growth. • Promote green businesses and jobs. • Provide and maintain infrastructure capacity in line with growth or decline demands.
Interwoven Equity "Ensure fairness and equity in providing for the housing, services, health, safety, and livelihood needs of all citizens and groups."	• Provide a range of housing types. • Plan for jobs/housing balance. • Plan for the physical, environmental, and economic improvement of at-risk, distressed, and disadvantaged neighborhoods. • Protect vulnerable populations from natural hazards.
Healthy Community "Ensure that public health needs are recognized and addressed through provisions for healthy foods, physical activity, access to recreation, health care, environmental justice, and safe neighborhoods."	• Reduce exposure to toxins and pollutants in the natural and built environments. • Plan for the mitigation and redevelopment of brownfields for productive uses. • Provide accessible parks, recreation facilities, greenways, and open space near all neighborhoods.
Responsible Regionalism "Ensure that all local proposals account for, connect with, and support the plans of adjacent jurisdictions and the surrounding region."	• Coordinate local open space plans with regional green infrastructure plans. • Delineate designated growth areas that are served by transit.

Source: David Godschalk and David Rouse, *Sustaining Places: Best Practices for Comprehensive Plans (PAS 578)* (Washington, DC: APA, 2015). 16-19, www.planning.org/publications/report/9026901/.

Exhibit 7.5 **Six Trends That Affect Comprehensive Plans, as Predicted by the American Planning Association**

Resilience	Increasing a community's ability to quickly recover from disruptive events, such as extreme weather events or other disasters
Systems Thinking	Viewing how traditional plan elements interconnect as a whole and using those interconnections to inform plan development
Community Engagement	Using digital technology to involve the community in the planning process
Equity	Addressing the needs of the disadvantaged, minority, and low-income populations
Implementation	Realizing tangible outcomes
Adaptation	Monitoring conditions and adjusting accordingly on an ongoing basis

Based on information from Godschalk and Rouse, *Sustaining Places: Best Practices for Comprehensive Plans*, 35-37.

Exhibit 7.6 **How Sustainable Planning and Codes Affect the Valuation Process**

Sustainable planning and codes affect the following:

- How we analyze and compare markets
- How we think about interrelationships between land uses
- How we describe and analyze the zoning of a subject property
- How we assess the consistency of existing improvements with local regulations
- How we analyze highest and best use
- How we think about location, access, and site configuration
- How we adjust comparable sales
- How we assess functional and economic obsolescence

Source: Gary R. Papke, "Sustainable Development Plans and Codes: Highest and Best Use and Market Value Problems and Solutions" (lecture, Appraisal Institute annual conference, Charlotte, NC, July 27, 2016).

Planning Codes and Zoning

Zoning regulations may require certain green standards (e.g., LEED Silver or equivalent) as a part of the base minimum code requirement. Or they may offer incentives such as a higher allowed density (floor area ratio or dwelling units per acre) for buildings that are LEED-certified or built to similar standards. Other green requirements such as bike racks, electric car charging stations, or transportation demand studies may also be specified in the zoning code. In addition, the amount of allowed parking may be curtailed to limit vehicle trips. In other words, the zoning may specify a parking maximum instead of a minimum. Making sense of this apparent reversal of policy is easier when viewed in light of the integration of sustainability principles into general plans, as discussed previously.

These requirements can affect the valuation process in several ways. Communities that require green building elements in the zoning code are effectively raising the bar for new construction. The market can respond to this in one of two ways. The market may view green building as the de facto norm for new construction. Conversely, if all new construction requires some level of green, then the market may view being "green" as requiring an increased level of effort. For example, if the building code effectively requires a LEED Silver certification or equivalent, property owners may choose to pursue higher levels such as Gold or Platinum to create market differentiation. Recertifying at a higher level or obtaining multiple certifications, such as a "triple platinum LEED" certification (which includes core and shell, commercial interiors, and existing buildings certifications) are other options some property owners have pursued. Still others may opt to add on certifications, such as NZE, the WELL Building Standard, or the Living Building Challenge, to cement the building's differentiation in the eyes of the market.

While planning and land use regulations have historically been under local control, regional and state-level regulations can also impact local planning decisions. Assembly Bill 32, known as the California Global Warming Solutions Act, passed in 2006 and is a clear example of how state legislation with sustainability-based objectives can filter down to local planning codes and subsequently affect land value and land use decisions. The act set the goal for the state to reduce greenhouse gas (GHG) emissions to 1990 levels by 2020, reflecting a 30% reduction, and to reduce GHGs to levels that are 80% below 1990 levels by 2050.[13] Largely in response to this policy goal, the state enacted Senate Bill 375, the Sustainable Communities and Climate Protection Act, two years later. This bill addresses one of the main contributors of GHGs in the state: passenger vehicles. The legislation calls on communities to coordinate transportation and land use policies in such a way as to reach mandated goals of reduced GHGs emissions from passenger vehicles. The primary mechanism employed is to develop regional land use transportation plans that will result in reduced total vehicle miles traveled (VMT) when approving new development.[14] The most common example is a preference for transit-oriented development (TOD) over more traditional automobile-centric suburban development, sometimes referred to as *sprawl* or *leap-frog development.*

In San Francisco, this legislation is a key driver of the Central SoMa Plan, which when adopted will become part of the city's general plan.[15] This plan seeks to re-zone a major corridor in the South of Market neighborhood from relatively low-density light industrial and service-commercial uses to high-density office use. Prior to this plan, the planning code had sought to protect this area primarily for light industrial and arts uses, which had been progressively squeezed out

13. In 2016, these targets were expanded to include a 40% reduction by 2030.

14. This is a radically different approach from what has historically been a locally oriented land use decision process, which typically did not involve cooperation with nearby communities and often lacked regional coordination.

15. Originally called the Central Corridor Plan, the Plan is now known as the Central SoMa Plan.

of other areas of the city by office and housing development. This major planning shift from preventing to encouraging higher-density office uses arose largely out of the requirements of Senate Bill 375. This area of San Francisco is under development with the new central subway project and is served by two of the region's major commuter rail systems (BART and Caltrain) and by the local municipal rail and bus system. This transit-rich environment made the area a prime target for new development that would accommodate economic growth while not adding to and potentially even reducing GHG emissions in the region. The original draft of the plan notes that locating jobs near transit is essential to achieving GHG emission reductions, and the zoning thus emphasizes commercial office use rather than residential uses.[16] At the same time, the plan seeks to protect existing light industrial and service commercial uses in the area.

The impact on land values due to the change in highest and best use has been, in some cases, significant and swift. For example, a nearly five-acre site that was previously zoned SALI (service/arts/light industrial) with height limits of 40 to 55 feet is proposed to change to an 85-ft. height limit with a portion up to 130 feet under the MUO (mixed-use/office) designation. Not only did the developable density more than double, but office uses that were specifically prohibited under the SALI zoning are now allowed under the MUO zoning. An assemblage of older industrial buildings that were owner-occupied was purchased for redevelopment as offices even before the zoning change was finalized. In this case, the state-level sustainability legislation resulted in changes to local-level land use regulations that ultimately changed the most probable buyer from an owner-user to a developer, changed the highest and best use from industrial to office, and caused the value of the site to significantly increase, due to the higher density allowed and the change in allowed uses. Exhibit 7.7 illustrates this trickle-down effect.

Building Codes

Building codes are the main mechanism used to set and enforce the minimum standards for new building construction and the renovation of existing structures. Building codes are periodically updated over time and have tended to become increasingly stringent as the underlying reference standards change. Energy efficiency is perhaps the most common example of this gradient. Building codes in some areas may also require certain green building characteristics, such as low-flow plumbing fixtures, water-efficient landscaping, and management of rainwater runoff. The cost of future renovations can be

16. San Francisco Planning Department, *Central Corridor Plan: Draft for Public Review* (San Francisco: San Francisco Planning Department; 2013), 4, www.sfplanning.org/ftp/files/Citywide/Central_Corridor/Central-Corridor-Plan-DRAFT-FINAL-web.pdf.

Exhibit 7.7 Sustainability-Oriented Policies Can Lead to Changes in Real Estate Values

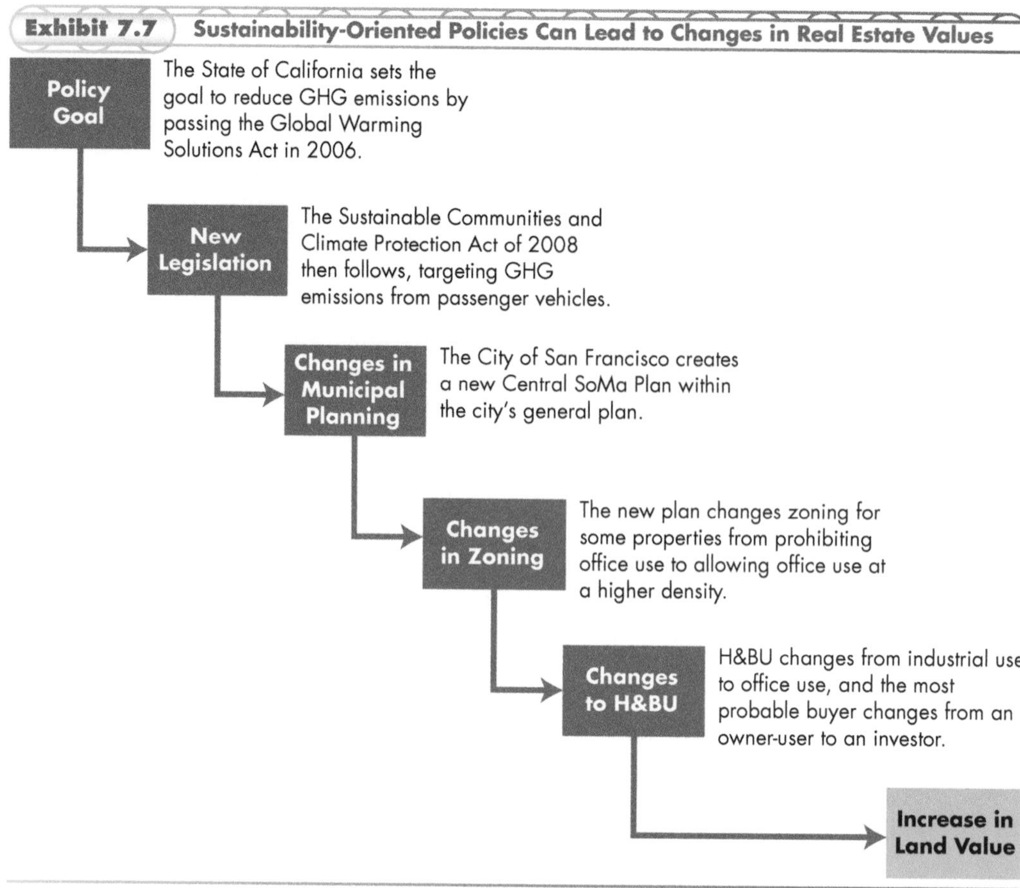

Policy Goal
The State of California sets the goal to reduce GHG emissions by passing the Global Warming Solutions Act in 2006.
New Legislation
The Sustainable Communities and Climate Protection Act of 2008 then follows, targeting GHG emissions from passenger vehicles.
Changes in Municipal Planning
The City of San Francisco creates a new Central SoMa Plan within the city's general plan.
Changes in Zoning
The new plan changes zoning for some properties from prohibiting office use to allowing office use at a higher density.
Changes to H&BU
H&BU changes from industrial use to office use, and the most probable buyer changes from an owner-user to an investor.
Increase in Land Value

affected directly by the higher cost of energy-efficient light fixtures and HVAC, for example, but can also be affected indirectly if the building permits required by periodic renovations such as tenant improvements trigger upgrades to the plumbing fixtures in the common restrooms or the common area lighting.

Building codes do not only affect new construction or renovations. Existing buildings may face obsolescence risk due to changing building codes, as discussed in the accompanying sidebar. The effect of energy efficiency and green building code requirements on existing buildings can be compared to the effect of the 1992 Americans with Disabilities Act (ADA). In both cases, there is a potentially significant capital cost that may or may not have an immediate economic return. Nonetheless, the capital expenditure is required for ongoing operation of the property.

Existing Buildings and the Risk of Building Code Obsolescence

Both market demand and policy are shifting—more frequently and more quickly in some markets than in others—towards the incorporation of green building standards into the built environment. This shift in market demand that encourages building owners to upgrade their properties concurrent with a rising minimum standard as mandated by building codes puts existing conventional buildings that do not meet current codes or that have not upgraded to meet current market demand at a heightened risk of obsolescence. As with any type of functional obsolescence, it is curable when the cost to cure the deficiency does not exceed the value added to the property in the after condition. Incurable functional obsolescence occurs when the cost to cure the deficiency exceeds the as-renovated contributory value of the component.

Existing conventional buildings fall into two main categories: those that can cost-effectively "green up" if property owners desire it or policy mandates it, and those that cannot meet the increasingly stringent building codes or market demand due to financial infeasibility or physical constraints. This dichotomy is not static. Existing buildings may be re-categorized as local market demand and supply evolve, policy and building codes change, technological advances provide new solutions, or existing technology becomes more financially feasible.

Existing conventional buildings may voluntarily "green up" as property owners seek to improve building efficiency to obtain lower operating expenses, improve marketability, and forestall obsolescence. Conventional existing buildings may also be required to incorporate green building components via policy mandates such as building codes and benchmarking requirements. These conventional buildings with green features may effectively compete with green buildings and may blur the distinction between conventional buildings and green buildings. Valuation professionals need to monitor their local markets for changes in supply and demand that may affect the competitive position of such buildings.

Older, unrenovated properties, particularly those located in areas with aggressively updated building codes, are at an increased risk of incurable functional obsolescence. This type of obsolescence requires special attention in the analysis of the highest and best use as improved as well as in the development of the cost approach.

As with any required upgrade, if the costs become too onerous, incurable obsolescence may affect the property, which could ultimately affect the property's highest and best use. All else being equal, a building that has not been recently renovated and is located in an area where building code requirements are regularly upgraded will face a greater likelihood of obsolescence than a comparable property that has been recently renovated. Conversely, the obsolescence risk is lower in areas where building codes are not regularly updated. The magnitude of obsolescence and its materiality to the valuation assignment will vary by locale and property type. However, it is increasingly necessary for valuation professionals to note the potential effect that changing energy and green building code requirements may have on renovation costs in the area.

The ongoing operational costs of a building may be positively affected by code-required upgrades that lower energy or water use. Thus, building code requirements and recent renovations, or the lack thereof, may be factors to be considered when analyzing and stabilizing operating expenses in the income capitalization approach. The code requirements also could be relevant in considering current or future tenant improvement costs, particularly for properties that have not been recently renovated.

The Impact of Resilience Planning on the Valuation Process

While environmental changes may not affect a particular region in the short term, buildings and particularly infrastructure are designed with long-term needs in mind, as noted by resilience expert David Singleton:

> Infrastructure investment decisions have long-term consequences, as the assets can shape development for decades – often beyond their lifetime. So decisions on infrastructure should anticipate the long-term environment, needs and constraints under which it will function.
>
> However, our ability to predict the future has been shown to be limited. Climate change is introducing deep uncertainty that makes this even more difficult. The environmental conditions under which infrastructure performs are likely to change radically and its design needs to take this into account.[17]

Severe storms such as Hurricane Katrina in 2005 and Hurricane Sandy in 2012 heightened awareness of the vulnerability of many cities–particularly coastal cities, where approximately 50% of the global population resides–to natural disasters and environmental challenges due to climate change.[18]

Hurricane Katrina is often credited with giving currency to the term *resilience* and the need for an urban infrastructure response from the public sector. But it was Hurricane Sandy that brought the financial implications of unanticipated weather events to the attention of mainstream commercial real estate owners, lenders, and insurers. The storm surge paralyzed Manhattan, the nation's largest real estate market and a global financial hub. The New York Stock Exchange was closed for two consecutive days, which hadn't happened since 1888 due to a severe winter storm.

Despite being downgraded below hurricane status by the time it flooded Goldman Sachs' headquarters in Lower Manhattan, Sandy revealed an unexpected environmental exposure that investors, lenders, and insurers would come to address as resilience. After all, if the site of One World Trade Center can end up nearly five feet un-

---

17. David Singleton, "Understanding Resilient Infrastructure," *Connectivity* (January 24, 2013), http://thoughts.arup.com/post/details/268/understanding-resilient-infrastructure. David Singleton is also the former global planning leader for ARUP, an independent firm of designers, planners, engineers, consultants, and technical specialists.

18. Sandy began as a Category 1 hurricane in the Caribbean, strengthened to a Category 3 hurricane, then transformed to a massive subtropical storm by the time it reached landfall near Atlantic City on October 29, 2012. Although its wind speeds clocked in below hurricane level, it created a storm surge due to its sheer size. The storm was essentially a massive wave that inundated portions of coastal New Jersey, Long Island, and Lower Manhattan with as much as nine feet of seawater. (Eric S. Blake, Todd B. Kimberlain, Robert J. Berg, John P. Cangialosi, and John L. Beven II, *Tropical Cyclone Report: Hurricane Sandy (AL182012)* (Miami, National Hurricane Center, 2013) hwww.nhc.noaa.gov/data/tcr/AL182012_Sandy.pdf); ULI (Uwe Brandes and Alice LeBlanc), *Risk and Resilience in Coastal Regions: A ULI Global Policy and Practice Forum Report* (Washington, DC: ULI, 2013), 8.

derwater due to a bad storm, what other environmental risks are we missing, and where?

What Is Resilience?

Three months after Hurricane Sandy, the ULI convened an interdisciplinary group with the express purpose to "explore the implications of new environmental risks in coastal regions on real estate practices and markets."[19] In a report published later that year, the ULI defines *resilience* as follows:

> Resilience–from the Latin *resilio*, meaning "to spring back"–is the ability to recover after an impact or misfortune. It is the ability to adapt to the consequences associated with an instance of failure or systemic breakdown.
>
> While there is no single professional or technical definition for the term, recently, in the wake of Hurricane Sandy and after several years of record losses from weather-related disasters, *resilience* is a term being used to describe the inherent qualities or capability of organizations and communities to recover quickly and resume their activities after natural catastrophes. In this context, resilience encompasses a wide variety of risk-mitigation strategies that seek to respond to vulnerabilities in communities and the built environment or to adapt to recent or anticipated risks associated with climate change.[20]

More succinctly, *resilience* can be defined as the ability "to prepare and plan for, absorb, recover from, and more successfully adapt to adverse events."[21]

From a valuation standpoint, it is reasonable to consider that a property with an improved ability to either withstand or recover from unexpected environmental risks may trade at a premium as compared to properties that do not have resilience built into the improvements or site. The ULI projects that "insurance and property markets will begin to price climate-change risks in a more thorough manner as those risks become more clearly characterized and widely accepted by market participants, policy makers, and regulators." Thus, the ULI contends that "project-based factors of resilience will become increasingly important for insurance, investment, and lending transactions."[22]

Resilient Infrastructure

Resilience and resilience planning are location-specific. What qualifies as a legitimate resilience concern along the Gulf Coast of Florida is different from what matters in upper Midwestern cities such as Minneapolis or in the desert southwest of Tucson. Resilience planning is a com-

---

19. ULI (Brandes and LeBlanc), *Risk and Resilience in Coastal Regions*, 2.
20. Ibid., 3.
21. Resilient Communities for America, National League of Cities, ULI, and USGBC, *Resilient Cities Summit: A Report of the 2015 Summit* (Aspen, CO: Resilient Communities for America, National League of Cities, ULI, and USGBC, 2015) http://uli.org/research/centers-initiatives/urban-resilience-program/reports/.
22. ULI (Brandes and LeBlanc), *Risk and Resilience in Coastal Regions*, 14.

munity-wide issue that is being integrated into the comprehensive or general planning documents of an increasing number of communities.

However, even though resilience risk tends to encompass more than just an individual property or property owner, the initiatives by communities to better prepare their jurisdictions for unforeseen environmental events can affect individual property owners via building codes and other regulations imposed on new and existing buildings. For example, green infrastructure is becoming an important aspect of a resilient built environment and could affect requirements for entitlements for new developments or limit development in areas shown to be more vulnerable to extreme weather or other environmental risks.[23]

But green infrastructure's appeal is not limited to low-lying coastal areas subject to tropical storms. Cities like Grand Rapids, Milwaukee, and Cincinnati are encouraging green infrastructure as a way to deal with combined sewer outflows (CSOs) that contaminate waterways with E. coli and other bacteria due to the mixing of storm and domestic wastewater. Cities in arid areas like Albuquerque view green infrastructure as a way to better manage water flows from infrequent, yet severe, storms, while capturing the water for later use during prolonged dry periods. In Los Angeles, a city that imports more than 80% of its water, the focus is on groundwater recharge, bioretention, and rainwater storage in preparation for drought, to aid in the reduction of the heat island effect, and to restore the community and natural connections to the long-channelized Los Angeles River.

Even without regulatory requirements enacted by local or state agencies, individual property owners may be interested in integrating resilience into their property's site and improvements as an operational best practice. For example, the Los Angeles Electrical Training Institute facility, run jointly by a partnership of the local union and electrical contractors association, learned from the 1994 Northridge earthquake how resilience was a weak spot in their business model. The magnitude 6.7 earthquake claimed 60 lives, damaged 112,000 structures, and resulted in $20 billion in property losses. In its aftermath, the local utility shut off electrical service while damage was assessed. Because their facility was without grid-supplied power and lacked a back-up power supply, there was no way to connect willing electricians with their member contractors. Lack of resilience infrastructure built into the facility undercut one of the primary functions of the organization–connecting its trained workers with their member employers–during a time of urgent need.

Learning from that disaster, the institute recently completed the second phase to their 140,000-sq.-ft. training facility, making it "NZE

23. Green infrastructure leverages existing site and climate characteristics with plant selection and site design to manage water flows from rain or flooding on site rather than sending the water off site, such as through the municipal wastewater treatment system.

plus." This means that the building generates significantly more electricity than it consumes. The property includes over 602 kWh DC of rooftop- and carport-mounted solar PV, plus a 300 kWh battery back-up capable of maintaining mission critical operations overnight, even if the grid goes down. In the future, the owner plans to increase the energy storage capacity to expand both the scope and duration of grid-independent operations.

Whether the response is from the public or private sector, resilience thinking and planning faces an inherent obstacle: How can significant up-front or ongoing investments for events that are severe yet

Resilient Infrastructure: Planning Ahead to Withstand the "Big Bad Wolf"

For the fabled Three Little Pigs, the quality of the built environment was critical to withstanding the effects of an unanticipated adverse outside influence. For property owners, cities, and communities facing unpredictable environmental risks, response to resilience risk is more complicated than simply choosing the right construction materials or enforcing basic building codes. The risks faced from unpredictable events such as rising sea levels, drought, or extreme weather are multifaceted, and some solutions remain untested. Response to the potential risks will vary depending on a variety of factors, including geography, the degree to which the individual property owner or community can afford to make resilience planning a priority, and regulatory influence. The examples profiled below involve risks ranging from flooding to drought. The responses of the property owners and communities to these challenges illuminate the cost and complexity of creating resilient infrastructure.

The Grand Ole Opry, Nashville, Tennessee

In May 2000, the Cumberland River rose to the unprecedented elevation of a 400-year flood, breaching the flood protection system after 13 inches of rain fell in 48 hours. The flood caused nine deaths, destroyed or damaged thousands of homes, and resulted in more than $2 billion in damages to the area.

Flood water stood four feet above the performance stage of the historic Grand Ole Opry House and inundated 800,000 square feet of the 4 million-sq.-ft. Gaylord Opryland Resort and Convention Center as well as most of its back-office facilities. Electrical switch rooms, all technology and communications infrastructure, miles of electrical wiring, and most of the facilities' kitchens and food storage areas were destroyed by the flood. Between the Opry House and the hotel and convention center, damages totaled more than $200 million. It took five months to complete remediation and refurbishment of the Opry House and six months to complete remediation and refurbishment of the convention center. As one of the area's major employers, the impact on the economy of the extended shutdown spread not only to the company's 1,800 employees but also to its suppliers, outsourcing companies, and transportation providers, not to mention taxes generated by the project, which make up more than 20% of the city's total hotel taxes.

The property owner's resilience response was to vertically extend a perimeter wall originally constructed after a 100-year flood that occurred just 35 years prior, in 1975. The brick and concrete wall protecting the 100+-acre site, which now stands up to 10 feet tall, cost a reported $17 million and was completed in 2012. In a flood event, groundskeepers can quickly install removable aluminum planks into the vehicular and pedestrian access points to maintain perimeter integrity.[24]

Lincoln Park and the Miller Creek Watershed, Duluth, Minnesota

Resilience and sustainability are closely related concepts, but they differ in two important respects. Resilience is designed to address a particular future adverse event or events and to permit a faster, less expensive, and less disruptive return to business as usual. It is primarily an adaptive response. Sustainabil-

24. For more information on this project, see ULI, "Returns on Resilience Case Study: Gaylord Opryland/Grand Ole Opry," accessed April 19, 2017, returnsonresilience.uli.org/case/gaylord-opryland-grand-ole-opry/.

ity, in contrast, is the overarching concept of balancing future needs with present needs. Resilience can be thought of as one of many tactics used to achieve a sustainability strategy. These are not competing but rather complementary ideas, as seen in this example from Duluth, Minnesota.[25]

Duluth is the third-largest city in Minnesota and has 86,238 residents. Duluth and Superior, Wisconsin, form the "Twin Ports," a metropolitan statistical area of almost 280,000 people. The two cities share a major deepwater port accessible to the Atlantic Ocean via the St. Lawrence Seaway. Duluth contains 68 square miles of dry land area, which is traversed by 47 separate creeks that empty into the St. Louis River or directly into Lake Superior. A natural bluff above the lake and river level divides the city as it drops 680 feet over the course of a mile. Like many older cities of the upper Midwest, it faces economic challenges to its traditional economic base of manufacturing and natural resource extraction.

Here, commercial development in the thriving "above-the-bluff" Miller Hill neighborhood caused negative storm impacts not only in Miller Hill but also downstream, in the economically disadvantaged Lincoln Park neighborhood below the bluffs, where Miller Creek flows into Lake Superior. Over the years, development in the Miller Hill commercial area removed wetlands that helped manage rainwater and replaced this natural infrastructure with impervious roofs and parking areas that reduced the capacity for on-site rainwater management. The water flow downstream was increased rather than being managed by natural features such as wetlands and pervious soils originally located above the bluff. In addition, the channelization of the creek that began as early as the 1930s created "choke points" during major storm events, creating localized flooding during severe storms when culvert capacity was exceeded.

In this case, the recommended course of action moved beyond simply managing the environmental concerns of the watershed to fostering economic development of the Lincoln Park neighborhood, a task that would require supportive social infrastructure. When posed with the question of how environmental resilience can coexist with economic and social development, the response of the ULI advisory panel was that it is not a question of whether it can be done but rather that there really is no other option. That is, environmental resilience is inextricably tied to the social and economic well-being of the community.[26]

La Cantera, San Antonio, Texas

In San Antonio, Texas, as in much of the arid west, drought is a way of life. Resilience in this context means the ability to prepare for, recover from, and adapt to drought. Planning a 323-unit apartment building as part of La Cantera—a resort-style, 150-acre, master-planned development—occurred during the 2011 drought and heat wave that caused 95 fatalities and $12 billion in damages across Texas and neighboring regions. The drought worsened in 2012, causing 123 deaths from a heat wave and $30 billion in losses primarily from crop failures across 22 states. It was the worst drought to affect the US since the 1930s.[27] Drought conditions would persist for three more years until a brief respite in 2015, when drought-related water use restrictions were briefly lifted in San Antonio, only to be reinstated several months later.

In this context, does it make sense to spend $1.4 million on a 1.5-acre park to provide a "resort landscape" experience when there could be a $425,000 bill to replant the park if damaged by recurring drought-related water use restrictions? The design team and developer chose to incorporate water conser-

25. As stated in the 2014 APA report, *Planning for Post-Disaster Recovery: Next Generation*, "It is important to embed the concept of resilience within the wider framework of sustainability. It is equally important that sustainability incorporate the concept of resilience. Resilience allows a community to respond to and recover effectively from specific events; sustainability is a frame of reference that aims to preserve for future generations the resources and opportunities that exist for current generations." (Allison Boyd, J. Barry Hokanson, Laurie A. Johnson, James C. Schwab, and Kenneth C. Topping, *Planning for Post-Disaster Recovery: Next Generation* (Chicago: APA, 2014), 6, www.fema.gov/media-library-data/1425503479190 22edb246b-925ba41104b7d38eddc207f/APA_PAS_576.pdf.)

26. For more information on this project, see ULI, *Duluth, Minnesota: Strategic Advice for Lincoln Park and the Miller Creek Watershed* (Washington, DC: ULI, 2016), http://uli.org/wp-content/uploads/2014/10/Duluth_PanelReport_web.pdf, 5.

27. National Centers for Environmental Information, "Billion-Dollar Weather and Climate Disasters: Overview," accessed April 19, 2017, www.ncdc.noaa.gov/billions/. Damage estimates are not adjusted for inflation.

vation, storage, and recycling infrastructure into the building and site design that minimized reliance on potable water use. The program included water-efficient fixtures and appliances in the units, drought-tolerant landscaping, and a recycled water system for landscape irrigation.

The La Cantera development includes the following features.

Building features:

- Energy Star dishwashers and appliances
- Low-flow faucets and shower heads
- Water heaters located close to fixtures to minimize water wasted while waiting for hot water

Site features:

- Native and drought-tolerant plants
- Minimum 4-in. mulch on all landscape beds to conserve irrigation moisture
- Mature, native live oak trees preserved for shade amenity in picnic area

Green infrastructure:

- Collection of unit air conditioner condensate
- Rooftop rainwater runoff collection
- 10,000-gallon underground storage cistern for AC condensate and rainwater
- Cistern monitoring to track daily collection

By monitoring the recycled water collection system, the owners now know that the landscape watering needs, which range from 1,000 to 4,000 gallons per day, can be met by on-site collection of condensate from the apartment units' air conditioners, which averages 4,500 gallons per day at full occupancy.

The park is part of the larger master plan design, and it has specific value to the residents. The unit premiums for park-facing units alone add over $25,000 per year to the income, which does not consider the inherent value of the park amenity to all units in the building. Reported savings on the water bill add nearly $9,000 to the bottom line. In addition to the $34,000 annual income benefit, the developer also sees a marketing advantage to the recycled water system: "Whenever we tell tenants, residents, and visitors about the water reclamation, people receive it really well. It is definitely a distinguishing feature."[28] Looking beyond the incremental rental premium and cost savings, this resilience strategy permitted the project to provide a "resort landscape" without the risk of losing the plantings due to drought-related water restrictions. Considering the $425,000 cost of replanting the park if damaged by drought, this strategy likely tipped the financial feasibility scales in favor of incorporating this amenity into the project. Put another way, had the project been built without this resilience, the value impact of the risk of future drought events on the project would likely have been significant and negative.[29]

unknown, uncertain, and often infrequent be justified? At least in the recent past, the answer to that question lies within the nature of the events themselves. The increased frequency and intensity of severe weather events often catalyzes action by creating a sense of urgency.

As the examples in the accompanying sidebar illustrated, resilience concerns affect a variety of property types and demographics and can have a profound effect on property value, land use policy,

28. ULI, "Returns on Resilience Case Study: The Residences at La Cantera," accessed April 19, 2017, http://returnsonresilience.uli.org/case/the-residences-at-la-cantera/.

29. For more information on this project, see ULI, "Returns on Resilience Case Study: The Residences at La Cantera," http://returnsonresilience.uli.org/case/the-residences-at-la-cantera/.

and social patterns. What resilience means, and its impact on a market or specific property, depends on the nature of the locational risks, decisions made by the property developer and owner, and decisions made by those completely unrelated to the property owner, including other property owners and policymakers.

Summary

To analyze the comparative advantages or disadvantages attributable to green building or sustainability faced by a given property, the valuation professional must first recognize the property's green design elements. Readily identifying green building and green features can be difficult without familiarity with green building design. Recognition can be enhanced by the following:

- Expanding one's visual database via education and other training opportunities
- Obtaining green building rating system scorecards or using green checklists, such as the Appraisal Institute's Commercial Green and Energy Efficient Addendum
- Disaggregating utilities for properties into separate categories for energy, water, and waste
- Actively considering the effect of site and locational factors such as transit proximity and walkability scores

Once the green elements are identified, the next step is incorporating them into the property and site analysis portion of the valuation process. Improvements descriptions for green buildings and features affect assignments involving green buildings and conventional buildings that have green building upgrades, performed either voluntarily or due to building code requirements. Additionally, properties selected as comparables may have green building elements that warrant identification, discussion, and appropriate adjustment for any value influence due to their green elements.

The impact of sustainability on future land uses also requires special attention in the appraisal process. Changes in federal, state, and regional policies and goals may affect community comprehensive plans and local zoning codes and alter the highest and best use analysis. In addition, ongoing, periodic building code changes and new mandates may require that green building features or design elements be incorporated in new buildings and renovations. For existing buildings, changes in building codes due to green building and sustainability may increase the risk of obsolescence. Integrating resilience planning and strategies into the built environment by communities and individual property owners may also have value implications.

8 Highest and Best Use Considerations

Highest and best use analysis is the nexus between market analysis and application of the valuation approaches. It is essential to selecting the appropriate valuation approaches and techniques, as well as selecting and analyzing rent and sale comparables. Ultimately, a well-reasoned and supported highest and best use analysis is the foundation of an accurate, reliable appraisal result.

Sustainability and green building considerations add new layers to this fundamental analysis. Green building and sustainability have altered market demand in many markets, while green building design, particularly passive strategies and energy-generating systems, has reshaped siting strategies and location desirability. In addition, resilience concerns and the goals of communities and property owners impact what gets built where and influence site and building design. Meanwhile, as discussed in the previous chapter, policy goals and comprehensive plans are altering the automobile-dominated planning model towards an emphasis on higher-density development utilizing alternate transportation modes including walking, biking, and public transit. This shift in policy and planning emerges in part from environmental concerns, but market demand from millennials and aging baby boomers for walkable, mixed-use neighborhoods with access to public transit, shopping, and entertainment is also a driving factor.

Accurately identifying and assessing any sustainability-oriented changes to a given market are particularly relevant for highest and best use analysis. Besides the effect on market demand, the influences of sustainability and green building are also changing what may be

Exhibit 8.1 Examples of Expanded Highest and Best Use Considerations Associated with Sustainability and Green Building

+ Site linkages and access
  - Walkability
  - Transit proximity
  - Active commute infrastructure proximity (bike and walking trails)
  - Access/proximity to shared natural areas, such as parks
+ Availability, impedance, or infringement of
  - Solar resources
  - Wind resources
  - Geothermal resources
  - Daylighting
  - Food production/urban agriculture
+ Climate factors
  - Temperature variation (diurnal, seasonal)
  - Humidity
  - Wind
  - Outdoor air quality (pollution, particulates)
  - Noise
+ Green infrastructure
  - Rainwater management
  - Rainwater harvesting
  - Groundwater resource
  - Heat island impacts
+ Federal, state, or municipal policy changes
  - New legislation
  - Changes to comprehensive plans
  - Changes to zoning codes
  - Changes to building codes
  - Green building incentives

legally allowed or physically required for new building development or existing building renovations, as discussed in Chapter 7. Financial feasibility and the analysis of maximum productivity of feasible uses may be affected.

The relative weighting of highest and best use criteria, whether physical, legal, or financial, may change due to the influences of sustainability and green building in a market. Even more importantly, the property characteristics that may need consideration when determining the highest and best use for a given property may expand, as shown in Exhibit 8.1. For example, aspects of site linkages and access that may not have previously been a material factor–such as walkability or access to shared open spaces–may now be a prominent issue to consider when analyzing highest and best use. Additionally, concerns about the availability of solar, wind, or geothermal resources or requirements for green infrastructure may become more relevant. Furthermore, local climate and ambient site factors such as outdoor air quality and noise may be critical issues when contemplating passive ventilation design strategies for green buildings.

This chapter focuses on the additional factors that may need to be considered when analyzing the three required conditions of the reasonably probable use–physical possibility, legal permissibility, and financial feasibility–as well as issues to consider when evaluating the maximally productive use.[1] Examples of these sustainability and green building-related considerations are summarized in Exhibit 8.2 and explored further in the following sections.

1. This text uses the definition of *highest and best use* that appears in the 14th edition of *The Appraisal of Real Estate*: "The reasonably probable use of property that results in the highest value." This definition assumes that a reasonably probable use meets the three conditions of physical possibility, legal permissibility, and financial feasibility. Identified uses that meet these conditions are then compared based on relative economic productivity.

Exhibit 8.2 Examples of Additional Considerations for Highest and Best Use Criteria Related to Sustainability and Green Building

	As Vacant	As Improved
Physically Possible	• What is the nature of the solar and wind resources for passive design and energy generation? • Are there any adverse influences (noise, odors, contaminants, or particulates) that might limit ventilation options? • Are there any biophilic site amenities, such as access to open space?	• How does existing orientation affect solar/wind resources? • Does existing structure physically allow for green renovation? Can it be altered? • Do occupants have access to quality views, natural light, or outdoor space?
Legally Permissible	• Do codes require green building? • Do codes incentivize green building?	
	• Do codes or mandates affect the size of the available building envelope? • Do codes affect or limit access to solar/wind resources or recycled water? • Is green infrastructure required?	• What is the status of the property's resource use systems (energy, water, waste, rainwater management, etc.), as compared to code requirements? • Do codes allow or restrict green upgrades?
Financially Feasible	• What are the cost implications for meeting or exceeding the code or market standard for green? • Are there incentives or cost reductions associated with green building? • Is there a competitive advantage to green buildings in this market? • Is there a competitive disadvantage to non-green buildings in this market? • Can any additional capital costs or cost savings of "green up" be passed on to end users?	
	• Is the ideal improvement green? If so, what is the ideal level of green?	• If market demand is green, can existing improvements be cost effectively altered to meet the market standard or expectation?

Highest and Best Use as Vacant

Highest and best use as vacant–i.e., unimproved–imagines the ideal improvement that would maximize site value. This analysis is performed for improved and vacant sites. In the case of the former, the conclusion of the ideal improvement is the benchmark against which the as-improved property is compared.

Central to this process is imagining the potential improvements and then selecting the ideal improvement that meets all three conditions and returns the highest value to the site. For a vacant site, the relevant question is if physical, legal, or financial factors influence whether green improvements or components should be considered in concluding the ideal improvement. Even for a site that is vacant and has never been improved, determining the highest and best use under each condition requires a consideration and comparison of alternate development scenarios. Thus, the examples provided in this section could in many cases also be applied to the as-improved highest and best use analysis.

Physically Possible Uses as Vacant

The physical limitations and opportunities of a vacant site to be considered in highest and best use analysis expand in the context of green building and sustainability. In addition to the conventional parameters of site size, configuration, topography, soil conditions, and public street access, other site characteristics may need to be considered or may take on greater weight.

For example, the configuration of the site may need to be assessed in light of its solar resource. That is, is the site suited to optimizing passive solar design or an on-site solar photovoltaic (PV) system? The former often involves an east-west axis to the building, which may not be feasible for a long, narrow site that is oriented north-south. Solar PV is optimized by unimpeded access to solar irradiation; therefore, it becomes important to consider existing or future structures on or off site, particularly tall buildings or trees that may cast shadows on a planned solar PV array, as shown in the accompanying photo.

The site's wind resource may also be a factor if the design team plans to use natural ventilation as the primary mode of air exchange or as part of a mixed-mode (natural plus mechanical) ventilation system. If wind turbines are contemplated, on-site and off-site obstructions may need to be analyzed and the wind resource evaluated.

Ambient environmental factors such as traffic or industrial noise, odors, contaminants, and other particulate matter (PM) such as pollens, pollution, or dust may also influence whether natural ventilation is possible or if operable windows would be prudent. Additionally, the site's capacity to manage and/or treat rainwater runoff or to process wastewater from on-site domestic use may be a factor to consider, particularly in municipalities where existing rainwater management or domestic water treatment facilities are at capacity.

Consideration of these additional site factors may influence the siting and configuration of potential buildings, as well as the size and configuration of the buildable envelope, leading to a highest and best use conclusion that would differ from a conclusion based solely on conventional design considerations. Green building may suggest improvements that may not maximize rentable area–which typically is an important factor in determining the maximally productive improvement–and instead focus on delivering space that more clearly aligns with market demand. For example, maximizing daylighting with narrow floorplates in a proposed office building may result in less rentable area, but the net result may be more marketable space that attains a higher rent per square foot due to the enhanced daylighting capacity and outdoor views provided by the narrower floorplate.

A mature tree shades the solar array of an adjacent building. Adjacent trees or tall buildings should be considered for their potential impact on planned solar arrays. In this case, the heritage redwood was protected by the local community and could not be removed.

Site considerations also extend beyond the four corners of the site to the linkages that the site has to the community. These linkages include access to streets, highways, and public transit and proximity to offices, housing, shopping, dining, entertainment, schools, parks, recreation, and other amenities. While these considerations are often subsumed under the banner of "location" in the conventional highest and best use analysis, proximity to transit, amenities, and the presence of walkable communities of mixed uses takes on greater importance when evaluating the full spectrum of environmental and social impacts of a proposed development, as is becoming increasingly common in the entitlement process. Put another way, if the community at large finds value in the health benefits of walkable communities or the environmental benefits of transit access, then these also need to be considered in the highest and best use analysis.

Legally Allowed Uses as Vacant

Legal constraints on land uses are typically found in the local planning and zoning ordinances and applicable building codes. These legal constraints may also include private use restrictions such as covenants, conditions, and restrictions (CC&Rs) or deed restrictions. The growing adoption of green building certification programs such as LEED has resulted in changes to zoning ordinances and building codes in many areas.[2] These changes incorporate sustainability and green building practices as either a minimum standard of compliance or as an incentive. Many of these changes are recent and ongoing, requiring regular review of zoning ordinances for recent modifications that include green building components. Furthermore, since building codes are upgraded on a periodic basis, recent changes

2. Further information regarding the effects of green building codes and sustainability-oriented planning and zoning ordinances can be found in Chapter 7.

may incorporate green building practices that raise the bar for new construction and renovation. CALGreen is an example of a statewide building code that incorporates some basic green building best practices pertaining to energy, water, and waste/recycling (among others) into the base building code for all construction in California. It first became effective in 2011 and was updated three years later.

A community that incorporates green building minimum compliance standards or incentives into its zoning ordinances and building codes would suggest some level of sustainability orientation of the market and would be a factor to note during the market analysis and when selecting and analyzing comparables. For the highest and best use as vacant, this discovery indicates that the market values green at some level, but it also means that every new building in the market will likely have at least some green attributes.[3] In this case, attaining distinction as a green building in the eyes of the market will likely require a more advanced level of green building practices on the part of the property owner. Additionally, incentive-based zoning that rewards higher levels of green building certification with expedited entitlements or a higher density may push the market toward a higher level of green building by creating an economic incentive to "go green."

Another area in which sustainability influences highest and best use is in the marginal impact of a proposed development on the existing infrastructure, including the domestic water supply and treatment systems, rainwater management, roads, transit, and the electrical grid. As the existing infrastructure ages, the impact of new development on system capacity is increasingly coming under scrutiny as communities seek to align who pays for new development with who benefits from it.

In the case of a new development seeking entitlements, developers may be asked to pay for resulting increases in automobile traffic, increased impact on water supply and treatment systems, or even electrical grid demand during peak usage periods. Encouraging alternatives to automobile use by locating trip-generating uses like office space close to transit and providing secure on-site bicycle storage and shower facilities at the office can reduce or eliminate the cost of transportation impact fees or allow for higher-density development because the traffic demand is mitigated. On-site rainwater management and reduced potable water use can reduce sewer fees and help avoid expensive public infrastructure bonds that would otherwise be passed on to ratepayers. The highest and best use analysis and conclusion may be affected to the extent that these impacts and associated costs

3. Note that while green codes may mandate a threshold for green building for new construction or major renovations, this does not mean that all buildings are green, nor does it equate with the market standard for green building. See the sidebar entitled "Do Green Codes Equal Green Buildings?" for further discussion.

are reduced or eliminated by incorporating green or sustainable elements.

Zoning and building codes may provide other advantages related to green building, such as allowing a larger building envelope. Alternatively, a larger building footprint may also be realized in areas where zoning regulations have changed from a traditional minimum parking requirement to a maximum allowed parking ceiling, thereby allowing the building to encompass a larger portion of the site.

Do Green Codes Equal Green Buildings?

Q: If the building code and/or zoning ordinance mandate green building, does that mean that all new buildings are green?

A: Not necessarily. While it is likely that the new buildings are, as a whole, greener than they would otherwise be, the relevant highest and best use questions to ask are as follows: What is the market standard for green? What do tenants respond to? What do they require? What will they pay more for? And most importantly, how do these market expectations and/or the demand for green building compare to the green building code or zoning-mandated standard for a green building?

On the other hand, if green building codes change market perceptions and expectations such that "new" is synonymous with "green/sustainable," then the real risk may be the accelerated obsolescence of existing buildings.

Other factors worthy of consideration include how the community's policies and codes may affect green building practices. For example, in one case, the height limit in the zoning code prevented the vertical axis wind turbines from extending above the roof line, which rendered the turbines largely ineffective. In another case pictured earlier in this chapter, heritage redwoods that cast shadows on the solar PV array of an office building renovation could not be removed due to their aesthetic value to the community.

Private restrictions on land use, such as CC&Rs that place limitations on green building components like solar PV installations, may also be relevant to the highest and best use analysis. These private restrictions, however, may be limited by so-called solar access laws that protect property owner rights to sunlight. Additionally, front yard landscaping requirements that limit non-turf coverings such as stone or mandate a minimum amount of turf could interfere with attempts to reduce outdoor water use for landscaping.

Legal constraints may also affect the type or extent of allowed green building improvements. Local ordinances and codes may not permit the use of gray water for landscape watering, for example. Composting toilets may require special exemptions or not be permitted at all in some areas. On-site water treatment systems that use rainwater harvested on site as a potable water source are likely to face rigorous approval standards due to public health concerns.

The Bullitt Center in Seattle is a prime example of the type of legal hurdles faced by an owner-occupant of a building that incorporates cutting-edge green practices. In order to harvest and treat water on site to meet the standards set by the Safe Drinking Water Act, the owner-occupant of the Bullitt Center had to gain an exemption from the Seattle Public Utilities jurisdictional monopoly, form an independent water utility, and agree to perform regular testing of the water certified by an independent third party. Initially, the owner-occupant attempted to gain an exception from the chlorination requirement of the local health department since chlorine belongs to a class of chemicals restricted by the Living Building Challenge rating system, the green building standard being pursued. After much dialogue with regulatory authorities, including the Administrator of the US Environmental Protection Agency, the owner-occupant of the Bullitt Center agreed to add a small amount of chlorine to the water to protect public health. As a result, the building was granted an exception under LBC certification.

Effects on Financially Feasible Uses as Vacant

The implications of sustainability for the financial feasibility of a property, whether vacant or improved, are fundamentally the same as they are for any conventional property: Is the marginal cost equal to or less than the marginal benefit of that improvement or component? The following sections consider the influence of sustainability and green building on financial feasibility that would apply equally to either the as-vacant or as-improved analysis.

Rent Premiums and Marketability

Measured rent premiums for green-certified or sustainable space, or for any other real estate feature for that matter, may or may not be supported in the market over the long term. Under the efficient market hypothesis, anyone else in the market could augment their property to meet the new demand for green space and thus dilute or eliminate the marginal rent premium, unless there is adequate demand and/or effective barriers to entry. This concept has important implications for income-based valuations and is no different from a perceived rent premium derived from any other non-green property characteristics, such as age, quality, prestige, or design.

The Bullitt Center building in Seattle. The owner-occupant of this building had some legal hurdles to overcome in order to meet the standards set by the Safe Drinking Water Act as well as meet the requirements of the Living Building Challenge rating system and the local health department. Photo by Joe Mabel.

Even when a rent premium cannot be unequivocally identified, the marketability of the space may be enhanced due to its perceived environmental sensitivity or its focus on occupant well-being. The economic impact of faster absorption should not be underestimated, as it can be more relevant to feasibility than the marginal rent premium that may or may not be durable going forward.

Cost Premiums

Cost premiums for green building construction can vary widely and often decrease significantly over time as the market becomes more familiar with green construction processes.[4] In addition, the impact of an integrated design often leads to cost synergies that lower the overall cost relative to the sum of component costs that may be reported in cost services or other à la carte costing sources.

As discussed in Chapter 3, sustainable building practices often incorporate a fundamental cost shift, whereby higher initial capital costs result in lower operational costs. This cost shift can obscure the true financial feasibility of a sustainable project if the ongoing operational cost savings are not fully internalized in the feasibility analysis. For example, economic feasibility tested using an income-based analysis should include the reduced operational cost associated with a green improvement that has a higher up-front cost. Alternately, some green features add to future operational or capital costs that need to be considered. For example, solar PV often significantly reduces energy (operational) costs. However, most inverters currently require replacement in Year 15 or so, which is a future capital cost that should be considered.[5]

Rebates and Incentives

Financial feasibility may also be impacted by rebates and incentives, such as preferential tax treatment. For example, even though many of the utility rebates for renewable energy are now exhausted, the federal Business Energy Investment Tax Credit for renewable energy systems was renewed in 2015.[6] It allows a 30% tax credit in the first year for both residential and commercial systems, such as solar PV. While most market value appraisals stop short of considering tax consequences to the ownership entity, these incentives may need to be considered if the market behavior clearly demonstrates that the incentive is a material factor in the purchase decision.

Similarly, incorporating green infrastructure to manage rainwater on site in some areas can make the property eligible for credits from the local water treatment utility. When determining the feasibility of including storm water retention ponds, underground cisterns, bioswales, permeable pavement, and other green infrastructure components on a property, available up-front or ongoing incentives should be considered.

---

4. Cost-related issues are covered in more depth in the cost approach section of Chapter 9.
5. Some inverters are now warranted for 25 years.
6. See Chapter 11 for more information on the federal Business Energy Investment Tax Credit (ITC).

Effects on the Determination of Maximum Productivity as Vacant

Using risk-adjusted rates of return are an integral part of analyzing which of the financially feasible uses result in the highest residual land value. As discussed more fully in the income capitalization approach discussion in Chapter 9, sustainability and green building can create material changes in the risk profile of a property and its potential uses. For example, a new non-green building in a market that values sustainability may be at greater risk of obsolescence than a new green building in that same market. This part of the analysis is highly dynamic in that the market expectation and market penetration of green and sustainability changes over time. Furthermore, the pace of the change can be more rapid than what is typical for other traditional real estate market characteristics. Heightened attention to market perceptions of and preferences for sustainability is therefore warranted, even when revisiting a familiar market or property type.

Sustainability and green building also have an impact when determining the ideal improvement. As noted in *The Appraisal of Real Estate*, the ideal improvement takes maximum advantage of the potential market demand for the site's highest and best use, conforms to market standards and the character of the market area, and contains the most suitably priced components.[7]

As discussed in previous chapters, market demand for sustainable and green property attributes can vary over time and between markets and property use types (e.g., industrial versus office versus retail). Valuers should be careful not to paint a given market or property type with a broad brush in terms of sustainability orientation when comparing and contrasting market demand for green building. Demand for green office space as measured by a rent or lease-up premium does not necessarily indicate the same premium in the retail or apartment sector, for example. In the case of the 1980s-era office park discussed in the sidebar in Chapter 7 on suburban sustainability (page 134), market demand for walkable amenities may mean that the maximally productive use as vacant or for an underimproved portion of the site is as a mixed-use retail/entertainment and residential building, even if another Class A office building might at first seem to be the logical choice. Additionally, green building codes and other development standards are dynamic, and what is considered a market standard today may change due to evolving standards. Lastly, as discussed in the previous section, costing of green components needs to be carefully weighed to assess whether and to what degree current cost premiums will persist.

Besides the three criteria noted above, the ideal improvement presumes no physical deterioration or obsolescence–i.e., no over-

7. *The Appraisal of Real Estate*, 14th ed. (Chicago: Appraisal Institute, 2013), 345.

improvement or underimprovement. Issues of superadequacy and obsolescence would need to be weighed carefully in all markets regardless of sustainability orientation, since the determination of whether the ideal improvement is overimproved or underimproved must always be made relative to the market. Indeed, a proposed improvement could be considered superadequate in one market but normative or even obsolete in another.

Highest and Best Use as Improved

The highest and best use analysis for an already improved site is typically focused more on the existing improvements than on the underlying site. All of the site factors noted previously still apply and should be considered. However, the relevant valuation question is whether the existing improvements should be physically modified in some way to enhance value. In other words, what physical alterations can be made to the existing improvements to bring them closer to the ideal improvements for the vacant site? Is renovation, conversion, or expansion possible? Should the improvement be demolished or retained?

In the case of existing buildings, the highest and best use determination of whether renovation is appropriate may be affected by green building code requirements, such as in cases when renovation triggers code upgrades that increase costs. Alternately, voluntary upgrading for market differentiation should be considered when there is evidence that market participants exhibit sustainability-oriented behaviors, such as a preference for green building in lease decisions or investors who incorporate sustainability into their operational best practices.

For an existing conventional building, the initial question may be whether green upgrades or green certification ought to be pursued. If "greening" the existing improvements is indicated, the next step is to address any physical constraints of the existing site and improvements. For example, in a market where energy efficiency is an important factor, older buildings may have aging mechanical systems that simply cannot be operated as efficiently as new HVAC systems. In addition, these buildings may also lack adequate roof and wall insulation or use single glazing rather than dual-glazed windows. Together, these physical limitations may render the building incapable of attaining Energy Star or other energy-efficiency certifications without the wholesale replacement of entire building systems and components. In extreme cases, partial or complete demolition is the ultimate modification. This may be warranted when market demand changes sufficiently such that the physical constraints of the property preclude cost-effective adaptation or policy and zoning changes alter the highest and best use of the site. The marginal costs of replacing existing non-green components or systems should include not just the cost of the new green component but also the cost of demolition, removal, and disposal of the obsolete conventional component.

If on-site renewable energy production is preferred by the tenant market or sought after by the investors as a way to lower energy costs, should a solar PV array be added? If so, what limitations might there be in terms of available roof space, orientation, or unshaded parking lot area for carport-mounted solar arrays? Can existing trees be removed, or are there local restrictions on tree removal? Does the zoning code limit the placement of ground-mount solar PV, such as a carport, due to setback or rear yard requirements? On the other hand, will the carport, which offers shade and weather protection, make the rentable building area more marketable and offset the added cost of the carport structure?

Buildings with large floor plates typically have limited daylighting options, which may be a factor in markets where tenants want open-plan space with views to the outdoors for everyone instead of just the occupants of perimeter private offices. In that case, does the highest and best use need to consider the cost to demolish what may be perfectly functional private offices before they reach the end of their economic lives in order to make the space "market ready?" Should a light well or atrium be carved out of the center of the building, reducing the rentable area but curing functional obsolescence? What other options might be available to bring a property that does not meet market requirements for green or sustainable space into line with market demand?

The practical limitations of traffic capacity of the existing roads and associated automobile infrastructure create a particular issue for properties such as suburban business parks, which typically lack robust public transit infrastructure. In markets where transit access is required to secure key tenants, private commuter buses and shuttles are increasingly common solutions. However, these solutions come at an ongoing operational cost.

The physical feasibility of these potential modifications leads logically to the financial feasibility of the upgrades. The essential test for financial feasibility of green or conventional alterations is whether the value in the "after" condition meets or exceeds the cost to cure the deficiency. While often a fairly straightforward test for conventional buildings, the financial feasibility of green building upgrades that reduce operational costs adds a wrinkle to the analysis, which should not be overlooked when comparing the marginal cost of the improvement to the value of the property in the "after" condition. Similarly, the potential for cost synergies (capital and operational) among green components should be considered.

The sustainability-related factors affecting the selection of the maximally productive use as improved are similar to the previously discussed effects on the highest and best use as vacant. However, in this analysis the maximally productive use focuses on which modifications to the existing, presumably conventional improvements are feasible (if any), and which provide the highest net return after considering associated costs. This analysis may incorporate, for example, evaluating whether a major energy-efficiency upgrade is warranted, if adding solar PV is justified, or if a lighting upgrade is economically viable. It may also compare the costs and benefits of each to determine which provides the greatest, or fastest, return on investment. Comparing the maximally productive use to the existing use can also identify areas of potential obsolescence.

Obsolescence Risk

As markets progress toward internalizing sustainability practices, expectations of the market shift. On a longer-term basis, this new market standard effectively raises the minimum threshold for entry into the market and creates de facto obsolescence for existing properties that lack these characteristics. At a certain point, the financial feasibility question then shifts to whether the proposed or existing project can afford *not* to incorporate sustainable building practices. In other words, how does *not* upgrading an existing property increase the risk of obsolescence? Is the obsolescence curable or incurable?

Changes in market demand and building technology may alter the traditional framework through which a building's improvements are considered obsolete. For example, there may be opportunities for existing conventional properties–such as Class B or C industrial or office buildings–to be candidates for sustainable renovations that raise their competitive position, thereby forestalling or eliminating obsolescence. The sustainable renovation described in Exhibit 7.3, Example 3 (page 138), is a prime example of how the sustainable renovation of a former racquetball club (constructed similarly to an office building) repositioned the improvements to a Class A-/B+ office building able to garner rents above its competitive set.

Superadequacy

Superadequacy is a special form of functional obsolescence. It can affect properties that incorporate green features or practices that the market does not fully recognize on a dollar-for-dollar basis, at least as of the date of value. One way to quantify this superadequacy is to compare the income and cost value indicators. However, market demand for green properties, at least at the early point in the cycle, is dynamic. Early indications are that the sustainability orientation of markets increases over time, with respect to both demand for green buildings and higher levels of green features and practices. As with external obsolescence, superadequacy with respect to the green characteristics of a building should be considered in light of the expected trajectory of the market's sustainability orientation. If there is in fact evidence that the market is moving in a direction of increased sustainability orientation, simply comparing the reported costs of an overimproved green building to the capitalized value based on market rent may overstate the amount of superadequacy. This situation is analogous to capitalizing the rent differential in a property due to a temporary market downturn. In such instances, it may be necessary to perform a discounted cash flow analysis of the income shortfall over the amount of time required for market demand to reach the point at which the marginal overimprovements are recognized by the market.

Alternately, if the overimproved green property results in added operating costs or the design characteristics affect its marketability, these impairments should also be considered in the highest and best use analysis. For example, if daylighting or a passive ventilation system precludes perimeter private offices in a market where window-line offices are the norm, this could impact the rent or marketing time (or both). The same would be true if the property lacks adequate on-site automobile parking to meet the market requirement. However, if the parking shortfall is accompanied by superior transit access and secure bicycle parking, the effect may be mitigated.

Case Study 8.A, Value Beyond Electrons, discusses an example of superadequacy.

Summary

Sustainability and green building continue to catalyze changes in construction requirements, building technology, and market demand. Since market demand underlies highest and best use analysis, any sustainability or green building-driven changes to market demand may ultimately affect the determination of highest and best use.

Most notably, sustainability and green building expand potential highest and best use considerations and may change their relative weighting in the highest and best use analysis. Whether such factors as walkability, transit proximity, green infrastructure requirements, impedance of or infringement upon solar or wind resources, or access to daylighting affect the highest and best use analysis varies between markets and property types and over time within a given market. Just as with any other potentially value-affecting property attribute, understanding, monitoring, and analyzing the potential for sustainability and green building to alter market demand is the essential foundation to incorporating these market influences into the highest and best use analysis.

Case Study 8.A Value Beyond Electrons

Certain forms of renewable energy generation provide a clear example of the special type of functional obsolescence known as superadequacy, particularly if the replacement cost exceeds the cost of another system that generates a similar amount of energy. In one project that included both a roof-mounted solar PV system and vertical axis wind turbines, the gross cost (before rebates and incentives or tax benefits) of the three vertical axis wind turbines was over $70.00 per watt of direct current (DC) of installed capacity, versus less than $5.00 per watt DC for the same energy capacity of the roof-mounted solar installation. This significant difference pointed strongly to superadequacy of the wind turbines, warranting attention in the cost approach. One way to estimate this superadequacy would be to measure the differential in the gross cost per watt, since electrons (at least theoretically) have the same market value no matter their source of generation.

In this case, solar PV installation on a cost-per-watt basis was significantly less than it was for the wind turbine installation. So why did the owner go ahead and install the wind turbines anyway? On the face of it, this decision may seem incongruent. However, the wind turbines in this particular project provided benefits to the owner-user that went beyond the value of the energy production. The building was a training facility for electricians, and the wind turbines provided an educational benefit to the students. Furthermore, beyond the distinctive architectural sculpture-like element they provided, the turbines sent a clear and prominent message to the community and the facility's contractor customers about the vision and mission of the training facility: Our students are the best and brightest and are trained in the latest technologies. That kind of perceived value accrues to that particular user and in this case would likely not translate to another buyer. Thus, the marginal cost premium may not fully translate to market value, unless there is clear evidence that other market participants would value it similarly for its aesthetic or other appeal.

The owner of this training facility for electricians installed both a solar PV system on the roof and wind turbines. The turbines provided benefits to the owner and users that went beyond the value of energy production.

9 The Three Approaches to Value

Previous chapters explored how green building and sustainability have changed building design and construction and have altered the types of properties that the market demands as well as the performance expectations for those properties. We have seen how these changes can affect aspects of the valuation process such as the scope of work, market analysis, property and site descriptions, and highest and best use analysis. How do these changes, in turn, affect the approaches used to render a defined value? What–if anything– needs to be done differently to value a green building or green features in a conventional building?

Appraisers typically use three approaches to value–the cost, sales comparison, and income capitalization approaches–when solving valuation problems. Green buildings, whether they are labeled as "green," "sustainable," or "high-performance," are no exception. While these assignments may require the appraiser to use these approaches in a different way or to gather and analyze data differently, the fundamental theory and practice of appraisal remains unchanged.

Green buildings can present the appraiser with significant new challenges, as discussed in previous chapters. Data availability is often an issue.[1] Assessing market demand for green space may require more extensive primary research, such as directly interviewing market participants, in cases where secondary sources such as

1. The paucity of comparable green data results from a variety of factors. First of all, green buildings are still a minority market share. Secondly, green buildings are not consistently identified within data services. Finally, apples-to-apples comparisons can be difficult when comparing green buildings, due to their heterogeneous nature.

third-party market reports would suffice for a conventional property. "Green" also tends to be a dynamic area of the real estate market, both in terms of technological advances and market adoption of green building practices. How much green building matters, and what components of green building matter in a particular market, can change over time. All of these factors have important implications in the application of the approaches to value.

Green Building Impacts in the Cost Approach

The cost approach takes on added importance for an emerging property type such as a green building, for which the sales comparison and income capitalization approaches may be weakened due to limited comparable sale and rental data. Furthermore, most green buildings are either new construction projects or involve significant renovation work, since the green sector is inherently new. In either case, the cost approach often becomes a more relevant indicator than might otherwise be the case.

In general, the application of the cost approach is the same for green buildings as it is for conventional buildings. However, green building design and construction can alter some of the finer points of the analysis. For example, replacement cost rather than reproduction cost is often the most commonly used method to estimate value in the cost approach. In practice, the information often provided to the appraiser is based on historical costs or a construction pro forma, and adjustments must be made to these reproduction costs to yield appropriate replacement cost estimates. This process is familiar to valuation professionals when it comes to conventionally designed and constructed buildings. However, as discussed in other chapters, cost considerations unique to green building design and construction can heighten the disparity between reproduction and replacement cost. For example, most conventional building construction costs are relatively stable, tending to trend upward primarily as a result of general inflation. This may not hold true for green buildings. If technological advances or market experience cause green building costs to decline, which can be common in the early phases of adoption, an obsolescence adjustment may be in order when relying on historical costs for a replacement cost estimate.

Thus, green building costs require additional analysis in the valuation process due to the nature of green building cost trends, the effect of synergies and integrated design, and the potential to double-count costs when using commercial costing services such as the Marshall and Swift Valuation Service or RS Means.

Green Building Cost Trends

Green building cost has been the subject of ongoing study and debate. Do green construction practices and processes cost more? If so, how much more does green building cost relative to conventional construction?

Many early projects reflected significant cost premiums to conventional construction. Over time, the cost premium has generally declined. This progression reflects several interrelated dynamics. First of all, building codes in many areas are progressively incorporating certain components of green building into the base level requirements for new construction and renovations. However, the commercial real estate industry remains unaware of these changes for the most part. Nonetheless, by raising the minimum standard for all construction, the cost premium over conventional construction shrinks. Secondly, as the design and construction industries are becoming more experienced with green building practices, the early learning-curve inefficiencies are giving way to a new "business as usual" and these new building practices are becoming more efficient. Finally, increasing demand for the new building products allows the early research and development costs to be recovered and prompts more producers to enter the market, causing costs to decline.

At the same time, a countervailing force is at work. Even as building codes and market participants incorporate green and sustainable building practices (pushing costs down), the baseline moves ever higher for what it takes to be considered "green" (pushing costs up). The Leadership in Energy and Environmental Design (LEED) program is a good example of the ratcheting up of market expectations for green buildings. The US Green Building Council (USGBC) periodically releases new versions of its LEED rating systems. Each version is incrementally more stringent. In addition, new certifications such as the Living Building Challenge, the WELL Building Standard, and Zero Energy (ZE)/Net Zero Energy (NZE) have also emerged. These new standards bring new construction costs and expertise requirements for the design team and contractors, which counters the downward pricing pressure of experience and competition. So even as competitive pressures and market knowledge exert downward pressure on the production side, higher expectations are pushing in the opposite direction.

The typical market cost cycle for new technology also plays a role. Costs typically decline initially and often quite rapidly in the early stages of development. As the technology scales, the cost declines decrease and the market moves toward a more stable and predictable cost pattern in which inflationary pressures tend to become the major influence and prices generally rise over time. Green building costs are likely to follow a similar pattern. However, for the foreseeable future, historical costs need to be viewed in light of the effects of these pricing dynamics, which are atypical in conventional commercial real estate and with which most appraisers may not be familiar.

The declining cost of green construction is evident in the US solar photovoltaic (PV) market, where the installed cost of rooftop (distributed) solar PV declined over 50% between 2008 and 2015, as shown in Exhibit 9.1. Costs are now stabilizing as the market matures. In a similar vein, market observers expect that energy storage costs such as batteries will also decline significantly in the future, as manufacturing capacity increases.[2]

Exhibit 9.1 tracks cost reductions in wind, solar, lithium-ion batteries, and light-emitting diode (LED) light bulbs since 2008 and illustrates how quickly and dramatically costs can decline over a relatively short period. In situations where cost is expected to rapidly decline, investors and property owners may conclude that it is more cost effective to wait for cost trends to normalize before investing in green building technologies. For example, in the case of LED light bulbs, it

Exhibit 9.1 **Cost Reductions in Wind, Solar, Lithium-Ion Batteries, and LED Light Bulbs Since 2008 in the United States**

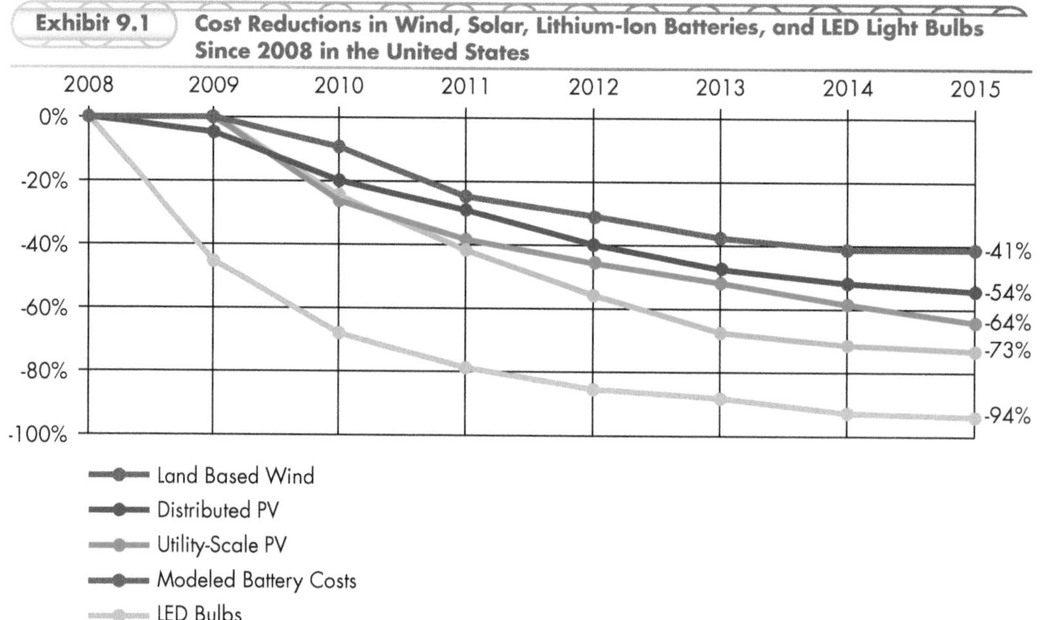

Source: US Department of Energy, "6 Charts That Will Make You Optimistic About America's Clean Energy Future," September 28, 2016, https://energy.gov/articles/6-charts-will-make-you-optimistic-about-america-s-clean-enerav-future.

2. For example, the 35 gigawatt-hour (GWh) production capacity of the 5.8-million-sq.-ft. "Gigafactory" being developed by Tesla and Panasonic will produce more lithium-ion batteries annually than the amount produced worldwide in 2013. This factory is expected to reduce the per-kWh price of batteries by 30% when it is completed in 2018. (Tesla, "Tesla Gigafactory," accessed March 28, 2017, www.tesla.com/gigafactory).

was clearly worth waiting for the price to decline before commencing a lighting retrofit incorporating LED fixtures. Put another way, the opportunity cost of investing in LED lighting in 2008 turned out to be quite significant, even though the magnitude and timing of the cost decline was unknown at that time. This is an example of the option value of waiting when prices are falling. As the rate of price decline decelerates, the option value of waiting declines as well, making investment in the new technology less risky. Subsidies by utilities or other entities may help bridge the cost gap initially, making upgrades to new technology financially feasible earlier in the cycle and thus effectively reducing the option value of waiting. Once costs stabilize, the option value of waiting to install LED lighting or other energy efficient technology may well switch to an option cost, as the opportunity cost of the energy savings outweighs potential future price declines.

Solar PV also demonstrates the potential for market expectations to change over time, often due to unintended or unexpected consequences. As solar PV has grown, so too have concerns over net energy metering (NEM) and grid capacity as the electrical grid adapts to distributed energy generation from intermittent sources like solar PV and wind. One solution is to add storage capacity to the grid. Regulatory and market forces may result in rooftop solar PV systems that include a battery back-up or energy storage. The current cost of storage renders solar PV with storage economically infeasible as of this writing, but that may change in the future as major battery manufacturing facilities are placed in service to meet the growing demand for electric vehicles.

While solar PV is an extreme case, the general decline in costs in the early stages of market adoption is a common trend in green building that heightens the importance of obtaining current cost estimates rather than relying on historical costs.

Component Costs, Systems Integration, and Synergies

Commercial cost services such as the Marshall and Swift Valuation Service and RS Means can be useful guides when the marginal cost of a particular item is needed, such as the marginal cost of triple-pane versus dual-pane windows or the added cost of wood that is certified as sustainable and carries a Forest Stewardship Council (FSC) rating. However, when these services are used to cost entire structures rather than component costs, caution is warranted to avoid unintended duplication (or double-counting) of costs.

Double-counting of green costs when using cost-estimating manuals and services can result from the following:

- Building code requirements that incorporate green components

- Misinterpretation or misapplication of total cost versus marginal cost for green components
- The effect on total costs of integrated systems and synergies

In the first case, green building costs could be double-counted due to the fact that certain jurisdictions may require green building components for all new buildings or major renovations. The statewide CALGreen building code in California is one example. Some municipalities even within California have enacted more stringent codes and requirements, such as mandating minimum levels of solar PV or requiring a vegetated covering for a portion of the roof. Since cost services base their estimates on local conditions, the cost service estimates should at least theoretically include the costs of the basic green components required to meet local codes. Assuming that the cost manual estimates are up to date, the costs of the vegetated roof and solar PV would therefore already be reflected in the base building costs in areas where these items are required by code. However, green building and green building requirements are evolving (sometimes rapidly), and it may be difficult for cost-estimating services to remain fully up to date. When developing a replacement cost estimate, research into the specific requirements of both state and local codes may be required, along with confirmation that the cost manual or service being used reflects these current requirements.

The second potential problem arises through a misinterpretation or misapplication of the green component costs reported by the cost service or another source, such as the construction cost budget. Component cost estimates for green features that represent the total cost of the system rather than the marginal cost over and above that of a code-compliant building would require a deduction for the cost of the conventional system that would be included in a code-compliant building. For example, assume that a conventional, code-compliant building is estimated at $175 per square foot, including local and time multipliers and based on a cost-estimating manual. In this area, the building code could be satisfied with a conventional roof-mounted package HVAC system. However, the subject property will have a geothermal heat pump system. In order to properly cost the building and avoid double-counting, only the marginal cost of the geothermal system over the conventional HVAC should be added to the $175 per square foot cost of the code-compliant building. So if the green component cost derived from the cost manual reflects the total cost of the geothermal system and not the marginal cost, then the avoided cost of the conventional system should be deducted from the geothermal system cost. Conversely, there would be no further necessary adjustment if the reported cost for the geothermal system is the marginal cost over and above that of a conventional system.

A "whole building" approach that results in an integrated design and synergies within building systems is a third area of potential double-counting when developing the cost approach. Component costs derived from cost-estimating manuals or services do not typically reflect potential synergies between green building components that may reduce costs or eliminate the need for a mechanical system or other feature. For example, automated shades that reduce heat gain to the building allow for a reduction in the cooling system capacity. Dual or triple glazing has a similar effect. Substituting LED for incandescent lighting will reduce heat gain from the lighting system. Exposing the concrete floors and walls to the ambient air to leverage thermal massing can also reduce heating and cooling loads. Adding a tightly sealed building envelope with above-standard wall and ceiling insulation furthers these same goals. When these strategies and features are implemented together in an integrated manner, a much smaller HVAC system is likely to be required. When a combination of design strategies or features is implemented in an integrated fashion, there are likely to be cost offsets in other areas of the project that may or may not be obvious but should be taken into consideration. Case Study 9.A illustrates how synergistic design strategies reduced the marginal cost of the sustainable improvements in a 1970s-era office building by nearly 50%, from $45 per square foot to $25 per square foot.

Case Study 9.A Reducing Costs through Synergies

The speculative shell renovation of an obsolete 1970s-era California office building was budgeted under two scenarios: as a conventional building and as a sustainable renovation. The latter scenario included significant upgrades to the building envelope, a mixed-mode ventilation system including operable windows with rooftop heat pumps, and a rooftop solar PV sized to provide 80% of the energy use for the building.

Before considering the solar PV, the sustainable renovation reflected a significant premium of $45 per square foot to conventional construction costs of $86 per square foot, or almost 50%. However, the sustainable premium was reduced to $25 per square foot (29%) due to a variety of offsets made possible by the sustainable renovation, as shown in Exhibit 9.2.

The major cost offsets included reducing the conventional package rooftop HVAC from over 100 tons to less than 20 tons, due to the building envelope upgrades and natural ventilation system. This change also reduced the need to upgrade the roof structure and eliminated the need for HVAC smoke detectors. The sustainable renovation also left the interior of the concrete tilt-up panel walls exposed to the interior to allow harnessing of the thermal mass effect, with insulation placed on the exterior. This design resulted in reduced costs for interior wall finishes. The open, exposed ceiling eliminated suspended acoustical tile ceiling finishes and reduced the cost of electrical distribution, resulting in further cost offsets.

Case Study 9.A (continued)

Exhibit 9.2 Cost Savings from Green Building Design Synergies

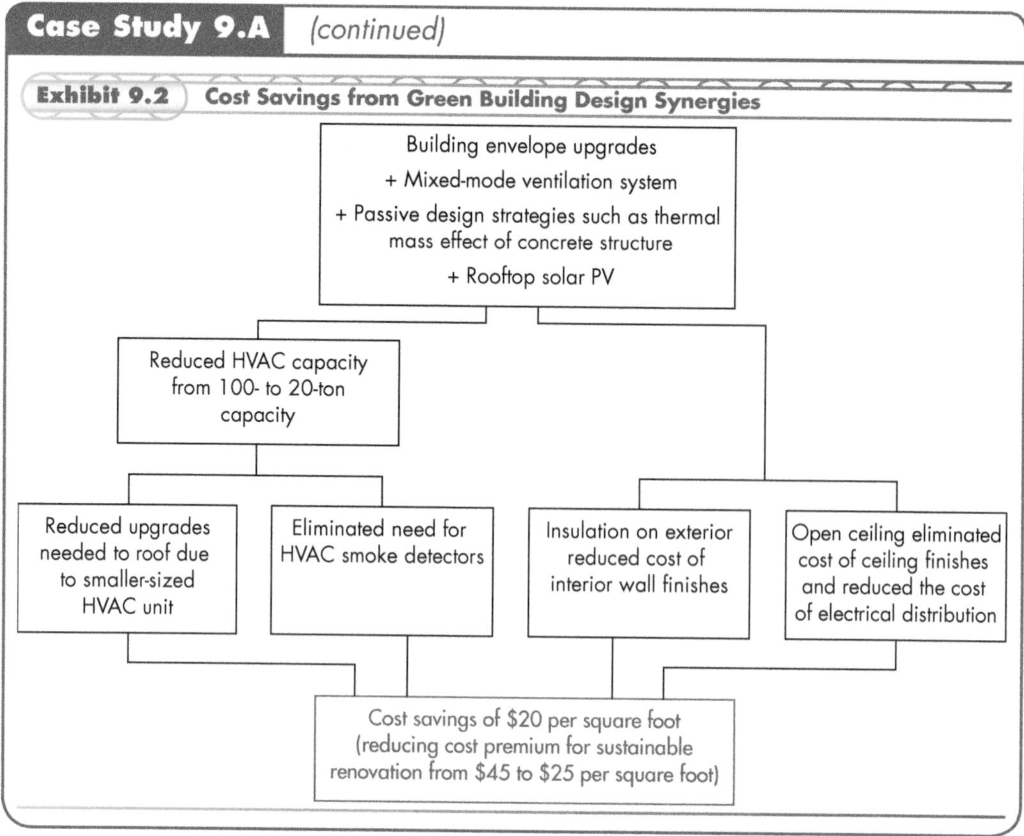

Building envelope upgrades
+ Mixed-mode ventilation system
+ Passive design strategies such as thermal mass effect of concrete structure
+ Rooftop solar PV
Reduced HVAC capacity from 100- to 20-ton capacity
Reduced upgrades needed to roof due to smaller-sized HVAC unit
Eliminated need for HVAC smoke detectors
Insulation on exterior reduced cost of interior wall finishes
Open ceiling eliminated cost of ceiling finishes and reduced the cost of electrical distribution
Cost savings of $20 per square foot (reducing cost premium for sustainable renovation from $45 to $25 per square foot)

Integrated systems may result in direct or indirect reductions in up-front costs. From a valuation standpoint, while the "whole building" approach and specifically the use of an integrative process is no guarantee that the project will achieve design, construction, and operational synergies, it significantly improves the likelihood that any potential synergies will be achieved. Perhaps even more importantly, it reduces the likelihood of direct and indirect conflicts between systems and components that might have a negative impact on the initial or operational cost or functional utility of the structure.

This design approach may also eliminate the need for capital costs that might otherwise be required for a conventional building, as seen in Case Study 9.B on the MIT Sloan School of Management.

Life-Cycle Costing

Green building practices often incorporate a shift in the timing and characterization of building costs, whereby lower operational costs over the building's life are traded for a higher up-front capital cost.

Case Study 9.B MIT Sloan School of Management Building E62

The MIT Sloan School of Management's Building E62 was conceived as a new headquarters for the business school.[3] The project's focus was on sustainability but had to meet the rigors of financial feasibility in order to obtain approval.

The six-story-plus-basement garage building is located at 100 Main Street in Cambridge, Massachusetts, and contains 215,000 square feet, excluding the 190,000-sq.- ft. underground garage. Reported construction costs totaled $142 million, or approximately $660 per square foot, excluding the garage. The design included operable windows, sunshades, a vegetated roof, and a high-performance building envelope consisting of high-performance fenestration (which includes triple-glazing, reflective finishes, and opaque glass used in various areas to manage heat gain), automated sun shades, a well-sealed building envelope, and added insulation. These design and construction practices allowed the HVAC system to be reduced by one-half, which was a direct offset to the added building envelope costs. The smaller HVAC also reduced the size of the electrical substation, resulting in an additional cost reduction. The design team reportedly used a life-cycle approach in selling the sustainable design approach to the owner by demonstrating a positive net present value of reduced energy costs relative to the initial up-front cost. The project got the go-ahead in 2007 and was completed in 2010. It was certified LEED Gold in 2011.

According to MIT, the building reportedly uses 42% less electricity than comparable MIT office/classroom buildings. Energy use for heating and cooling is about 70% lower, which translates to annual energy cost savings of $500,000 ($2.23 per square foot of above-grade space). The marginal cost of the sustainability features were reportedly $2.3 million, or 1.6% of the construction budget. The net incremental cost was reduced to $340,000 when the avoided capital cost of expanding the campus central plant was considered, which would have been required to meet the added heating and cooling demand of the building if it had been built to conventional standards.

The MIT School of Management's Building E62 in Cambridge, Massachusetts. This building renovation employed an integrated design process, which harnessed synergies resulting in significant construction cost and operational efficiencies within the building. Additionally, the reduced energy of the project meant that costly expansions to the campus heating and cooling systems could be avoided. The combination of building construction cost synergies, operational cost savings, and the avoided capital cost of the central plan expansion facilitated the project's feasibility. Photo by Sloancondev.

3. For more information, refer to Nina Kruschwitz' article titled "MIT for Managers: Can You Afford to Build Green?" *MIT Sloan Management Review* (April 11, 2016) at http://sloanreview.mit.edu/article/mit-for-managers-can-you-afford-to-build-green/?utm_source=twitter&utm_medium=social&utm_campaign=sm-direct, and the capital project overview for this building at http://capitalprojects.mit.edu/projects/mit-sloan-school-e62.

Case Study 9.B *(continued)*

This case study is atypical in that the owner of the building is the occupier, and yet the decision on whether to "go green" was predicated in large part on the same financial test an investor or owner would apply to a conventional office building–i.e., whether the added cost is justified by the measurable economic benefits. This case study also points to the importance of considering the full range of economic benefits attributable to the green or sustainable components, which in this case included the avoided cost of an expansion of the central plant to accommodate the new building's HVAC requirements.

These types of integrated systems and synergies can affect how green component costs are interpreted. Just as combining a smorgasbord of green features without consideration of each feature's impact on the operation of other systems and the whole building operation is not likely to result in positive synergies in cost, operation, or function, simply aggregating individual green component costs without regard to integrated design synergies will not yield a credible current replacement cost estimate.

For example, above-standard insulation required to meet energy performance goals will add to the construction cost of the project relative to a code-built building. Occupancy and daylight sensors for lighting are more expensive than traditional manually operated switches. The same is true for digital HVAC controls, which allow for more precise monitoring and more efficient operation of the space conditioning system. However, the higher up-front capital costs of these above-standard features (relative to a code-compliant building) are accompanied by lower operational costs in the form of reduced energy costs for operation.

While these operational cost savings may not normally be considered when analyzing the construction cost budget, they reflect a real economic benefit to the property over its economic life. The sustainability orientation of green building emphasizes considering all costs of the property over its economic life–a concept known as *life-cycle costing*. In a life cycle cost analysis, the operational and end-of-life (demolition/renovation) costs are considered together with the up-front costs, also called *first costs*, in order to more fully capture the total cost of the property from cradle to grave. The example in Case Study 9.B illustrates how life-cycle cost analysis of a project can allow for a more accurate accounting of the costs of the project over time. This practice is fundamentally different than typical construction costing practices, such as minimum bid and value engineering. These practices emphasize attaining the lowest up-front cost regardless of potentially higher operational costs, which may not be evident to the owner until the building is up and running.

Conventional appraisal theory and practice draws a clear distinction between capital costs and operational costs. However, there is clearly an interaction between the two, and the distinction may not be entirely clear in some cases. This life-cycle emphasis of green building may be one of the more challenging aspects to incorporate into appraisal theory. Nonetheless, the notion that there is a relationship between initial cost and operational or life-cycle cost is clearly embedded in the appraisal concept of economic life. A lower-quality component typically has a shorter economic life but a lower initial cost than a higher-quality component. The lower-cost component may also require a higher level of maintenance. For example, a good-quality, wood-frame office building with a painted wood exterior may have an economic life of 50 years and require repainting every five to 10 years. In contrast, a good-quality steel frame office building with a glass exterior has a much higher up-front cost, but a longer economic life of 60 years and no periodic repainting cost.

In the same vein, green building components that extend the economic life of the improvements or reduce repairs, maintenance, or re-tenanting costs may justify their higher up-front costs with lower operational costs or a longer economic life. For example, under-floor air distribution (UFAD) systems add to the initial cost for the build-out of the space relative to conventional office tenant improvements, even after considering the avoided cost of ductwork. However, the flexibility of the design, in which wiring and air distribution is contained in chases beneath a raised floor, allows for lower cost when the space needs to be reconfigured for a new tenant. Occupant comfort is often improved, since the conditioned air is distributed up from the floor and closer to the occupants, and occupants are able to control the temperature via adjustable diffusers mounted on the floor. When considering whether the higher cost of this type of build-out system contributes to market value, it would be relevant to consider the lower future tenant improvement costs as well as the potentially enhanced occupant satisfaction that may reduce turnover and thus downtime between lease-up over the asset's economic life. In addition, since UFAD systems typically reduce tenant improvement costs, their presence may be worth considering when adjusting for landlord-provided tenant improvement allowances in the market rent analysis.

Cost Allocation

In addition to a cost shift between capital and operational budgets, green building design may also alter how initial construction costs are allocated compared to a conventional building's construction budget. For instance, a construction budget for a green building may reflect higher indirect or "soft" costs than a conventional building, due to new and/or more complex design and construction processes and the use of an integrative process. Certain aspects of the green building project, such as energy or daylight modeling or working with advanced mechanical systems, may also require additional architectural and engineering design time. Third-party commissioning of the systems at start-up can also add to construction costs. These additional services will increase project costs to varying degrees. Conversely, unexpected reductions in the development budget may occur. For example, greater-than-expected demand for space in one major green renovation project resulted in pre-leasing of the project, thereby eliminating the projected absorption period and associated rent loss during stabilization.

For the valuation professional, the potential for shifts in the timing (capital versus operational) and composition (indirect versus direct) of total construction costs requires thoughtful consideration when comparing and adjusting costs for a given project. Traditional "rules of thumb" may not be as relevant for green projects, particularly when analyzing and stabilizing construction budgets.

Depreciation

In appraisal practice, depreciation is defined as "a loss in property value from any cause" or "the difference between the cost of an improvement on the effective date of the appraisal and the market value of the improvement on the same date."[4] Deductions for all applicable forms of depreciation–including physical deterioration, functional obsolescence, and external (economic) obsolescence–are a necessary step in estimating depreciated replacement cost in the cost analysis.

Physical Deterioration

Physical deterioration (often referred to less precisely as physical depreciation) is the wear and tear of the property, usually attributed to use and the elements. Physical deterioration estimates for green components may or may not be identical to those for conventional components. While sustainability may seem to imply durability of materials, a variety of other factors may play into the choice of materials used for a building. Some materials may indeed be chosen for their durability, indicating an extended economic life. Others may be selected for their ability to be recycled or reused, because they come from a rapidly renewable natural resource like bamboo, or because they are manufactured from recycled materials, such as carpet made from recycled water bottles. The six-story Bullitt Center office building in Seattle was constructed primarily of engineered wood, essentially heavy timber construction. This material was selected in large part due to the carbon sequestration feature of the wood. The wood-frame structure acts as a carbon sink, keeping the carbon out of the atmosphere. Since the

4. *The Dictionary of Real Estate Appraisal*, 6th ed. (Chicago: Appraisal Institute, 2015), 63.

manufacturing of the cement used in concrete is a carbon-intensive process, using concrete for the entire building instead of just the foundation and podium levels would have added carbon to the atmosphere instead of removing it through the use of the heavy wood framing.

Roof coverings for vegetated roofs and some "solar-ready" roofs may have longer expected economic lives and/or warranties to avoid the cost of removing the vegetation or solar equipment. Here the difference between conventional and green construction may be relatively obvious, especially if the roof covering has a longer warranty. In other cases, the difference may not be as obvious. LED lighting may look identical to conventional lighting such as fluorescent or halogen lighting, but it has a much longer service life and a higher up-front cost.

Physical deterioration deductions for green buildings should account for the same factors that affect conventional features. However, due to their relative novelty in the market, the appraiser may need to perform additional research to determine if green components differ materially from their conventional counterparts in terms of durability and economic life. Some materials may be specifically selected for their durability and/or ease of maintenance, which would suggest a reduced exposure to physical deterioration. Other components may have reduced durability and/or increased maintenance requirements.

Functional Obsolescence

Functional obsolescence can originate from either a deficiency or flaw in the structure, materials, or design of a building's improvements, or from a superadequacy of the improvements. In either case, the critical determinant is how the improvements compare to market norms and expectations.[5] It may be easiest to consider how green building may result in an overimprovement, or superadequacy; this issue is discussed in the following section. However, it is also possible that a green building feature or design strategy may lead to a functional deficiency. In one case, the use of a mixed-mode HVAC system that incorporated operable windows for natural ventilation created a noise nuisance on one side of the building. This side of the building faced an industrial warehouse building, and that neighbor's loading activities created an unwanted disturbance throughout the day that could have been eliminated with a different design choice. In this example, the adverse influence is eliminated when the windows are closed. Failing to anticipate this adverse influence in the design process created a functional flaw in the property.

Conversely, in markets where green buildings are more common and sustainability orientation is high, buildings that do not meet minimum standards expected by the market may face a competitive disadvantage, creating a functional deficiency. In some Class A office markets, LEED certification is required in order to remain on the

5. *The Appraisal of Real Estate*, 14th ed. (Chicago: Appraisal Institute, 2013), 623.

short list of properties toured by the most desirable tenants. In markets where sustainable features are expected or required, the functional utility risk to existing buildings can be measured as the cost to cure the deficiency if the cost to cure is less than the incremental value enhancement (curable obsolescence).

Perhaps the greater risk in such markets is incurable obsolescence, when correcting the defect is either financially infeasible or physically impossible. If the cost to cure exceeds the value enhancement, the property suffers a permanent diminution in value known as *incurable obsolescence.* Consider an office market where tenants now prefer small floor plate space with shallow bay depths so that all employees have views of the outdoors and daylighting strategies are optimized. A large floor plate back-office building of 1980s vintage may not be adaptable to this new market standard at any cost, which could relegate the property to a lower market tier and adversely impact value. Furthermore, if the tenants also desire access to public transit that the property's suburban office park location lacks, this functional deficiency could affect marketability, attainable rents, and the property's market position. In an extreme case, significant obsolescence can raise a highest and best use issue and demolition and redevelopment may be the most productive use of a site improved with obsolete improvements. In this respect, understanding the sustainability orientation of the market becomes relevant to both the obsolescence estimate and the highest and best use analysis.[6]

Superadequacy

The special form of functional obsolescence known as superadequacy can impact green buildings just as it can affect conventional buildings.[7] Superadequacy may in some cases require a negative adjustment if, for example, a component of the property adds additional maintenance or other costs to the property. In the case of an oversized solar PV system, the replacement cost estimate would assume an appropriately sized system, which would essentially subsume a depreciation deduction for the superadequate component. As long as the midterm capital cost of the inverter replacement was based on the appropriately sized PV system, there would not likely be additional deductions for superadequacy from the replacement cost estimate.

Market conditions may also change what is considered superadequate over time. For example, high-performance features such as electrical vehicle charging stations might have been considered atypical in a given market five years ago, but may now be demanded by the market or even required by local building codes. In the previous case of

6. Chapter 8 explores the effects of sustainability and green building on highest and best use analysis.

7. The process for considering the presence of superadequacy and adjusting appropriately is discussed in more depth in *The Appraisal of Real Estate*, 14th ed.

a building with an oversized PV system, the oversized system may provide capacity for increased demand for daytime EV charging, as market demand changes. In this case, the superadequacy would be temporary.

External Obsolescence

External obsolescence arises from externalities, which in appraisal are factors outside the property that nonetheless affect property value.[8] Externalities can have a positive or negative effect on property value. Common examples of negative externalities include street noise or an off-site odor. Proximity to transit or well-maintained properties are examples of positive externalities.[9]

A preference for alternate means of commuting and proximity to walkable amenities could become a negative externality for an aging suburban office park constructed in an area with limited access to transit and few on-site amenities. While single-use office and business parks with abundant parking situated adjacent to the freeway were state-of-the-art suburban developments when they were originally constructed, market tastes and desires have shifted in many areas toward mixed-use developments offering the opportunity to live, work, and play in one place, without sole reliance on automobile transportation. The cost to subsidize the local public transit system or to provide private shuttles would be one way to measure the impact of the lack of transit externality using the cost approach. The negative externality of a lack of on-site walkable amenities may be reflected in several ways:

- The opportunity cost of converting previously high office rent-generating space to lower-rent amenity space that might include multiple food vendors, child care, or education services
- The marginal cost of subsidizing certain desirable amenities
- The cost to convert the space and build it out for the new use

In more extreme cases, the demolition of existing office buildings may be necessary to facilitate "placemaking" via a mixed-use retail-entertainment facility with multifamily housing. This would create the walkable amenities in place of what was previously a primarily single-use office park.[10]

While it may not always be curable, external obsolescence can be temporary. For example, the external obsolescence adjustment to a

---

8. This definition of *externalities* is specific to real estate. Inasmuch as the effect is outside the property or transaction but is nonetheless value-affecting, it echoes the definition of *externalities* offered in Chapter 4 as it pertains to sustainability: "Externalities are the effects of an activity not anticipated or paid for at the time of the event. Externality risk is the risk that these costs will be charged back, or internalized, to the source."
9. *The Dictionary of Real Estate Appraisal*, 6th ed., 83.
10. The sidebar on suburban sustainability in Chapter 7 (page 134) showcases the example of the Bishop Ranch suburban office park development, which has taken steps to address external obsolescence.

conventional building for a temporary market downturn that creates adverse market conditions and depressed rents should reflect the likely duration of the downturn and the likelihood of the market recovering to healthy conditions. In such a case, simply capitalizing the rent differential may overstate the external obsolescence affecting the property.

Similarly, there may be inadequate market evidence to support the cost of green features, particularly in early-stage, sustainability-oriented markets. For example, the higher cost of the green features may not be fully justified by currently attainable market rents, improved marketability leading to faster absorption and reduced downtime, reduced operating cost, lower risk, or other measurable indicators. However, to the extent that the obsolescence is due to the market's sustainability orientation or appetite for green buildings, any adjustment should also consider the potential for the market to move toward a greater sustainability orientation, as well as the likely pace of such change. Finally, since appraisal theory assumes a knowledgeable buyer, the potential for increased market awareness may affect the demand for green features in the future.

Rebates and Incentives

Certain green building components and practices may qualify for direct rebates, sales tax abatement, property tax abatement, income tax credits, accelerated depreciation, or in some areas, Renewable Energy Credits, also known as RECs.

The role of rebates and incentives in the cost approach is to reduce the cost disparity between conventional and green building materials and practices. Rebates and incentives are often temporary in nature and may decline over time, or have a specified life. In the cost approach, these incentives should be considered to the extent that the market considers them and only if they are commonly available *at the time of the appraisal* to all market participants. Chapter 11 further discusses the effects of rebates and incentives on the valuation process.

Green Building Impacts in the Sales Comparison Approach

The sales comparison approach to value relies on the direct comparison of transactions of comparable properties to the subject property. As such, the approach relies on an active transactional market of similar properties. The approach is "applicable to most types of real property interests when there are sufficient recent, reliable transactions to indicate value patterns or trends in the market."[11] The lack of comparable green, sustainable, or high-performance properties is often cited as a weakness of this approach and may even be put forth

11. *The Appraisal of Real Estate*, 14th ed., 380.

as an argument that no value enhancement accrues to the property for its green features. While data limitations are real and likely to continue to be a factor for the foreseeable future, the mere fact that comparable properties are not readily available does not necessarily mean that the market does not value these features or properties.

Commercial appraisal is rife with instances in which cost-based or income-based adjustments are required to properly adjust comparable sale transactions. For example, consider a residential condominium project in which the subject units have homeowner association (HOA) dues that are significantly higher than those of comparable units. It is not uncommon to apply an income-based adjustment using a discounted cash flow (DCF) analysis of the HOA differential over the expected tenure of the typical owner. Similarly, income-based adjustments for signs or cell towers may be necessary when those features contribute measurable value but comparable market data is lacking. The typical rent loss and lease-up cost analysis for a non-stabilized property is, essentially, a cost-based adjustment applied to the income capitalization approach, and often the sales comparison approach as well.

The following sections discuss implementation of the sales comparison approach when some level of green, sustainable, or high-performance data is available. It also offers examples of income-based and cost-based adjustments that can be considered when more directly comparable data is lacking.

Elements of Comparison

Identifying the relevant characteristics for comparison purposes is central to the successful implementation of the sales comparison approach. Referred to as *elements of comparison*, these characteristics are used to compare the comparable properties to the subject property as well as to each other and form the basis for the adjustment process. Property rights conveyed, market conditions, location, and economic characteristics are but a few of the common elements of comparison for a conventional commercial property.

For green properties, these elements of comparison still apply. However, there are additional elements of comparison to consider, the identity and relevance of which may vary with the local market. Identifying what elements matter requires market research, beginning with identification of the most probable buyer.[12]

Who Is "The Market?"

Market value is what "the market" values. The goal of identifying elements of comparison is to set the stage for relevant and supportable adjustments that narrow the range of the comparable property purchase

12. The *most probable buyer* is not an individual but rather a class of buyers who share common characteristics. Examples of classes of most probable buyers are owner-users and investors.

prices, facilitating the development of a credible value conclusion from the sales comparison approach. Thus, before any element of comparison can even be judged for relevancy, the most probable buyer–"the market" for the asset–must be identified. Identifying the most probable buyer is usually accomplished as part of the highest and best use analysis.

Investors often have different thresholds and metrics for value than owner-users, whether the property is green or conventional. As a result, the elements of comparison most relevant for owner-users may not matter as much or at all to investors. Consider the case of a predominantly vacant commercial building. The user sees the vacancy as a positive feature in terms of its utility in meeting the user's space needs. The investor, in contrast, may view the vacancy as upside potential but will also likely consider the costs necessary to stabilize the asset. In this case, the element of comparison–occupancy–requires very different adjustments depending on the most probable buyer.[13]

In the case of a green building, identification of the most probable buyer is just as critical. Whether an adjustment for green features is indicated, for precisely what characteristics, and the magnitude and direction of the adjustment may hinge on whether the most probable buyer is a sustainability-minded owner-user, a small investor focused primarily on near-term returns, an institutional investor with sustainability-reporting requirements, or some other class of potential buyers.

Furthermore, the relevant element of comparison may differ among asset classes even within the same buyer class. Investors who buy both retail and office properties may look to different elements of comparison for green and conventional features when assessing each of these property types. Energy Star ratings and energy use intensity (EUI) may be more important in the office portion of that investor's portfolio–in which the leases are full service gross and the landlord therefore captures the energy savings–than they are in the retail portion of the portfolio, in which the triple-net lease structure apportions the energy cost savings to the tenant.[14] On the other hand, the energy metrics of both components of the portfolio may be important to the institutional investor in order to calculate whole-building energy use and greenhouse gas/carbon intensity for sustainability-reporting purposes.

As these examples illustrate, correctly identifying the most probable buyer is the critical first step when judging which elements of comparison are worthy of consideration in the adjustment process. Some of the potential elements of comparison unique to green buildings are discussed in the sections that follow.

---

13. For example, if the most probable buyer is an owner-user, no adjustment may be indicated. Conversely, if the most probable buyer is an investor, a downward adjustment for stabilization costs is likely necessary.

14. EUI is discussed later in this chapter as well as in the sidebar on site versus source energy use (page 192).

Third-Party Certification

In some markets, a third-party green building certification, such as a LEED certification, may be what the market uses to differentiate these properties from their conventional counterparts.[15] However, many certification rating systems, including LEED, certify at incrementally more stringent levels. Thus, what may matter more than the mere presence of a particular certification is the specific certification award level. In other words, it may not be enough to just be LEED-certified at any level (Certified, Silver, Gold, or Platinum), but rather, the market may require at least a LEED Gold certification to meet Class A office building standards. In addition, the minimum threshold may increase over time due to competitive pressures, motivating building owners to recertify their buildings at higher levels to maintain competitive position or attain a market advantage. Finally, since the green building certification standards typically increase in rigor over time, certifying a building under the more recently released standard, such as LEED Version 4, may reflect or imply a superior level of "greenness" relative to a building certified under an earlier version.

Comprehensive rating schemes such as LEED, Green Globes, the Building Research Establishment Environmental Assessment Method (BREEAM), and the Living Building Challenge (LBC) focus on multiple attributes. More recently, certifications that focus on a single attribute or area have emerged. For example, space users who value occupant health and well-being may see the more recently released WELL Building Standard or Fitwel certification as important characteristics. The SITES certification focuses on sustainable site development and landscaping practices. In addition to its comprehensive rating, the LBC also certifies projects as ZE based on an analysis of post-occupancy energy use over a 12-month period.

Because certifications and labels vary in what they measure and certify, the valuation professional must be familiar with both what the market views as relevant and what the particular certification represents. Understanding what the market reacts to is most relevant for selecting the elements of comparison for the sales comparison approach, while understanding what the certification represents has implications that extend to the other approaches to value. In other words, it may be enough to know that the market is cognizant of green certifications and that these spaces tend to lease faster or attain a rent premium for the green certification to be considered an element of comparison. However, making an adjustment based on that element of comparison likely requires an understanding of how various green certification ratings differ in terms of what they measure and how the certification is earned.

15. See Chapter 2 for an in-depth discussion of the types of rating systems and how they may affect the valuation process.

Using Modeled or Predicted Energy Performance in the Valuation Process

Actual building performance is influenced by a variety of factors that are outside the control of the designers, engineers, and construction contractors. Most notably, occupant behavior and the owner's operational decisions can confound the most rigorous and well-supported energy modeling assumptions. Predicting actual energy performance is not unlike modeling future cash flows in a DCF analysis for a multitenant property in that the actual cash flows rarely match the prediction. This fact alone does not make the DCF an unreliable indicator of value, particularly if market participants use it and the appraisal assumptions align with those of the market. However, DCFs are not always the best *predictors* of future cash flows. Even so, if similar assumptions are applied, the DCF can be an excellent tool for comparing financial performance between comparable properties or between the subject and the comparable properties. It can also be used as a sensitivity tool to measure the impact of a changing rental growth rate or turnover cost assumptions.

In the same vein, energy modeling can be a reliable tool for comparing properties and as an indicator of which property has the potential to operate more efficiently. Assuming that the energy modeling assumptions are reliable, a building *designed* to be 25% more energy efficient than a code-compliant building should be expected to *actually perform* more efficiently and use less energy than a comparable code-compliant building. All else being equal, the more efficient building should still have a comparatively lower EUI than the code-compliant building even if occupant density is higher—resulting in a higher energy load from the HVAC—or the tenants work longer hours than predicted, resulting in higher lighting and plug loads.

There are pros and cons to relying on modeled versus actual performance. Appraisers are more experienced dealing with actual, measured performance in the form of historical operating expenses including energy, water/sewer, and other building expenses. The weakness of this approach is that occupant and owner behavior can skew the results, often without the appraiser's knowledge.

Consider two multitenant suburban office buildings that are of similar size, construction, and vintage located side by side in the same market. They are exposed to identical climate and market forces. They have the same level of insulation, the same HVAC vintage, and the same lighting. They are leased on a full-service basis at a similar rent for five years, with the landlord being responsible for the utilities. Theoretically, the energy cost should be the same or very similar for these buildings. However, if Building A is occupied at a density that is 30% higher than its neighbor Building B and includes an energy-intensive server room that Building B lacks, the energy use profile of Building A will be higher. If the operating expenses for Building A are stabilized based on a historical operation that is 25% higher than Building B, the net operating income (*NOI*) of Building A will be reduced by the marginally higher energy cost and the value by the income capitalization approach will be negatively impacted.[16] Should the higher energy use of Building A's occupant make the building worth less than its neighbor? Put another way, by analyzing actual energy use in direct capitalization, is it the building or the occupant behavior that is being valued?

In this respect, a predictive energy model may be a more reliable indicator of the energy efficiency of the building itself than the actual measured performance, unless the appraiser considers the differences in occupancy and operation. Ideally, both modeled and actual performance data should be obtained, and any differences reconciled. However, in the everyday world of appraisal practice, this level of detail is not likely to be common. Whether actual or modeled performance is a more reliable measure for appraisal purposes is arguably less important than being clear on which data set is being relied upon.

In this office building example, the valuation question echoes the "mark-to-market" debate. If additional operating expense comparables supported significantly lower energy costs similar to Building B, it may be prudent to use the lower market-based utility expenses in developing the *NOI* for direct capitalization. Then the appraiser can adjust for the higher utility cost borne by the landlord until the lease expires as a line-item adjustment based on the discounted present value of the over-standard expense for the remainder of the lease term.

16. This situation highlights one of the cost-benefit misalignments that green leases seek to address through, for example, the submetering of energy and water for equipment that places above-standard demands on these resources (see the sidebar titled "What Is a Green Lease?" later in this chapter (page 213)).

As discussed in Chapter 2, many certification systems focus mostly or entirely on the design and construction aspects of the property rather than its operation. Thus, these design-focused certifications may not measure actual post-occupancy performance, such as energy or water use. It may be relatively easy to identify the construction cost approach impacts of such certifications but not so easy to identify operational impacts. If the certification is based on design and construction and does not also measure post-occupancy performance, the impact of the green features on the operating expenses in the income capitalization approach may not have the needed support until the property has been up and running at stabilized occupancy. The accompanying sidebar on using modeled, or predicted, energy performance in the valuation process discusses the potential pitfalls surrounding the use of modeled energy performance data.

The various rating systems differ in terms of whether certifications rely on predicted (modeled) or actual (historical) performance. There may be differences even within the same certification program. For example, the USGBC's LEED program consists of a variety of tracks that apply to various types of buildings. Most of the initial LEED tracks applied to new construction or renovation projects and were originally referred to as New Construction (NC). They are now referred to under the umbrella category of Building Design and Construction (BD+C).[17] For projects focused on interior renovations such as tenant improvements, the original track was labeled Commercial Interiors (CI) but is now referred to as Interior Design and Construction (ID+C). The names of each of these certification tracks illustrate their focus on design and construction. They were not originally intended to certify actual performance. The USGBC subsequently developed ratings for existing buildings, originally labeled as Existing Buildings Operations and Maintenance (EBOM), which is now referred to simply as Operations and Maintenance (O+M). The O+M tracks are focused on the ongoing operation of the property and thus include measured performance metrics such as energy and water use, which other LEED tracks generally do not.

In some cases, LEED or other green building certifications may be less important than energy use and/or greenhouse gas emissions. In these cases, the Energy Star certification and associated rating may be the more relevant element of comparison. NZE buildings (also known as *zero energy buildings*) may also appeal to markets where energy use and greenhouse gas emissions matter to the occupants, owners, or both. Alternately, EUI may be important to a property owner reporting energy use as part of a sustainability reporting program required by investors, such as the Global Real Estate Sustain-

17. The BD+C category encompasses new construction and major renovations. In the current version of LEED (v4), the category is further divided into New Construction, Core and Shell, schools, retail, data centers, warehouses and distribution centers, hospitality, and healthcare.

ability Benchmark (GRESB), the Global Reporting Initiative (GRI), or the Sustainability Accounting Standards Board (SASB).

Energy Use Intensity

In addition to certifications and ratings, the energy use of a building can be used to compare the relative efficiency of a property's design, construction, and operation. EUI is the element of comparison in this case. EUI is most often based on gross "conditioned" building area, meaning the area serviced by HVAC, but it can also be based on the number of full-time equivalent occupants or the economic production of the space. The most common energy measurement is in thousands of British thermal units (kBtus), but kilowatt-hours (kWh) may also be used. In most cases, measurement is taken at the utility meter. This measurement is referred to as *site energy use.* However, some databases use source energy, which includes the energy lost in generation and transmission, as discussed in the accompanying sidebar on site versus source energy use.

EUI has intuitive appeal as an element of comparison metric in the sales comparison approach. Like historical operating income and expenses, EUI is an actual, measured quantity that is free of the ambiguities of projected, modeled estimates.

Site EUI for the subject property can be calculated rather simply based on actual energy use as reflected in the utility meter bill for electricity or natural gas. In the case of a delivered fuel like heating oil, site EUI for the subject property can be calculated based on energy use as reflected in the quantity delivered on the fuel invoice. The various fuel amounts can be converted to a common basis such

Site versus Source Energy Use

Energy use in buildings is often compared using EUI. It is typically expressed as kBtu of energy used per square foot and can be thought of as analogous to *NOI* per square foot. However, unlike *NOI*, lower is better with EUI.

While EUI is usually measured in kBtus, it can be measured in kWh per square foot as well.[18] So far, this metric is fairly clear and straightforward. As long as you keep your kBtus and kWhs straight and use a common building area measurement, everything should work out, right?

Not quite so fast. As it turns out, *where* you measure the energy use also matters. Is the energy use measured at the site via a utility meter or at the source of generation, such as the power plant? Why does it matter?

The difference has to do with whether the energy is delivered in a raw state or a finished, ready-to-use form. Raw energy such as natural gas or fuel oil is referred to as a primary energy source. It needs to be combusted on site to provide heat or to run a steam turbine that generates electricity, as happens in an on-site cogeneration (cogen) or combined heat and power (CHP) facility.[19] In contrast, a secondary fuel source like electricity or district steam arrives on site ready to use in its finished form. No additional processing is required. However, what arrives on site represents only a fraction of the total energy that was used to generate the ener-

18. Building area is usually gross "conditioned" building area, meaning space that is heated and cooled. This could include an enclosed garage in some climate zones. Care should be taken to discern the building area basis used, since the inclusion of a large parking garage could affect the EUI of a building relative to one without a garage.

19. Combustion is the most common method of converting raw fuel to useable energy. However, fuel cells convert raw fuels to energy via a chemical reaction that does not involve combustion.

gy and then transport it to the site. In the process of burning the fossil fuels or other fuel to generate the electricity, energy is lost, primarily to heat. The process of transmitting the energy across high-voltage power lines, including stepping up the voltage and then stepping it back down, results in yet another point of energy loss. By the time it reaches the site, less than one-third of the total energy used to generate and transmit the delivered electricity remains. In contrast, 95% of the source energy of a primary fuel source like natural gas arrives at the site. Thus, site energy measurements do not fully capture the cost of the energy that arrives on the site. Perhaps more importantly, comparing energy use metrics like EUI at the site can be misleading since comparing primary energy to secondary energy is like comparing apples to oranges in terms of total energy use.

The following example compares a hypothetical building's energy use based on six different heating systems with varying efficiency and fuel mixes. The heat load is held constant, and the resulting energy use (both site and source) is shown for various fuel mixes. Depending on the fuel mix, site energy use varies from 250 to 1,818 MBtus, while source energy use ranges from 785 to 3,140 MBtus. Interestingly, however, the least efficient option on a source basis (electrical resistance such as base board heaters) would be the third *most* efficient option on a site energy basis, behind only the two heat pump systems. Also worth noting is that while the air source heat pump uses less than 40% of the site energy of a district steam system, the source energy use of both systems is nearly identical. In both of the examples noted, the energy embedded in the generation and delivery of electricity explains the different rankings when energy use of these heating system options is compared on a source-versus-site basis.

Exhibit 9.3 Efficiency Comparison of Energy Sources

					Energy Use (MBtus)		
	Heating Fuel	**Heating System**	**System**	**Efficiency**	**Site**	**Source**	**Source-to-Site Ratio**
A	Electric	Resistance	N/A	Inefficient	1,000	3,140	3.14
B	Natural Gas	Boiler	55%	Inefficient	1,818	1,909	1.05
C	Natural Gas	Boiler	80%	Efficient	1,250	1,313	1.05
D	District Steam	Steam	95%	Efficient	1,053	1,264	1.20
E	Electric	Air Source Heat Pump	COP 2.5*	Efficient	400	1,256	3.14
F	Electric	Geothermal Heat Pump	COP 4.0*	Highly Efficient	250	785	3.14

* COP = Coefficient of Performance, a measure of heat pump efficiency. Higher COP = more efficient.

Source: Energy Star, "Portfolio Manager Technical Reference: Source Energy," accessed March 29, 2017, www.energystar.gov/buildings/tools-and-resources/portfolio-manager-technical-reference-source-energy.

So, if source energy is the superior metric, why is site energy used so widely? Perhaps the main reason is that measuring energy use at the meter is easy to do. In addition, when comparing similar properties within a local market, the fuel source is often similar and the site-to-source conversion does not impact the results. Furthermore, building codes and standards typically focus on what happens inside the four walls of the building. They often do not apply to (and may lack authority over) what happens before the energy or materials reach the site.

Finally, when design teams pursue high-performance ratings like NZE status, the impact of off-site energy losses is diminished. If a building generates electricity on site such as with solar PV, the fuel cost is essentially free of generation and transmission losses, other than the system losses inherent in the solar PV system itself.

While site EUI may be the metric most often encountered by the valuation professional in the field, databases maintained by the Department of Energy and the Energy Star Portfolio Manager use source EUI as the default. This convention can lead to confusion, particularly when seeking comparative EUI data. An option is often (but not always) provided to switch between the two. Whether source or site energy is used to measure building performance, the important point for valuation professionals is to use care not to mix comparisons of site versus source energy use when analyzing and reporting data.

as kBtus using appropriate conversion factors. Conversion factors for common fuels follow:

Electricity:	1 kilowatt-hour = 3.412 kBtu
Natural gas:	1 cubic foot = 1.028 kBtu*
Heating fuel oil:	1 gallon = 137.381 kBtu*

* Based on US consumption, 2014

Source: US Energy Information Administration, www.eia.gov/energyexplained/index.cfm?page=about_energy_conversion_calculator.

While energy use data for the subject property can be obtained from historical utility bills, energy use for the comparable properties may be more difficult, depending on the property location. In certain cities and at least one state (California), benchmarking and disclosure laws require property owners to periodically report energy use. A map of jurisdictions where benchmarking laws are in effect as of February 2017 is shown in Exhibit 9.4.[20]

Other sources of energy use data include national databases such as the Commercial Building Energy Consumption Survey (CBECS), a periodic survey of the actual energy use of a variety of building types across the United States. The US Energy Information Administration (EIA) collects and reports on a wide variety of energy use data as well.

The Building Performance Database (BPD), maintained by the US Department of Energy's Office of Energy Efficiency and Renewable Energy, is purported to be the nation's largest dataset of information about commercial and residential buildings' energy-related characteristics.[21] The information is culled from a variety of federal, state, and local private and public sources and is reported anonymously. This database has filters for a variety of building characteristics including use, location, physical characteristics, and operating/occupancy characteristics. Its primary limitation is data availability, particularly for some use types and geographic areas. However, it is nonetheless a useful source for assessing general property operational ranges.

In practice, using EUI data as an element of comparison may not always yield expected results. Issues such as differences in occupancy and occupant-dependent energy use can distort apples-to-apples comparisons. Case Study 9.C discusses the limitations of using EUI data as an element of comparison by examining four different Class A properties in the same CBD in terms of various factors, including EUI. This study reveals some surprising results regarding the use of EUI data when analyzing and comparing properties.

20. Benchmarking requirements are particularly fluid and geographically disparate. For current policies in the United States, visit www.imt.org/resources/detail/map-u.s.-building-benchmarking-policies.

21. https://energy.gov/eere/buildings/building-performance-database

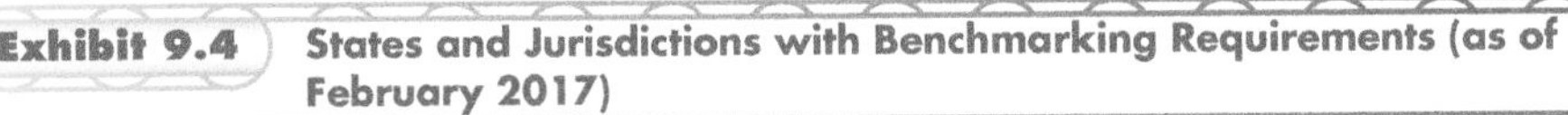

Exhibit 9.4 **States and Jurisdictions with Benchmarking Requirements (as of February 2017)**

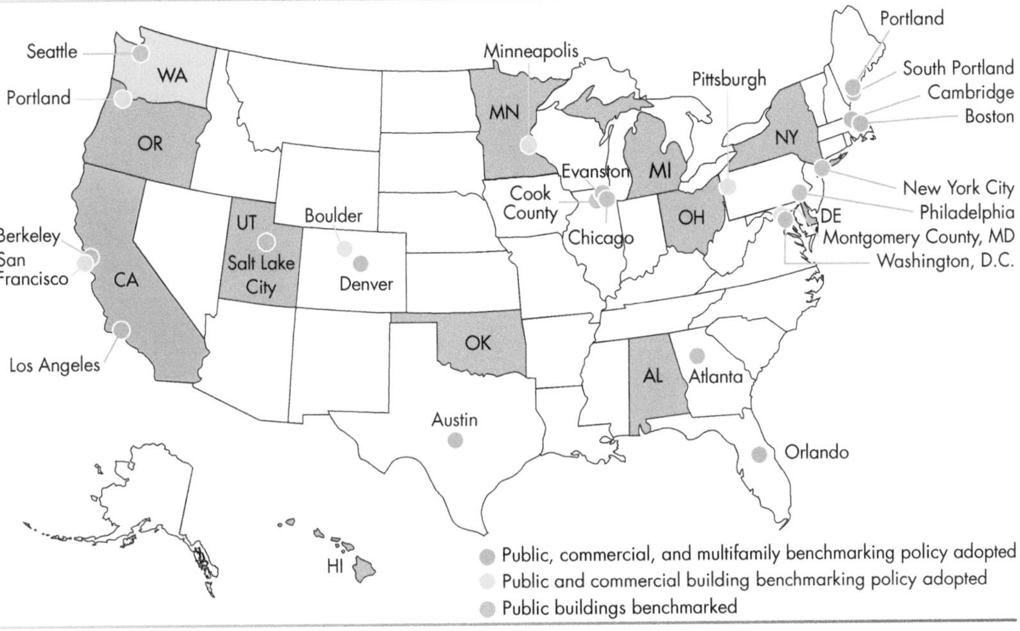

Graphic by the Institute for Market Transformation (IMT).

Case Study 9.C Energy Use Intensity as an Element of Comparison

Analysis of publicly available benchmarking data can lead to some unexpected results and point out the limitations of relying on EUI alone to assess building energy efficiency. Consider the following reported EUI data from five large office buildings located in the same CBD, as shown in Exhibit 9.5.

Comparables A and B are similar in size and vintage, so they were likely built to the same building codes. Yet Comparable A uses almost twice as much energy as Comparable B, even though it has a higher LEED rating. In contrast, Comparable C is almost 80 years older than Comparable B and has a similar LEED certification level, yet it uses less energy than Comparable B and achieves a respectable Energy Star rating of 83.

Comparable D is located across the street from Comparable A and is 37 years older, yet it uses half the energy of Comparable A. However, Comparable D's Energy Star rating of 61 is far inferior to the rating of Comparable C, which is 41 years older.

Comparable E, built in 1958, uses more energy per square foot than any of the other properties, even more than Comparable C, a pre-World War II building that was built 27 years earlier. Comparable E earned an Energy Star rating of 6, meaning that 94% of Comparable E's peers use less energy than it does.

Case Study 9.C *(continued)*

Exhibit 9.5 **Energy Use Intensity Data for Five Office Buildings**

	Comparable A	Comparable B	Comparable C	Comparable D	Comparable E
Year built	2009	2010	1931	1972	1958
Gross sq. ft.	2,245,112	2,152,863	2,812,739	1,188,090	849,024
Stories	55	44	102	41	38
Site EUI (kBtu/sq. ft.)	209.4	109.7	82.2	103.8	218.9
LEED	Platinum	Gold	Gold	N/A*	None
Energy Star Rating	Not rated	Not rated	83	61	6

* LEED certification for two small tenant interiors only

Source: The City of New York, "Energy and Water Data Disclosure for Local Law (2014 NYC)," accessed June 5, 2017, https://data.cityofnewyork.us/Environment/Energy-and-Water-Data-Disclosure-for-Local-Law-201/jzst-u7j8.

This data raises a number of interesting questions, including the following:

- If building energy codes get more efficient over time, why is the oldest building (Comparable C) the most efficient?
- If building energy codes apply equally to all buildings, how can buildings that were built at essentially the same time (A and B) have such widely disparate energy usage?
- If energy efficiency is part of being a green building, how can the three LEED-certified buildings have such differing energy usage?

This comparison highlights the importance of occupancy and operating practices on building energy use. It also demonstrates the importance of understanding how building vintage and design affect energy use. Finally, this example illustrates the critical role of energy-efficiency upgrades during renovations that can significantly improve a building's energy performance.

Comparable A is the Bank of America headquarters building at One Bryant Park in Midtown Manhattan. Hailed as the "world's greenest skyscraper" when it was completed in 2009, it came under criticism for its high energy use once the initial New York City energy benchmarking data was released. Much of the building's high energy use is attributed to the 24-7 operation of the trading floors that represent a substantial portion of the building. These floors were designed to operate at full lighting and HVAC capacity despite the fact that off-hours occupancy was only a fraction of daytime capacity. Post-occupancy commissioning revealed that over-ventilation of the building contributed to the above-standard energy use. Subsequent analysis also concluded that design decisions related to the sizing and controllability of the HVAC system significantly constrained the ability to reduce building energy consumption. In fact, post-occupancy energy use was 12.7% *below* design, so in this case, the actual measured energy use corresponded to the

Case Study 9.C *(continued)*

modeled perfomance.[22] This example demonstrates how important design decisions are to the ultimate long-term operation of the property.

Comparable C, the oldest of the comparables, is the Empire State Building. The superior performance of this building is likely due in large part to its comprehensive energy-efficiency retrofit completed in 2010, in connection with a major renovation and asset repositioning. The $550 million renovation included $106 million for energy-efficiency upgrades, consisting of a chiller re-build, refurbishing the 6,514 existing windows to improve their energy efficiency, and instituting a tenant-based energy performance program. As of 2014, the building reportedly saved $2.8 million, or 25% of its pre-renovation annual energy use.

In addition to the energy-efficiency-focused renovation, the design and construction material used may also be a factor in the low EUI of this building. All of the other comparables were built after World War II in a modern style with glass curtain walls. This type of building envelope, with the relatively high window-to-wall ratio that is ubiquitous in modern CBDs, is inherently less efficient than the lower window-to-wall ratio that characterizes the building envelope of many pre-World War II buildings like the Empire State Building. The accompanying photos illustrate this point. Interestingly, both the One Bryant Park building and the Empire State Building were built with dual-pane glass windows with an R-value of 2.[23]

As part of the Empire State Building energy retrofit, all 6,514 of the original dual-pane, double-hung windows were removed and remanufactured on-site adding insulating spacers, inert gas, and a layer of heat-reflective film, which increased the R-value from 2 to 8. For the Empire State Building, the window refurbishment was responsible for more energy savings than any other energy-efficiency measure (EEM) undertaken. Together, these EEMs reduced building energy use enough that a planned additional new chiller to serve common areas could be avoided. Rebuilding and reusing the existing chiller avoided in a $17 million capital cost.

Comparable E is the Seagram building, located at 375 Park Avenue in Midtown. This Modernist icon was built in 1958 and designed by Ludwig Mies van der Rohe and Philip Johnson. It has the highest EUI in the comparable set. The high energy use may have any number of origins, such as occupant behavior or density, the age of the mechanical systems, or building operation practices. A comprehensive energy audit by an energy consultant would be required to determine the source of the high energy use for a building such as this and to separate the building-related energy use from occupant-related energy use. Without such an assessment, it would be virtually impossible to meaningfully assess the value impact of this above-standard EUI beyond the impact of the high energy cost on the *NOI*.

22. Michael Donnolo, Vincent Galatro, and Lucas Janes, "Ventilation in Wonderland," *High Performing Buildings* (Summer 2014): 50-58.

23. R-value is resistance to heat transfer. A higher R-value indicates a more efficient insulator.

Case Study 9.C *(continued)*

Architectural design changes and construction materials used for the building envelope can affect energy use. Pre-World War II building, such as the Empire State Building, shown above, were built with lower window-to-wall ratios than post-World War II modern skyscrapers. The window-to-wall ratio of the Empire State Building is 32%.

Post-World War II modern skyscrapers, such as the One Bryant Park building shown above, tend to feature glass curtain wall exteriors with high window-to-wall ratios. The window-to-wall ratio for this building is 62%.

In summary, this EUI comparison highlights some of the challenges in using EUI as an element of comparison. It is often difficult to distinguish whether an abnormally high or low EUI is due to building characteristics, occupant characteristics, or a combination of the two.

Asset Score

The Building Energy Asset Score is a rating system devised by the US Department of Energy that is intended to rate the energy efficiency of the physical structure and the major systems of a building. The system also provides suggestions for energy-saving renovations and upgrades. The Asset Score is available online for building owners and others to use.[24] It relies on a series of inputs regarding the building's

24. More information on the Asset Score can be found at https://energy.gov/eere/buildings/building-energy-asset-score.

physical characteristics combined with localized climate information and compares the subject building to the data from similar buildings. The Asset Score uses an energy model to predict energy use based on the provided inputs and rates buildings on a scale of 1 to 10, with 10 being the best.

The appeal of the Asset Score is that it removes the occupant-influence variable from the equation and thus provides a snapshot of only building-related energy use characteristics. As a predictive model, it faces the same limitations of any model, in that the results are only reliable if the inputs are representative of the physical conditions of the property. In other words, while the Asset Score is useful for comparison among similar properties, it may not be an accurate predictor of actual property performance (just as with comparing properties). Furthermore, the construction and mechanical details required for accurate results may not be available for comparable properties, which could limit its utility for comparative analysis.

Individual Green Building Features and Characteristics

In addition to certifications, some markets may look for specific features regardless of whether a certification is attached. Examples of building features that may be considered as elements of comparison include operable windows for natural ventilation, access to natural light and views of the outdoors, transit proximity, secure bike storage, shower facilities for bicycle commuters, communal gardens or eating areas, electric car charging stations, and on-site renewable energy generation.

Proximity to non-automobile commuting modes such as public transit, bike trails, and dedicated bike lanes can be measured by Transit Score and Bike Score. These algorithms rate relative convenience to these modes of transit on a score of 0 to 100, with 100 being the best. Similarly, Walk Score rates proximity to a wide variety of area amenities including restaurants, cafés, bars, grocery stores, parks, schools, shopping areas, and entertainment. While there are inherent limitations to these scoring systems, they do provide a general guide to the relative appeal of an area based on metrics that are often considered in assessing the attractiveness of a property's location.[25]

Identifying the relevant green element or elements of comparison is best achieved through market research, just as one would identify conventional elements of comparison. Both primary and secondary sources can be used and may be identified in the market analysis process discussed in Chapter 6. Interviewing brokers and property owners can provide useful insights, but so can observing other market behaviors. For example, office leasing flyers that include a map of the nearest commuter rail stop and shuttle schedule would indicate that transit access is an important factor in that market. Apart-

25. More information on these scoring systems can be found at www.walkscore.com.

ment brochures that quote the Walk Score, Transit Score, or Bike Score suggest that these are relevant in the eyes of the target market. The accompanying photo shows parking lot lighting standards that incorporate mini solar PV and wind turbines located prominently at the main entry to a shopping center. This visual cue may reflect the sustainability orientation of the market, whether or not the impact on energy use is measurable. Similarly, evidence of separate landfill recycling or compost bins in public venues as seen in the accompanying photo or as seen curbside on trash day suggests that the community is cognizant of the benefits of reducing waste and encouraging recycling and composting.

Other readily observable examples of a community's sustainability orientation in public spaces might include dedicated bike lanes painted on public streets, bike share and bike rental stands, electric car charging stations, low-flow bathroom fixtures, hybrid-electric and biodiesel public buses, use of gray water for landscape watering, drought-tolerant landscaping and xeriscaping, green infrastructure such as vegetated roofs, permeable pavement, and bioswales. The presence of informational marquees touting the benefits of these features to the public can provide additional cues that these types of features matter in that market. For example, signs such as those seen in the accompanying photos explain the varied community benefits of the vegetated roof at Milwaukee's Mitchell Airport.[26] Chapter 6 delves more deeply into the steps that can be taken to ascertain a given market's sustainability orientation and proclivity for green features and green building.

Academic studies may help identify appropriate elements of comparison to consider for a particular property type and geographic area. Research is beginning to focus on disaggregating the "green premium" to better understand precisely which green building characteristics are most in demand and therefore most likely to influence rents and prices. In 2014, researchers identified the green building attributes most important to tenants using a series of focus groups comprised of commercial real estate market participants (tenants, project managers, brokers, developers/designers, property managers, and appraisers/researchers) in four geographically representative cities: Chicago, Denver, Washington DC, and San Francisco.[27] Across all four focus groups, the most popular green building features were access to natural light, convenient public transportation, good indoor air quality, and occupant-controlled interior temperature. The next

26. The individual components discussed here are meant to be illustrative rather than comprehensive.

27. Robert A. Simons, Spenser Robinson, and Eunkyu Lee, "Green Office Buildings: A Qualitative Exploration of Green Office Building Attributes," *Journal of Sustainable Real Estate (JOSRE)* 6, no. 1 (2014): 211-232.

Parking lot lighting standards that incorporate mini solar PV and wind turbines prominently displayed at the main entrance to a shopping center may suggest that the market is sustainability-oriented, even if the impact of these features on energy use is nominal.

These segregated bins for landfill, compost, and recycleable waste in a public area provide an indicator of the sustainability orientation of the market.

A sign details the community benefits related to the vegetated roof at Milwaukee's General Mitchell International Airport.

Another sign explaining the benefits of a green roof at Milwaukee's General Mitchell International Airport may suggest that green features matter to the market.

most important features were efficiency-related and included energy-efficient HVAC and lighting and green leases that reward green behavior. LEED certification ranked 11 out of 19, and Energy Star certification did not rank at all.

Subsequent research published in 2016 involving the same researchers analyzed willingness to pay for specific green features based on a much broader sample that included 708 tenant respondents in 17 US metropolitan areas.[28] The results indicated that, once again,

28. Spenser Robinson, Robert A. Simons, Eunkyu Lee, and Andrew Kern, "Demand for Green Buildings: Office Tenants' Stated Willingness-to-Pay for Green Features," *JOSRE* 38, no. 3 (2016): 424-453.

improved indoor air quality and access to natural light scored highest overall. The results also showed that public companies and energy and information technology companies are most likely to pay for green-labeled buildings. Regional differences in green feature importance also exist, underscoring the importance of localized market analysis.

Ultimately, the element or elements of comparison that matter to the most probable buyer or occupant are identified through a diligent application of market research. In the valuation process, appraisers need to be aware of the potential for overarching and emerging market influences, such as sustainability, to play a role in the decision matrix of the market participants to determine if green building features breach the threshold of relevance for consideration as a material element of comparison. Thus, the valuation professional must not only recognize green features and evidence of green certifications but also recognize the behavioral cues in the market that indicate these characteristics play a role in real estate market behaviors.

Comparative Analysis

Once the relevant green element or elements of comparison are identified, the appropriate adjustments can be applied to the comparable properties to derive a value indication for the subject property. These adjustments should be supported in the same manner as adjustments for conventional features. The best support is almost always direct extraction from the market– i.e., paired sales. When such support is not available, alternate proxies for market preferences may need to be developed and relied upon. For example, it may be necessary to use a measured rent differential for green buildings in the market to support an adjustment in the sales comparison approach, assuming the connection is supported. Alternately, it may be necessary to use some proportion or all of the marginal cost of the green components to adjust non-green comparables. Whatever adjustment method is used, appropriate market research is critical to a credible result.

Studies and Secondary Support

When direct market evidence is lacking, additional support for green building adjustments may be derived from secondary sources, including academic research. A fairly substantial body of literature has emerged on the value premiums associated with commercial properties with green and energy-efficient certifications.[29] Much of the early literature relied on statistical analyses of US office buildings based on national data provided by a single provider reporting generally positive and consistent rent and value premiums for LEED-certified or

29. For a concise summary of the early literature on green building rental and value premiums, see Hans Op't Veld and Martijn Vlasveld, "The Effect of Sustainability on Retail Values, Rents and Investment Performance: European Evidence," *JOSRE* 6 no. 2 (2014): 163-167.

Energy Star-rated office buildings.[30] The single-source nature of the data has been cited as a potential weakness in the reliability of these studies along with the fact that the measured value effect may capture other building characteristics such as size, quality, age, and location.[31] The national scope of the data set and the extended time frame of the data collection may also mask the effects of local and market conditions. Finally, rent premiums were typically measured using self-reported asking rents, which may not reflect actual achieved rents or concessions such as tenant improvements and free rent.

More recent research has sought to address these concerns and refine the predictive reliability of the research results by investigating topics such as the dynamic and unique effect of LEED and Energy Star certification across time and markets, the market-specific effect of spatial distribution and transit proximity on certified buildings, the effect of property size on green premiums, the specific characteristics of green buildings for which tenants are willing to pay, and the concentration and dispersion of green buildings in prime locations.[32]

While national data and out-of-area studies may lack the local focus necessary for use in the adjustment process of an appraisal report, studies can nonetheless be useful for identifying trends in the market and providing secondary support for adjustments. For example, researchers Avis Devine and Nils Kok examined actual performance data over a 10-year period for a portfolio of 291 office buildings in Canada and the United States, totaling 68 million square feet.[33] The study measured financial performance based on rents and occupancy as well as resource use (energy and water), with some limited non-financial measures, such as tenant satisfaction and lease renewal rates. The results of the study, published in 2015 using data

30. Examples include Norm Miller, Jay Spivey, and Andrew Florance, "Does Green Pay Off?" *Journal of Real Estate Portfolio Management* 14, no. 4 (2008): 385-400; Piet Eichholtz, Nils Kok, and John M. Quigley, "Doing Well by Doing Good? Green Office Buildings," *American Economic Review* 100, no. 5 (December 2010): 2492-2509; and Franz Fuerst and Patrick McAllister, "Green Noise or Green Value? Measuring the Effects of Environmental Certification on Office Values," *Real Estate Economics* 39, no. 1 (2011): 44-69.

31. For example, see Spenser Robinson and Andrew Sanderford, "Green Buildings: Similar to Other Premium Buildings?" *The Journal of Finance and Economics* 52, no. 2 (February 2016): 52: 99-116; and Spenser Robinson and Patrick McAllister, "Heterogeneous Price Premiums in Sustainable Real Estate? An Investigation of the Relation between Value and Price Premiums," *JOSRE* 7, no. 1 (2015): 1-20.

32. Prashat Das and Jonathan A. Wiley, "Determinants of Premia for Energy-Efficient Design in the Office Market," *Journal of Property Research* 31, no.1 (2014): 64-86; Sofia Dermisi, "A Study of LEED vs. Non-LEED Office Buildings Spatial and Mass Transit Proximity in Downtown Chicago," *JOSRE* 6, no. 2 (2014): 115-142; Robinson and McAllister, "Heterogeneous Price Premiums in Sustainable Real Estate," 1-20; Robinson et al., "Demand for Green Buildings," : 424-453; Thomas Braun and Sven Bienert, "Is Green (Still) a Matter of Prime? Stylized Facts about the Location of Commercial Green Buildings," *JOSRE* 7, no. 1 (2015) 160-182.

33. Avis Devine and Nils Kok, "Green Certification and Building Performance: Implications for Tangibles and Intangibles," *The Journal of Portfolio Management* 41, no. 6 (2015): 151-163.

from 2004 to 2013, included the results pertaining to rent, occupancy, and energy performance shown in Exhibit 9.6.

Rent and occupancy premiums are consistent across both the US and Canadian portions of the portfolio. The reported premiums are also consistent with previously published literature.[34]

The energy use effects are less consistent and somewhat unexpected in that LEED buildings in Canada report slightly higher energy use than the portfolio average. In addition, Energy Star-certified buildings (which are limited to the US only) report significantly higher energy use. The researchers explain that this paradoxical result could reflect a number of factors, including differences in occupant density, operating hours, use of the space, or the proclivity for a building owner with high utility bills to pursue Energy Star certification in an effort to understand and reduce energy costs.

The study also found that in the Canadian portfolio (similar detailed leasing data was not available for the US portfolio), a green certification had a positive impact on the effective rent for buildings offering rent concessions.[35] In the portfolio, buildings offering rent concessions reported effective rents that were 11% lower than buildings not offering concessions. However, the effective rents were only 7% lower for buildings offering concessions that also had a green certification, reflecting a four percentage point improvement. This finding could imply a positive stabilization effect of green certifications on occupancy.

The study also attempted to assess tenant retention as measured by likelihood of renewal, with generally inconclusive results. The results of a single year of tenant responses to the question regarding overall satisfaction in the Canadian portfolio did indicate some level

Exhibit 9.6 Performance Data for US and Canadian Office Buildings, 2004-2013

	Rent Premium		Occupancy Premium		Energy Use	
	US	Canada	US	Canada	US	Canada
LEED	3.7%	10.2%	4.0%	8.5%	-14.3%	4.4%
Energy Star	2.7%	N/A	9.5%	N/A	25.8%	N/A
Walk Score*	0.4%	1.2%	N/A	N/A	N/A	N/A

* The Walk Score premium is measured as a percent increase in rent per Walk Score point.

Source: Avis Devine and Nils Kok, "Green Certification and Building Performance: Implications for Tangibles and Intangibles," *The Journal of Portfolio Management* 41, no. 6 (2015): 151-163.

34. See Eichholtz et al., "Doing Well by Doing Good," 2494-2511; Piet Eichholtz, Nils Kok, and John M. Quigley. "The Economics of Green Building." *The Review of Economics and Statistics* 95, no. 1 (2013): 50-63; and Franz Fuerst and Patrick McAllister, "Green Noise or Green Value? Measuring the Effects of Environmental Certification on Office Values," *Real Estate Economics* 39, no. 2 (2011): 45-69.

35. The Canadian sample included LEED and BOMA Best certifications.

of increased tenant satisfaction in green-certified buildings overall, although the result in LEED buildings was not statistically significant.

In addition to studies on certifications and energy use, research has recently migrated toward occupant health and well-being. In particular, the relationship of occupant health and well-being to occupant productivity has emerged as an area of intense focus, as tenants seek to attract and retain talented workers, particularly knowledge-based workers in areas like technology. However, no matter the industry, commercial real estate is increasingly being viewed as more than simply a fixed cost and instead as part of a strategy to attract and retain the best and brightest workers and improve their productivity.

In 2015, researchers found a correlation between increasing the rate of air changes per hour in office buildings and occupant productivity.[36] Cognitive ability as measured by tests that assess decision-making increased by 8%, which was equated to a $6,500 annual increase in per-employee productivity. The study further concluded that the associated cost of $40 per employee (in increased energy costs) could be offset by the use of an energy recovery ventilator (ERV). This study provides an intriguing example of an area of potential value impact that may be unfamiliar to many in the commercial real estate industry. Yet it is an area that warrants monitoring due to the significant potential impact of even a small increase in occupant productivity.

In summary, statistical studies and other academic research can be useful tools to support adjustments in the sales comparison approach when paired sales and other forms of direct market evidence are lacking, incomplete, or inconclusive. While caution is always warranted when using studies to support an explicit adjustment, these studies should not be dismissed simply because they are not local or because they use statistical modeling or other techniques that market participants may not use. Particularly when benchmarked against local, primary, and secondary research, such studies can provide an important supplementary tool to assist in solving the valuation problem. Furthermore, statistical techniques such as hedonic modeling can leverage data to uncover relationships that might otherwise go unnoticed using conventional appraisal methods and practices.

Cost- and Income-Based Adjustments

Cost- and income-based adjustments can be helpful when the comparable sales data does not offer the direct market evidence necessary to support an adjustment that may otherwise be indicated, particularly for green features. Solar PV is a common example. Both the

36. Piers MacNaughton, James Pegues, Usha Satish, Suresh Santanam, John Spengler, and Joseph Allen. "Economic, Environmental, and Health Implications of Enhanced Ventilation in Office Buildings," *International Journal of Environmental Research and Public Health* 12, no. 11 (2015):14709-14722.

depreciated replacement cost and the avoided cost of the electricity due to the electrical generation can generally be estimated with some level of reliability. The valuation of solar PV is discussed in greater detail in Chapter 10.

Replacement cost estimates for specific green features, such as a vegetated roof or electro-chromic glass, can be benchmarked using cost comparables (when available) and commercially available costing references such as RS Means and Marshall and Swift Valuation Service, as discussed earlier in this chapter. Replacement cost is generally preferred to reproduction cost and current cost estimates are likely to be more accurate than older data, due to the declining costs of many green building technologies in the early stages of market adoption. Cost adjustments should include all applicable forms of depreciation, as discussed previously.

A measured rent premium in the market could be used to make a discrete adjustment in the sales comparison approach. Care should be taken to consider the durability of the rent premium in light of the property's ability to fend off future competition and maintain the rent premium. If the rent premium is likely to be diminished or eliminated in the foreseeable future, a DCF over a defined period rather than a direct capitalization of the rent premium may be a more reliable indicator of the market's view of the contributory value of the green features or certification. Conversely, improved marketability and tenant retention could result in faster absorption, fewer months of vacancy between leases, reduced concessions, and lower turnover, all of which would positively impact the effective gross income. Even if the green building contract rent is no higher than that of a conventional building, the effective rent net of concessions, vacancy, and turnover certainly would be.

An individual green feature like a solar PV array that generates a predictable, measurable amount of energy for an extended period of time is a logical choice for the application of an income-based adjustment in the sales comparison approach.[37] As discussed in detail in Chapter 10, this approach uses the present value of the avoided cost of the electricity generated by the system over its remaining economic life to estimate the contributory market value of the PV array.

In addition to the energy production of a solar PV array, energy savings due to building design, construction, or specific features can provide a similar identifiable, predictable income stream that lends itself to an income-based adjustment. An NZE building is an example of this combination of design, construction, and distinct features that significantly reduces energy use in a building, typically by 30%-50% as compared to a conventional (code-compliant) building. Assuming the energy savings is well supported and the energy use of a compa-

37. This discussion pertains to owned rather than leased systems.

rable conventional building can be reliably estimated, the avoided energy use can be translated into a discrete value adjustment in the sales comparison approach using either direct capitalization or DCF and supported by the cost approach.

Case Study 9.D focuses on a suburban office building energy-efficiency renovation and provides a detailed analysis of the application of cost- and income-based adjustments in the sales comparison approach.

Green Building Impacts in the Income Capitalization Approach

Of the three approaches to value, the income capitalization approach may be the most sensitive of all to the commercial real estate market's changing attitudes, desires, and tastes. The power of the income capitalization approach in this respect is that it provides the ability to measure several areas in which a new market or property characteristic like green building could potentially affect value:

- Top-line (gross) income effects, such as rent premiums and marketability
- Operating cost effects
- Risk effects as reflected in overall rates and yield rates

Income Effects: Measuring the Space User Market Response

The response of the occupier to green real estate can be measured in several ways, including rent differential, enhanced marketability, and tenant satisfaction.

Rent Premiums

For leased space, rent premiums for green space relative to conventional space may (or may not) be detectable in the market, using a conventional paired comparable analysis. When a rent premium is identified, care should be exercised to avoid inadvertently capturing other building attributes in the green rent premium while analyzing green versus non-green rent comparable pairs. For example, if a rent premium is detected for LEED certification, is it independent of another variable such as age? If all of the LEED buildings are new and the non-LEED buildings are not new, it is possible that the rent premium detected in the market is due in whole or in part to some other characteristic associated with the age of the LEED buildings. It is also worth investigating what characteristics are in fact contributing to the perceived rent premium. Such insight is often gained through market participant interviews. Case Study 5.A in Chapter 5 (page 91) provides an example of how interviews with the tenant and the local leasing

Case Study 9.D Cost- and Income-Based Adjustments in the Sales Comparison Approach

In the renovation of a four-story, 45,000-sq.-ft. suburban office building, the property owner incorporated a series of energy-efficiency upgrades based on an audit performed by an energy consultant. The building was originally constructed as an industrial building in the 1960s and was last renovated in the 1980s to convert it to office use.

The energy consultant's recommendations included installing an energy management system and making elevator, water, lighting, and control upgrades at a total estimated renovation cost of approximately $250,000.[38] Comparable properties with similar energy-efficiency upgrades were not available; therefore, the contributory value of the proposed energy-efficiency renovation was estimated using cost- and income-based adjustments.

Exhibit 9.7 summarizes the costs and projected annual savings from the various recommendations. Taken together, the four EEMs reflect a total net cost after rebate of $250,984, or approximately $5.58 per square foot. The projected annual cost savings in the form of reduced electricity and gas use is $38,425 per year, or $0.85 per square foot per year. The simple payback period of all EEMs together is 6.5 years. The payback periods range for 0.2 to 22.5 years. The longest payback period is for the elevator motor upgrade. The other EEMs reflect payback periods of less than five years.

Exhibit 9.7 Summary of Costs and Savings from Energy-Efficiency Measures Associated with the Renovation of a Four-Story Suburban Office Building

	Project Cost				Annual Energy Savings				
Energy Efficiency Measure	Total Cost	Rebates/ Incentives	Net Cost	Net Cost per Sq. Ft.	Electricity (kWh)	Natural Gas (therms)	Annual Cost Savings	Cost Savings per Sq. Ft.	Simple Payback (Years)
Lighting & controls	$81,580	($7,240)	$74,340	$1.65	94,568	–	$17,023	$0.38	4.4
Energy management system w/DDC	$82,000	{$11,653)	$70,347	$1.56	48,290	6,542	$16,543	$0.37	4.3
Elevator upgrade	$109,350	($3,085	$106,265	$2.36	26,280	–	$4,730	$0.11	22.5
Water	$140	($108)	$32	$0.00	–	108	$129	$0.00	0.2
Total	$273,070	($22,086)	$250,984	$5.58	169,138	6,650	$38,425	$0.85	6.5

Contributory Value of the Energy-Efficiency Measures

In this case, the search for comparable sales with similar energy-efficiency upgrades was not fruitful, so direct extraction of the appropriate adjustment from the market was not possible. However, considering the fact that the owner was spending over $250,000 and would save over $38,000 per year assuming the proposed

38. This amount reflects the net cost, after deducting applicable rebates and incentives.

Case Study 9.D *(continued)*

energy-efficiency work was completed, consideration of the value impact of these EEMs was supported. The contributory value of the EEMs was estimated using both cost and income-based adjustments.

For the cost indicator, the replacement cost new was based on the reported cost net of incentives and rebates, which were widely available in the market as of the date of the appraisal. Depreciation of all types was considered. Since the improvements are new, no physical deterioration is indicated. No evidence of functional obsolescence was observed. Since the EEMs improve the efficiency and/or extend the economic life of the mechanical systems, no evidence of external obsolescence was noted. Furthermore, the EEMs were projected to have an associated cost savings, and the payback period averaging less than five years fell within typical investor thresholds. Based on this analysis, no evidence of external obsolescence was indicated. Using the cost approach, the contributory value of the EEMs was therefore estimated at $250,000, or $5.56 per square foot.

The income capitalization approach adjustment used the projected energy savings associated with the EEMs as the estimate of the anticipated future benefit for adjustment purposes. The EEMs were projected to reduce energy costs by a total of $0.85 per square foot, or $38,425 per year. While this cost savings would positively impact the *NOI* on a dollar-for-dollar basis, the long-term durability of the cost savings was uncertain. For example, the two largest cost-saving components–the light fixtures and controls and the energy management system–may need to be replaced in 10 to 15 years. Together, these two EEMs represent 87% of the total cost savings. The elevator motor upgrade, in contrast, would likely be much longer lived but represents only 13% of the cost savings.

Therefore, direct capitalization was not deemed an appropriate technique to value the contributory value of the EEMs for the purposes of an income-based adjustment in the sales comparison approach. Instead, the present value of the energy cost savings was discounted over the expected life of the EEM improvements. A 12-year discounting period was concluded, giving credit to the longer-lived elevator component but considering the shorter life of the energy management system and lighting upgrades. A discount rate range of 8.5%-9.0% was concluded, reflecting a slight premium to the discount rate for the underlying real estate to allow for the risk that the projected energy savings may not be fully realized. The present value at the indicated discount rate range is shown in the table below. The income-based valuation agrees with the cost-based estimate of $250,000.

Discount Rate	Present Value
8.50%	$252,120
8.75%	$249,335
9.00%	$246,598

Case Study 9.D *(continued)*

The contributory value of the EEMs was reconciled at $250,000, or approximately $5.56 per square foot. The adjustment was applied to each of the comparable properties that lacked similar energy-efficiency upgrades.

broker helped identify the specific factors that were driving the rent premium and provided support for the green rent premium.

Rental rates and by extension rent premiums are also dynamic, perhaps more so than any other component of the valuation process. Rental rates can respond almost immediately to new market information and typically do so far more quickly than other metrics such as construction cost or sale prices. The dynamic nature of rental rates, together with the market forces of supply and demand, can also affect the durability of the rent premium. In a generally efficient market, new market information such as rent premiums detected for green buildings would be disseminated throughout the market. Owners of conventional buildings would logically consider whether they, too, should attempt to meet the new market standard for green. For some properties, it may not be physically possible or financially feasible. For others, a risk adjustment as discussed later in this chapter may be appropriate. At least some of the properties that can "green-up" physically and in a financially feasible manner are likely to complete the upgrades required to meet market demand for green buildings and attempt to capture the premium. If demand and supply rise more or less in tandem, the green premium may prevail. However, if supply outpaces demand, the premium may diminish or evaporate entirely. If a sufficient critical mass of properties become green, the market standard or minimal threshold may shift so that green is the new standard in the market for that type of space. Conversely, if demand outstrips supply, then the premium may expand, so long as the demand continues and supply is unable to effectively satiate all demand for green buildings in that market.

Longitudinal studies (repeat studies of the same data set at different time periods) are ideal for isolating the unique physical and locational aspects of real estate, but it can be difficult to gain access to the necessary data for portfolios or markets over long time periods. One previously discussed study analyzed the US and Canadian portions of a 291-building, 58 million-sq.-ft. portfolio over a 10-year period.[39] In that study, the researchers Devine and Kok found measurable rent and occupancy premiums and detected a positive correlation between Walk Score and rents.

39. Devine and Kok, "Green Certification and Building Performance," 151-163.

In addition to a rent premium, the rate of growth in rental income may be affected by the green characteristics of the property. The projected market rent growth rate is one of the direct inputs in the DCF analysis. It may also be relevant as a consideration in the overall rate selection in a direct capitalization analysis if the rental growth rate for green buildings is expected to exceed that of conventional buildings.

Marketability Effects: Lease-Up and Renewal Probability

The marketability of green buildings relative to conventional buildings may also impact the income potential of the property. If green certification or green features accelerate the leasing velocity of vacant space, reduce landlord concessions such as free rent or tenant improvements, or result in more satisfied tenants who are more likely to renew, then the effective gross income could be positively impacted. In the Devine and Kok study noted above, occupancy was 4.0%-9.5% higher in the LEED- or Energy Star-certified buildings. The same study also found that among buildings that offered concessions, certified buildings showed reduced concessions relative to non-certified buildings.

Reduced downtime between leases, reduced concessions, and higher renewal probability each can be modeled individually in commercially available DCF programs. In a static direct capitalization analysis, future renewal probability and landlord concessions would be subsumed within the overall rate. A reduced initial lease-up would also have a positive impact on the as-is value for a new or recently renovated but vacant property.

In practice, green buildings and features are typically perceived as enhancing quality and creating a higher quality product relative to conventional buildings. It is also possible, however, that certain green building features could impair marketability, detract from occupant productivity, or create a deterrent rather than an incentive to potential lessees. For example, a naturally ventilated building may have unwanted noise or contaminants from the outdoors or create a real or perceived security vulnerability or loss of privacy for the occupants. This potential negative impact, while considered unlikely in most cases, should not be eliminated from consideration when evaluating the potential value impacts for green properties.

Operating Expense Effects

Green features can have a wide range of impacts on the operating expense profile of a building. These impacts are most often positive in that they reduce the cost of operation, but operating costs can also increase due to green building practices. Appropriately and equitably balancing the cost of green improvements with the associated operational savings is a critical valuation issue, whether the lease structure is full service gross or triple net. The accompanying sidebar on green leases explains how green leases and green lease clauses can influence the financial feasibility and performance of green building renovations and projects. Some of the most common operating expense impacts include energy, water/sewer, repairs and maintenance, insurance, management, and replacement reserve allowances.

Energy

Green buildings are generally expected to be more energy efficient than their conventional peers, meaning that they have a reduced energy use profile or EUI. However, this expectation is not always borne out in practice. Therefore, it is worth investigating whether or not the energy use and cost is materially different for a green building relative to its peers. Even buildings designed to use significantly less energy than mandated by code may not achieve design performance due to occupant behavior, conflicts between systems, or other factors including mechanical systems that fail to operate as initially planned.

The more complex the systems are, the more likely some additional ongoing monitoring and corrective response may be necessary. This requirement could result in additional operating expenses for the property in the form of a building engineer's salary, use of an outside consultant such as a commissioning agent, or increased property management time and expense. In the extreme case of NZE buildings for which the goal is to generate as much energy on site as is consumed, the advanced mechanical systems may require additional monitoring and adjustment to detect system failures, conflicts such as heating and cooling systems simultaneously operating in the same space, or the motion-activated lighting controls being inadvertently activated by the automatically controlled operable windows. In the case of an NZE bank branch in Florida, a service call for an electrical issue resulted in the inadvertent disabling of a portion of the solar PV array, which was not discovered until several months later. A more robust monitoring system was subsequently implemented to prevent a recurrence.

Building performance can also deteriorate over time if not monitored and adjusted regularly, a phenomenon known as "drift." The attainment of reduced energy use in one year, for example, does not ensure that performance will continue unless a measurement and verification protocol is in place to monitor and adjust the mechanical systems as necessary. Periodic commissioning of the building systems or in some cases ongoing monitoring (sometimes referred to as *continuous commissioning*) may be required for more complex facilities.[40]

When green building systems operate as planned, the results can be material and impact value. Exhibit 9.8 summarizes the 12-month operating data for two office buildings located across the street from

40. See the sidebar titled "What Is Building Commissioning?" in Chapter 2 (page 31) for more details on commissioning and the ramifications to the valuation process.

What Is a Green Lease?

One of the barriers often cited by landlords and tenants regarding energy and other efficiency upgrades is that the party who pays the capital cost of the upgrade may not benefit from the operational cost savings. As a result, the landlord has little incentive to pay for capital improvements like a more efficient HVAC system or lighting upgrade if only the tenant benefits from the upgrade in the form of lower operating costs. Referred to as the "split incentive," this misalignment of benefit and cost is most obvious under a net lease in which the tenant pays for operating costs such as energy and water, but the landlord is responsible for the build-out, including the HVAC, lighting, and plumbing fixtures. However, the split incentive can also occur under a gross lease in which the landlord pays all the operating expenses, leaving the tenant with no incentive to reduce energy use.

Green leases seek to equitably align the cost and benefit of energy and other efficiency upgrades to buildings so that the property can be operated most efficiently while meeting the needs of the owner and the occupant. They may also be referred to as *aligned leases, high-performance leases,* or *energy-efficient leases.*

While green leases typically focus on energy use and energy efficiency, they may contain a wide range of clauses relating to sustainable building operating practices targeting four main areas: recovery of capital costs, the operation and maintenance of the property, specification to use green or sustainable materials in tenant improvements or common areas and the resource-efficient operation and maintenance of the building, and reporting requirements related to sustainability goals and benchmarking regulations. Examples of each type may include:

- Capital cost recovery

  Balance the cost of capital improvements and the subsequent savings resulting from those improvements

  - Cost recovery provisions for improvements that reduce operating costs
  - Limit cost recovery pass-through to tenant cost savings from that improvement
  - Cost recovery for certifications such as LEED and Energy Star
- Building operations

  Cooperation between landlord and tenant to operate the building in an efficient, sustainable manner

  - HVAC temperature set points and operating hours
  - Energy use parameters, maximum occupant density
  - Green cleaning requirements—e.g., janitorial products and equipment
  - Landlord provision of recycling facilities for tenant
  - Tenant participation in landlord's recycling program
  - Tenant requirement to purchase renewable energy produced on site
  - Landlord requirement to procure renewable energy for tenant
  - Tenant credit for reduced energy/water use
  - Submetering of tenant's high energy use equipment
- Materials use and purchasing

  Ensure use of green/sustainable materials for tenant improvements, common areas, or building maintenance and operations-related purchases

  - Sustainable purchasing requirements (Energy Star equipment, FSC-certified wood, recycled content furniture, formaldehyde prohibition)
  - Landlord approval of tenant improvements, including lighting and plumbing fixtures
- Reporting requirements

  Compliance with statutory-mandated reporting of resource use such as water and energy, as well as voluntary green building/sustainability certification and reporting requirements

  - Cooperation/compliance with energy reporting and benchmarking requirements

- Rights to measure, verify, and disclose tenant energy, water, and waste
- Access to tenant energy and water usage data
- Submetering of electricity, gas, and water
- Landlord/tenant cooperation with the other's respective sustainability goals
- Tenant cooperation with the landlord's green building/sustainability certification
- Tenant participation in landlord occupant surveys

Besides these four main areas, green leases may also expand the scope of what may be included in a lease. For example, typical lease language concerns who is responsible for maintaining and replacing the roof as needed. However, a green lease may include language that specifies whether the landlord or tenant retains the rights to the rooftop for solar PV installation.

Green leases and green lease language can have important implications in the valuation process. First, the mere presence of green leases is a clear indication of the sustainability orientation of a market. Since both parties have agreed to abide by the specified terms, the green lease shows that the sustainability-oriented mindset has progressed from intent to practice on both sides of the transaction. This evidence of sustainability-oriented behavior may be a factor to consider when weighing the degree to which green features, certifications, and other green building practices are assessed in the comparable properties and the subject property.

Secondly, depending on the nature of the green lease language and the viewpoints of the landlord and tenant, the green lease language could have a positive or negative impact on the marketability of the property. A negative marketability effect could arise if the tenant views the landlord's green lease requirements as too restrictive. Some tenants, for example, may resist participating in the landlord's green certification program or may not be willing to voluntarily disclose energy and water usage, for fear of a negative reaction by outside stakeholders. Alternately, the landlord's commitment to sustainability as demonstrated by rigorous requirements in the green lease may signal to the sustainability-minded tenant that the landlord is serious about green building and sustainability and that the marketing claims have merit. In this case, the green lease acts as a market signal telegraphing the landlord's intent.

Specific green lease language can also directly impact the valuation process. For example, a green lease clause for an NZE building might include an expense stop on the electricity expense that limits the landlord's obligation under the full service lease to the amount of energy generated on site. If the tenant uses more than the amount generated, they are responsible for the remainder. This type of clause would provide protection to the landlord from unexpected tenant energy use as well as any potential fluctuations in the on-site energy production. It would also shift these risks to the tenant, which could affect how this expense is stabilized and the growth rate is applied, which may be a consideration in the overall rate and discount rate analyses.

Finally, the proactive use of well-crafted green leases and green lease language that equitably aligns costs and benefits suggests that the landlord is operating the facility in accordance with the operational best practices, which may make the property more appealing to the investor market.

each other that are owned and occupied by the same entity. The older building is a conventional building built in the 1980s that has been renovated and updated periodically. The newer building was designed and has been independently verified as operating as an NZE building. In this case, the NZE building uses 62% less energy than the conventional building, and the energy cost is $0.26 per square foot annually, or 92% less than the conventional building's energy cost of $3.21 per square foot.

NZE buildings combine reduced energy use design and mechanical systems with an on-site energy source, typically solar PV.[41] In

41. NZE buildings and on-site energy generation are discussed in more detail in Chapter 10.

Exhibit 9.8 **Energy Use Intensity Comparison of Conventional and Net Zero Energy Buildings**

	Conventional	NZE
Year built	1986	2012
Building area (sq. ft.)	22,550	49,161
Occupant count	37	98
Sq. ft. per occupant	609	502
Gross Annual Energy Use (before Solar PV)		
Gas (therms)	1,702	0
Converted to kWh	49,881	0
Elec (kWh)	371,666	351,303
Total Energy Used (kWh)	**421,547**	**351,303**
EUI (kWh/sq. ft./yr.)	18.7	7.1
EUI (kBtu/sq. ft./yr.)	63.8	24.4
Energy Cost		
Gas	$1,795	$0
Electricity*	$70,624	$12,883
Total	$72,419	$12,883
Per sq. ft.	$3.21	$0.26
Per kWh	$0.172	$0.037
Annual Energy Generated		
Electricity (kWh)	0	418,037
As % of use	NA	119%

* Includes all local utility transmission and distribution charges plus user taxes.

this case, the NZE building generated almost 20% more energy than it consumed over the year. However, even without considering the on-site energy generation, the NZE design and construction resulted in an EUI of 24.4 kBtus per square foot per year for the NZE building compared to 63.8 EUI for the conventional building. In other words, the NZE-designed building used roughly one-third of the energy per square foot of the conventional building.

New buildings are not alone in the potential to reduce energy use in a material way. Significant operational cost savings can be realized by upgrading aging systems in existing buildings.

For example, in the case of a large (1 million+-sq.-ft.) multitenant, 20-story building built in the 1960s and last renovated in 1995, energy-efficiency upgrades led to significantly lower energy costs over a five-year period (2008-2012). Beginning in 2009, the property owner undertook a series of energy-related renovation projects, including a major lighting upgrade (of fixtures as well as daylight and occupancy sensors), installation of a cogeneration facility, and heating and cooling equipment replacements and upgrades, including variable frequency drives (VFDs) on chiller pumps and air handlers.[42] Solar film was also replaced on the windows. Operational changes included switching off the escalators during off-hours and encouraging occupants to power down computers and other equipment at the end of the day. The costs of the renovations related to energy efficiency completed between 2009 and 2012 are summarized in Exhibit 9.9.

As a result of these measures, energy cost declined 32% from $1.97 to $1.34 per square foot, as shown in Exhibit 9.10. For comparison purposes, market expenses for comparable buildings as reported by the BOMA Experience Exchange Report (EER) were significantly higher ($2.47 in 2008) and declined only modestly (8%) during the same five-year period. Energy costs for the property that were 20% lower than market levels in 2008 declined to 41% below market levels as a result of the energy-reduction upgrades.

This example underscores the importance of understanding the nature and extent of energy-use renovations to the subject property and their impact on market value. Accurate stabilization of the energy expenses requires an understanding of the nature of the work completed and its expected impact on energy use and energy cost, particularly for a property that is already operating at levels below what is reported

Exhibit 9.9 **Energy-Efficiency Renovations: 2009 - 2012**

Year	Scope of Work	Cost/sq. ft.
2009	Lighting upgrade: fixtures + sensors	$3.48
2010	Replace 8 air handling units, 28 motors w/VFDs	$1.18
2010	HVAC optimization/cogeneration facility	$1.61
2010	Commissioning	$0.13
2012	Solar window film replacement	$0.20
Total		$6.60

Exhibit 9.10 **Energy Cost per Square Foot**

Year	Subject $/sq. ft.	BOMA $/sq. ft.
2008	$1.97	$2.47
2009	$1.63	—
2010	$1.66	—
2011	$1.62	—
2012	$1.34	$2.28
2013 (budget)	$1.03	—

42. Cogeneration involves electricity generated on-site, usually using natural gas, with the waste heat cycled through the boiler to reduce heating costs. VFDs can be an important component of energy-efficient HVAC systems and are discussed further in the Green Feature Gallery in Appendix A (pages 292-293).

in the market. Simply stabilizing the energy expense at the BOMA levels under a "mark to market" approach or utilizing a mid-point between the subject's historical level and market level would lead to an inaccurate prediction of this operating expense and have a direct impact on value. For example, the difference between the BOMA 2012 energy cost of $2.28 per square foot and the subject's actual $1.34 cost is $0.94 per square foot, which is a variance of 70% from the actual reported 2012 cost. In other words, stabilizing this expense at the BOMA levels would have resulted in an expense that was 70% higher than the actual cost.

Accurate stabilization of expenses also requires an understanding of the nature of the cost or expense comparables relative to the subject. In this case, comparable building expense information from the appraiser's files supported the BOMA energy cost estimates as being market-oriented. However, the expense comparables did not have the same level of energy-efficiency upgrades as the subject property and thus were not reliable indicators of energy use for a property such as the subject.

Water and Sewer

Green buildings typically employ strategies that reduce potable water use both within and outside the building envelope. Common practices include installing low-flow faucets, urinals, and toilets. "Low-flow" is a relative term and is likely to reflect a different nominal flow rate in different jurisdictions. For example, 1.6 gallons per flush may be considered low-flow in one area, while 1.28 may be the standard in another. Furthermore, the threshold in a jurisdiction may change over time, typically toward a lower flow rate.

Water use outside a commercial building is generally focused on landscape watering. Drought-tolerant landscape design and xeriscaping practices that eliminate or reduce landscape watering from potable sources have become commonplace in the arid regions of the country. Strategies to achieve this goal include plant selection, planting density, reducing the total landscaped area, and replacing water-intensive ground covers such as turf with alternate material such as stone, wood chips, or recycled concrete. Potable water use outdoors can also be reduced by harvesting gray water from the building or rainwater on site using rain barrels, cisterns, and bioswales that capture and collect rainwater from impervious surfaces for later use.

Despite its relative scarcity in many areas, the cost of water has historically been low relative to other building operating expenses. In the preceding example, the water cost is roughly 10% of the energy cost. Therefore, even large reductions in water use and cost may not ultimately result in a measurable value impact. However, the impact is often more noticeable for older properties and properties that may have undetected water leaks. Case Study 7.A in Chapter 7 (page 132) demonstrates the bottom line impact of fixing water leaks and upgrading fixtures. Here, simple repairs and fixture upgrades that reduced the water/sewer expense increased the *NOI* by almost 3.5%, which increased the value indication from the income capitalization approach by a similar amount.

Another example of significant water savings achieved in an older building is the case of the 1960s-era office building discussed in the previous section on energy use. Along with the energy use reduction upgrades, the owner also undertook water conservation renovations in 2010 that included replacing existing plumbing fixtures with dual-flush toilets, low-flow urinals, and aerators on the faucets to reduce water flow. As a result of these changes, water usage declined by a total of 43% over the five-year period, during which time occupancy was stable. The water cost per square foot, which had nearly doubled in the three years from 2008 to 2010, declined to $0.09 per square foot immediately following completion of the fixture replacement, reflecting a 40% reduction from the baseline cost in 2008 and a 65% reduction from the peak cost in 2010. Exhibit 9.11 summarizes water consumption both before and after the 2010 fixture replacement.

The cost of the project was $1.25 per square foot. Based on the annual savings (2010 versus 2011) of $0.17 per square foot, the simple payback period is just over seven years.

The previous calculation assumes a more or less fixed cost of water, but that may be an erroneous assumption in the future. While water currently remains relatively inexpensive, its cost is expected to increase more rapidly than general inflation in many areas due to scarcity, other environmental factors, and the need for municipalities to fund replacements of aging infrastructure.

In this particular area, an independent consultant's January 2014 report to the local water utility recommended water rate increases over the 2014–2018 five-year period of 12%, 12%, 10%, 10%, and 8% per year, respectively, or a simple average of 10.4% and a compounded total of 64%. By comparison, a 2.5% inflation rate, as might be used to model inflation in DCFs over five years, reflects a compounded total of 13%.

Properties that use reclaimed or recycled water for non-potable uses such as landscaping and toilet fixtures may benefit from the lower

Exhibit 9.11 Water Usage per Square Foot Before and After Fixture Replacement

Year	Subject $/Sq. Ft.	Gallons /Sq. Ft.
2008	$0.15	7.98
2009	$0.23	—
2010	$0.26	—
2011	$0.09	—
2012	$0.09	4.56

cost of such water from the local water utlity. Collecting and reusing rainwater on site would further reduce this cost.

Waste Diversion

Green building operational best practices usually include reducing waste sent to landfills and encouraging the recycling of suitable waste material. This process is often referred to as *waste diversion*. Waste diversion can range from simply separating waste that can and cannot be recycled to more elaborate triple waste stream systems that separate compostable material as well. Municipalities vary in their capacity to process multiple waste streams, which can present a limitation for some green building operations. In other areas, triple waste stream management is the norm and may even be mandated by local ordinance. Cost savings can be realized in some cases by implementing a recycling program that allows the property owners to reduce the number of landfill bins for which they pay. For example, communities may encourage recycling and composting by offering these bins for free but charging for landfill bins. If a review of historical operating expenses reveals a notable decline in trash costs, it may be worth investigating if the landlord or waste management company recently changed its waste management practices.

In addition to the potential cost savings realized from employing a multiple waste stream system, there may be additional costs to consider as well. Trash collected from the tenant spaces may still need to be sorted, even if multiple bins are provided in the tenant suites. This sorting process requires a dedicated space and personnel. Compost bins may need to be regularly cleaned to manage odor and pest problems. These requirements could impact labor and equipment costs for ongoing maintenance. Food-intensive operations such as hotels, grocers, and retail facilities with multiple restaurants may incur added costs for dedicated composting or compacting recyclables.

Green Cleaning

Green cleaning refers to cleaning practices, products, and equipment that reduce the adverse impacts of the cleaning process on the environment, workers, and occupants both within and outside the building. The intent of green cleaning practices is well captured in the intent statement for the high-performance green cleaning program under the LEED Operations and Maintenance rating system:

> "To reduce the exposure of building occupants and maintenance personnel to potentially hazardous chemical, biological and particulate contaminants, which adversely affect air quality, human health, building finishes, building systems and the environment, by implementing, managing and auditing cleaning procedures and processes."[43]

---

43. US Green Building Council, "High Performance Green Cleaning Program EQ3.1: Intent," accessed April 3, 2017, www.usgbc.org/credits/eq31.

The products associated with green cleaning practices may reflect marginally higher costs relative to conventional custodial cleaning products. Likewise, cleaning equipment such as green-labeled vacuum cleaners that meet specified particulate containment criteria and that operate below specified decibel levels could potentially affect the janitorial costs. Staff training may also add some marginal cost, at least initially.

Other Operating Expenses Including Repairs and Maintenance

Individual green features may need to be evaluated for their potential to contribute to increased operating costs or operational cost savings. For example, a vegetated roof or an interior living wall require some level of additional ongoing maintenance cost, but they may not require more than a marginal increase in the landscape maintenance expense. Likewise, solar PV arrays may initially appear to require significant additional maintenance. In practice, the marginal operating cost of solar PV may include occasional cleaning (which may not be indicated depending on the locale) and monitoring of the energy production (which can be accomplished through a web-based interface). Typically, the only significant capital expenditure during the life of the system is replacement of the inverter(s), a cost which is more akin to a capital expense than an operating expense given its magnitude and infrequency of replacement (approximately every 15 years or more). Even that cost may become obsolete for newer systems, which are delivered with inverters that in some cases are warranted for up to 25 years, approaching the expected 25+-year economic life of the solar modules.

Whether these costs are more appropriately included in the operating expenses or as part of the reserves allowance will depend on market practice in light of the specific valuation technique applied. For example, if the solar PV system is valued separately from the building improvements using a DCF analysis, the line item cost for replacement of the inverter could be included in the DCF at the appropriate time. Alternately, it could be included as part of the ongoing operations and maintenance allowance.

Some property insurers offer modest (5%) discounts for green buildings. There may be other incentives or rebates available for various green building characteristics. For example, on-site rainwater management strategies such as permeable pavement, bioswales, or cisterns may qualify properties for reduced wastewater discharge fees in some locales. These operating cost offsets would be appropriately considered when stabilizing operating expenses, so long as they are recurring and not one-time benefits or of limited duration.

Management Expense

In addition to utility, repairs and maintenance, and insurance cost effects, the effect on the ongoing management of the property should be considered. Advanced, interrelated systems may require additional ongoing monitoring, measurement, and verification, or ongoing commissioning in order to operate as intended. Thus, a marginally higher maintenance expense may be warranted. However, these costs may not extend beyond the initial commissioning in the first year or two of operation, and may not differ substantially from the process required for a conventional building. When properly designed and calibrated, it is also possible that automated systems may reduce management involvement in the ongoing operation of the building.

Replacement Reserves

The potential for added or reduced future capital costs should be considered in estimating the replacement reserves allowance. Some green features may warrant additional reserves allowances, while others may reduce future capital outlays. A building design that reduces the mechanical heating and cooling load significantly, as discussed in Case Study 9.A. Reducing Costs through Synergies, will require proportionately lower reserves for replacement of the HVAC units at the end of their useful lives. Conversely, when the benefit of the lower energy cost from a solar PV array is incorporated into the stabilized operating statement in the form of reduced energy expense, then the associated capital costs of replacing any short-lived items such as the inverter and the modules at the end of their respective economic lives should also be reflected in the replacement reserves allowance.

Overall Capitalization Rate and Discount Rate Considerations

Green building features and characteristics expand the array of factors that warrant consideration in developing the overall rate or discount rate for commercial properties. These rates incorporate a return *on* and a return *of* capital, and are adjusted positively or negatively for the perceived risk of the underlying asset.

The available scholarly literature and market activity indicate that green buildings may reflect a lower rate of return profile than conventional properties. For example, a 2010 study by Gary Pivo and Jeffrey D. Fisher using a data set from the National Association of Real Estate Investment Trusts (NAREIT) found that overall capitalization rates were 52 basis points lower for Energy Star-labeled buildings as compared to non-labeled buildings.[44] This conforms to the 55-basis-point reduction in overall rates for LEED- and Energy Star-certified build-

44. Gary Pivo and Jeffrey D. Fisher, "Income, Value and Returns in Socially Responsible Office Properties," *Journal of Real Estate Research* 32, no. 3 (2010): 243-270.

ings as reported in a 2008 study by Norm Miller, Jay Spivey, and Andrew Florance drawing from CoStar data.[45] Pivo and Fisher also found that proximity to transit (a fixed-rail station) was associated with a basis point reduction of 40 (in suburban areas) to 150 (in the central business district) in the overall capitalization rate.

Xudong An and Gary Pivo studied default risk in a pool of 22,813 commercial mortgage-backed security loans for the effect of various sustainability-related features.[46] They found a 30% lower default risk for properties within one-quarter mile of a fixed-rail station, a 20% lower risk for Energy Star-rated properties, and a 13.5% lower risk for a Walk Score that is one standard deviation higher. (A score of 75 indicates that a location is "Very Walkable" and a score of 44 indicates that a location is "Car Dependent.")

In addition to the academic literature suggesting that a reduced risk profile may apply to green properties, some lenders are acknowledging that reduced risk. In 2016, Fannie Mae began offering preferential loan pricing for multifamily properties certified under certain green building rating systems, such as LEED. In addition, their Green Rewards program offers discounted loan pricing and up to 5% additional loan proceeds for energy- and water-efficiency upgrades or on-site renewable energy generation. The Green Rewards program offers up to a 25-basis-point reduction in the interest rate and requires projects to demonstrate at least a 20% reduction in energy or water use. Properties must also monitor and report performance using the Energy Star Portfolio Manager program. The loans are then packaged and re-sold in the secondary market as part of Fannie Mae's Green MBS program, which targets environmentally focused investors. Freddie Mac offers a similar program called Green Advantage, with preferential financing terms for multifamily properties performing energy- and water-efficiency upgrades as well as for green-certified properties. HUD offers reduced mortgage insurance rates (20-45 basis points) on FHA loans for energy-efficient renovations and new construction.

In March of 2016, Lloyd's Banking Group of the United Kingdom announced a £1 billion fund offering interest rate discounts of up to 20 basis points for loans of £10 million properties. The program requires properties to meet specific performance targets regarding energy use or carbon emissions reductions, with tiered loan pricing depending on the level of performance actually achieved.

These lending programs demonstrate a lower risk perception for green properties from lenders. They also suggest that market behav-

45. Miller, Spivey, and Florance, "Does Green Pay Off?" 383-399.

46. An Xudong and Gary Pivo, "Default Risk of Securitized Commercial Mortgages: Do Sustainability Property Features Matter?" (paper presented at 2015 Real Estate Research Institute Conference, March 30, 2015. Revised April 16, 2015).

ior is now recognizing what the scholarly literature has previously detected through statistical analyses.[47]

All else being equal, a lower overall rate typically reflects either a lower perceived risk profile for the property, a greater reliance on appreciation versus initial cash flow, or a combination of both. A reduced risk premium would affect the overall rate selection in direct capitalization analysis. In the DCF, the reduced risk premium could potentially influence both the discount rate and the exit (reversionary) overall capitalization rate. A greater reliance on appreciation could signal that investors perceive superior income growth relative to other properties, lower expense growth, or a lower exit overall capitalization rate expectation, which would imply lower exposure to future risks. The DCF permits individual adjustments to each of these parameters, whereas these parameters are subsumed in the overall rate when performing direct capitalization.

An illustrative application of this academic research is shown using the three comparables from Case Study 5.A. Elements of comparison common to conventional building overall rates are listed, such as age, occupancy, credit quality, and the relationship of the in-place *NOI* to market rent. Location, which can sometimes influence overall rates, was deemed sufficiently similar in this case, so that no adjustment was applicable. In addition to the conventional elements of comparison, several green elements of comparison are also included: Walk Score, Transit Score, and distance to the nearest commuter rail station. The adjustments are shown in the overall capitalization rate (*OAR*) grid in Exhibit 9.12.

The credit tenancy adjustment was extracted from separate sales. The below-market rent adjustment to Comparable 3 was based on the estimated impact for this lease over the remainder of the lease term. No explicit adjustment was applied for the Walk Score, since the available evidence shows a limited impact on risk. The impact is perhaps more readily discernible in the price-per-square-foot adjustment of the sales comparison approach.

The Transit Score was only available for one of the comparables, which is not uncommon since the algorithm relies on data provided voluntarily by local transit agencies. Instead, rail station proximity was examined, and a downward adjustment of 25 basis points was applied to all three comparables for the subject property's superior (0.2 mile) proximity to commuter rail. The comparable range was 0.4 to 1.4 miles. An additional downward adjustment of 25 basis points was applied for the LEED certification, based on primary market research that revealed tenant and user demand in the market. Finally,

47. See, for example, Gary Pivo, "The Effect of Sustainability Features on Mortgage Default Prediction and Risk in Multifamily Rental Housing," *JOSRE* 5, no. 1 (2013): 152-173.

Exhibit 9.12 **Overall Capitalization Rate Grid**

	Subject	Comparable 1		Comparable 2		Comparable 3	
Year built/renovated	1990/2005	1988		1946/1999		1989	
Net rentable area (sq. ft.)	23,915	13,928		55,000		27,975	
Occupancy		96%, 8 tenants		100% single tenant		100% single tenant	
NOI @ market?		Yes— *NOI* @ mkt.		Yes— *NOI* @ mkt.		No— *NOI* below mkt.	
Credit quality		Average		Credit tenant		Credit tenant	
Walk Score	49	74		84		56	
Transit Score	N/A	N/A		N/A		43	
Distance to rail station	0.2 miles	1.4 miles		0.4 miles		0.9 miles	
Unadjusted *OAR*			**7.00%**		**6.54%**		**6.30%**
Credit tenancy		No	0.00%	Yes	0.50%	Yes	0.50%
Below-market rent		No	0.00%	No	0.00%	Yes	0.25%
Within 0.25 mi of rail station?	Yes	No	-0.25%	No	-0.25%	No	-0.25%
LEED certified?	Yes, Silver CI*	No	-0.25%	No	-0.25%	No	-0.25%
Energy Star?	No	No	0.00%	No	0.00%	No	0.00%
Adjusted *OAR*			6.50%		6.54%		6.55%

* Commercial Interiors

neither the subject nor the comparables were Energy Star-certified, so no adjustment was applied for this factor.

As a result, the overall rate range was compressed from an adjusted range of 6.30%-7.00% to an adjusted range of 6.50%-6.55%.

Summary

Despite the fact that green building and sustainability affect the valuation process in many ways, the fundamental theory and practice of appraisal remains unchanged. The basic three approaches to value–cost, sales comparison, and income capitalization–are all potentially valid methods for deriving a defined value for green buildings and conventional buildings with green features. To appropriately utilize these three approaches, valuation professionals need to be able to identify and understand new property characteristics and technologies and to recognize the degree to which sustainability, as an emerging market influence, affects demand in the subject's market.

Cost Approach

The cost approach is a useful method for analyzing green buildings. However, care must be taken to consider the unusual cost dynamics associated with green building, whereby costs decline over time, particularly in the early uptake phase of market adoption of green building practices. However, when current replacement cost is used with proper adjustments for all forms of depreciation as well as applicable rebates and incentives, the cost approach can be one of the more reliable approaches used to estimate market value for green buildings. Cost-based analyses can also be used to adjust for green building components in the other approaches, especially the sales comparison approach, when directly comparable data is limited or lacking.

When costing green building components using cost-estimating manuals or services, special care is needed to avoid double-counting under three scenarios. First, in areas where code-compliance mandates green building components, care should be exercised not to add costs for items already required by code. Secondly, appropriate interpretation of the data contained in the cost manual or construction budget is required regarding whether the reported cost is a total or marginal cost for the green component. Third, cost manuals or services may not account for cost synergies obtained through integrated design of the building's systems.

The cost approach can also serve as a benchmark that identifies the risk inherent in value indicators from the sales comparison or cost approaches for both green and conventional properties. While cost may not necessarily equal market value, cost is typically viewed as a de facto upper limit to value and is also the threshold test for financial feasibility in the highest and best use analysis. While there are instances when market value may be higher than replacement cost, those instances are temporary and may be reliant on certain barriers to entry in a more or less efficient market. Situations in which the market value conclusion exceeds cost implies an above-standard risk that should be considered in the valuation process for all properties, regardless of whether they are green or conventional.

Sales Comparison Approach

Identifying market-based support for specific adjustments in the sales comparison approach can be a challenge even for conventional commercial properties. This challenge is exacerbated in the green building sector by the paucity of green building-related data in most markets. Application of an income-based or cost-based adjustment is one way to overcome limitations in the availablity of comparable data.

Appraisers can also look to their own primary market research, secondary market research, academic research, and other studies to provide evidence to support adjustments that are relevant to the market. Central to this process is the identification of the most probable buyer and the sustainability orientation of that buyer as well as selection of the appropriate elements of comparison. As with conventional buildings, the relevant elements of comparison for green properties may vary from market to market, by property type or owner type, and over time. By properly identifying the appropriate buyer and elements of comparison and executing adjustments based on market-derived support, credible valuations of green buildings can be rendered, even when comparable market data of similar properties is lacking.

Income Capitalization Approach

The income capitalization approach allows the appraiser to quantify many of the ways in which green buildings perform differently from their conventional counterparts. Market influence can be directly measured by demand from end users in the form of market rent, marketability, and tenant satisfaction and retention. Operating cost differences relating to energy, water/sewer, and waste are readily measurable and thus can be easily translated into a value impact using either direct capitalization or a DCF analysis. Risk differentials and appreciation expectations can be directly measured in the market or inferred from market participant behaviors and applied as appropriate to the overall capitalization rate, income and expense growth rates, or yield rates. In this respect, the income capitalization approach techniques of direct capitalization and DCF are well suited to capturing the value impacts of new market influences, building technologies, and operating practices typical of green buildings. These same techniques can also be used to address the effect of these characteristics on conventional buildings.

10

Distributed Energy Generation

Much of this book has thus far emphasized the integrated interconnectivity of green building design and construction. Distributed energy generation systems, seen most commonly in the current market as solar photovoltaic (PV) systems, present a departure from this "whole building" concept. Unlike most other green building design features, distributed energy generation systems can often be "bolted on" to existing, decidedly non-green buildings with little change or accommodation to the other components of the building.[1] While this type of "bolt on" does not make a conventional building green, it nonetheless has a material impact on the energy costs and warrants attention in the valuation process.

With distributed energy generation systems such as solar PV proliferating in various markets across the country, this ability to "bolt on" an on-site energy generation system to a conventional building dramatically increases the likelihood of a valuation professional encountering this type of green feature. As discussed in Case Study 5.B: What Went Wrong? in Chapter 5 (page 95), it is not uncommon for assignments to be awarded without adequate information regarding green features such as solar PV systems. Or, as discussed in the example of the 1960s-era public library assignment in Chapter 5 (pages 97-100), there may be no information provided at all about the presence of on-site distributed energy systems. These scenarios of scant or missing information on these types of green features present a conundrum for valuation professionals who may not yet feel comfortable valuing on-site energy generation or who are seeking to avoid green assignments.

1. On-site energy generation systems are also often part of the integrated design of a green building.

Compounding this competency risk to valuation professionals is the fact that on-site, energy-generating systems are one of the most likely green building features to affect the valuation process. Without a fundamental understanding of on-site energy generation, a valuation professional will be unable to determine the degree to which the system affects value.

What Is Distributed Energy Generation?

When one thinks about energy generation, what most often comes to mind is the conventional, centralized energy generation and distribution model that has dominated the electrical utility business since electrical power became widely available in the developed world in the early twentieth century: Large-scale utility providers operate regionally and provide electrical power from a centralized plant, which is then transmitted to individual buildings via an electrical grid.

Distributed energy generation, on the other hand, refers to energy generation sources that are localized relative to the consumption source or load. The generation source may service a single building, or–in the case of community or district systems–a neighborhood, campus, or community. Distributed generation is, by definition, small in scale relative to conventional centralized generation sources such as hydroelectric, coal-fired or nuclear power plants, or utility-scale solar and wind.

Distributed energy generation can employ a variety of technologies. The most common example of distributed energy generation is rooftop solar PV arrays on homes and commercial buildings. Other examples include wind turbines, concentrating solar power (CSP), small-scale hydroelectric, fuel cells, and combined heat and power (CHP) systems. Each of these systems shares the distinction of converting a fuel that carries non-electrical energy into electrical energy on site. However, each approach varies in its technology, cost, efficiency, fuel source, and applicability to small-scale installations.

While distributed energy generation systems may operate independently from the grid, these systems usually remain grid-tied, or interactive with the local electrical grid, primarily because most renewable energy systems generate energy intermittently–i.e., only when the sun is shining or the wind is blowing. Grid-tied distributed generation allows the distributed energy source to supply all or a portion of the property's needs when the intermittent source is active and draw conventionally sourced electrical power from the grid when necessary. In areas where net energy metering (NEM) is available, being grid-tied may also allow the distributed energy generator to effectively "sell" any excess electricity back to the grid.[2] Distributed

2. NEM rate structures, also referred to as *tariffs*, vary geographically and are in flux. The ability of a distributed energy generator to sell back excess energy production to the grid is a salient issue in the valuation process and is discussed in more depth later in this chapter.

generation can also be employed as part of a *smart grid*, which utilities use to better manage peak demand and intermittent supply and avoid the capital cost of added generation capacity.[3]

Valuing Solar PV Systems

This chapter focuses on valuing solar PV, since it is by far the most common type of distributed generation and therefore most likely to be encountered by valuation professionals.[4] Many of the concepts and techniques applicable to solar apply equally to other forms of on-site energy generation, or can be modified as needed to address the differences relevant for valuation. Like many other green building characteristics, valuing solar PV requires an understanding of new concepts and vocabulary. The accompanying sidebar on solar PV key terms and concepts discusses some of the more common terminology associated with solar PV systems.

Solar PV Key Terms and Concepts

Alternating Current versus Direct Current

Alternating current (AC) reverses direction periodically, whereas *direct current (DC)* flows in one direction only. In the United States, alternating current, commonly known as "household current," reverses direction 120 times per second, or 60 cycles (hertz), in the form of a sine wave. This is the type of electricity that powers household appliances and office equipment. In contrast, direct current is what cell phones and laptop computers use. An *inverter* changes the current from DC to AC, a process which involves a loss of energy.

Azimuth versus Tilt Angle

Similar to a compass bearing, the *azimuth* is the angle that a solar array faces relative to a reference point. It is expressed in degrees, in a clockwise direction, relative to true north (zero degrees). Thus, due east is 90 degrees, due south is 180 degrees, and due west is 270 degrees. The optimal azimuth for solar PV production is directly facing the sun. For a fixed-mount (non-tracking) system in the northern hemisphere, the optimal azimuth is due south (180 degrees). In the southern hemisphere, the optimal azimuth is due north. In contrast to fixed arrays, tracking arrays allow the azimuth to change diurnally, such that the azimuth is optimized based on the time of day.

The *tilt angle*, in contrast, is the angle between the solar array and the horizontal plane. For a fixed-tilt array, the tilt angle is typically set to maximize either seasonal or annual energy production. A lower tilt angle (closer to horizontal) maximizes summer production, since the sun travels through the sky at an angle that is closer to vertical. In the winter, the sun arcs across the sky at a lower angle, so a more vertical tilt would maximize winter solar PV production. Tracking arrays with two axes of rotation can change both tilt and azimuth to optimize electrical production from a solar array.

3. The role of commercial buildings in utility smart grids, including a discussion of the components such as distributed generation resources (DGRs), energy storage systems (ESSs), and microgrids, is covered in the article "Commercial Buildings: Energy Efficiency and Reliability with Electric, Smart, and Microgrids," by Stephen Seawalk et al., *Journal of Sustainable Real Estate* 8, no. 1 (2016): 20-61.

4. While this chapter covers the fundamental concepts related to valuing solar PV, the reader is encouraged to conduct further study regarding specific valuation practices. Coursework such as the Appraisal Institute's *Residential and Commercial Valuation of Solar* provides additional information and case studies to help prepare the valuation professional for real-world assignments.

Btus, Therms, kWh, and kW (DC)
Building energy use and production is measured using a variety of metrics depending on either the fuel source or the intent of the measurement. Consider the following examples:

- Natural gas use is measured in therms.
- Electricity use and generation is typically measured in kilowatt-hours (kWh).
- Solar PV systems are sized based on kilowatts of direct current (DC), or kW DC.
- Whole building energy use metrics, such as Energy Use Intensity (EUI), use kBtus per square foot.

A *kilowatt (kW)* is equivalent to 1,000 watts. It is a measure of instantaneous energy use or generation, but it does not consider the length of time the energy is used. A kilowatt is a measure of peak load or generation capacity.

In contrast, the *kilowatt-hour (kWh)* adds a time dimension reflecting overall consumption (referred to as "load") or "production" (if generating) during a defined time period such as a month or year. The volumetric portion of an electric bill is measured in kWh, and electricity is priced as cents per kWh. This is also the metric used to measure solar PV production over the month or year. One kWh is equivalent to 0.293071 kBtus.

The *kW (DC)* rating of a solar PV array reflects its peak generating capacity, measured in direct current (DC), when the solar module is new and exposed to a prescribed amount of light under standard test conditions (STC) at the factory. Field conditions typically reflect a lower level of peak kWh production. This "nameplate rating" is how solar PV modules and arrays are sized. It may be expressed as kW DC (STC), kW DC, or kW dc, and is typically noted, along with the measurement protocol, on the manufacturer's label on the back of the module. An individual module may have a nameplate rating of anywhere from less than 200 to over 400 watts DC, depending on the type of silicon used, the manufacturer, and the vintage of production, among other factors.

The system size (expressed as kW (DC)) and its annual production capacity (expressed as kWh) are related, but should not be confused. In a given climate or geographic region, the relationship between kW (DC) and annual kWh production should remain fairly constant, assuming similar module composition (monocrystalline versus polycrystalline) and efficiency, as well as similar tilt, azimuth, shading, soiling, and system age. If any of these factors are suboptimal, then the annual kWh production will likely be adversely affected.

A *British thermal unit (Btu)* is the amount of heat energy required to raise one pound of water from 60°F to 61°F at one atmosphere of pressure. One Btu is equivalent to 3.41214 watts, or 1,055 joules. One kBtu is equivalent to 1,000 Btus. A *therm* is equivalent to 100 kBtus, or 100,000 Btus.

Like kWhs, kBtus measure energy use or production over time, but each metric is used in different contexts. Electricity use and generation is expressed as kWh. However, when whole building energy use is measured, the convention used is kBtus. Converting back and forth between kBtus and kWh is often necessary when analyzing building energy use and on-site energy production. The conversion factors are as follows:

1,000 watts = 1 kilowatt (kW)
1 kilowatt-hour (kWh) = 1,000 watts × 1 hour
1 kBtu = 3.41214 kWh
1 kilowatt (kWh) = 0.293071 kBtus
1 therm = 100 kBtus (100,000 Btus)

Building Integrated Photovoltaics
Building integrated photovoltaics (BIPV) are photovoltaic materials that replace conventional building materials in parts of the building envelope such as the roof, skylights, fenestration, or facade.

Derate Factor
The *derate factor*, also known as the *system losses*, account for total electrical losses throughout the solar PV system when operating under field conditions. System losses occur due to a variety of factors including shading, module soiling, ambient temperature, inverter inefficiency, wiring, and connection losses and

equipment mismatch. The derate factor is applied to the nameplate rating of the PV modules or array to determine production capacity based on the site's solar resource and the orientation of the array.

Inverters and Microinverters
An *inverter* processes direct current (DC) electricity generated by solar PV modules, changing it into alternating current (AC), which is the standard household current used by most electrical loads. There are three categories of inverters:

- Grid-interactive inverters, which are connected to the electrical grid
- Stand-alone inverters, which have no connection to the grid and rely on batteries
- Bimodal inverters, which can operate in either grid-interactive or stand-alone mode

String inverters connect to multiple modules, while *microinverters* control only one module. Microinverters result in higher per-module power output but are more expensive than string inverters. *Central inverters* connect large numbers of modules and are usually found in commercial installations.

Load
The *load* is the total electrical demand on an energy-producing system, or the energy consumption of equipment.

Maximum Power Point Tracker
A *maximum power point tracker* (*MPPT* or simply *PPT*) is a device that optimizes the power output of a PV module under all conditions by identifying the point of maximum power production of the solar modules.

Microgrid
A *microgrid* is a localized electricity distribution system consisting of loads, distributed generation, and storage that is normally connected to the local electrical grid but is capable of operating independent of the grid. *Islanding* or *islanded operation* refers to the ability of a microgrid to continue to power its loads independent of the grid for an extended period of time. This type of islanding is referred to as *intentional islanding* and requires disconnection from the grid. Unintentional islanding occurs when a distributed generator continues to supply energy to the grid when the grid has failed. This can produce a hazardous condition. Therefore, inverters typically include automatic anti-islanding capabilities that prevent electricity from distributed generators from being sent back to the grid when the grid is not powered.[5]

Power Purchase Agreement
A *power purchase agreement (PPA)* is a contract between a power generator and a power consumer whereby a property owner, referred to as a *host*, agrees to allow a third party to install a solar PV system on the host property. In return, the host agrees to buy the entire electrical output for a predetermined period of time at the rates and terms set out in the agreement. Under a PPA agreement, the solar PV system remains the property of the third party, who also maintains the system. PPAs and leased systems are referred to as *third-party owned (TPO)* systems.

Shading Analysis
Shading analysis is the process of determining the influence of obstacles, such as structures and vegetation that obstruct direct solar irradiation on a solar array, on electrical production. It is usually performed by the system installer prior to installation.

Silicon
Silicon (Si) is a chemical element that is most commonly used as a semiconductor material for PV cells due to its ability to generate an electrical current when exposed to light. It is used in solar PV cells in one of three forms:

- *Monocrystalline silicon*, also known as *single-crystal silicon*, is the base material used in electronics and high-performance PV cells. Monocrystalline silicon is grown in cylindrical ingots. As a result, the cells

5. The largest private microgrid in the US is located at Hudson Yards, the 17-million-sq.-ft. redevelopment on the far west side of Manhattan. The first three buildings will be serviced by a microgrid that will permit the buildings to remain powered (island) even if the grid is de-powered in the event of a natural disaster, such as a hurricane.

are usually square with "clipped" corners, yielding an octagonal shape with four long sides and four short sides. Monocrystalline silicon produces the highest efficiency solar PV cells (≥20%) and is typically more expensive than polycrystalline silicon.

- *Polycrystalline silicon*, also known as *polysilicon* and *multicrystalline silicon*, consists of multiple small crystals (crystallites) that give the cells their distinctive metal flake appearance. Because polysilicon is cast into rectangular ingots rather than grown as a crystal, the cells are typically rectangular in shape. These characteristics make polysilicon cells readily distinguishable from monocrystalline cells. Polysilicon is both less expensive and less efficient (typically <20%) than monocrystalline silicon.
- *Amorphous silicon* is a non-crystalline form of silicon that is manufactured by deposition from a gas in a series of thin films onto a substrate such as glass, metal, or plastic. Amorphous silicon can be applied to a wide variety of materials and used in applications requiring curves and flexibility when crystalline silicon is not suitable. Amorphous silicon is much less efficient (~10%) and degrades faster than crystalline silicon, but it is also less expensive.

Solar Cell, Module, Array, and Balance of System Components

The *solar cell* is the smallest component of the solar PV system. Solar cells are combined into *modules*, which are encased in tempered glass and commonly referred to as *solar panels*. A grouping of electrically connected modules is an *array*. The remaining components of a solar PV system are collectively referred to as the *balance of system (BOS) components*, and include the wiring, mounting hardware, inverter(s), and any other equipment such as maximum power point trackers, batteries, and switching gear. These definitions are summarized in the following list:

- Multiple solar cells sealed in tempered glass = module (aka panel)
- One or more modules connected electrically = array
- Array plus balance of system (BOS) = solar PV system
- Balance of system = wiring, mounting hardware, inverter(s), etc.

Solar PV String

A solar PV *string* refers to multiple photovoltaic modules connected electrically in series to produce a specified operating voltage.

Standard Test Conditions

The term *standard test conditions (STC)* describes a defined set of conditions under which PV module electrical production is tested in a laboratory or factory.

Tariff

Tariff refers to the rate schedule and other terms of service approved by the regulatory body that oversees the public utility service provider. Rate schedules are structured in a variety of ways, and may include the following:

- *Demand charges* are most often found in commercial, agricultural, and industrial tariffs. Demand charges are based on peak demand during a billing cycle and are thus a hybrid between fixed and volumetric charges.
- A *feed in tariff* is a rate structure designed to incentivize distributed renewable generation by offering a volumetric price premium, often for a specific contract period, for renewable energy sent back to the grid.
- *Fixed charges*, also known as *grid charges* or *non-by-passable charges*, are the portion of the rate schedule that is independent of the amount of energy used and are typically not offset by net overgeneration under a NEM tariff. Fixed charges are generally intended to cover the utility service provider's fixed costs.
- *Net energy metering (NEM)* is an electrical rate structure, also referred to as a *tariff*, that allows a grid-tied distributed energy generator to offset the future use of grid-supplied electricity with on-site generation that exceeds instantaneous demand. NEM tariff structures vary by utility jurisdiction but typically allow credits for excess generation that can be applied to offset future demand, often limited to a specified time period, such as a year. Depending on the utility service provider, credits for excess generation may reflect all or a portion of the full retail rate at the time of generation or may be based on something less than the retail rate, such as the wholesale electricity rate.

- A *tiered rate* schedule is one that includes progressively higher volumetric rates (¢/kWh) as consumption increases. Tiered rates are more common in residential tariffs than commercial or industrial tariffs.
- *Time of use (TOU) rates* are volumetric electricity rates that vary with the time of day and/or the season. TOU rates are usually positively correlated with overall load (demand) on the grid.
- *Volumetric charges* are the portion of the tariff based on the amount of electricity use, typically expressed as ¢/kWh. Volumetric charges are typically most sensitive to the cost of fuel used to generate electricity.

Tilt Angle
The angle at which a fixed-mount PV array is set relative to horizontal is called the *tilt angle*. The tilt angle for a fixed-tilt array can be set or adjusted to maximize either seasonal or annual energy collection.

Tracking Array
A *tracking array* is a PV array that is capable of following the path of the sun diurnally (daily) and/or seasonally to maximize the electrical production of the modules. The two most common orientations are:

- Single-axis tracking, which is a mounting system that allows the array to rotate diurnally, east to west, changing only the azimuth of the array
- Dual-axis tracking, which is a mounting system that allows the azimuth to change with the time of day and the tilt to change with the season, allowing the maximum electrical production from the array

Tracking arrays are typically associated with higher output than fixed arrays, as well as elevated operations and maintenance (O&M) costs relative to fixed-tilt arrays.

Uninterruptible Power Supply
An *uninterruptible power supply (UPS)* refers to a system that encompasses a back-up power supply using battery storage to provide a continuous supply of power to loads in the event that the primary power source is disrupted.

Market Characteristics

Although solar PV technology has been commercially available for more than 40 years, it has remained a niche until very recently. In 2000, installed capacity was 2 gigawatts DC. The market grew to more than 900,000 installations with an installed capacity of 25.6 gigawatts DC as of December 2015, with 90% of that growth (over 23 gigawatts DC) installed between 2011 and 2015.[6] Total installed capacity is expected to reach 97 megawatts by 2020. The majority of the new capacity in that time frame is expected to be utility-scale (centralized) projects.

A number of factors have contributed to the market expansion of distributed solar PV. Perhaps more important than any other single factor is the presence of NEM that is now mandatory in 39 states, the District of Columbia, and four US territories, as seen in Exhibit 10.1. NEM is an electrical utility rate structure, also referred to as a *tariff*, that requires electrical service providers (utilities) to reimburse distributed generators for electricity generated in excess of instantaneous demand and allows the distributed generator to draw energy from the grid when demand exceeds supply. This mechanism can

6. Solar Energy Industries Association, "Solar Market Insight 2015 Q4," www.seia.org/research-resources/solar-market-insight-2015-q4.

Exhibit 10.1 **States with Mandatory Net Metering Rules (as of April 2017)**

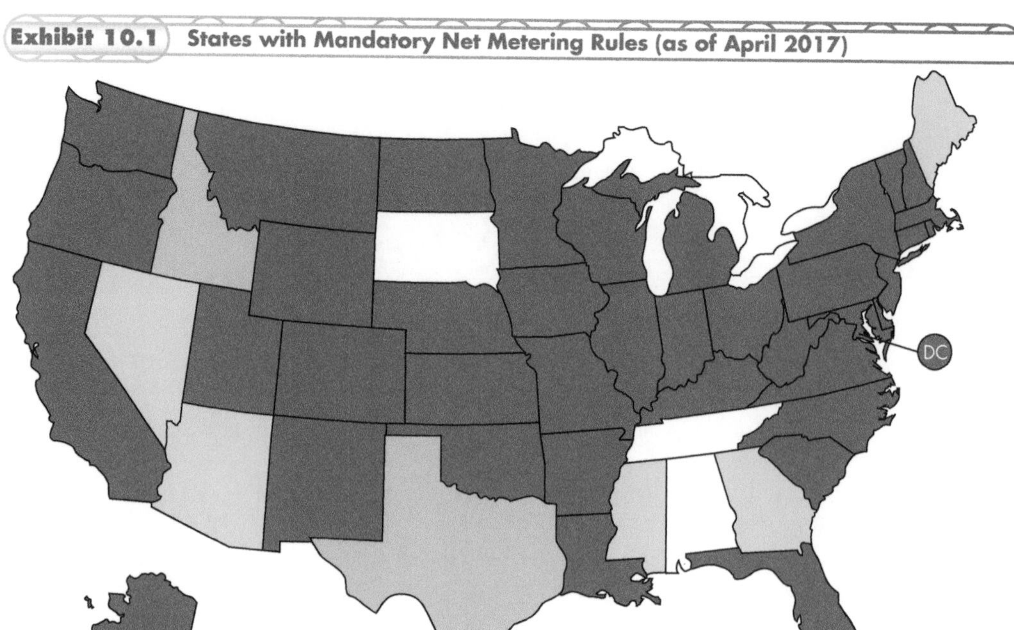

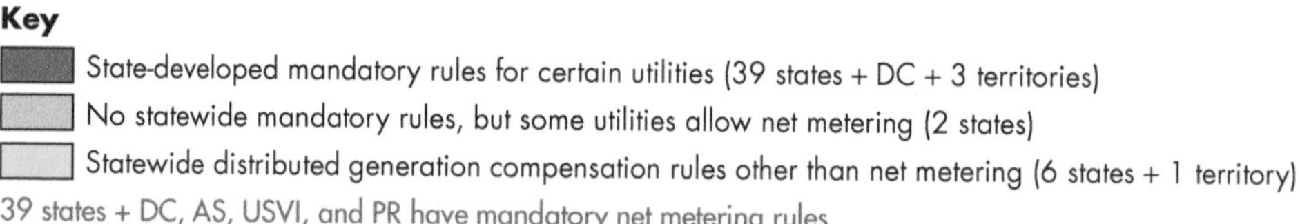

Source: Database of State Incentives for Renewables and Efficiency, "Detailed Summary Maps: Net Metering, April 2017," www.dsireusa.org/resources/detailed-summary-maps/.

reduce or effectively eliminate the need for on-site energy storage for intermittent energy generators, such as solar and wind. Eliminating the need for battery storage greatly enhances the economics of distributed solar PV.

Other factors, including declining component costs, have also played an important role. Financial incentives in the form of rebates from local utilities, tax credits such as the federal Investment Tax Credit (ITC), and accelerated depreciation for commercial installations (as discussed in Chapter 11, pages 264-265) have all contributed to the proliferation of solar PV and other renewables. While the utility-based rebates have been fully subscribed and are thus no longer available in most areas, the federal ITC was extended at the end of 2015. This 30% tax credit will likely continue to be a factor in the expansion of both distributed commercial and utility-scale renewable energy projects until it begins to sunset in 2020.[7] These types of financial incentives and their effect on the valuation process are discussed in more detail in Chapter 11.

Describing the Solar PV System Equipment

Most solar PV systems consist of two basic components: the solar collectors (cells) and one or more inverters to convert the electricity from direct to alternating current, the form most often used in buildings. Additional components such as mounting hardware, wiring, and in some cases, maximum power point trackers, comprise the remaining elements of a typical commercial solar PV system. Some systems may also include energy storage in the form of batteries.

Cells and Inverters

Solar PV cells are manufactured from silicon, which has the unique ability to create an electrical current when it is exposed to light energy. The most common rooftop solar system utilizes either polycrystalline or monocrystalline silicon modules. A collection of cells comprise a *module*, also referred to as a *panel*. A grouping of solar panels is referred to as a *solar array*.

In addition to crystalline silicon solar panels, thin-film solar cells have also been developed that are flexible and can be laminated on or into building materials, including roof shingles and glass. Thin-film solar cells typically have lower efficiency and a shorter life than crystalline silicon cells; however, their light weight and flexible nature offer greater flexibility in terms of installation and application.

The energy production of crystalline silicon declines very slowly over time, a process referred to as *degradation*. The rate of degradation ranges from approximately 0.25 to 1.0% per year for crystalline modules, and 1.5% or more annually for thin-film products. Polycrystalline modules, which are the most common modules on the market, are expected to degrade at approximately 0.5% per year. This rate of degradation would indicate that the panel would still be producing more than 87% of its initial production capacity when new at the end of the typical 25-year warranty period.

The electricity generated by the solar cells is then fed via electrical wires to one or more inverters. These inverters convert the direct electrical current into alternating current. There are three general types of inverters: grid-interactive inverters, stand-alone inverters, and bi-modal inverters. An array may have one inverter, several inverters for the array (known as *string inverters*), or as many as one per module (known as *microinverters*).

7. Tax policies are subject to change. For current tax credit information, see www.seia.org or www.dsireusa.org.

Grid-interactive inverters are capable of working in concert with the local electrical grid, such that excess electricity generated by the system can be sent back to the grid when it is not needed on site. Conversely, when on-site generation is inadequate to meet on-site needs, electricity can be imported from the grid. Grid-interactive systems are by far the most common type of solar PV installation.

Solar PV systems are also capable of operating independently from the grid, in which case the system requires a stand-alone, or grid-independent, inverter. Grid-independent systems require an energy storage mechanism, typically consisting of one or more batteries, in order to provide electricity at night. Alternately, a back-up power source such as a propane or diesel-fired generator could be used instead of the battery storage. Bi-modal inverters are a hybird inverter capable of operating in stand-alone mode as well as in grid-interactive mode.

Inverters historically have had a service life that is roughly half the typical module warranty period of 25 or more years. Common inverter warranty periods have increased from 10-15 years to 20-25 years, as the technologies have matured.

The accompanying sidebar on microinverters, string inverters, and maximum power point trackers provides additional information regarding inverter types.

Microinverters, String Inverters, and Maximum Power Point Trackers

Most inverters, which convert the DC electricity generated by solar PV modules into AC electricity, are grid-interactive, or grid-tied. That is, they are designed to be connected to, and function in concert with, the local electrical grid. Stand-alone inverters, in contrast, are not capable of interacting with the electrical grid and are designed solely for operation independent of the grid, relying on batteries for energy storage. Bimodal inverters are capable of operating either as grid-interactive or in stand-alone mode, using battery storage.

The second level of distinction for inverters is whether they are dedicated to an individual module or control a series of modules. Microinverters are installed one per panel, while string inverters are connected to multiple modules. Large arrays may use one or more central inverters, which are essentially string inverters connected to a large number of modules. Microinverters tend to be more expensive than string inverters, but typically result in higher electrical production. Microinverters are most appropriate when one or more of the modules is subject to shading, or when the array faces different directions. With a string inverter, the output of all modules in the string is limited by the module with the lowest output. If one module is 50% shaded, then the output of the entire string is limited to 50%. Similarly, if one module fails, the output of the entire string falls to zero.

In contrast, since microinverters control only one module, shading or module failure affects the production of that module only. Microinverters also allow module-level monitoring of energy production, facilitating fault detection and correction. Microinverters tend to have longer warranties of up to 25 years, whereas string inverters may only be warranted for 5 to 10 years.

Inverters may also incorporate MPPT technology, which enhances power output. The maximum output of a solar PV module is a function of two factors. The first is sunlight intensity, which varies seasonally, diurnally, and also potentially by shading and soiling. The second factor is the characteristics of the connected electrical load. MPPT technology adjusts the electrical load to the module to find the optimal level of power transfer (maximum power point) based on instantaneous sunlight intensity. By finding the optimal match between sunlight intensity and load, the overall power output of the module(s) is maximized.

Mounting Hardware and System Monitoring

Ancillary system components (referred to as *balance of system*, or *BOS*) include the mounting hardware, which often consists of aluminum frames and mounting brackets. Fixed-tilt systems, which are most common, are attached to the roof or ground at a set angle (tilt) relative to horizontal, and a direction (azimuth) relative to due north.

Solar arrays are most commonly affixed in a permanent orientation, but they may also be mounted in such a way that the panels are capable of moving in one or two planes, referred to as *single-axis* or *dual-axis tracking mounts.* Single-axis mounts allow the panel to track the sun's daily arc across the sky, optimizing the azimuth throughout the day and thus improving energy production. Dual-axis mounts allow the tilt to be adjusted as well, which adjusts for the variation in the seasonal tilt of the earth as it rotates around the sun.

System monitoring is typically conducted at the inverter level, and a web-based interface that tracks the ongoing energy output of the system

Is Solar PV Real or Personal Property?

Whether solar PV is considered real or personal property is a common question and an appropriate starting point when approaching a valuation assignment involving on-site energy generation systems. The answer depends on several factors, including how it is affixed, the ownership of the equipment, and whether the system is designed specifically to export energy to the grid. To frame the thought process, it is useful to review how appraisers differentiate between real and personal property.

Real property is defined as "items that have been installed or attached to the land or building in a permanent manner."[8] Examples of real property include:

- Land
- Buildings
- Fixtures—e.g., plumbing, lighting, heating, and air-conditioning[9]

Personal property, in contrast, is defined as "moveable items of property that are not permanently affixed to, or part of, the real estate."[10] Examples of personal property include:

- Furniture and furnishings not built into the structure, such as refrigerators and freestanding shelves
- Items such as bookshelves and window treatments installed by a tenant that, under specific lease terms, may be removed at the termination of the lease[11]

Here, the primary distinction is whether or not the item is physically attached to the underlying structure and/or the land. By this distinction alone, most distributed solar PV systems would qualify as real property.[12]

8. *The Appraisal of Real Estate*, 14th ed. (Chicago: Appraisal Institute, 2013), 7.
9. Ibid.
10. Ibid.
11. Ibid.
12. Some rooftop solar PV modules are held in place by ballast only, with no apparent permanent attachment to the underlying structure. This may place the modules in a "gray area" between real and personal property. However, it is likely that the balance of system components such as the wiring and inverters are permanently attached and integrated into the operation of the structure's electrical system.

In addition, the *real property* definition's example of fixtures as the mechanical systems in a building would seem to include, by extension, distributed electrical generation systems such as rooftop solar PV. Conversely, the second example under the personal property definition implies that under certain circumstances, attached property may remain personal property, based on the intent of the parties as called out in a lease.

Generally, but not always, the physical attachment of a fixture to real property constitutes unity of ownership, although there are exceptions. The most common examples of this situation are leased solar PV systems and PPAs. Here, there is a lack of unity of ownership despite physical attachment, and thus the systems would be classified as personal property. Such systems are referred to as TPO, or third-party owned. The underlying solar PV lease or PPA for a TPO system usually clearly states that the equipment remains the property of the solar leasing company (or the seller), and may grant the property owner (referred to as the *host*) the right to purchase the equipment at prescribed time periods and/or relocate the equipment within the same utility territory.

Trade fixtures such as certain built-in kitchen equipment in a restaurant may be paid for by the tenant, may be separately financed, and may be removable at the end of the lease term. It is possible that solar PV, under certain circumstances, could be viewed as a trade fixture that is intended to remain under the ownership of the tenant and removed at the end of the lease term, despite its physical attachment to the real estate. Whether or not such systems qualify for treatment as real or personal property is specific to the situation and may depend largely on the intent of the parties and the nature of the documentation in the lease.

IRS Guidelines

The Internal Revenue Service (IRS) provides additional insight into the classification of solar PV as real or personal property, plus additional guidance on the treatment of solar PV installations intended for net energy export, in its 2016 real estate investment trust (REIT) reporting guidelines.[13] While these IRS guidelines are specific to tax treatment of assets for REITs and thus do not necessarily reflect appraisal thinking, the criteria identified and the thought process presented are useful in establishing whether a solar PV installation is considered real property or personal property (or a mix of the two) in the valuation process.

These guidelines specifically address solar PV in the provided Examples 8 and 9, in which the IRS differentiates between a solar PV installation intended to generate electricity for export and sale to a third party (i.e., a solar farm, Example 8), and a similar solar PV installation sited adjacent to a building (Example 9). In the latter case, the intent is to supply electricity to the adjacent building but not primarily for export and sale. In the solar farm example, the solar modules are considered personal property much like machinery, because of their active function (converting solar energy to electricity for sale to a third party) and because they can be easily disconnected and removed. Thus, the IRS concludes that the modules in this case are personal property rather than real property.

In contrast, the mounts and exit wire are considered real property. The mounts consist of poured concrete, and the exit wire is buried underground and permanently connected to the transmission line. The IRS concludes that the mounts and exit wire are real property because they:

- Are permanently affixed to the land
- Are not designed to be removed
- Are to remain affixed to the land after the tenant vacates
- Would require significant time and expense to remove

Thus, in the case of a solar farm or utility scale solar PV installation, the solar PV system is considered a hybrid of real and personal property by the IRS. This conclusion is logical and appears to be soundly reasoned, but it may or may not coincide with the conclusion that is appropriate for non-REIT investors and/or outside of income tax situations.

The IRS' Example 9 is more typical of the type of distributed generation installation encountered in commercial appraisal. In this case, the solar PV system is identical to the system in Example 8, except that it was designed and sized to meet only the needs of an adjacent office building that is under the same own-

13. See IRS, "Definition of Real Estate Investment Trust Real Property," August 31, 2016, www.federalregister.gov/documents/2016/08/31/2016-20987/definition-of-real-estate-investment-trust-real-property.

ership as the solar PV site. In this case, the IRS concluded that the entire system, including the modules, wiring, and mounts, is real property because the solar PV system components:

- Are expensive and time consuming to install and remove
- Will be damaged upon removal
- Were sized specifically to serve only the office building
- Serve a utility-like function to the office building
- Serve the office building functions of containing, sheltering, and protecting tenants
- Produce income in the form of consideration for the use and occupancy of the office building
- Will remain in place when the tenant vacates the office building

The guidelines conclude that this type of installation is entirely comprised of real property, even though the solar PV system may have been added after the office building was constructed. Furthermore, the guidelines note that the conclusion would not change if the building roof covering consisted of shingles containing solar PV modules or cells instead of an adjacent ground-mount or carport-mount system. This example suggests that the typical distributed generation system, such as rooftop or carport-mounted solar PV, is considered real property, assuming unity of ownership.

Tests for Determining if Solar PV is Real or Personal Property

By synthesizing these two approaches, five tests emerge that can be applied to discern between real and personal property. In order to be considered real property, all of the following questions must be answered affirmatively.

- Is the solar PV system permanently affixed?
- Is it designed to support the use of the property?
- Is it intended to be permanent?
- Is it under the same ownership as the real estate (unity of ownership)?
- Is it subject to damage or likely to cause damage to the underlying real property if removed?

Based on these criteria, a TPO system such as a PPA or leased solar PV system would not qualify as real property because it would fail the fourth test, unity of ownership. Even though the equipment may be permanently attached, designed for the specific installation, and possibly intended to be permanent, a TPO system would be considered personal property rather than real property due to the lack of unity of ownership. In contrast, a solar PV system that is owned by the property owner, or "host-owned," would be considered real property so long as it is physically attached with the intent to be permanent and designed to meet the property's energy needs.

Solar PV installations designed to export energy for sale, such as solar farms, present a special case that may result in a hybrid classification of both real and personal property. Mounts and wiring may be clearly classified as real property due to the physical and ownership characteristics. However, if the solar modules can be readily removed without significant damage to either the real property or the modules themselves, then it could be argued that the modules represent personal property. This approach is consistent with the most recent IRS guidelines for REITs.

Battery Storage and Other Ancillary Energy Generators

Battery storage systems, small-scale wind turbines, cogeneration plants, fuel cells, and other similar distributed energy generation sources can also be screened using the same criteria as that used for solar PV. Battery storage systems could be considered real or personal property, but the scale of commercial battery systems and their integration into the distributed energy generation system favors a real property classification. Ancillary energy sources like wind turbines, fuel cells, and cogeneration plants are typical site-specific installations tailored to the energy loads of the associated land and improvements. Unless they are clearly designed for impermanence—such as a trailer-mounted portable generator—or are separately owned and leased to the property owner, such systems likely fall into the category of real property.

may be available. Monitoring systems provide a useful tool for measuring and verifying actual system production over time. Even when complete physical specifications are unavailable for an operating system, accessing the monitoring system often provides enough information to develop a value opinion. Monitoring systems are also useful for detecting system failures or malfunctions that affect energy production.

Key Value-Affecting Elements of Solar PV Systems

One of the first questions related to the valuation of on-site energy generation such as solar PV systems is whether it is considered real or personal property. The accompanying sidebar discusses this important initial question.

Assuming the system is determined to be real property (in addition to the equipment constituting the solar PV system), other equally important issues require consideration in order to appropriately determine the contributory value of the solar PV system. For example, whether the system is owned or leased, the nature of the local electrical rate structure, and the system's production capacity (among other issues) can positively or negatively affect value.

Owned versus Leased

Solar PV systems can be owned or leased. The ownership of the system is a key consideration in the valuation of solar PV systems, since (as with any valuation assignment) understanding the property interest appraised is a critical starting point in the analysis.

If the solar PV system is purchased outright by the owner of the underlying real estate and is attached to the land or buildings, the property rights appraised are essentially the same as the underlying real estate. Unless the benefit of the energy generated has been transferred elsewhere (say to a specific tenant), any value added by the solar PV system should accrue to the underlying real estate.

However, if the solar PV system is leased from a third party or the property is encumbered by a PPA, then the solar PV system is owned by a third party. This type of arrangement is often called a third-party owned (TPO) system. Leases and PPAs are two types of financing structures for TPO distributed generation systems. In both cases, a third party owns the equipment, while the property owner, referred to as the *host*, agrees to buy the electricity generated by the TPO system. The primary substantive difference is that in the case of a PPA, the host agrees to buy all the electricity generated by the system at a predetermined rate per kWh, which typically escalates over time. In contrast, a lease reflects a fixed monthly payment that does not depend on the amount of electricity the system generates.

In the case of a TPO system (leased or PPA), the solar PV system is not unlike leased fixtures in a commercial facility, such as large-scale commercial washers and dryers that are permanently affixed to a hotel but are leased from a vendor. The market value of the underlying real estate could be impacted positively or negatively by this type of agreement.

Positive impacts may occur if the solar PV lease or PPA resulted in a below-market price for the electricity generated. This could result from favorable lease payments that are lower than the energy cost purchased from the utility in the case of the former, or from a rate schedule that reflects a below-market electricity price per kWh in a PPA. A positive impact could also arise from a fully prepaid solar PV lease.

Negative value impacts of leased solar PV systems could arise from one of three areas:

- Rate structure or tariff (NEM)
- Marketability at re-sale
- Power production during periods of vacancy

Rate structure or *NEM tariff risk* pertains to the risk that the rate structure in the lease or PPA may not dovetail with market rates over time. For example, the rate structure stipulated in the lease may reflect above-market rates and/or above-market annual rate increases. In one case, a commercial building owner entered into a 15-year PPA for a 268 kW DC rooftop solar PV system, with an initial contract price of $0.15/kWh. The rate schedule escalated at a rate of 3.5% per year to $0.245 per kWh by Year 15. At the time of the appraisal in the seventh year of the PPA, the contract rate was $0.184 per kWh, essentially at parity with the average rate for the all-in cost of utility-sourced electricity ($0.185). However, as the PPA contract rate at the time of appraisal was at the upper end of the range of grid-purchased electricity and the PPA escalation rate is above both inflation and historical electricity price increases, the PPA rate could begin to outpace the grid rate in the future. As a result, the cost of energy for this property owner could exceed the cost of buying it from the grid for some or all of the remainder of the PPA term. Assuming that the electricity rates increase in line with inflation projections of 2.0 to 2.5% per year, the likely value impact was estimated to be $20,000 to $30,000 in this case.

Alternately, PPAs and leases offer greater certainty over future electricity cost and protection from unexpected electricity price increases due to unexpected fuel cost increases or other factors as compared to grid-purchased electricity. Leases and PPAs also insulate the solar PV energy user from the risk of changes to the NEM tariff that could negatively impact the solar PV system's value.

Marketability risk should also be considered. In the above example, if the next buyer did not want to assume the PPA agreement or was in some way prevented from doing so, then the owner would be left with three options: move the system to another location in the same utility territory, exercise one of the purchase options, or pay the termination fee. In this case, the purchase option would only apply if the potential sale coincided with one of the purchase option dates (end of Year 5, 10, or 15).

Exiting the PPA any time outside the purchase option windows would necessitate exercising the termination option. In this example, termination of the agreement would require payment of a termination fee plus the cost of removing the system. The termination fee began at over $3.9 million in the first year, then stepped down rapidly over the first five years, reflecting the accelerated depreciation recapture exposure of the PPA provider. At Year 6, the termination fee was approximately $950,000. As of Year 7, when the property was appraised, the fee was approximately $859,000. The fee continues to decline throughout the term until it reaches $189,000 in Year 15.

This example illustrates the potential relative magnitude of marketability risk. While the $20,000-$30,000 impact associated with the rate structure risk may reflect a nominal value impact, a potential marketability impediment of $859,000 is almost certainly material to the valuation.

Vacancy risk is a unique risk that pertains to the nature of PPA and lease agreements. The obligation to pay for the electricity generated on-site in the case of the former, or to pay the lease in the case of the latter, represents an ongoing obligation that does not exist in a conventional building that buys its electricity from the grid. While there are varying levels of fixed charges for grid connection and services, taxes, surcharges, and in many cases, demand charges to provide for peak usage capacity, the bulk of conventional grid-supplied electricity charges are volumetric. In other words, the charge is variable, based on the kilowatt-hours used. If you are not using electricity, you do not pay for it. Solar PV PPAs and leases differ in this respect, in that the obligation continues whether or not there are occupants in the building to use the electricity. If the electricity is not used, it can be resold to the grid in most states, under net metering tariffs. However, the extent to which the cost of that excess electricity can be recouped by reselling it back to the grid depends on the nature of the local net-metering tariffs. In most areas, a distributed generator is limited as to how much energy can be generated and resold to the grid, and the buy-back rate is often less than the retail rate.

System Size

The sizes of solar PV systems are most often reported based on peak output under factory conditions referred to as standard test conditions (STC) and are reported as kilowatts DC (direct current), or kW DC. The production capacity of an array is the cumulative output of the modules. Thus, 25 240-watt modules would result in a 6,000-watt system, expressed as 6.0 kW DC.

The amount of energy produced by this 6.0 kW DC system depends on a number of environmental and installation-specific factors. Environmental influences include the number of hours of sun available (solar irradiance), humidity, cloud cover, ambient temperature, and shading from nearby trees and buildings. For example, humidity can negatively affect solar production, because the sunlight is diffused by the water vapor in the air. Similarly, high temperatures can reduce the output of the solar modules. Soiling of the modules can also impact performance. Solar installers consider all these factors when estimating the output of the system.

The configuration of the installation also impacts solar energy production. Fixed-tilt arrays, if mounted on a flat roof typical of commercial buildings, are usually oriented at an angle that optimizes the solar module production. For pitched roofs, the mounting angle is typically the roof pitch, which may or may not be optimal and thus may affect production. Finally, the array's orientation relative to due north (azimuth) affects the production as well. Solar installers consider all of these site-specific installation factors when estimating production.

While the solar installation contract may vary in the level of detail provided, it is often the single best source of information pertaining to system size and other physical and energy production-related characteristics. Most include, at a minimum, the number and type (brand) of modules, the total system size, the number and type of inverters, and some reference to the nature of the mounting hardware. The warranty periods of the modules and the inverter(s) are also typically reported in the installation contract.

Installation contracts also note, at a minimum, the estimated first year energy production in kilowatt-hours. This estimate takes into account local climate and solar irradiance characteristics, shading, and the specifics of the installation, including azimuth and tilt. Some contracts also include detailed projections of future production reflecting deterioration of the modules (known as *degradation*), as well as soiling and any other sources of production loss. Single and dual-axis tracking mounts reflect a proportionately higher level of production than fixed arrays, but reflect a higher cost. Carport mounting can add 20%-30% to the installation cost relative to a conventional roof mount.

Solar installation contracts also include the total gross cost, detail any rebates or incentives, and note if the installer or property owner is to claim them. Some contracts also reflect a deduction for the ITC and may even show the impact of accelerated depreciation. Thus, when inquiring about the cost of a system in absence of the contract, it is important to ascertain whether incentives, rebates, tax credits, or depreciation have been deducted from the reported cost.

In the absence of the contract, the installer may have records of the installation and be able to provide system size and production estimates, as well as the installation date. Modules are labeled on the back with the manufacturer, model number, and production capacity. As a result, the system size could also be estimated by multiplying the module count by the individual module production capacity as noted on the back of the module. However, since modules have widely ranging production capacities (180 to 420 watts, for example), simply counting the modules from an aerial photograph would not provide sufficient information to estimate system size unless the individual module capacity, or model number, was known.

Production Capacity

The predicted production capacity of a solar array is reported as kilowatt-hours per year (kWh per year), and is estimated by the solar installer. For an operating system, the monitoring software typically tracks the actual production since the system was installed and is a useful source for production capacity, especially when the installation contract is unavailable. It is also useful as a check on predicted production from the installation contract. If actual reported production is much lower than predicted, it could be a sign of a system fault or failure(s). Solar PV production can also be estimated using web-based resources, including PVWatts, or market data on similarly oriented systems in the local market.[14]

Production capacity is also influenced by the system age. Production for crystalline modules typically declines up to 0.5% per year, and thus a 15-year-old system would be expected to produce more than 90% of the same system if it were new.

Module Warranty, Inverters, and System Economic Life

Solar PV modules are typically warranted for 25 years, and sometimes for as long as 30 years. For valuation purposes, the economic life of the system is often pegged to the warranty term on the modules. The rationale behind this convention is that most roofs last approximately that long, and it may not be cost effective to reinstall the old modules after the roof is replaced, even if the modules continue to generate energy.

While the modules may last 25 to 30 years or more, inverters have historically required replacement mid-term, usually projected for Year 15. Technological advances have extended the service lives, and warranties of up to 25 years are not uncommon for inverters. The current thinking is to include an allowance for a midterm replacement, but this assumption could change over time if inverters continue to improve in durability. Solar installers can provide current replacement cost estimates for this component of the system, which

14. More information on the PVWatts Calculator can be found at http://pvwatts.nrel.gov/.

can be used to project this future cost. For older, existing systems, it is important to ascertain whether or not the inverter(s) have been replaced, particularly for systems that are 10 or more years old.

Approaches to Value

Unlike many other green building features, the contributory value of owned solar PV systems can be readily valued as a discrete building component using the cost and income capitalization approaches. The applicability of the sales comparison approach may be impaired by the lack of comparable sales data that includes owned solar PV. However, to the extent comparable data is available, this approach would be applicable and should always be explored. Elements of comparison to consider for adjustment purposes would include the system's physical characteristics such as system age, orientation, and size.

Income Capitalization Approach

The income capitalization approach to valuing a solar PV system is based on the premise that the present value of the avoided cost of electricity is a proxy for the value of the system to the property owner. This premise holds even for owner-occupants and other property owners for whom the primary motivation for ownership of the property is not necessarily the income-generating capacity, so long as the occupant has an ongoing use for the energy produced. The alternative for a property occupant is to buy power from the grid, and so the income capitalization approach applies a unit electricity cost drawn from the local market. This cost is then applied to the annual kWh production, resulting in a gross "income" reflecting the avoided cost of grid-purchased electricity. Due to the typical expected economic life of approximately 25 years, a discounted cash flow (DCF) analysis is a more reliable method of estimating the contributory value of the solar PV system than direct capitalization.

While solar PV systems have ongoing operating costs, these costs are relatively limited. There are no moving parts, and so long as production is monitored regularly to identify any faults or failures, solar PV systems are relatively low maintenance.[15] Washing the modules may be indicated in some geographic areas, but natural precipitation is often adequate for cleansing the modules. The modest gain in production due to cleaning the modules may not justify the cost of cleaning or the potential risk of damage to the glass surface due to etching in areas where the groundwater has a high mineral content. A midterm inverter replacement allowance is typically incorporated into the cash flow, either as a line item or as part of the ongoing operations and maintenance allowance.

---

15. The exception is tracking arrays, which have moving parts and likely have higher operations and maintenance (O&M) costs as a result.

Valuation by the income capitalization approach requires, at a minimum, a set of data inputs as summarized in Exhibit 10.2 and discussed in the following section.

Annual kWh Production

Annual kWh production information is typically available from the installation contract, the monitoring software, or online sources such as PVWatts. It can also be estimated based on local production data for similarly sized systems.

System Age and Module Warranty

The system age and module warranty can be obtained from the installation contract, the property owner, or in some cases the monitoring software.

Inverter Replacement Cost

The inverter replacement cost is best sourced from knowledgeable local installers. For systems that have been in service for 10 years or longer, it is prudent to inquire as to whether the inverter has already been replaced. Current estimates depend on the number and type of inverters, as well as system size. Inverter cost per kW is generally inversely related to size, with larger systems generally reflecting lower per kW cost, all else being equal.

Cost per kWh of Grid-Purchased Electricity

The avoided per kWh cost of grid-purchased electricity can be derived from several sources, including a review of the subject property's electric bills, electrical costs for comparable properties, or various databases that track the cost of electricity, such as PVWatts, which uses the US Energy Information Administration (EIA) data.

The strength of using historical, local data from the subject or the marketplace is the same as that for using local market data for any other operating income or expense estimate. The subject and local data best reflect the nuances of the local climate, the local utility rate structures, and use patterns. Data reported from large national databases like the EIA is also useful, particularly when local data is not available. However, this type of data tends to lag in reporting.

When analyzing the cost per kWh of grid-purchased electricity, the practices summarized in Exhibit 10.3 and described below may prove useful when determining the appropriate cost to use for a given assignment.

Exhibit 10.2 **Minimum Data Inputs Required for Valuing Solar PV via the Income Capitalization Approach**

- Annual kWh production
- System age
- Module warranty
- Inverter replacement cost
- Cost per kWh of grid-purchased electricity
- Electricity cost growth rate projection
- Appropriate discount rate

Use Comparable Data from the Same Utility Territory

Electric rates are highly sensitive to the source of fuel used to generate electricity, and therefore rates between utility territories can vary widely. Furthermore, investor-owned utilities (IOUs) typically have different cost structures than municipally owned utilities. These two factors can result in very different per kWh (volumetric) rate structures in adjacent territories that have otherwise similar geographic and climatic conditions.

Exhibit 10.3 Useful Practices for Determining the Cost per kWh of Grid-Purchased Electricity

- Use comparable data: similar size and use type within the same utility territory
- Separate fixed charges from volumetric charges
- Use the weighted average over the year rather than "spot" rates
- Consider the effect of net-metering rules
- Consider future load profiles

For example, as of 2016, the Sacramento Municipal Utility District (SMUD) reported commercial rates that are on average 24% lower than the rates in the adjacent Pacific Gas and Electric (PG&E) territory. SMUD is a municipally owned utility that derives 20% of its capacity from hydroelectric generation. PG&E is an investor-owned utility that derives only 6% of its capacity from hydroelectric generation. Hydroelectric is one of the least expensive sources of electrical energy generation. The combination of differing generation sources, and differing ownership structures, contributes to the disparity in electric rates.

In addition, rates vary widely based on the type of user. Industrial, manufacturing, and large commercial users are typically charged lower rates than small commercial users. Using cost comparables that are of the same use and size and that are located in the same utility territory is key to an accurate estimate of electricity cost for the subject.

Separate Fixed Charges from Volumetric Charges

Utility tariffs often include a fixed charge and a volumetric charge. The fixed charges are generally intended to reflect grid infrastructure costs, while the volumetric charge (per kWh) is generally more closely tied to the cost of the fuel source: coal, natural gas, hydroelectric, nuclear, wind, or solar. Fixed charges may also include demand charges for larger commercial customers to compensate the utility for the marginally higher cost of providing electricity at times of peak demand, when higher-cost "peaker" plants have to be used, or higher-cost electricity has to be imported from outside the area at spot pricing that reflects peak demand.

In some areas, additional charges are now being added to net-metering tariffs for distributed generation sources, which will reduce the net benefit of the avoided electricity cost. These unavoidable charges should be considered in light of the avoidable (volumetric) portion of the bill.

Use the Weighted Average Over the Year Rather than "Spot" Rates

The volumetric component of electrical rate structures vary widely based on use and the local territory, but generally consist of combinations of one or more of the following structures:

- Flat rates, in which all electricity costs the same no matter when it is purchased
- Tiered rates, in which higher per kWh rates apply for higher volume use (use more, pay more per kWh on average)
- Time of use (TOU) rates, which depend on when electricity is consumed: summer versus winter, morning versus afternoon, peak versus part-peak versus off-peak, or combinations of all of the above

No matter the structure, the best indicator of actual volumetric (per kWh) electricity cost is the actual, weighted average cost per kWh over a typical year for a given property, net of any fixed charges that would remain in place. The best source of this data is likely to be the subject's historic electric consumption, derived from a review of electric bills and supported by market data for similar properties.

Consider the Effect of Net-Metering Rules

Note that if the state where the system is located does not offer net-energy metering (as shown in Exhibit 10.1), then the value of any instantaneous energy generation that exceeds on-site demand at that point in time will not be realized unless there is a storage component, such as a battery.

In the same vein, the local utility's NEM policy for reimbursing for excess energy generation may affect the valuation of the avoided electricity. For example, some NEM tariffs reimburse at full retail cost, while some reimburse at a wholesale rate. This distinction has important implications for sizing the system and may play into the price per kWh electricity rate used in the DCF analysis. If excess generation yields only a fraction of the retail price of purchased electricity, then the optimally sized system from a financial perspective would be one that minimizes excess generation. If the system is already in place and generates significant excess energy, the price per kWh of avoided electricity input into the DCF may need to be adjusted to reflect a weighted average retail/wholesale rate.

In some areas, NEM tariffs may be guaranteed, or "grandfathered," for a specified period of time, while in others, the NEM tariffs may change based on a predetermined schedule that reduces net excess generation reimbursement over time. A favorable tariff that is grandfathered for an extended period would be a factor to consider in the discount rate selection.

Consider Future Load Profiles

Solar PV is typically sized to the demand (load) of the current building and its occupants. It is worth considering if the current load is typical of the market for this type of property. A system sized for an above-market load may indicate potential superadequacy, a risk that would not exist for an undersized system. Conversely, this potential superadequacy risk may be offset by growing demand for electrical vehicle (EV) charging stations.

Electricity Cost Growth Rate Projection

The future rate of growth for electricity can be projected in much the same manner as other operating expenses in a conventional DCF, which are typically expected to grow more or less in line with inflation. Historically, electricity costs have trailed inflation, and projections for future increases range widely depending on the source. Future electricity costs are difficult to predict due to the wide range of influences that can sometimes have countervailing or unexpected consequences.

For example, renewable portfolio standards that mandate utilities to source specified portions of their energy from renewable sources like wind and solar were expected to increase electricity costs above historical levels in states that adopted those requirements. Similarly, cap and trade schemes enacted in the Northeast US and California were also expected to put upward pressure on electricity prices. However, at about the same time these regulatory requirements were enacted, technological advances that enabled hydraulic fracturing greatly increased the supply of domestic natural gas, significantly reducing its cost. The price of natural gas declined 67% from a peak of $7.97 per thousand cubic feet in 2008 to $2.66 per thousand cubic feet in 2012.[16] This reduced fuel cost impacted electric rates in areas where natural gas is a large component of the fuel mix, because fuel cost is one of the factors considered when rates are periodically reviewed and reset. There is often a delay of several years, however, between the fuel cost change and the effect on electric rates. In the case of the electric rate for Southern California Edison, where natural gas represented 38% of its fuel mix in 2014, the reduced cost of natural gas contributed to a 22% reduction in the summer peak time-of-use volumetric rate (¢/kWh) under one commercial tariff when rates were reset in 2016.

Appropriate Discount Rate

A discount rate is comprised of several components, including return on and of capital, and a consideration of the risk of the asset relative to alternate investments. A single discount rate is typically (but not always) applied to both the operating income stream and the

16. US Energy Information Administration, "US Natural Gas Wellhead Price, Annual," accessed March 28, 2017, www.eia.gov/opendata/qb.php?category=457054&sdid=NG.N9190US3.A.

reversionary value resulting from ultimate resale at the end of the investment term. This is the rate reported in commercially available investor surveys commonly used in commercial appraisal.

Common considerations in developing a discount rate include the age, condition, and quality of the asset, economic conditions affecting the geographic area, market conditions of the particular property type, barriers to entry for new competitive developments, and the risk profile of the income stream, which may include factors such as tenant credit quality and rollover exposure.

A logical place to start in determining the appropriate discount rate for a solar PV installation would be the appropriate discount rate for the underlying asset. From that base, adjustments can then be applied for the various differences between the quality, quantity, durability, and timing of the projected income stream relative to the underlying property.

Solar PV differs in several key respects from a typical real estate income stream, and these differences warrant consideration in selection of the discount rate. The major differences between the "cash flow" represented by the avoided cost of electricity in a solar PV DCF and the cash flow derived from a typical leased commercial property include:

- Risk of unfavorable changes to the NEM tariff that defines the income stream of the solar PV DCF
- Any difference between the electricity growth rate projection in the solar PV DCF and the market rent growth rate in the real estate DCF
- The extended projection period of the solar PV DCF relative to the real estate DCF
- The lack of any reversionary value of the solar PV system incorporated into the DCF

Net Energy Metering Risk

Electrical tariffs are revisited periodically and adjusted as often as every three years. This practice can expose the solar PV owner to potential market risk if the rate structure is revised in an unfavorable way. Much like a market-rent readjustment in a lease that has no floor, there is a risk the tariff could become less favorable unless NEM tariffs for pre-existing systems are protected or grandfathered. In many areas, initial net-metering laws were relatively generous with respect to reimbursement for excess generation within the course of a year. If the system overproduced in the summer, the customer banked a credit based on retail rates at that time that could be used to offset periods in the winter or at night when grid-sourced electricity was purchased, often at a lower unit cost. So long as the customer did not produce more than was consumed when netted out over the course of a year, the distributed generation customer was able to use the grid as a virtual "battery" to capture excess generation during peak production and draw on it when demand exceeded supply.

As distributed generation (particularly solar PV) proliferated, some IOUs became increasingly concerned that investor returns would diminish under existing NEM tariffs, particularly if the adoption of distributed generation became widespread or if customers ultimately disconnected entirely from the grid. The IOUs also argued that current NEM tariffs unfairly shifted the cost of maintaining the grid to customers without distributed generation. This position has been countered by a number of studies that point to the benefit distributed generators add to the grid, primarily due to the avoided cost of building new generation capacity and infrastructure, as well as reducing peak demand. The ultimate goal is fair compensation to both sides of the transaction, but the final solution may take time to evolve, and the resolution will likely vary depending on the geographic area.

Net-energy metering programs are likely to remain in flux in many parts of the US for the foreseeable future, which is a risk factor for solar PV. The overall trend that is emerging appears to be toward an increase in fixed grid charges such as standby charges, demand charges, or flat monthly fees for distributed generators. There is also a trend toward reducing the buy-back rate for instantaneous excess generation. NEM risk is reduced in areas where existing customers' NEM tariffs are protected for a period of time.

Electricity Growth Rate

If the growth rate applied to the initial per-kWh price of electricity used in the solar PV cash flow model differs from that used for the market rent growth rate of the underlying real estate, the discount rate for the solar PV may need to be adjusted. A higher or lower growth rate for the electrical rate would correspond to a similar directional (if not magnitude) adjustment to the solar PV discount rate, relative to the discount rate for the underlying real estate. This adjustment is similar to the effect of adjusting the market rent or expense growth rate in the DCF for a conventional commercial property.

Extended Projection Period

All else being equal, a longer projection period would reflect greater exposure to uncertainty, and therefore higher risk. This factor tends to elevate the solar PV discount rate relative to the underlying real estate.

Lack of Reversion

A typical solar PV DCF valuation consists of annual cash flow only. The reversionary value is expected to be negligible, which differs from the underlying real estate in a typical commercial property for which the present value of the reversion may represent half or more of the total DCF value. The reversionary component of the value is riskier than the value of the interim cash flows, due to the inherent uncertainty associated with predicting market conditions and investor expectations in the future. This uncertainty is reflected in the investor surveys that consistently report exit overall rates that are higher than the corresponding going-in (initial) overall rates. All else being equal, since the solar PV DCF does not rely on reversionary value, the reduced risk would tend to lower the discount rate for the solar PV component, relative to the underlying real estate.

Cost Approach

When valuing solar PV, the cost approach provides an important benchmark to the income capitalization and sales comparison approach indicators. As with the cost approach applied to the underlying real estate, the reliability and accuracy of the result requires using current replacement cost rather than historical cost and appropriately considering all forms of depreciation. Furthermore, since incentives such as rebates and tax credits are widespread and often inconsistently reported, clarifying the cost reporting basis is critical. In other words, it must be determined if the reported cost is on a gross basis (before incentives) or a net basis (after incentives). If the reported cost is after incentives, the specific incentives considered–rebates, tax credits, or accelerated depreciation–must also be determined.

Gross cost is the total, installed cost of the solar PV system before considering any available rebates, tax credits, or accelerated depreciation. It is usually the top line figure reported on the installation contract, prior to deductions for any incentives. However, the cost reported by the property owner may or may not include deductions for various incentives such as rebates and tax credits.

The gross cost, i.e., replacement cost new, of a solar PV system is what is most often used as the starting point for a cost approach. Current replacement cost is particularly important for solar PV, since the cost of installed PV has been declining as deployment has scaled. A declining cost environment presents special challenges when relying on historical cost as an indicator of current replacement cost new.

Once current (gross) replacement cost is determined, all forms of obsolescence are then evaluated. Physical deterioration, functional obsolescence, and external (economic) obsolescence all have the potential to affect solar PV installations and should be considered.

Physical deterioration will be applicable to all existing systems to some degree. Physical deterioration can be estimated using straight-line or another appropriate method, typically using the warranty period of the modules as the economic life.

Functional obsolescence can affect solar PV due to a suboptimal installation. The physical constraints of the site or improvements may dictate that the solar PV array is oriented at a less-than-optimal tilt or azimuth. For example, an array facing due south (in the northern hemisphere) normally produces the greatest energy production. However, the orientation of the building or site may preclude a 180° due-south azimuth, which will likely affect production. Similarly, shading from nearby buildings or structures could diminish production. Web-based solar PV tools like PVWatts can be used to quickly estimate the functional obsolescence of a suboptimally oriented array, simply by comparing the output with the actual, installed azimuth to the output with the optimal 180° due-south azimuth.

External obsolescence also affects most solar PV systems as reflected in the presence of incentives such as rebates and tax credits. If these incentives are widely available and considered in the purchase decisions of the market participants, they may be viewed as a proxy for external obsolescence. Utility rebates clearly fall into this category. The US federal ITC tax credit also meets these criteria, as it is available to all US taxpayers, is claimed in the year the installation commences, and has consistently been a material factor in the economic feasibility of most solar PV systems to date. While there are some market participants such as non-profits and institutional owners who may not have a federal tax liability and thus cannot avail themselves of this particular incentive, the majority of market participants seem to view this incentive as an immediate economic benefit, and it has therefore been internalized into the market.

All or part of the five-year Modified Accelerated Cost Recovery System (MACRS) depreciation may be put forth as an incentive as well. Unlike the ITC, however, the beneficial treatment (if any) arises from the short term of the depreciation schedule, which is an IRS determination. If it were not subject to five-year MACRS, it would presumably be depreciated over a longer period, so any net benefit is limited to the marginally faster depreciation. Finally, the impact is further reduced by the requirement that the MACRS depreciation basis is reduced by one-half of the ITC claimed. In other words, the marginal benefit is 85% of the theoretical margin between a longer depreciation schedule and the five-year MACRS.[17]

Case Study 10.A Valuing Solar PV

To illustrate the concepts discussed in this chapter, consider the following case study. This case study concerns an existing solar PV system that was installed on a commercial building approximately two years prior to appraisal. The system consisted of a rooftop polycrystalline silicon array with a fixed tilt. The original installation contract was not provided, and the solar installer was unavailable. Therefore, the tilt, azimuth, and estimated annual kWh production were not

17. The marginal benefit is calculated as: 1 – (30% ÷ 2) = 85%

Case Study 10.A *(continued)*

provided. The property owner provided access to the monitoring software and historical electric bills.

Historic actual kWh production was derived from the online monitoring system, from which future production was estimated. Review of the property owner's annual net-metering "true-up" bill revealed that the project was significantly undersized relative to demand, meaning there would be little risk of overproduction, even at peak production times. Based on a review of the electric bill and other research, the avoided cost of the electricity (volumetric portion) was estimated by deducting the fixed portion of the electric charges from the total, yielding an estimate of the anticipated cost.

The azimuth of the roof-mounted system was estimated at 215° (southwest) using online aerial imagery.[18] As a result, the potential for functional obsolescence to affect the system was noted as it was oriented 35° off due south (180°).

Review of the comparable sales data revealed no sales of properties with solar PV systems, so the sales comparison approach was not considered a viable option. The income capitalization and cost approaches were considered to be the most reliable indicators of value for estimating the contributory value of the subject solar PV system.

Income Capitalization Approach

The array was valued using a spreadsheet DCF over the remaining 23-year estimated economic life of the system. A 0.5 degradation factor was applied to the energy production. A 2.5% growth rate was applied to the per kWh electricity rate.

Ongoing operations and maintenance (monitoring, periodic cleaning, and upkeep) was estimated at 5% per year. The inverter replacement was estimated separately in current dollars based on market information and experience with other projects of this size. The inverter cost was escalated at 2.5% per year to the thirteenth year of the analysis, when the system would be 15 years old.

The discount rate was estimated based on a review of investor surveys and considered the extended discounting period balanced with the lack of reversion. The risk of unfavorable changes to the net metering rate structure was considered to be below average, as this existing system would be grandfathered under current legislation in California. While some risk remained to the rate schedule, the system size was well below maximum demand. Therefore, the risk to the rate of reimbursement for excess generation was deemed limited. The discount rate was concluded to be similar to the discount rate applicable for the underlying asset. The present value of the avoided electricity costs, net of expenses, was estimated at approximately $2.36 per watt.

As a check of reasonableness, the first year's "income" reflecting the avoided cost of electricity in Year 1 is compared to the present value, resulting in an imputed first-year overall rate that was 150 basis points *higher* than the discount

18. Google Earth Pro or Solmetric Azimuth Tool are two online tools for estimating the azimuth. The azimuth can also be estimated on-site using a compass or smartphone app.

Case Study 10.A (continued)

rate. This relationship may at first appear counterintuitive. Investor surveys historically report discount rates that are 100 to 200 basis points higher than the corresponding initial overall rate. However, this apparent incongruity can be explained by the lack of reversion for the solar DCF. The solar PV overall rate is higher because the income stream must allow for both return on and of investment within a 23-year time frame. In this respect, the income stream for a solar PV system is more similar to a leasehold investment in which there is no reversion, and thus the leasehold owner must recoup 100% of the initial investment plus a return on that investment through cash flow only. As a result, overall rates for leasehold interests are, all else being equal, higher than they are for comparable fee-owned properties, and the marginal premium is inversely related to the remaining term.[19] A similar relationship is to be expected when valuing a solar PV system with no anticipated reversionary value.

Cost Approach

Market research at the time of appraisal revealed that the current replacement (gross) cost of a similar new fixed-tilt, rooftop-mounted system, before considering incentives, was approximately$4.00 per watt DC. Physical deterioration based on a straight-line basis was estimated at 8% (2 years old ÷ 25-year economic life).

Functional obsolescence was identified as a potential consideration due to the orientation of the array being southwest, rather than due south. The effect of this suboptimal configuration was tested by a comparative analysis changing only the azimuth, using the PVWatts software tool. The effect was found to be inconsequential, so no deduction was applied.

External obsolescence was estimated at 30% of the replacement cost new, net of the physical depreciation already deducted. This obsolescence estimate was based on the 30% ITC tax credit. As a ubiquitous public subsidy, this tax credit can be viewed as a proxy for economic obsolescence for all qualified renewable distributed generation resources. No additional rebates or incentives were available.

After deducting all forms of depreciation from the current replacement cost new estimate, the estimated contributory value of the solar PV system to the value of the underlying real estate was estimated as follows:

Replacement cost new	$4.00 per watt DC
Less physical depreciation (8%)	($0.32)
Subtotal	$3.68
Less functional obsolescence (0%)	($0.00)
Subtotal	$3.68
Less external obsolescence (30%)	($1.10)
Depreciated replacement cost	$2.58 per watt DC

19. In other words, the shorter the term, the higher the premium, all else being equal.

Case Study 10.A *(continued)*

Reconciliation

The contributory value of the subject's solar PV system was estimated using the income capitalization and cost approaches, resulting in the following value estimates:

Income capitalization approach	$2.36 per watt DC
Cost approach	$2.58 per watt DC

The cost approach is typically considered the upper limit of value, based on the principle of substitution. However, it is vulnerable to inconsistencies between the appraiser's estimate of obsolescence and the market's view of obsolescence. Nonetheless, the cost approach provides an important test of reasonableness to the income capitalization approach, which is susceptible to changes in the NEM tariff.

The strength of the income capitalization approach is that it values the anticipated economic benefit of the solar PV. The net energy generated is readily measurable and can be monetized as the avoided cost of grid-purchased electricity. The DCF used in the income capitalization approach is also capable of modeling nuanced assumptions pertaining to the projected income stream. Both approaches were considered in reconciling a contributory value between the two indicators.

Emerging Topics in Distributed Energy Generation

While solar PV installations are increasingly common now, particularly in some markets, this was not always the case. Rapid changes have occurred in many areas related to energy and building technology. For example, the last several years have seen a growing emphasis on issues related to energy storage, microgrids, and creating "net zero energy" buildings.

Energy Storage and Microgrids

The intermittent nature of most distributed renewable energy requires a secondary energy source to supply power when the sun is not shining or the wind is not blowing. This secondary energy source is most commonly provided by the existing electrical grid, facilitated by NEM tariffs. However, it can also be supplied by other sources, including:

- Conventional generators (diesel or other fuel sources)
- Combined heat and power systems (CHPs) that generate heat and electricity on site
- Fuel cells that generates electricity from natural gas or other fuel without combustion
- Energy storage in the form of a battery

While any of these options would allow for grid-independent operation, only battery storage offers the option to operate on a fully renewable basis.[20] This is one factor that is motivating a growing interest in on-site battery storage. The other major concern driving interest in incorporating batteries into distributed renewable energy systems is the possibility that NEM tariffs may be less favorable in the future, which may have a negative impact on the economics of distributed energy generators.

Batteries are also viewed as a strategy to bolster grid resilience, particularly for mission-critical operations. Uninterruptible power supplies (UPS) have been used in this manner for data centers and other critical enterprise functions, often in conjunction with back-up generators. Batteries can be used to "peak shave," or shift load from peak demand times when electricity is most expensive, and to avoid or reduce demand charges for peak usage. Batteries are an essential component of microgrids, which are a small interconnected network of generation, storage, and loads designed to operate independent from the grid.

The market for battery storage is currently relatively small, but projected to grow rapidly as increases in manufacturing capacity lower battery production costs. As of 2016, the annual deployment of energy storage is projected to exceed 2.0 gigawatts by 2021, reflecting a nine-fold increase over the deployment of 226 megawatts in 2015. Of this projected amount, half will consist of "behind-the-meter" installations in commercial and residential buildings, with the remainder reflecting utility installations. By comparison, only 15% of the installations in 2015 were "behind the meter," so the projection is for a far greater growth rate in the behind-the-meter distributed energy sector.[21]

A variety of battery technologies are available for use in commercial building installations. By far the most common is lithium ion (> 90%), the same technology used in most laptop and electric vehicle batteries. Other technologies include conventional lead-acid, sodium chemistries, flow-vanadium, and flow-zinc.[22] Batteries also vary in how often they are capable of charging and recharging, a process referred to as *cycling*. Generally, batteries meant for rapid cycling are more expensive than back-up batteries designed for infrequent cycling.

Batteries remain a relatively expensive option as a secondary energy source, especially relative to relying on the grid via NEM. However, battery costs are declining and are expected to decline

20. Fuel cells that operate on methane recovered from agricultural processes such as dairies would also be considered a renewable energy source, but not if the fuel source is natural gas.

21. GTM Research/Energy Storage Association, "US Energy Storage Monitor: Q4 2016 Executive Summary," December 2016. www.wou.edu/~mcgladm/Geography%20470%20Energy/US-Energy-Storage-Monitor-Q4-2016_Exec-Summary.pdf, 9.

22. Ibid., 5.

substantially as new large-scale manufacturing facilities come on line in the US and elsewhere. The current thinking is that the interest in electric vehicles will fuel demand for battery production at a scale that will significantly decrease the cost of energy storage. In addition, battery storage needs at the utility scale, required to manage the intermittent nature of renewable sources of energy that are becoming a larger portion of utility portfolios under renewable portfolio standards requirements, are also driving demand. As with solar PV and wind in its early stages, utility incentives are available in some areas, mandated by the regulatory agencies, which can significantly reduce the cost to the end user.

Net Zero Energy Buildings

Net zero energy (NZE) buildings, sometimes referred to as zero net energy (ZNE) and zero energy (ZE) buildings, focus on a building's balance between energy use and on-site energy generation. This type of building is typically viewed as one that uses no more energy than it generates on-site over the course of a year. NZE buildings share two important characteristics: significantly reduced energy use compared to a conventional building of similar type, with any remaining energy use supplied by an on-site renewable energy source, as shown in Exhibit 10.4.

NZE buildings typically remain connected to the local electrical grid. By remaining grid-tied, these buildings obviate the need for energy storage to accommodate periods of energy demand unmet by real-time energy production. Local net-metering regulations may also provide an economic incentive to stay connected to the local grid.

Exhibit 10.4 NZE Buildings Combine Significantly Reduced Energy Use with On-Site Renewable Energy Generation

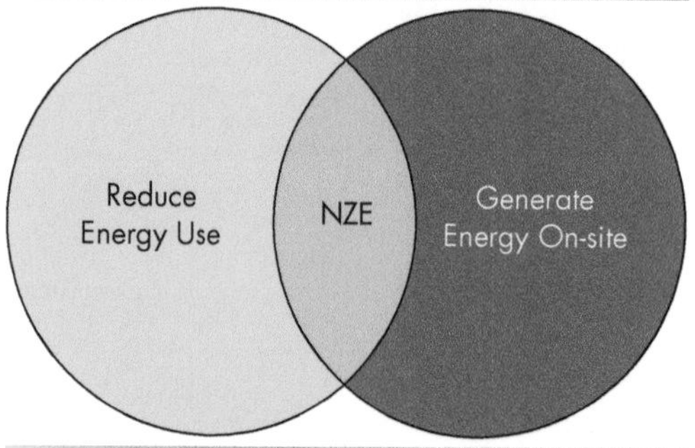

Source: Timothy P. Runde, "Net Zero Energy Buildings: An Introduction for Valuation Professionals," *The Appraisal Journal* (Spring 2015): 141-149.

While it may be presumed that NZE buildings are green buildings, this is not necessarily true. NZE buildings are defined by their energy consumption net of on-site energy production, whereas green buildings take into account other attributes beyond net energy use, such as occupant health and experience and environmental impacts beyond energy consumption.

In the United States, two organizations currently offer verification and/or certification of net zero energy status: the International Living Future Institute (ILFI) and the New Buildings Institute (NBI). The NBI tracks verified and planned NZE buildings in the US. In their 2016 report on NZE buildings, NBI reported a 35% increase in the number of buildings verified as NZE between 2015 and 2016, and a nearly twofold increase in the number of buildings they define as "emerging" NZE buildings.[23]

While it is not required that NZE buildings be more energy efficient than conventional buildings, the physical limitations of the site and/or economic barriers would most likely preclude the ability to provide sufficient on-site energy generation from a renewable source without concerted efforts to reduce on-site energy demand. NZE buildings, therefore, commonly utilize complex design strategies and technologies to facilitate a much-reduced energy load as compared to conventional buildings. For this reason, the valuation of an NZE building presents a particularly challenging assignment, requiring the valuation professional to understand not only these more complex systems related to energy use but also how to value on-site energy generation.[24]

Summary

Distributed energy generation refers to small-scale, energy generation sources that are either on-site or localized relative to where the energy is being used, in contrast to the large-scale, centralized energy generation and distribution model that has been common for the past century. Distributed energy generation systems can be grid-tied or operate independently from the grid.

Rooftop solar PV arrays on homes and commercial buildings are currently the most common type of distributed energy generation. Several factors have contributed to growth in the market for solar PV in the United States. While NEM rules may vary across the country, they generally provide an economic benefit for distributed generation such as solar PV by reducing or eliminating the need for on-site energy storage. In addition, financial incentives such as utility rebates and federal tax credits have spurred growth in solar PV installations.

Solar PV systems consist of solar collectors (cells) and one or more inverters that convert the electricity generated from direct current (DC) to the more commonly used alternating current (AC). Systems can be mounted on the roof of a building or carport, or fixed to the ground. The tilt and azimuth of the array affects production capacity. While fixed-tilt systems are most common, tracking arrays that change

23. New Buildings Institute, "2016 List of Zero Net Energy Buildings," http://newbuildings.org/wp-content/uploads/2016/10/GTZ_2016_List.pdf. The number of verified NZE buildings grew from 39 to 53 in the year prior to September 2016; "emerging" NZE buildings grew from 152 to 279. The NBI defines emerging NZE buildings as those with a stated goal of reaching NZE status that have not yet met that goal due to being in the design or construction phase, or not yet having a full year's data demonstrating net zero achievement.

24. For more in-depth information on valuing NZE buildings, see Timothy P. Runde's article entitled "Net Zero Energy Buildings: An Introduction for Valuation Professionals," *The Appraisal Journal* (Spring 2015): 141-149.

the azimuth and/or tilt of the modules result in increased energy production, as well as increased operation and maintenance costs.

Key aspects of solar PV systems that affect value include whether the system is owned or leased, the size of the system, its production capacity, and its economic life. While all three approaches to value are applicable, the sales comparison approach may be challenging due to a lack of comparable sales data that includes solar PV at this time. When valuing solar PV using the income capitalization approach, the following minimum data inputs are required: annual kWh production, system age, module warranty, inverter replacement cost, cost per kWh of grid-purchased electricity, a growth rate projection for electricity, and an appropriate discount rate. The cost approach provides a useful benchmark to the income capitalization and sales comparison indicators. Current replacement cost rather than historical cost is used as a starting point, after which all forms of depreciation (physical, functional, and external) as well as any incentives such as tax credits or rebates are considered and deducted appropriately.

Emerging topics related to distributed energy generation include energy storage systems such as batteries, microgrids, and net zero energy buildings. While these types of systems or features are not currently as common as solar PV, these technologies warrant monitoring by valuation professionals for possible entry into their markets.

11 The Role of Incentives in Green Building Valuation

A wide variety of incentive programs are available for energy-efficiency improvements, solar PV and other renewable energy improvements like solar water heating, and other components of comprehensive green building certifications. Various incentive programs available at the federal, state, and local levels include both direct financial incentives–such as rebates, tax abatements, grants, and financing programs–as well as indirect incentives, such as expedited permitting programs and density bonuses.

These programs are designed to encourage the adoption of green building practices that are viewed as beneficial to the public but may be more costly to implement than conventional building practices. In this way, such programs affect supply and demand for green building, as discussed in Chapter 4.

In the United States, the Database of State Incentives for Renewables and Efficiency (DSIRE) is a repository of energy-efficiency and renewable-energy policies and incentive programs for each state.[1] While it is a good starting point for available incentives in a particular area within the US, this database may not include every available program for certain types of green building incentives that are not directly related to energy efficiency and renewable energy generation, such as green infrastructure. The local municipality and local utilities, such as the water and sewer authority, may be the best source of informa-

1. See www.dsireusa.org.

tion relating to any available green building incentives that may not be directly related to energy efficiency or renewable energy generation.[2]

Types of Incentives and Impact on the Valuation Process

Incentives raise a variety of valuation issues. Incentives can include rebates, tax effects, and special financing programs available for green-related improvements, any of which may affect the valuation process. The nuanced yet critical question of how incentives differ from concessions from a valuation perspective is discussed in the accompanying sidebar. While this distinction may initially seem to be little more than a point of semantics, whether the offset is classed as an incentive or concession changes how it is analyzed within the appraisal process.

Incentives or Concessions?

Incentives for green building improvements, such as energy-efficiency upgrades and on-site energy generation, are sometimes confused with concessions offered by sellers or landlords at the time of transaction. However, there are important differences between the two. While a seller- or landlord-provided concession may in some cases function as an incentive in that it facilitates a sale or lease transaction, seller- and landlord-provided concessions are treated differently in the appraisal process.

Third-party incentives in the context of green building differ from seller-provided concessions in two important respects: the funding source and the timing. Exhibit 11.1 breaks down the various scenarios that may be encountered for a subject property and comparable properties that receive proceeds related to green building improvements. As seen in the graphic, the first step is determining *when* the proceeds are provided, followed by identifying *who* is providing the funds. That is, the first question is whether the proceeds are transferred at the time of the transaction or independent of the sale or lease transaction, and second, whether the proceeds are being provided by the seller/lessor or by a third party.

As the exhibit shows, proceeds for green improvements are generally considered to be concessions if they were provided by the seller at the time of a transaction, whereas such proceeds would be considered incentives if they were provided by a third party independent of a particular transaction. The exception occurs when a third-party incentive is transferred by the seller to the buyer as part of a transaction. This situation could occur in cases of rebates for green improvements offered by the local utility or government that a developer/builder may assign to the buyer at the time of sale, such as a rebate for an energy-efficient lighting upgrade. In that case, while a third party is the ultimate source of the funds, it is the seller who is providing them to the buyer as part of the bundle of rights transferring at the time of sale, with the seller acting as a conduit for the incentive. In contrast, if the proceeds are third-party provided without passing through the seller, and assuming that the benefit would be available to any prospective buyer, this would not be considered a concession. Preferential Fannie Mae financing terms for green multifamily properties would be an example of a third party-provided incentive that may be tied to a particular transaction.

---

2. A number of communities offer such programs through the water and sewer utility. For example, see the information on green infrastructure funding available through the Milwaukee Metropolitan Sewerage District at www.mmsd.com/mmsd-news/green-infrastructure-funding-available. The Milwaukee area and other Great Lakes communities deal with rainwater runoff in the watershed. Other areas in the country face other water-related issues and may offer similar green infrastructure incentive programs.

Exhibit 11.1 **Are Proceeds for Green Improvements Incentives or Concessions?**

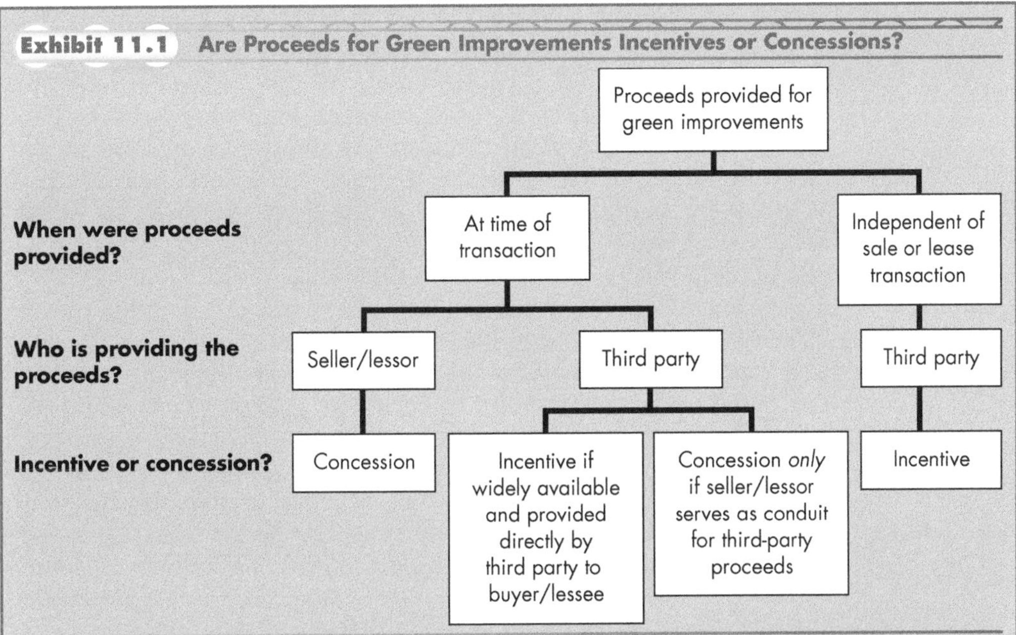

This distinction between incentives and concessions can impact the analysis of a subject property and its comparable properties. While both incentives and concessions have the effect of reducing the net cost of the green improvements to the recipient, they are treated differently in the appraisal process. Seller-provided concessions are typically treated as a line-item deduction from the gross sale price in order to normalize the price absent the effect of the seller-provided concession. Similarly, landlord-provided concessions reduce the effective rental rate paid by the tenant. Third-party incentives, in contrast, typically function independently of a particular transaction. Therefore, unless the third-party incentive is specifically tied to the transaction, it would not normally be a consideration when analyzing the current sale price of the subject property or a comparable property in the sales comparison approach.

Third-party incentives are, however, a relevant consideration when analyzing the current or historical cost of a property or an improvement to a property. For example, if rebates for energy-efficiency improvements are widely available in the current market, they should be considered when evaluating the contributory value of the improvements in the cost approach or cases when a cost-based adjustment is used in another approach. If the rebate program has expired and rebates are no longer available, they no longer represent a reduction in the current replacement cost of the improvement and would not be considered.

Ongoing incentives may also need to be considered in the appraisal process. For example, suppose that the subject property or one of the comparable properties benefits from an ongoing incentive such as a feed-in-tariff (FIT), a scheme whereby excess electricity generated by an on-site renewable energy system is reimbursed at a premium rate. If this incentive is no longer available in the market, this financial benefit represents a unique attribute of the property for which an appropriate adjustment would need to be made, assuming it could be transferred to another buyer.

Rebates, Grants, and Other Direct Reimbursements

Rebates are direct payments to the property owner to offset some or all of the cost of qualified improvements. Rebate programs are usually administered locally by the utility or municipality and are often funded through a ratepayer surcharge or another means. Rebate programs vary widely but may apply to energy-efficiency upgrades such as insulation, high-efficiency windows or HVAC equipment, solar PV, battery storage, or low-flow plumbing fixtures. The programs often have a defined time period or a maximum subscription amount.

For example, in some areas, distributed solar PV systems were initially eligible for rebates that declined in amount per watt installed based on the total amount of installed capacity in the utility service territory. In many areas, solar PV rebate programs have been fully subscribed and new installations are no longer eligible for utility rebates. However, rebates for solar hot water heating systems or energy-efficiency improvements may still be available. Rebates may also be available for green infrastructure improvements such as permeable pavement, bioswales, and rainwater detention or treatment improvements (such as cisterns). The availability of these programs varies with the local jurisdiction's priorities and funding capacity.

Rebates reduce the cost of the qualified improvements to the property owner on a dollar-for-dollar basis. They are normally deducted from the current replacement cost new as a line item in the cost budget at the level currently available in the market.

Grants function in much the same manner as rebates, reflecting a direct reimbursement to the property owner for qualified green improvements. Grants are often targeted to cutting-edge technology and other high-cost improvements that are seen as beneficial but may not otherwise be implemented due to a high initial cost. Examples of grant programs include battery storage as well as weatherization and other energy-efficiency improvements for low-income housing.

Rebates, grants, and other forms of direct reimbursements affect the cost approach to the extent that they are widely available to the market and are being used by market participants. If they are no longer available, historical rebates should not be applied to a current replacement cost estimate. This type of incentive also affects any cost-based adjustment to the income capitalization or sales comparison approach for the contributory value of green-related improvements by reducing the net cost to the property owner. Primary market research may be necessary to discern the extent to which the market is incorporating these direct reimbursements into its view of the contributory value of the improvements.

Tax Effects

Tax credits and other tax implications of real estate are usually not considered in the process of a market value appraisal. However, the market reaction to the federal Business Energy Investment Tax Credit (ITC) and its importance in the continued expansion of solar PV and other forms of renewable energy should be considered in the appraisal of properties with distributed energy generation capacity.

The ITC is a tax credit available to US taxpayers as a dollar-for-dollar reduction in tax liability taken at the end of the year that the project is placed in service. The current rate for commercial properties is 30% of the qualified basis through 2019, declining to 26% in 2020, 22% in 2021, and then 10% in 2022, where it remains indefinitely.[3] Solar PV is eligible, as are a variety of other renewable technologies. However, some technologies have maximum limits and/or more attenuated credit reduction.

The ITC is widely credited with facilitating the growth in distributed solar PV. The market appears to have internalized this expectation, and the solar installation industry widely employs its benefit when selling systems to prospective clients. Because it is available virtually everywhere in the United States and can be monetized in the first year by any US taxpayer with an adequate tax liability, all or a portion of the federal ITC is typically viewed in the marketplace in the same manner as other incentives, such as rebates and grants. In the context of the cost approach, the ITC shares the characteristics of external obsolescence to the extent that it affects all properties similarly, reduces the cost equally, and is external to the parties to the transaction. However, the ITC is subject to a five-year recapture for commercial properties, which may reduce its value, particularly for properties that are expected to transfer within five years of installation.

Accelerated depreciation may also be presented as a direct financial benefit of renewable distributed energy systems like solar PV. Renewable energy systems are eligible for federal Modified Accelerated Cost Recovery System (MACRS) tax deductions, as discussed in Chapter 10. There may also be favorable state-level depreciation deductions available. While it is possible that accelerated depreciation may reflect some level of financial benefit to property owners in certain markets, the extent of that benefit would be limited to the marginally faster cost recovery relative to the cost recovery available for other, similar property improvements. Furthermore, the timing of the benefit would need to be considered, which could entail comparing the present value of the alternate depreciation schedules.

3. For residential installations, the ITC declines to 10% in 2020, where it remains indefinitely. Tax policy is subject to change. See www.dsireusa.org or a similar database for up-to-date incentive availability, including tax credits.

Financing-Related Incentives

Financing programs are also available for a wide range of energy-efficiency and green building improvements, as well as renewable energy generation. The various programs may offer below-market interest rates, favorable underwriting standards, or a combination of the two. For example, Fannie Mae began offering a green building incentive financing program for multifamily projects that meet certain green building guidelines in early 2016. The program uses conventional underwriting but allows a 25 basis point reduction (or more) in the interest rate.

The treatment of favorable financing programs for green building-related improvements is similar to the manner in which favorable financing for conventional buildings is handled in the appraisal process. For example, the benefit of the 25 basis point reduction in the interest rate could be estimated as the present value of the difference between the respective loan payments at market rates versus the favorable rate, discounted at the market rate.

Property Assessed Clean Energy (PACE) programs, sometimes also referred to as C-PACE for commercial properties, are a special type of financing program that can be used for a variety of green improvements, including energy-efficiency upgrades and renewable energy systems. PACE programs allow the property owner to finance qualified improvements with the payments added to the property tax bill, much like a special assessment for a municipal bond. The programs vary in terms of requirements and may be offered by a municipality or private sector entity. The program may or may not require an appraisal of the underlying real estate. Underwriting is often less rigorous than it would be for a conventional loan, which adds to the program's appeal. Furthermore, PACE loans are typically transferrable upon sale to the new owner, unlike conventional loans, and because they are billed with the property taxes, may be viewed as a priority lien on the asset. If the interest rate on the PACE loan is above market, the PACE encumbrance may need to be evaluated for its effect on marketability and/or the potential purchase price.

The effects of PACE financing on the valuation process may vary and can be complex to analyze. The last section of this chapter delves into some of the more nuanced appraisal issues that may develop due to PACE financing.

On-bill financing is similar to PACE financing, except that instead of being billed with the property taxes, the payment for the loan is included with the local utility bill. On-bill financing impacts depend on the nature of the program, the magnitude of the monthly payment, and whether the financing follows the property or the property owner in the event of transfer.

Other Incentives

Some of the other more common but indirect incentives for green building-related improvements include expedited entitlement processing, density bonuses, Renewable Energy Certificates and Credits, and FITs.

Entitlement benefits such as expedited permitting and density bonuses may also be available in certain areas for green building-related improvements. Some programs specify a certain level of LEED certification or an equivalent. While the value of expedited permitting may be more difficult to quantify, the effect of a density bonus, particularly in higher-density urban and transit-oriented suburban areas, may be more readily quantifiable.

Renewable Energy Certificates and Credits (RECs) are tradable representations of the environmental benefits of renewable energy generation that are sold separately from the electricity generated.[4] They are also known as "green tags," "green certificates," and "tradable renewable certificates." RECs are typically traded in a minimum of 1 megawatt-hour (MWh) increments.

RECs are available for purchase by virtually anyone, but the primary customers are electrical utilities in states where renewable portfolio standards (RPS) requirements can be met by purchasing RECs. They may be traded in an open market or bought and sold in a more controlled setting, depending on the market. Open-market pricing tends to be more volatile, as it is sensitive to the spot pricing impacts of supply and demand. In addition, the purchase contract may extend over multiple years, and the price per MWh may be structured to decline over time. While these incentives may represent a significant financial incentive to the property owner, they are typically considered to be an intangible component of value and are reported separately in the market value appraisal of real property.

FITs are not common in the United States, although they have been used widely in other areas, such as Germany. FITs reflect a utility tariff wherein a distributed energy generator such as a rooftop solar owner receives a premium from the utility over the cost of grid-purchased electricity for net electrical generation provided to the grid. These tariffs are usually intended to facilitate the local utility in reaching its RPS requirements. The impact of a FIT would depend on the degree to which the reimbursement rate is above the price of grid-purchased electricity, the duration of the agreement, and whether it is transferrable to a new owner. Some of the same risk considerations would apply to FITs as to NEM tariffs, as discussed in Chapter 10.

4. RECs are referred to as Solar Renewable Energy Certificates (SRECs) in some markets.

PACE Financing

PACE financing is sometimes advertised as adding value to a property, which is misleading. PACE is simply a financing vehicle. While the improvements that PACE finances may, and often do, materially affect market value, the benefit must be reported in light of the priority lien that a PACE encumbrance represents. What can be confusing to all involved is that market value appraisals typically assume ownership free and clear of liens or encumbrances, yet the PACE encumbrance is a priority lien billed with the property taxes.

As a financing vehicle, PACE encumbrances, particularly PACE loans for improvements that affect the operating expenses like energy-efficiency upgrades and distributed generation, require attention in both the development and the reporting of the appraisal. The developing and reporting are interrelated, and care is required to be internally consistent within the report and to be consistent with how the PACE encumbrance is reported in the appraisal.

Appraisal Development Issues

The primary issue when developing the appraisal for a property with an existing or proposed PACE encumbrance is whether the reported value conclusion will include the value of the PACE-financed improvements. If the reported value includes the benefit of the PACE-financed improvements, the reported value conclusion should also reflect the associated encumbrance. If the appraisal of a property does not include the benefit of the PACE-financed improvements, the reported value conclusion becomes a hypothetical value, unless the improvements have not yet been completed. No matter how it is developed and reported, the optimal solution is best attained during the process of developing the scope of work with the client at the outset of the assignment.

Appraisal Reporting Issues

Once the appraisal development concerns have been addressed through the scope of work, two important appraisal reporting considerations should be kept in mind in order to avoid reporting a misleading result. First of all, the PACE encumbrance should be clearly disclosed and reported throughout the report, and best practices would include the PACE encumbrance everywhere the as-proposed value is reported. Second, particularly for lender assignments, the client may require a separate income statement that reflects the reduced expenses due to the solar PV-generated electricity, energy-efficiency improvements, or other cost reduction measures such as water or waste stream considerations. This as-proposed *NOI* could then be used for underwriting purposes, more accurately reflecting the cash flow available for debt service.

In this second instance, several important issues should be kept in mind when reporting an as-proposed *NOI*. If the improvements include items like a solar PV system, which is expected to have an economic life that may be less than the overall property, then an adjustment to the replacement reserves should be considered in order to reflect the cost of replacing the system in the future. The cost of replacing the inverter(s) should also be included. These costs could be included in a variety of ways: as a separate line item, in the repairs and maintenance category, or in the replacement reserves allowance. Similarly, the operating costs may also be affected by any required costs of ongoing commissioning, maintenance, and repairs of complex systems.

PACE versus Infrastructure Bonds

PACE encumbrances are sometimes viewed as analogous to publicly issued bonds for infrastructure improvements associated with new development projects. While there are similarities, there are also important distinctions that may determine how the client views the PACE payments from an underwriting standpoint and how the PACE encumbrance is reported in the appraisal.

Infrastructure bonds typically pertain to improvements that benefit one or more privately owned parcels but are situated on contiguous, publicly owned land. In contrast, PACE is used to finance improvements to privately owned buildings situated on private land. Secondly, infrastructure bonds are imposed by collective vote and cover an entire class or group of properties. In contrast, PACE financing is voluntary, pertains to a single property, and is at the discretion of the private property owner. While it might be argued that infrastructure bond assessment payments reflect a tax and thus are part of the governmental powers exception that prevails over fee simple ownership, the private property owner's control over participation and direct ownership of the PACE-financed improvements do not fit the common definition of a governmental imposition or tax.

This distinction may be important in determining how a lender client views the PACE payments from an underwriting standpoint and how the PACE encumbrance is reported in the appraisal.

Case Study 11.A PACE Financing

As discussed in the previous section, PACE financing allows property owners to borrow money to finance green improvements. The payment is added to the property tax bill, and lending requirements may be less stringent than they would be for a typical loan. Valuing a property with a PACE encumbrance may be relatively uncomplicated. On the other hand, complexities can quickly arise, even from projects that may at first seem straightforward.

Case Study 11.A *(continued)*

Overview

A property owner of an 82,400-sq.-ft., 1980s-era, single-tenant industrial manufacturing building located in the Silicon Valley of Northern California wants to finance a $2.25 million solar PV project without paying out of pocket for the up-front costs. In addition, the owner would like to pass along the cost of the PV system to the tenant, who will be the primary beneficiary, since the tenant's electricity bill would be eliminated by the installation of the solar PV system.

The property is leased for a remaining term of nine years to a high-tech electronics manufacturer. Under the triple-net lease, the tenant pays 100% of all building expenses, except structural reserves. The tenant's current monthly electric bill averages almost $20,000, excluding fixed charges, representing 1,200,000 kWh of electricity load per year. The property owner wants to install a 750 kW DC solar PV array to essentially supply the tenant's entire electricity load, making the facility net zero energy (NZE).

Adequate roof area is not available to accomodate a system of this size, so approximately one quarter of the modules need to be situated on carport mounts in the parking lot. The carport mounts are more expensive than roof mounts, but they also provide a shade amenity for parked cars, which is a desirable amenity for the tenant's employees in this climate.

The installed cost of the system is summarized in Exhibit 11.2. As indicated in the table, the solar PV system cost includes the carport mounts. Replacing the roof was deemed necessary due to its age and the costs of removing and reinstalling the modules during their expected economic life of 25 years. The reported costs are gross costs, before considering any available incentives.

Exhibit 11.2 Breakdown of the Cost for the Solar PV System

Solar PV system	$1,812,000
Re-roofing	$377,000
PACE closing costs	$61,000
Total system cost	$2,250,000
Installed cost per watt	$3.00 per watt

In this utility territory, all utility and municipal rebates and incentives have been fully subscribed and are no longer available to new solar PV projects. The 30% federal ITC is available for the qualified portion of the project. Solar PV installations also qualify for accelerated depreciation under the five-year MACRS schedule. The project parameters are summarized in Exhibit 11.3.

Case Study 11.A *(continued)*

Exhibit 11.3 Project Overview

Property type	1980s-era industrial manufacturing building
Property size	82,400 square feet
Amount to be financed	$2,250,000 gross system cost
Size of solar PV system	750 kW DC
Projected electricity generation	1,200,000 kWh per year (Year 1)
Lease term remaining	9 years
Current electricity cost	$20,000 per month (1)
Gross avoided electricity cost	$238,000 per year (2)
O&M allowance ($30/kW DC/yr.)	($22,500) per year (3)
Net avoided cost of electricity	$215,500 per year
Utility and municipal rebates?	No
Tax credit?	Yes 30% ITC available
Accelerated depreciation?	Yes 5-year MACRS

(1) Net of fixed charges
(2) System sized to provide 99% of predicted electricity load
(3) Annual allownace for inverter replacement, monitoring, and maintenance

Potential Benefits of Using PACE Financing

In looking at this project from the points of view of the landlord (property owner), tenant, and lender, a variety of potential benefits can be seen. The primary potential benefits of using PACE financing for the landlord include:

- No need to refinance the existing mortgage
- No out-of-pocket cost
- No personal credit guarantee–real estate is sole security for the loan
- All or a substantial portion of the system cost paid directly via the tenant's property tax bill
- Free and clear ownership of a 10-year old solar PV system once the PACE loan is paid off
- May provide a financing option for owners in cases when sourcing additional equity or debt are not viable or are forbidden by the existing loan covenants

The primary potential benefits for the tenant include:

- Fixed electricity costs for the remainder of the lease term
- Marketability of carbon-free manufacturing to clients
- The potential to build in electrical grid resiliency by adding battery storage

For the existing lender in first lien position, the main benefit of consenting to allow a PACE encumbrance to step ahead of the first mortgage in lien priority is

Case Study 11.A *(continued)*

to maintain an existing customer relationship. There may be few other benefits to the primary lender.

Does the PACE Solution Pencil Out?

Exhibit 11.4 shows the key parameters of PACE financing proposed for this project.

Exhibit 11.4 Summary of Key Parameters of the PACE Financing Proposal

Amount financed	$2,250,000
Term	10 years
Payments	Biannual
Interest rate (nominal)	5.65%
Annual PACE payment	$321,500 per year (1)
Net avoided electricity cost	$215,500 per year (2)
Payment premium with PACE	$106,000 per year

(1) Includes reserve for initial year payment (as reported by landlord)

(2) Net of operations and maintenance (O&M) allowance

This situation presents an intriguing scenario. As noted in Exhibit 11.4, the proposed financing would require the tenant to pay a 49% premium, or $106,000 more per year for electricity. Unless the tenant agrees to pay this premium for renewable energy, this solution would not appear to meet the property owner's stated requirements of avoiding up-front costs for the solar PV system.

What else might explain why this proposed solution might be acceptable to both the property owner and the tenant?

There may be several reasons for tenants to consider a scenario in which they pay a premium for this type of on-site renewable energy:

- The lease includes language that requires it (i.e., the tenant signed a "green lease," as described in the sidebar titled "What Is a Green Lease" in Chapter 9 (page 213)).
- The tenant perceives other benefits, such as the business benefit of advertising carbon-neutral manufacturing to the clients.
- The tenant perceives a benefit in fixing electricity costs for 10 years, which exceeds the 49% electricity cost premium.
- The tenant can reap some or all of the associated tax benefits.

In this particular case, the tenant was a part owner of the building and thus was able to derive partial benefit from the 30% federal ITC and five-year MACRS accelerated depreciation deduction. However, without these tax benefits, selling this program to the tenant would likely be a struggle. Alternately, the landlord could fund the shortfall, which would be offset by the same tax credit and depreciation benefits during the first five years.

Case Study 11.A *(continued)*

Potential Risks of PACE Financing

Assuming all parties agree to the proposal, what are the risks to the property owner (landlord) and tenant in this case?

- Vacancy risk
  PACE payment continues for 10 years even during vacancy, when the property does not benefit from the avoided electricity cost. The risk accrues primarily to the landlord.
- Superadequacy risk
  Is PV capacity consistent with market demand for electricity for the most probable user? In other words, will the business needs of the current tenant change the amount of electricity needed for the remaining lease term? Will more energy-efficient equipment reduce the electrical load in the future? This risk accrues primarly to the tenant since the PACE loan term and the remaining term of the lease closely coincide in this case.
- Negative leverage risk
  Negative leverage occurs when the PACE payment is greater than the operating cost savings due to short amortization, interest rate, or operating cost savings that do not justify up-front cost. In ths case, the risk accrues primarily to the tenant.
- Marketability risk
  Will the investment and leasing markets view the PACE encumbrance as a negative factor? This risk accrues to the landlord.
- NEM risk
  The current NEM tariff may change unfavorably at some point in the future, reducing the value of the avoided electricity cost.[5] In this case, the risk accrues primarily to the tenant.

These risks are not materially different than the risk any property owner faces for a non-green renovation or tenant improvement project. No tenant equals no rent, and specialized improvements may or may not garner the same rent premium in the marketplace as generic improvements, which could result in superadequacy and/or negative leverage. These risks are inherent in all real estate, green or conventional. However, the origin and nature of the risk may be unfamiliar to the valuation professional and the property owner accustomed to conventional real estate risk/return analyses. For example, NEM risk analysis requires some level of understanding of the behavior of the regulatory authorities who set NEM tariffs, as well as the susceptibility of the tariff-setting process to political influence from IOUs. In some utility territories, existing NEM tariffs may be grandfathered and thus protected from changes for a specified period, such as 20 years.

5. See Chapter 10 for more information on NEM and NEM risk.

Case Study 11.A *(continued)*

Superadequacy risk from the tenant's perspective includes risk specific to the current tenant's business and the larger business sector in which the tenant operates. If demand for the tenant's products or services decreases or the overall business sector declines, the tenant may be locked into a fixed-cost arrangement when demand is variable and has declined. Technological advancements could also reduce demand, as new equipment and building components become more energy efficient, either voluntarily or due to code upgrades. This risk cuts both ways, however, as shifts toward electrical vehicles that require daytime charging stations, for example, may more than offset the reduced demand from technological advances, building code changes, or changes in the specific business or sector.

What about the risk to the first lien holder, that is, the lender who has an existing first trust deed in place and may be asked to consent to a PACE priority lien? Primary concerns of the first mortgage lender include:

- Vacancy risk
  Who pays the PACE debt service if the tenant vacates?
- Underwriting risk
  How do the loan-to-value, debt coverage ratio, and other underwriting parameters change with the PACE loan? Does this affect the landlord's ability to make timely loan payments on the first mortgage?
- Regulatory compliance risk
  Will the bank regulators change how the loan is classified due to the PACE encumbrance?
- Default risk
  Just like property taxes, the lender is ultimately responsible for the PACE payments if the borrower fails to stay current. However, there is some protection for the primary lender, as the PACE loan usually cannot be accelerated in the event of default. In other words, the primary lender cannot be required to pay off the outstanding balance on the PACE loan just because the borrower falls behind on the PACE payments.
- NEM risk
  Does the tenant's ability or willingness to pay deteriorate if the NEM tariff changes such that the avoided electricity cost to the tenant is reduced?

Lender risk concerns are likely to be commensurate with the magnitude of the PACE encumbrance. A PACE encumbrance of less than 5% of the asset value is likely to warrant less concern and scrutiny from the lender than the present example, in which the $2.25 million PACE encumbrance could approach 20% of the market value of the underlying asset.

Summary

Green building incentives provided by utilities, public agencies, or other third parties result from policies intended to encourage green building practices. A wide variety of incentives exist for green building-related improvements that can have material impacts on the appraisal process. These programs may be direct subsidies such as rebates, tax benefits, or favorable financing, as well as less direct material benefits such as expedited entitlements or density bonuses. Understanding the market's perspective on the incentive, as well as the extent of its availability, is critical to properly addressing the market value impact of green building incentives.

PACE programs provide financing options for energy-efficiency, distributed-generation, and other green improvements that may not otherwise be feasible due to liquidity limitations, existing loan covenants, or leases that do not permit these costs to be recovered. As a financing vehicle for improvements that often affect the operating expenses of a property, special care is required in the development and reporting of the appraisal. There are a variety of ways to accurately incorporate the value effect of the improvements and the underlying encumbrance in a clear manner that is not misleading. Engaging the client in this discussion early when developing the scope of work is central to a satisfactory outcome for both the client and the appraiser.

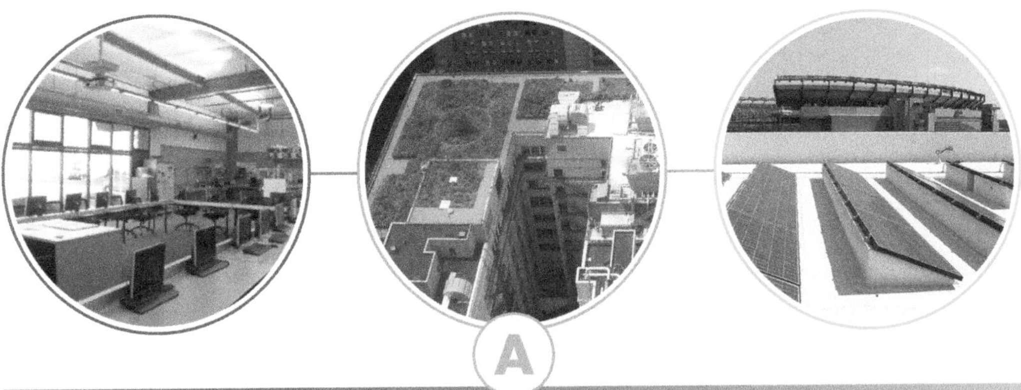

A Green Feature Gallery

Green features are property characteristics that achieve green or sustainability objectives, such as resource efficiency, enhanced occupant health and well-being, or the minimization of the environmental impacts of real estate development. Green features are not exclusively found in green buildings; they can exist in conventional buildings as well. As green building becomes more common, either through voluntary adoption or policy mandates, existing conventional building stock is increasingly incorporating green building design and features through retrofits and renovations. This infiltration of green building features into existing buildings makes it increasingly likely for valuation professionals to encounter green features in their course of work.

Green buildings are not merely random assemblages of green features. As Jason McLennan, creator of the Living Building Challenge rating system described in Chapter 2, puts it, "Sustainable design is much more than a shopping list of technologies and strategies that can be found in any particular building."[1] However, recognizing common green features is key to describing and valuing the property. Even if the building does not meet the definition or market standard for a green building per se or is a decidedly non-green building, specific green features may have direct or indirect value impacts that warrant consideration. Furthermore, the identification of one or more green features may spark additional relevant inquiry into the building's physical or operational characteristics.

1. Jason F. McLennan, *The Philosophy of Sustainable Design* (Kansas City, MO: Ecotone Publishing, 2004), 98.

Green features, however, are not always obvious. The often seamless integration of green elements within a building and its site can make it difficult to identify them, particularly for those who may not be regularly involved with green buildings. This Green Feature Gallery provides examples of various green features and includes brief descriptions, photos, and discussion of their potential impact on value. It is meant to be illustrative, but not exhaustive.

The green features discussed here are grouped into five broad categories:

- Site and location characteristics
- Structural and building envelope features
- Mechanical, electrical, and plumbing (MEP) components
- Interior build-out
- On-site energy generation systems

Due to the interrelated nature of many green building elements, keep in mind that these categories are used to organize the following discussion and not meant to imply that a green feature only impacts a single category or system. For example, daylighting strategies have been categorized in this Appendix in the interior build-out category, but daylighting can also have meaningful impacts in the mechanical systems category and affect the building envelope.

Bioswales can be used in all types of locales and property types. This bioswale is located in front of a residence hall at the University of Wisconsin-Stevens Point. Note how the gutter and downspout system funnels rainwater from the roof into the bioswale, thereby keeping the rainwater from entering the municipal sewer system.

Site and Location Characteristics

Bioswales and Other Rainwater Management Strategies

Bioswales, rain gardens, underground cisterns, and on-site retention and detention ponds are site improvements that facilitate on-site rainwater management. This approach of managing and treating the rainwater where it falls differs from conventional construction practices, which contain and control rainwater in order to transfer it safely off site to a municipal sewer system or other natural receptacle such as a river, stream, or wetland. Besides reducing demand on the municipal infrastructure, on-site rainwater management helps maintain natural underground aquifer recharge and reduces pollutant flows into nearby waterways. Underground cisterns may be used to collect and store rainwater for watering landscaping during dry periods and to control or prevent off-site flows during periods when the municipal system is overwhelmed, holding the water for release at a later time when the treatment system is not at or over capacity.

The Packard Foundation's headquarters in Los Altos, California, features a wide variety of rainwater management strategies, including rain gardens, a green roof, and a 20,000-gallon underground cistern. The cistern allows rainwater to be collected for landscaping and for toilet flushing within the building. A detention basin, seen here, serves as a protective measure in case the cistern reaches capacity. A detention basin (or pond) differs from a retention pond in that it is meant to handle overflow water as needed in heavy storms and allow for the slow release of that water, whereas a retention pond is designed to hold water for indefinite periods of time.

At Persimmon Place, a LEED Gold-certified retail shopping center in Dublin, California, this bioswale populated with drought-tolerant plant species captures rainwater runoff from the parking lot.

Cherry Gardens, a LEED-certified multifamily project in Charlotte, North Carolina, has a site size of less than one acre and was deemed to be too small for traditional above-ground rainwater treatment options. Instead, an underground system designed to detain rainwater and remove particulates from it was installed. Two systems were installed—one under the parking lot behind the building and one in front of the building.

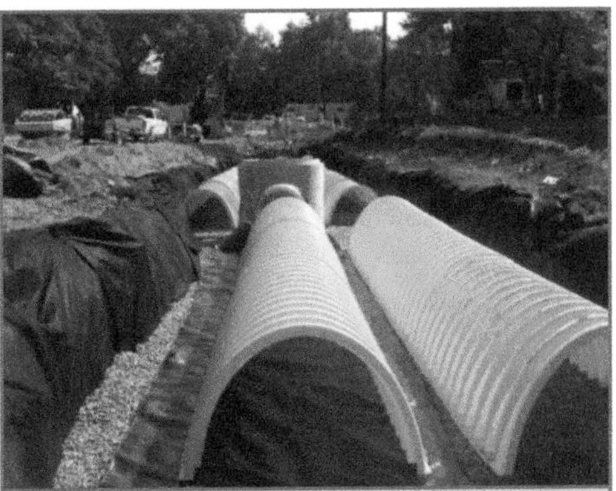

A close-up of the underground system designed to detain and treat rainwater at the Cherry Gardens project. Photograph courtesy of Jimmy Royster, Project Manager, The Affordable Housing Group of NC.

On-site water management features can be difficult to discern from conventional landscaping features, and their costs may not be much different than those for conventional landscaping features. Cisterns and water re-use systems add to the cost of a project, which may be mitigated operationally to some extent by lower municipal water/sewer charges or infrastructure impact fees.

Drought-Tolerant Landscaping

Drought-tolerant landscaping practices, sometimes referred to as *xeriscaping*, reduce or eliminate outdoor plant water use. These practices are becoming so common in water-stressed portions of the United States, such as the West, that it is influencing the overall design aesthetic, changing the usual color palette from lush greens to one that incorporates more warm browns, yellows, and grays. In arid areas, a common strategy involves native species planted at low density, surrounded by thick mulch to retain soil moisture. These plantings are often combined with various crushed decorative stone or some other type of permeable hardscape surface, such as decomposed limestone, in place of more hydrophilic turf that dominated landscapes as recently as the 1980s and 1990s. When turf is included, it may be artificial. Instead of using conventional broadcast sprinklers, water is delivered via a timer-controlled drip irrigation system that waters each individual plant. Timers with weather- or soil moisture-sensing controls are now mandatory minimum requirements of the California green building code, CALGreen.

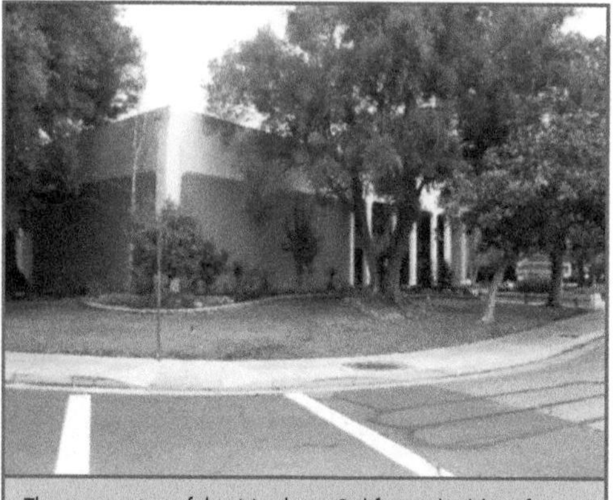

The renovation of this Northern California building from a fitness facility to net zero energy office space utilized drip irrigation to reduce the amount of water used for landscaping. This photo shows the building before renovation, with traditional water-thirsty turf ground cover.

This photo shows the same yard area planted with drought-tolerant rosemary bushes and covered with wood-chip mulch.

Alternative Modes of Transport

Property owners and developers are finding it increasingly necessary to support and facilitate alternatives to traditional automobile commuting. The impetus for this comes not just from sustainability-oriented policy but also from practical limitations of the existing automobile infrastructure and the high cost of expanding it. Demographics are also in play, as millennials in particular demonstrate less affinity for automobiles and a greater reliance on alternate modes of transport such as bicycles, walking, and public transit.

Active commuting options such as bicycling require changes to the building's parking capacity and configuration to include secure bike storage, lockers, and shower facilities. Proximity to dedicated trails and bike lanes plays a bigger role in enhanced locational appeal when occupants engage in active commuting. Access to ride-hailing services may affect the appeal of a particular location. Access to existing public transit options means the property owner may avoid the ongoing operational cost of private shuttles.

Other evidence of an emphasis on supporting alternate transport modes includes priority car pool and van pool parking, bike share facilities, shower and locker facilities, parking spaces dedicated

This sign, located at the entrance of a retail shopping center in the Bay Area of Northern California, is a clear indication that this shopping center is located within walking distance of the regional rail system (BART).

The property owners of this Midtown Manhattan office building converted one of its loading docks into tenant bicycle storage.

This Silicon Valley office building features secure bike storage. These metal containers are a good example of how a green feature might go unnoticed or be misattributed without proper knowledge. Unless one is a bike commuter or is told specifically what these containers house, how would one know they are meant for bike storage?

to car share services, and subsidized transit vouchers. These programs may be voluntary, compulsory due to entitlement or zoning requirements, or reflective of green building credit achievement. While parking lot signs may be quite obvious, the only evidence of a shuttle service or voucher program may be a line item in the building operating statement. The cost may also be entirely obscured within another expense category.

The sidebar in Chapter 7 titled "Suburban Sustainability" (page 134) discusses some of the issues faced by a property that lacked transit proximity and the subsequent changes made by the property owner to address this shortfall.

Walkable Amenities

The emphasis on mixed-use projects that create a live-work-play environment has heightened the focus of a project's linkages to daily needs such as retail, restaurants, entertainment, child care, medical services, and education providers. *Walkability* has emerged as the term to describe a basic locational characteristic: How convenient is this site to what else the occupants do every day?

Walk Score uses a proprietary algorithm to rate an area's relative proximity to a variety of services on a scale of 0 to 100. The higher the score, the less a motor vehicle is required to meet daily needs. Transit Score and Bike Score are related scoring systems by the same organization that provides Walk Score. They can be helpful in ranking locational appeal in markets where these attributes matter to the end users.

Another aspect of walkable amenities is access to open space and walking trails. In suburban areas, open space is typically not at the premium it is in more urban settings. However, lack of sidewalks in suburban areas can inhibit pedestrian access to both open space and daily needs. Furthermore, the distribution of open space may not facilitate regular ac-

Walkable amenities can include access to open or green spaces. In New York City, an abandoned railroad trestle was transformed into a public park. The High Line opened in phases, beginning in 2009.

The High Line serves as a park to neighborhood residents and visitors.

cess by residents and workers. In urban settings, cities may mandate that new developments set aside a certain amount of publicly accessible open space. In New York City, an abandoned former elevated freight rail line on Manhattan's West Side was transformed into an elevated public park called the High Line, as shown in the accompanying photographs.

The High Line also mitigates the negative effects of rainwater runoff, functioning similarly to a green roof.

Structural and Building Envelope Features

Atypical Insulation Techniques

The three accompanying photographs illustrate an atypical wall insulation technique designed to improve the thermal comfort of a building's interior while reducing its energy use. In this example, a 5⅝-inch layer of rigid foam insulation was applied to the exterior of the existing 6-inch concrete tilt-up walls and then encapsulated in a rigid, laminated composite exterior finish. While exterior finish insulation systems are not unique to green building, this wall assembly is unusual in terms of the amount of insulation used and the fact that the concrete wall interior is left exposed to the interior air of the building. This is a fundamental departure from a conventional approach, in which the interior walls would be furred out with wood and finished with gypsum board. Filling the cavity between the gypsum board and the concrete wall with fiberglass batt insulation may or may not be performed, depending on the local code and climate conditions.

Mounting the insulation on the exterior and leaving the concrete walls exposed to the interior air allows the thermal mass properties of the structural concrete walls to contribute to stabilizing the internal temperature of the building. The combination of increasing the R-value of the building envelope and enhancing the thermal mass properties of the structure reduces the amount of energy needed to mechanically heat and cool the interior and maintain thermal comfort for the occupants.

Applying the insulation to the building exterior also creates a natural inset for the windows, which can help control glare and unwanted solar heat gain. As seen in the first of the three accompanying office building photos, the deep inset also allows the aluminum window frames to function as light shelves, reflecting light into the interior of the building.

Besides affecting the nominal increase in usable floor area that would otherwise be lost to the studs and gypsum board walls, this insulation strategy affects various cost elements of the property. Initial capital costs will be affected by the reduced size of any required mechanical HVAC equipment. Additionally, the added cost of the exterior insulation system will be accompanied by a reduction in cost due to the lack of furring, drywall, and interior insulation. Operating costs will likely be reduced due to decreased energy consumption and the fewer maintenance needs of a smaller HVAC system. If the HVAC system includes a cooling tower, water use will also likely be reduced due to the reduced cooling load. Lastly, future capital costs for replacement of the downsized HVAC system will also be affected, reducing the required reserves allowance.

Observing this type of atypical construction technique is a clue that the building's design team focused on building energy use. This should prompt questions about whether other areas of building energy use, such as lighting and HVAC, were also addressed.

In this renovated office building, the nearly 6-inch exterior-applied insulation creates natural shading of the inset glazing. The brushed aluminum horizontal portion of the window frame separating the view glass from the transom simultaneously functions as a solar shade for the view glass below it, and as a light shelf that reflects daylight through the transom glazing above it, into the interior of the building. There, the natural light reflects off the underside of the reflective metal ceiling, bringing glare-free natural light deeper into the interior of the building.

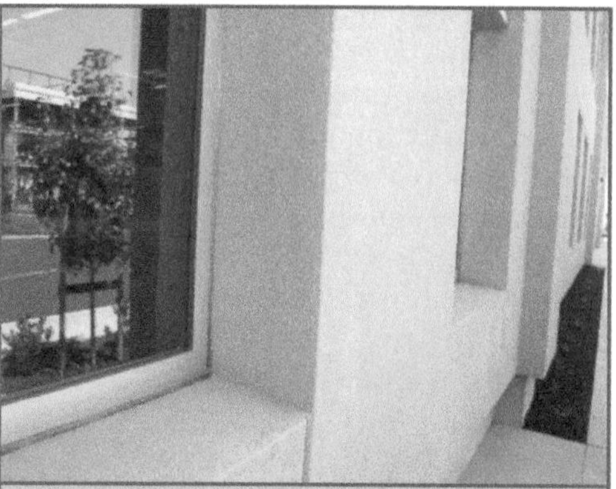

Atypical insulation techniques may be difficult to spot upon physical observation. However, the unusually deep window bays of this Northern California net zero energy office building, seen in this exterior view, should prompt further investigation.

An interior view of a window in this same building shows that the concrete wall is exposed to the interior in order to leverage thermal mass.

Cool Roofs

Cool roofs, also referred to as *white roofs* or *high-albedo roofs*, are roof coverings that have both highly reflective surfaces and the ability to emit absorbed heat. Cool roofs are widely, but not universally, used on new and re-roofing installations in many areas, particularly in warm climates. According to the Cool Roof Rating Council (CRRC), "A cool roof is one that strongly reflects sunlight and also cools itself by efficiently emitting radiation to its surroundings."[2] Coolness is measured by two properties, solar reflectance (SR) and thermal emittance (TE). Both properties are measured on a scale from 0 to 1; the higher the value, the "cooler" the roof.

Commercial cool roofs commonly consist of flat or low-slope roof coverings that incorporate a highly reflective finish (white or silver) rather than the conventional black tar or tar and gravel roof coverings. However, cool roof coverings for both flat and conventionally sloped roofs are now available in a wide variety of formats, from factory-coated metal and cap sheets to shingles, tiles, and field-applied coatings. Some cool roof products are dark in color and therefore may not be easily identified by visual observation alone.

By reflecting solar irradiance and emitting excess heat gain, cool roofs can significantly reduce thermal heat gain penetrating through the roof structure to the interior of the building, thereby reducing cooling load requirements. According to the CRRC, cool roofs can reduce cooling needs by 7% to 15%.[3] Cool roofs also reduce an individual building's contribution to the *heat island effect* that is common in urban areas. The heat island effect describes the phenomenon whereby constructed materials such as concrete and asphalt absorb solar irradiance at a greater rate than natural vegetation does, causing the ambient temperature to rise in areas of dense urban and suburban development. Cool roofs may increase heating costs during the winter months in cold-weather climates. According to the CRRC, however, the effect is nominal in most climate zones due to the low angle of the winter sun and the presence of snow on the roof.

Cool roofs can be part of new construction or incorporated onto existing buildings, such as the one seen in this photo of a building in Milwaukee's historic Third Ward warehouse district.

The widespread use of cool roof coverings in warmer climates means that a cool roof covering alone may not

2. Cool Roof Rating Council, "Cool Roofing Information for Home and Building Owners," accessed April 27, 2017, http://coolroofs.org/resources/home-building-owners.

3. Ibid.

indicate a green or highly efficient building. However, it may indicate that further investigation of other building components is warranted. A cool roof coating used in conjunction with a foam roofing system or with a composite roof insulation system (which uses a sprayed-on rigid foam covering with a cool roof coating on the exterior and fiberglass batt insulation on the interior) suggests that the design intent was a highly efficient building envelope. As a result, there may be other areas to consider, such as the wall insulation and glazing.

Vegetated (Green) Roofs

Roofs covered with vegetation provide several benefits to the building: insulation, rainwater management, and in some cases, biophilic appeal. Like cool roofs, vegetated roofs also reduce the building's

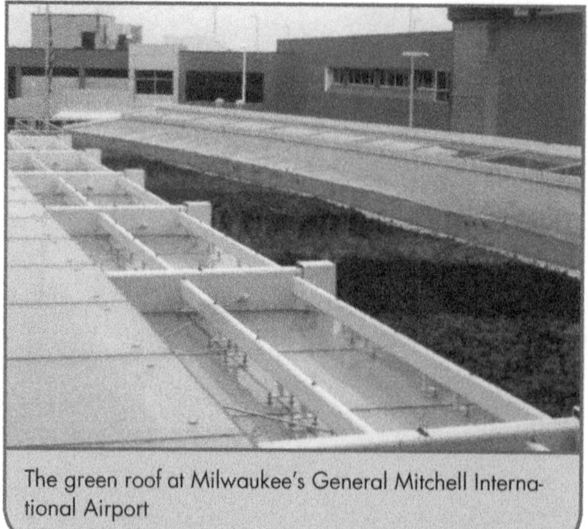

The green roof at Milwaukee's General Mitchell International Airport

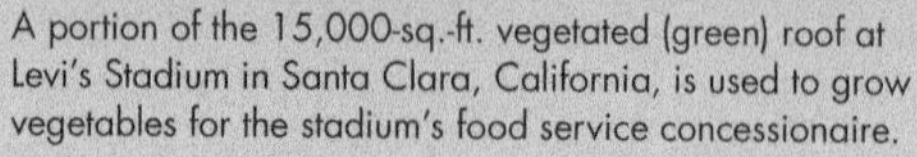

A portion of the 15,000-sq.-ft. vegetated (green) roof at Levi's Stadium in Santa Clara, California, is used to grow vegetables for the stadium's food service concessionaire.

This green roof at the University of North Carolina's Nursing School in Chapel Hill provides an outdoor amenity space for students and faculty. Photograph courtesy of the UNC Chapel Hill School of Nursing.

UNC Chapel Hill School of Nursing's green roof also reduces rainwater runoff and urban heat island effect. Photograph courtesy of the UNC Chapel Hill School of Nursing.

contribution to the heat island effect. The soil and vegetation act as insulation that controls solar heat gain, and the vegetation and soil provide rainwater management services by reducing and controlling the rate of rainwater flow. The latter benefit may be of greater concern in areas where municipal systems for processing rainwater are at, near, or over capacity. If the vegetated roof cover is also visible to the building occupants–either from the occupied space or from an outdoor roof deck–then the vegetated roof may also function as a biophilic design element (providing a view to nature) that enhances the quality, appeal, and marketability of the space or as a building amenity where herbs and vegetables can be grown.

Vegetated roofs require some level of additional ongoing maintenance as compared to conventional roofs. Vegetated roofs are often made up of a conventional roof membrane covering with a component rack and tray system that holds the plants, facilitating periodic plant maintenance and replacement. Green roofs are found in a wide range of climate zones and may be part of a variety of commercial building types, such as offices, educational facilities, multifamily structures, sports facilities, and even airports, as shown in the accompanying photographs.

This multitenant office property in the Tri-Valley area of Northern California added a green roof to the conference center located beyond the waterway.

The green roof atop the conference center is visible from both the rooftop patio and the office space situated across the waterway.

High-Performance and Electrochromic Glazing

Single-pane glazing is not only relatively inefficient in terms of energy use, but it can also detract from the occupants' comfort. When windows do not insulate well against the outside environment, internal thermal currents develop that create an unpleasant, drafty interior environment. High-performance glazing employs technologies that reduce the thermal transfer between the exterior and interior. Strategies

Electrochromic glazing changes tint to control thermal heat gain and glare without the need for blinds or other window coverings while preserving occupants' views to the outdoors, as shown in this photo taken inside a Northern California office building.

include dual and triple glazing, specialized low-emissivity (low-e) coatings, and replacing the ambient air in the cavities between the window's glazing layers with inert gases like argon, krypton, and xenon. These gases are more dense and more resistant to thermal transfer than ambient air. Dual and triple glazing also offers improved acoustical performance over single glazing, which may be as or more important than the energy-efficiency benefit, particularly in dense urban areas where unwanted noise is abundant.

Dynamic or *electrochromic* refers to glass with glazing that changes its tint to control solar thermal gain and glare, obviating the need for shades or blinds. In this way, it can facilitate daylighting and enhance biophilic design by preserving views of nature while managing the unwanted influences of glare and direct heat gain. Variable opacity glazing, such as electrochromic glass, works by passing an electrical current through a laminated coating on the glazing, which changes the tint of the glass to control glare and heat gain while maintaining occupants' views through the window.

Electrochromic glass represents a cost premium as compared to conventional glass, and is most effective when incorporated into a building or energy management system. The cost premium should be considered in the context of the cost savings due to reduced energy use for cooling, as well as the potential to downsize the HVAC system by reducing peak load requirements. For example, a 2010 study found that electrochromic glass uses 20% less energy than conventional dual glazing and 45% less energy than conventional single-pane glass.[4] In addition, the avoided cost of interior shade controls (such as roller shades or blinds) or exterior shade controls (such as light shelves or exterior blinds) may be a consideration. Electrochromic glass is typically most effective on facades that face south, west, and east, for which managing direct sunlight is of the most concern.

Operable Windows

Operable windows may seem like a "throwback" in terms of commercial construction technique, but they can play a valuable role in green building design and construction. While they are common in multifamily buildings of any vintage, operable windows in new office

4. Paladino and Company, *Performance Assessment of SageGlass Electrochromic Coatings and Control Scenarios*, June 2010, www.sageglass.com/sites/default/files/whitepaper_final.pdf.

buildings or other types of commercial buildings are likely to be part of a larger green building strategy and may be a signal that the design team is incorporating natural ventilation into the interior thermal conditioning system. Commercial green buildings most commonly incorporate natural ventilation with a mechanical HVAC system in a mixed-mode hybrid ventilation system. Operable windows may be actively controlled by the occupants or mechanically controlled by the building management system (BMS). Some advanced building management systems notify occupants of optimal times to open the windows, as well as times when keeping the windows closed is optimal for energy efficiency and interior thermal comfort. Other systems open and close the windows automatically. Operable windows can help reduce energy use by using outside air for daytime cooling during appropriate seasons or incorporating automated techniques like night flushing, in which naturally cool nighttime air is used to remove the daytime heat gain from inside the building. Operable windows can also provide the biophilic benefit of enhancing occupants' connection to nature.

Traditionally, operable windows have been more common in low-rise than high-rise buildings. However, the PNC Tower in Pittsburgh is a 33-story, 800,000-sq.-ft. high-rise office building that incorporates operable windows, a double-skin facade, and a vertical "solar chimney" to use outside air inside the building for five months out of the year. The building is designed to use half the energy of a conventional code-built building.

While operable windows can contribute to lower energy use and enhanced indoor air quality, they also have some limitations. Controlling unwanted noise, humidity, outdoor air pollens, particulates, and pollutants while providing privacy to occupants proximate to the open windows can be potentially problematic. Seasonal outdoor temperature variability may also render this option to be of limited appli-

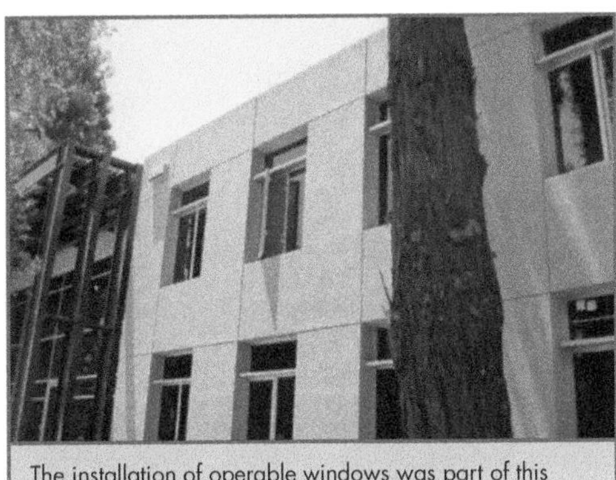
The installation of operable windows was part of this Silicon Valley building's sustainable renovation.

Operable windows and exterior solar shades on a LEED-certified residence hall on the University of Wisconsin-Stevens Point campus

cability in some climate zones. For example, PNC Tower is only able to use natural ventilation for five months out of the year due to the temperature, humidity, and pollen counts of its upper-Midwest climate.

Heavy Timber Construction

Heavy timber or "mass timber" construction is not new to commercial and industrial buildings. Before the advent of poured-in-place concrete, heavy timber construction, combined with masonry bearing walls, was common in the warehouse districts of large cities around the turn of the twentieth century. It was commonly referred to as "mill" construction and traditionally denoted timber with a minimum diameter of eight inches. Such wood was typically harvested from virgin, old-growth forests.

Wood construction has typically been limited to low-rise buildings due to structural limitations and building codes. However, it is now being deployed for taller buildings in some areas, such as the nine-story Murray Grove residential building in London and the seven-story T3 office building in Minneapolis, which is reportedly the largest wood building in North America. Wood offers cost and environmental benefits relative to conventional steel and concrete construction.

In green building design and construction, *heavy timber* typically refers to reclaimed, recycled, or engineered wood. Engineered wood is a composite wood material that is typically glued and laminated into larger-dimension stock. A more recent engineered wood product is cross-laminated timber (CLT), which can reportedly match the strength of concrete and steel. CLT can be used for structural compo-

Heavy timber in the form of engineered wood and structural wood plank floors was used in the green-certified Bullitt Center office building in Seattle, shown here. Exposing the wood to the interior provides biophilic benefits to the occupants.

Heavy timber construction is not unique to green buildings. It was also used in the original construction of this historic 1920s-era hotel in Yosemite National Park. One can see common features between this hotel dining room and the modern office interior shown in the prior photo, seemingly disparate properties built nearly a century apart.

nents of commercial buildings, such as the columns, beams, rafters, and purlins.

In Seattle's Bullitt Center–a six-story commercial office building built in 2012 and certified under the Living Building Challenge–heavy timber was reportedly chosen for the upper four floors due to its inherently renewable nature, to avoid the greenhouse gas emissions associated with concrete and steel production, and to take advantage of the carbon sequestration benefit of wood. The timber was also locally sourced. Exposing the wood to the interior, as shown in the accompanying photograph, also provides biophilic benefits to the occupants. In the Bullitt Center, wood was also used for the floors, which were constructed of two-by-six lumber pieces set on edge and covered with a lightweight concrete slab.

Limitations of heavy timber construction may include local building/fire code restrictions, pests, and the temperature and humidity sensitivity of the material, which results in seasonal expansion and contraction. Wood floors and stairs may also be susceptible to noise transfer and squeaking due to the material's flexibility. Construction cost impacts are likely to be specific to the project and design. Fire insurance rates could potentially be affected by this type of construction.

Mechanical, Electrical, and Plumbing Components

Passive Design Strategies

Passive design strategies are often used in green buildings to augment or replace conventional mechanical HVAC systems and electrical lighting. Passive systems can be very easy to miss during site visits, as they often mimic conventional design and construction techniques. For example, the exterior solar shades shown in the accompanying photographs could easily be mistaken for an architectural element rather than a green building feature. However, they are carefully designed to allow light directly into the building in the winter, but shade it in the summer. By directing available light from the windows, they control unwanted glare and solar heat gain. They can also be used in connection with light shelves inside the building to bring natural light

This new multifamily property in the Hayes Valley neighborhood of San Francisco uses perforated metal exterior solar shades on the south and west elevations to help manage solar heat gain yet allow some daylight to pass through to the glazing. Note how the orientation of the shades differs for the south elevation of the darker portion of the building (on the right side of the photo), versus the west elevation (on the left side of the photo), reflecting the differing angle of incidence of the sun on each facade throughout the day. The solar shades have a different configuration on the white portion of the same building (at the far left), yet provide the same function.

deep into the space. In turn, this reduces lighting and heating requirements as well as increases the availability of natural light to the interior of the space, thereby enhancing its desirability.

Passive design strategies can include daylighting, natural ventilation, and various passive heating and cooling systems, which are discussed in greater depth in the sidebar in Chapter 3 titled "Harnessing 'Free' Energy: Passive Design Basics" (page 58).

The solar shades on the upper floor exterior of this recently constructed office building in Madison, Wisconsin, are placed above the vision portion of the glazing to control glare and below the transom glazing to maximize daylighting effects. The louvered design of the solar shades, including the spacing and precise angle of the metal slats as well as the 2.5-ft. depth, are all part of the climate-specific design intended to simultaneously shade the vision glazing while maximizing natural light reaching the interior throughout the year.

Variable Frequency Drives

Variable frequency drives (VFDs), also known as *variable speed drives*, consist of an electronic controller that permits motors to run at varying speeds, making them more energy efficient. Motors are a major use of energy in HVAC systems, and conditioning the interior air typically accounts for one-third of the energy use in a conventional office building. In a traditional large office building, motors drive pumps and compressors for the chillers as well as the fans in the air-handling units (AHUs) and cooling tower.

Because the relationship between energy use and speed (output) in motors is not linear but exponential, doubling the speed of a fan requires roughly eight times the energy, a relationship known as the *fan affinity laws*. This also means that reducing fan speed by 50% results in an 87.5% energy savings relative to running the motor at full speed. Electrical motors are typically sized for maximum load and are limited to operating at only one speed because they run on AC power. Adding a VFD to a fan, pump, or compressor motor allows for significant energy savings by permitting the motor speed to be optimized for the load. VFDs are a component of a high-efficiency HVAC system and are typically controlled by a BMS consisting of software, sensors, and controls that manage the mechanical systems in the building.

VFDs are usually mounted near the motor they control and come in a variety of shapes and sizes. While VFDs can greatly reduce energy costs, they are not always readily identifiable and may be present as part of an energy-efficiency upgrade in an otherwise non-green building. They may be seamlessly integrated into a larger package HVAC unit and thus not visible at all. The building engineer may need to be consulted to determine if the exhaust fans, compressor pumps, and/or circulation pumps have VFDs.

All else being equal, an HVAC system with VFDs in place will operate more efficiently and at lower energy cost than a comparable system without such controls. However, adding VFDs to various components of the HVAC system may deliver differing energy savings, depending on the application and other components in the system. Furthermore, optimal operation requires knowledgeable staff in order to realize the potential of these components. Initial commissioning and ongoing monitoring and adjustment will likely be necessary to realize the potential efficiencies. In an older building where codes may not have initially required VFDs, this type of upgrade will likely reduce energy use relative to historical levels and should be considered when stabilizing the operating expenses. Such an upgrade may also provide a visual clue that the owner is focused on energy-efficient operation. Further investigation into the presence of a building or energy management system and other efficiency upgrades is warranted.

The VFD units shown in this photo were installed in a new green building located in Menlo Park, California.

This VFD unit is located in a 1980s-era office building in San Francisco. Compared to the two units in the prior photo, one can see that many size and shape variations are possible for VFD units.

VFD units can be located in various areas of the building or site. This VFD unit at an electrician's training facility in Los Angeles is located outside the building, adjacent to the cooling tower.

Building Management Systems

The computer-based *building management system (BMS)*, sometimes also referred to as a *building automation system*, controls the building's electrical and mechanical systems including the lighting, HVAC, and power systems. Life safety and security systems may also be incorporated. Energy management systems (EMSs) are a subset of BMSs that are focused solely on the energy-using components of a building. These systems incorporate sensors, controls, and a software interface; they may vary widely in terms of sophistication. Most modern large buildings include some type of BMS. The more advanced the building systems, the more important a BMS will be to attaining the projected performance. Physical evidence of these systems is typically limited, particularly during the site visit. The presence or absence of a BMS may need to be ascertained through interviews with the property manager or engineering staff or a review of third-party reports.

The accompanying photograph shows the dashboard display of a BMS for a net zero energy (NZE) building that provides touch-screen access for all of the building's real-time energy use metrics, such as lighting, HVAC, plug load, and the on-site renewable energy system. This dashboard is evidence that the building has a fairly sophisticated BMS that can monitor the type and location of energy use, track faults in the system, and provide ongoing management of the building's energy use and generation.

As with VFDs, the mere presence of a BMS does not guarantee the superior performance of a building. Knowledgeable engineering staff performing ongoing monitoring and adjustment, including

The electrical box in a building's mechanical penthouse shown here is the only observable evidence of the building's BMS and illustrates how the BMS can be the "Invisible Man" of green features: It controls many of the major energy-using systems of the building and can be instrumental to the efficient operation of a property but may hardly be detectable.

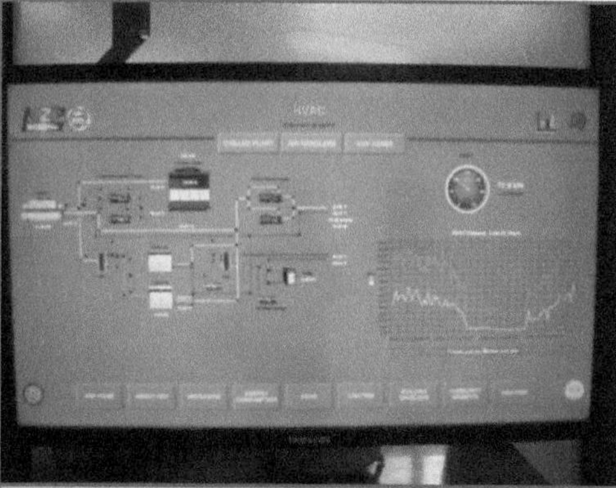

This computer monitor in a building's common area serves as a more visible and sophisticated BMS than the system shown in the prior photo. The dashboard display provides touch-screen access for all of the building's real-time energy use metrics, including lighting, HVAC, plug load, and the on-site renewable energy system.

timely response to faults and conflicts that are noted by the BMS, are important to realizing the potential performance enhancement of the system. For advanced, high-performance buildings such as NZE buildings, an outside consultant such as a commissioning authority (agent) may need to be retained either periodically or on an ongoing basis to ensure that systems operate as planned.

Non-Potable Water Systems

Non-potable water systems collect, treat, and re-use water collected from a variety of sources. These sources may include rainfall collected from the roof and site, or water used on-site and collected from bathroom sinks, showers, and laundry facilities (often termed *gray water*). The water is typically filtered and treated, then re-used on-site for non-potable uses, such as toilet flushing and irrigation. Non-potable water may be collected and re-used on site, or it may be accessed via a municipal system.

The 700,000-sq.-ft., 55-story office and condominium tower at 181 Fremont Street in San Francisco is incorporating a non-potable water collection and treatment system into a new high rise that is expected to collect and treat over one million gallons of water annually. The system is expected to reduce annual costs for water and sewer charges. The

Local municipal codes mandate appropriate signage for systems using non-potable water.

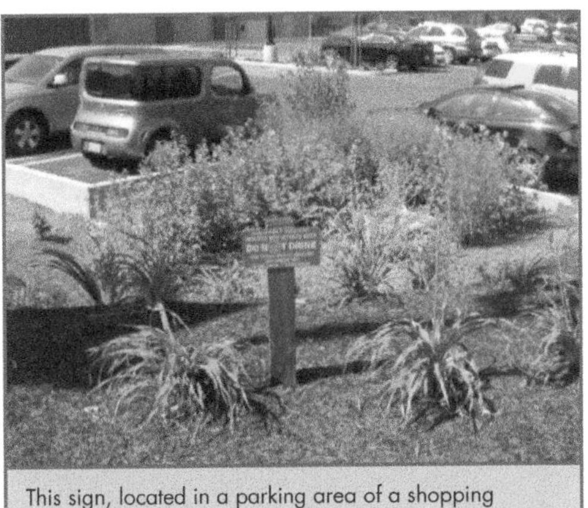
This sign, located in a parking area of a shopping center, indicates that the bioswale is being irrigated with non-potable water.

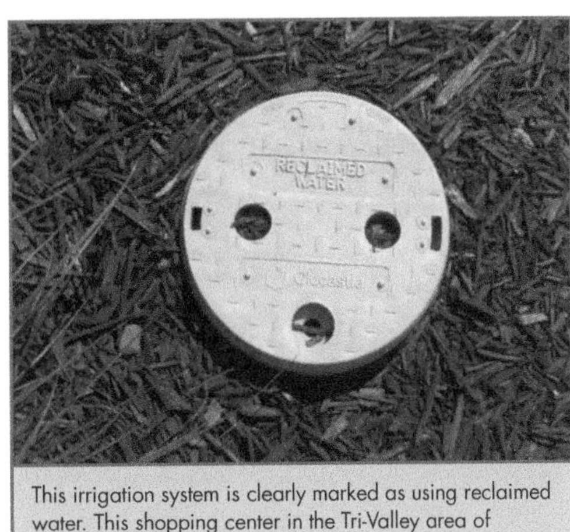

This irrigation system is clearly marked as using reclaimed water. This shopping center in the Tri-Valley area of Northern California obtains its non-potable water through a municipally operated system.

developer's motivation was reportedly the project's sustainability orientation, including LEED Platinum certification, and compliance with the San Francisco Stormwater Management Ordinance.

Under-Floor Air Distribution

Raised floor systems such as *under-floor air distribution (UFAD)* systems elevate the finished floor above the slab and use the resulting plenum in lieu of ducting for conditioned airflow and raceways for wiring. This design saves energy by reducing the amount of fan power required for air distribution. It is also typically more efficient to condition the air in the lower portion of the room where occupants are located rather than distributing conditioned air at the ceiling level, as is typical with most conventional HVAC systems. Other benefits of UFAD systems include greater occupant control over temperature, since the air diffusers located in the raised floor can be adjusted manually by the occupants as needed.

UFAD systems are also typically easier and less expensive to reconfigure for new build-outs or workspace configurations, which is often noted as an offset to the added up-front cost of this system. The up-front cost can also be offset by the reduced ducting that would otherwise be required for a conventional HVAC system. UFAD systems are particularly well-suited to open floor plan configurations.

A partially installed UFAD system in a new shell office building in the Mission Bay neighborhood of San Francisco. Note how the flooring is elevated, allowing the space below the floor to function as a plenum for airflow and a raceway for electrical and computer cabling.

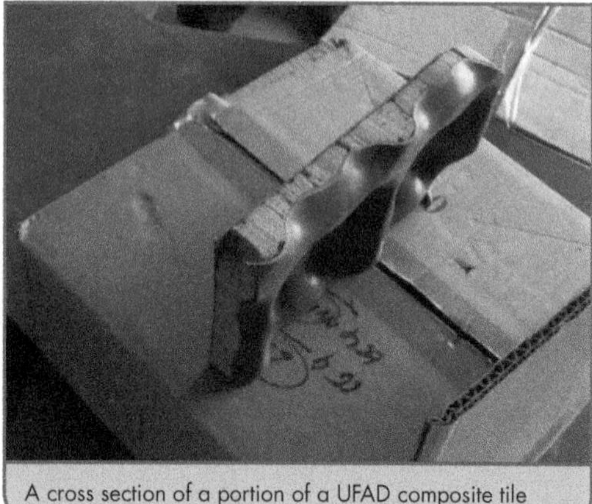

A cross section of a portion of a UFAD composite tile

Hydronic Heating and Cooling

Hydronic heating and cooling systems rely on water or another fluid to transfer heat *to* or *from* a conditioned space in order to optimize occupant comfort. Since fluids of a given volume are capable of carrying more energy (higher enthalpy) than gases such as air, less energy is required to move the heating or cooling medium in a hydronic system than in an air-based HVAC system.

Conventional steam boiler/radiator systems and radiant heat using tubes embedded in the flooring are common hydronic heating systems and have been in use for many years. More recently, hydronic cooling systems such as *chilled beam systems* have been implemented in commercial buildings. *Chilled beam* is somewhat of a misnomer, since the system can be used for both heating and cooling. The ceiling-mounted cooling units are typically six feet long and are connected to a two-pipe hydronic loop (for cooling only) or a four-pipe system (for heating and cooling). Chilled beams can be active or passive, with the former relying only on convection, with no fan-driven air flow. In contrast, active chilled beams, which are more suitable to most commercial applications, use a high-velocity air flow that passes over the coils in the chilled beam unit, transferring room heat to the hydronic cooling loop and thus cooling the ambient room air. Chilled beam systems allow the sizes of the ducting and air handling fans to be significantly reduced (by 60%), resulting in up-front cost savings as well as up to 40% less fan energy for conditioned air distribution.[5]

The nondescript chilled beams in this Northern California office building can be seen in the upper right-hand quadrant of this photograph. This heating and cooling system blends seamlessly with conventional ceiling treatments and may be difficult to discern.

The Sacramento Municipal Utility District (SMUD) facility in California features a partially open ceiling that includes a chilled beam installation with the labeled supply and return pipes visible. It is somewhat easier to identify the hydronic HVAC components in this building than the building shown in the prior photo.

5. Peter Rumsey and John Weale, "Practical Implementation of Chilled Beams for Offices," *Engineered Systems* (January 2011): 30-36, http://thermairsystems.com/wp-content/uploads/2011/10/Chilled-Beams-Rumsey-2011.pdf

Chilled beam systems can also be paired with a water-side economizer, which is similar to a conventional air economizer but instead uses evaporative cooling. Such a system was a key component of the high-efficiency HVAC system implemented in the Packard Foundation headquarters in Los Altos, California, which was previously featured in the section on bioswales and other rainwater management strategies. This system relies on nighttime evaporative cooling to provide "free" cooling (that uses no compressor energy), which is stored in an insulated tank for daytime use via the hydronic cooling loop serving the chilled beams.

Air- and Ground-Source Heat Pump HVAC Systems

Heat pumps use a reversible mechanical compression cycle to heat or cool space using a refrigerant. Heat pumps typically consist of two parts: an indoor air-handling unit and an outdoor heat pump, which functions much like an air conditioner. Depending on climate conditions and heating load, an air-source heat pump uses outdoor air as a source of heat or as a receptacle to reject unwanted heat, depending on whether the system is in the heating or cooling mode. Ground-source heat pumps (GSHPs) use the earth instead of the outside air for heat source and rejection and are often necessary in more extreme climates. GSHPs use a bore field that is drilled on site containing pipes through which a fluid is pumped, and heat is either absorbed or rejected from the fluid in the process.

Heat pump systems can be difficult to identify by casual observation. Two examples are shown in the accompanying photographs. While the first photo shows clearly labeled, insulated pipes in the subterranean garage of a three-story Wisconsin office building, the mechanical equipment is in a secure area and not readily observable. These labeled pipes lead to the bore field surrounding the building, which is also virtually invisible, with nothing to indicate the boreholes that extend 250 feet below grade. The second photo shows ground source heat pumps in a more accessible, easier-to-detect location.

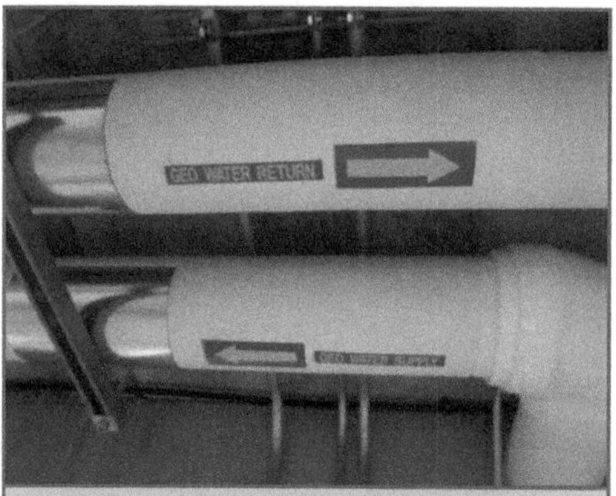

In this green office building in Wisconsin, the mechanical equipment is located within a secure mechanical room. The only visible clue that there is an atypical HVAC system in this building is the labeling on the pipes suspended from the garage ceiling, which could be very easy to miss.

Sometimes, it is what is missing that provides the most information. An aerial view of the Wisconsin building showed virtually no rooftop mechanical equipment. The roof is the most common location for the HVAC system in a conventional, low-rise suburban office building such as the one in this example. A careful eye may also have noticed the limited amount of small diameter duct work and lack of variable air volume units visible in the open ceilings of the tenant spaces. This duct work provides fresh air to the space via a dedicated outside air system (DOAS) but does not heat or cool the space.

In general, heat pump systems tend to be more efficient than conventional forced-air HVAC systems since the heat-containing medium they use is a liquid, which is more energy dense than air. Furthermore, heat pump systems eliminate the amount of energy lost due to duct leakage.

In contrast to the example in the first photo, the ground-source heat pumps are clearly visible in this basement garage of a Northern California green office building.

Variable Refrigerant Flow HVAC Systems

A *variable refrigerant flow (VRF)* HVAC system is a sophisticated heat pump system that can be connected to a conventional boiler/chiller water loop, or alternatively use either air or the ground for heat source/rejection. VRFs differ from conventional heat pumps in that the variable level of refrigerant flow allows them to simultaneously operate in heating and cooling mode, "moving" heat from where it is unwanted to where it is desired (heat recovery). Since most commercial buildings require cooling in some portion of the building all year, even when heating is required in other portions, VRFs allow for an efficient transfer of heat from where it is needed to where it is not. VRFs are not yet widely used in the United States but are becoming more common. They have been widely used in Japan since the 1980s.

VRF systems are typically more expensive than conventional heat pump systems but are more energy-efficient due to the variable speed of the pumps and the ability to heat-recover between zones. They also use less interior space and have lower maintenance costs. Because the compressors in VRF systems are centrally located away from tenant spaces, they may avoid the unwanted compressor noise associated with the interior units of conventional heat pumps, particularly in larger applications.

The air-source VRF system in the Northern California office/educational facility shown here uses ambient air to reject excess heat as well as to draw heat when needed.

Energy Recovery Mechanisms

Heat recovery ventilators (HRVs), also known as *heat recovery wheels* and *energy recovery ventilators (ERVs),* belong to a class of HVAC components that allow for an exchange of heat between outside (intake) air and exhaust air without mixing the two. Energy recovery mechanisms can be configured in a variety of ways, but generally most share a common design: separate intake and exhaust ducting that utilizes a conductive material, usually metal, which conducts heat from the warmer air to the cooler air. The primary difference between an HRV and an ERV is that the latter is designed to address higher humidity conditions in which the water content of the air is a larger component of the enthalpy, or embodied energy, of the air.

One of the most common types of energy recovery mechanism is a *heat wheel,* also known as an *energy recovery wheel.* The metal wheel spins slowly through the outside and exhaust air ducts, absorbing heat from the warmer air and releasing it to the cooler air without mixing the two air flows. Heat wheels can be used when either heating or cooling the interior is required. In a cooling situation, the heat transfers from the outside air intake to the exhaust air, which has been mechanically cooled. Thus, the embodied energy of the cooled air is "recycled" into the intake air, reducing the cooling load for the HVAC system. When in heating mode, the opposite occurs. Heat from the exhaust air is transferred to the intake air, warming it and reducing the energy needed to condition the cold outdoor air.

This type of equipment is particularly important for tightly sealed building envelopes. Energy recovery mechanisms can also mitigate the additional cost of increased outside air conditioning required by higher ventilation requirements due to building codes or green building rating systems or to enhance occupant comfort and productivity.

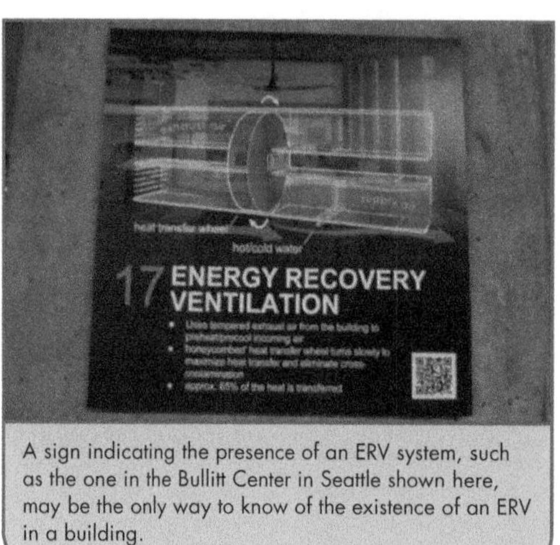

A sign indicating the presence of an ERV system, such as the one in the Bullitt Center in Seattle shown here, may be the only way to know of the existence of an ERV in a building.

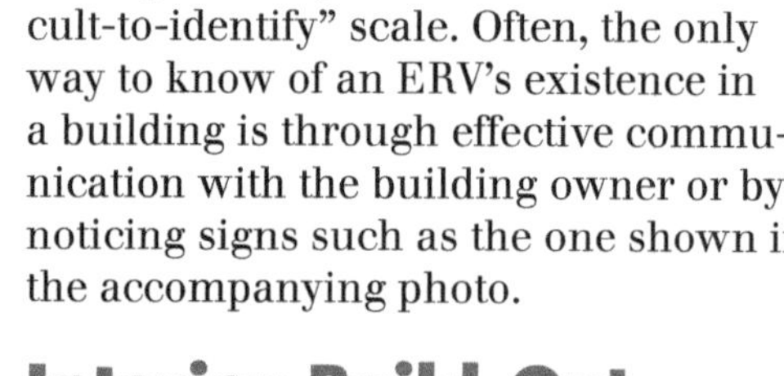

ERVs tend to be a very well-hidden green feature; they may rival building management systems on the "difficult-to-identify" scale. Often, the only way to know of an ERV's existence in a building is through effective communication with the building owner or by noticing signs such as the one shown in the accompanying photo.

Interior Build-Out

Daylighting

Daylighting, as defined within the LEED green building rating system, is "the controlled admission of natural light into a space, used to reduce or eliminate electric lighting."[6] Daylighting intends to bring light into the interior build-out so as to provide occupants with natural light as well as to reduce reliance on artificial lighting. Paints and materials with high light reflectance values (LRVs) are typically used in the interior to disperse the natural light throughout the interior. Substituting natural daylight for electric light reduces energy use and lighting heat load, but it is also thought to create a more desirable environment that may enhance productivity, health, and well-being. Daylighting practices include a wide range of building design and construction considerations, including building/glazing orientation, window-to-wall ratio, floorplate depth, and ceiling height. Natural light can also have negative effects, such as glare and heat gain, which must be managed or mitigated. Common strategies to address these unwanted effects include diffusers, solar shades, awnings, light shelves, interior or exterior automated blinds or other window coverings, and laminates such as fritting applied to the glazing that absorb or reflect heat and glare but permit visible light to pass, so that views to the exterior are protected.

In addtion to the building's fenestration, skylights, solar tubes that use lenses to intensify light, and roof monitors can also be used to bring natural light to interior spaces that are distant from perimeter walls, as seen in the accompanying photograph. Once natural light has been brought to the interior, low workstations and highly reflective finishes on paints and furniture can be used to amplify the light's effectiveness and bring it further into the interior. Daylighting generally works best with open floor plan space, but perimeter private offices that use glass interior walls or doors can effectively allow much of the

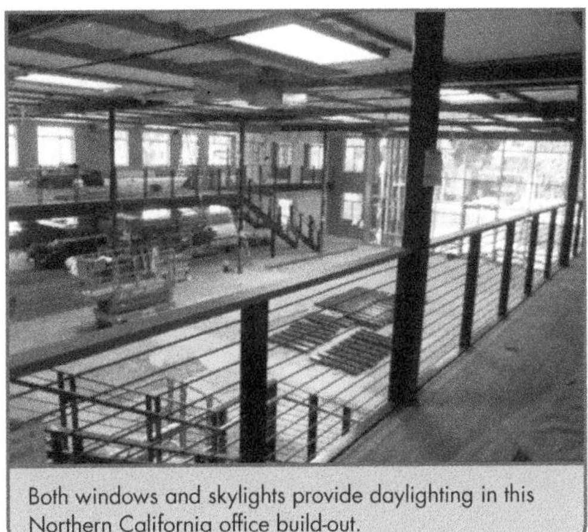

Both windows and skylights provide daylighting in this Northern California office build-out.

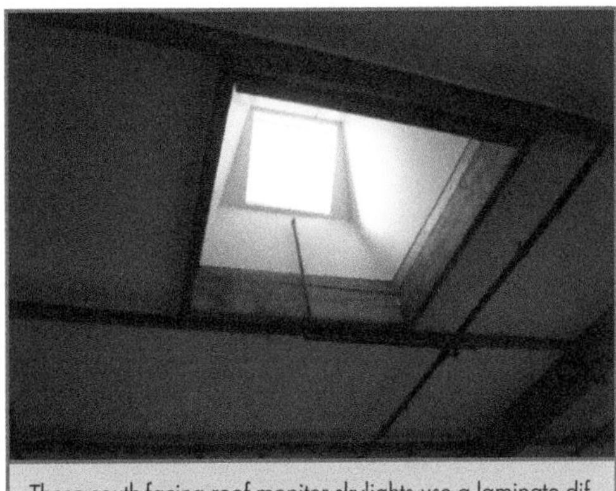

These south-facing roof monitor skylights use a laminate diffuser to control glare. They are also operable and function as part of the passive ventilation strategy for the building.

6. US Green Building Council (USGBC), LEED *Reference Guide for Green Building Operations and Maintenance*, 2009 ed. (Washington, DC: USGBC, 2010), 493.

Reflective blinds, as seen here, can be installed to help deflect light deep into a building's interior.

perimeter source daylight to enter the building's interior. The Sacramento Municipal Utility District (SMUD) building in California uses a combination of reflective interior blinds and light-colored, highly reflective paint to enhance daylighting capabilities for a new multistory NZE building with a relatively low window-to-wall ratio and deep floorplates.

Energy efficiency gains from daylighting can be enhanced by incorporating automated daylight-sensing controls that automatically dim artificial lights when ambient natural lighting is adequate. Another daylighting strategy involves "tuning" the light levels so that they are appropriate for the task at hand. Rather than lighting the entire space at a single foot-candle level, common areas may be lit at a lower level than conference rooms and work stations may use high-efficiency task lighting, such as LED desk lights.

Biophilia

Biophilia is the concept that humans have an innate connection to the natural environment. Biophilic design incorporates natural elements into the built environment. Biophilia, as discussed in the sidebar in Chapter 2 titled "Biophilia: The Human Connection to Nature," (page 40) can incorporate a wide range of building elements and design strategies, some of which are more obvious than others. A "living wall" prominently displayed in the lobby of a large office building or a

This outdoor courtyard, which separates two wings of a building's U-shaped floor plate, is an example of biophilic design.

This living wall serves as a natural and architectural element. In addition to making use of the concept of biophilia, living walls can also reduce interior noise and improve air quality in a building.

vegetated roof visible from the building interior are readily noticed. Other less-obvious biophilic elements may also signal the intent to enhance the quality of the occupant experience. Using exposed natural materials such as wood, brick, and stone, incorporating natural shapes and colors into the interior design, or adding views to nature by screening a neighboring wall or parking lot with vegetation are all common biophilic design strategies that may not at first appear to be directly related to green building or sustainable design.

In this South San Francisco office building, the semi-exposed walkways that straddle the cavernous atrium and connect the office floorplates demonstrate the biophilic design concept of *peril*. Note also the exposed natural wood and views to nature.

Biophilia can also incorporate a concept known as *risk* or *peril*. This is the idea that humans enjoy exploring an area that seems a little dangerous or risky but that has implied safeguards. Frank Lloyd Wright's iconic structure at Taliesin features a walkway dubbed "The Birdwalk." It is a long and narrow protruding balcony that is often cited as a prime example of this type of biophilic design.

Prominent Stairwells

A building design incorporating a grand staircase that is more obvious than the elevator bank may at first seem to be little more than

At the Bullitt Center in Seattle, the "irresistible staircase" rises six stories set within three walls of glass, offering a 270-degree view of the surrounding city. Not only is the stairwell a prominent design feature from the exterior, but finding the elevator "hidden" behind the stairwell requires passing through a separate set of doors and turning a corner. By making the stairwell easier to find than the elevator, the building design intends to enhance occupant health.

In this owner-occupied office building in Northern California, the elevators are tucked away to the side of the main entry. The lobby design draws the visitor into the seven-story atrium, which this stairwell seems to invite visitors to explore.

a design quirk. However, creating inviting opportunities for daily exercise in the work or home environment can be part of encouraging the health and well-being of occupants, which is part of the intent of green building and certain green building rating systems such as the Living Building Challenge and the WELL Building Standard. For example, the "irresistible staircase" in the six-story Bullitt Center (shown in the accompanying photo) is not only easier to find from the building lobby than the elevator, but the glass-enclosed stairwell offers 270-degree views of the surrounding Seattle area.

On-Site Energy Generation Systems

Solar Photovoltaic Arrays

Solar photovoltaic (PV) arrays are not a new technology. At its core, solar PV is very simple. Crystalline silicon, when exposed to light, creates an electrical current. That direct current (DC) is then changed to alternating current (AC) when it passes through an inverter. Solar PV technology can encompass a wide variety of installations and has wide-ranging applications from powering an individual device to powering entire buildings, businesses, or communities.

A typical solar PV array consists of a collection of modules, also referred to as solar panels. A typical module consists of an assembly that includes crystalline solar cells laminated beneath glass and mounted in an aluminum frame. Modules vary in their output based on the type of silicon used (i.e., monocrystalline or the less-efficient polycrystalline), the way they are manufactured, and other factors. The balance of system components include one or more inverters, which convert the DC output of the modules to AC. String inverters handle a series of modules or an entire array and are more cost-effective than module-level microinverters, which offer superior performance. The mounting system can include a fixed or mobile (tracking) system. Fixed arrays attach to the roof, ground, or other portion of the structure. Carport mounts also offer shade and weather protection for vehicles, but at an added cost relative to roof or ground mounts. Tracking systems incorporate one or two axes of rotation, which allows the modules to maintain the optimal orientation to the

This commercial building in Moraga, California, was originally built in the early 1900s and recently renovated. The roof shingles are embedded with solar PV modules capable of powering the building. Building-integrated photovoltaics (BIPVs) like this are indistinguishable from conventional shingles from ground level. A zoomed-in photo taken from the second floor of the office building across the street was required in order to properly show the shingles.

This massive 295.8 kW carport-mounted solar PV array looks like it could power a small village. In fact, it creates enough power to meet 55% of the projected needs for this 13,000-sq.-ft., LEED-certified organic grocery store constructed in 2007 in Grass Valley, California. The 16,800-sq.-ft. array exceeds the footprint of the building it services and illustrates the energy demands of 24-hour refrigeration and long operating hours for a modern grocery store.

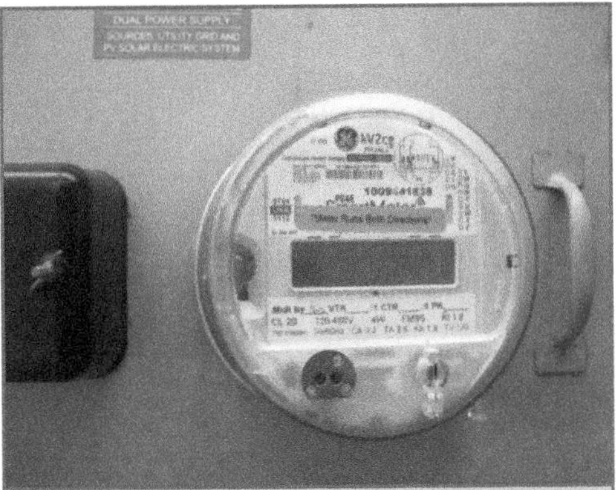

The label on this electrical meter reads, "Meter runs both directions." While electrical meters can run backwards under net metering tariffs, not every meter is labeled as such.

sun on a daily and seasonal basis. Solar PV systems and other types of on-site distributed generation are discussed further in Chapter 10.

Concentrating Solar Power

Concentrating solar power (CSP), also known as *concentrating solar thermal*, is a process that uses mirrors to focus sunlight on a tube through which a liquid is passed. The energy from the super-heated liquid is transferred to water, which is used to power a steam turbine that generates electricity. CSP is usually reserved for large-scale applications such as utility-scale solar projects but has also been applied at the building level. The appeal of concentrating solar power is that the heat energy can be stored and used to run the turbine when the sun is not shining. CSP differs from conventional solar PV in that the former does not involve silicon semiconductor material as a solar collector. The accompanying photo shows a micro-concentrating solar array on the rooftop of an

This photo shows a portion of a roof-mounted, concentrating solar array that uses mirrors to focus sunlight onto a water-filled tube in the middle of the collector. The superheated liquid is then used to pre-heat the return air for a conventional HVAC system to heat domestic hot water and to power a 50-ton, double-absorption chiller that converts the heat energy into chilled air to cool the interior of this office building. CSP is typically employed at utility scale, but this micro-concentrating solar thermal system powers a four-story, 45,000-sq.-ft. suburban office building in the East Bay area of Northern California.

office building. In this particular case, the micro-CSP collector was paired with an absorptive chiller so that the building could be both heated and cooled with the help of solar energy.

Solar Thermal Systems

Solar thermal systems used for heating domestic hot water (DHW) are sometimes confused with solar PV arrays used to generate electricity. At first glance, solar thermal systems and solar PV arrays share similarities. However, there are notable distinctions between the two, as shown in the accompanying photo. Unlike solar PV, solar thermal DHW systems are designed to heat water rather than generate electricity. Solar thermal systems are connected to plumbing, usually at the top and bottom of the panel. In addition, solar thermal collectors are usually solid black, while solar PV modules often have a distinctive rectangular or octagonal pattern. Solar thermal hot water systems in commercial applications usually include a back-up electric heating element.

Solar thermal used for domestic hot water often has a similar shape and panel configuration to solar PV. However, solar thermal collectors have a tell-tale plumbing connection rather than the electrical connection typically found at the back of a solar PV module. In addition, the face of the solar thermal panel is typically flat black, with no horizontal or vertical markings.

Solar PV modules have distinctive horizontal and vertical delineations on the surface, and there is no plumbing connection. Instead, the modules are connected by wiring. The modules shown here are monocrystalline, as indicated by the generally square shape with clipped corners. Polycrystalline modules would likely have a rectangular rather than square delineation on the surface, with no clipped corners.

Energy Storage Systems

Battery back-up and uninterruptible power supplies are two examples of energy storage systems. Energy storage typically takes the form of a series of batteries contained within a nondescript metal cabinet. A variety of technologies can be used, from lead acid car batteries to lithium-ion or other chemical technologies. Energy storage can be an important part of a resilient building infrastructure as well as a strategy to manage peak energy demand.

The grey units in this photo and the next are central inverters, while the white units are battery cabinets. The two inverters are part of a 602 kW roof and carport-mounted solar PV system that provides more energy than this 141,000-sq.-ft. electrician's training facility in Los Angeles consumes annually, thus making it a net zero plus (NZP) facility.

The total 300 kWh battery capacity and the over-standard PV array of this Los Angeles electrician's training facility are part of the owner's resilience strategy for its mission-critical operations that would allow the facility to remain operational by disconnecting from the grid in the event of grid failure.

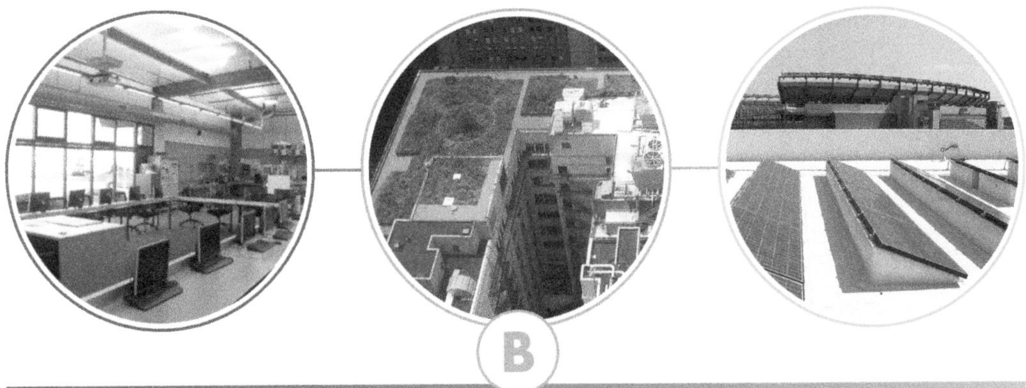

B

Commercial Green and Energy Efficient Addendum

The Appraisal Institute's Form 821: Commercial Green and Energy Efficient Addendum, is a tool that appraisers can use to identify green buildings and green features. This form is available for use by all appraisers, not just Appraisal Institute professionals. This and other Appraisal Institute forms, including Form 820.05: Residential Green and Energy Efficient Addendum, are available through the following software vendors:

- ACI
- a la mode
- Bradford Technologies
- HomePuter®
- SFREP

More information about the form can be found at www.appraisalinstitute.org.

 AI Reports® Form 821*	Client File #:		Appraisal File #:	
	Commercial Green and Energy Efficient Addendum			
	Client:			
	Subject Property:			
	City:		State:	Zip:

Additional resources to aid in the valuation of green properties and the completion of this form can be found at
http://www.appraisalinstitute.org/education/green_energy_addendum.aspx

The appraiser hereby acknowledges that the information provided within this addendum:

- has been considered in the appraiser's development of the appraisal of the subject property only for the client and intended user(s) identified in the appraisal report and only for the intended use stated in the report.
- is not provided by the appraiser for any other purpose and should not be relied upon by parties other than those identified by the appraiser as the client or intended user(s) in the report.
- is the result of the appraiser's routine inspection of and inquiries about the subject property's green and energy efficient features. Extraordinary assumption: Data provided herein is assumed to be accurate and if found to be in error could alter the appraiser's opinions or conclusions.
- is not made as a representation or as a warranty as to the efficiency, quality, function, operability, reliability or cost savings of the reported items or of the subject property in general, and this addendum should not be relied upon for such assessments.
- is not to be construed as a replacement for an appraisal report but is an Addendum to an appraisal report. This Addendum is not designed to assign value to each of the components identified. The Addendum is provided as a part of the description of the properties' special characteristics that have been included in the analysis and value conclusions in the appraisal report. It also serves the client in securing adequate information on the property type to assist in hiring the appraiser with knowledge and experience in this special property type.

Green Building: The practice of creating structures and using processes that are environmentally responsible and resource-efficient throughout a building's lifecycle from siting to design, construction, operation, maintenance, renovation, and deconstruction. This practice expands and complements the classic building design concerns of economy, utility, durability, and comfort.[1] High Performance building and green building are often used interchangeably; however, they do have different definitions.

High Performance Building: A building that integrates and optimizes all major high-performance building attributes, including energy efficiency, durability, life-cycle performance, and occupant productivity.[2]

Six Elements of Green Building: A green building has attributes that fall into the six elements of green building known as (1) site, (2) water, (3) energy, (4) materials, (5) indoor air quality, and (6) maintenance and operation. A Green Building will be energy efficient but an energy efficient building is not synonymous with Green Building.

Property Type

Category of Property: (explain) ______________________

This Addendum is for property types that include multifamily, all types of commercial, and industrial use properties. The Addendum can be used for proposed or existing structures including retrofits.

Who may complete this Addendum?

The Addendum may be completed by any of the following:

- LEED AP serving on project's charrette
- Green Rater that rated the project
- Developer/builder involved in developing the project
- Investor with sufficient information and documents to support the data
- Appraiser

The appraiser must have sufficient knowledge and experience of the property type to review an Addendum completed by others and comment on any inconsistencies or omissions noted. The person completing the Addendum should complete the "Completed by" Section of this Addendum.

The objective of this Addendum is to standardize the communication of the green and/or high performing features of commercial properties. Identifying the features provides a basis for comparable selection and analysis of the features.

The Addendum will assist the client in extracting the documents necessary to expedite the appraisal process by having a better understanding of the special property features. This will assist the client in securing the appraiser with knowledge and experience in the property type.

The Addendum can be attached to the listing of the property, which will allow the appraiser more detail on sales and listings of similar properties.

The Addendum may be used in its entirety or only the pages that apply.

Intended Users of this Addendum: Lender as part of their scope of work, appraisers as a supplement to the appraisal report, investors as a summary of special green/energy features, and/or real estate agents as a supplement to a listing.

---

[1] U.S. Environmental Protection Agency at www.epa.gov/greenbuildings/pubs/about.htm

[2] Energy Policy Act of 2005 (Public Law 109-058) at http://www.nibs.org/?page=hpbc

Client:		Client File #:	
Subject Property:		Appraisal File #:	

Documentation to Appraiser

The client should supply the qualified real estate appraiser with the following documents and information for analysis. This information should be supplied in advance of the appraisal bidding process to allow the appraiser full disclosure of the potential scope of work. Check the items that will be made available to the appraiser.

1. **LEED checklist** (if appropriate). Alternatively, if certified by another organization the checklist used by the certifier should be provided to the appraiser. (The checklist is the worksheet used by the green certified to award points for the green rating. The green score may be presented as a preliminary score on proposed construction and subject to a final inspection upon completion of construction. The appraiser should be presented with the final rating prior to the final inspection.) The checklist will address the six elements of green building identified earlier in this Addendum.

   Comment: This document assists the appraiser in understanding the shade of green and areas that received most points. For instance, a commissioned building will have a checklist used by the rater. The checklist is extremely useful in documenting the details on the subject property. The checklist will address in detail the materials element that appraisers may not be qualified to identify.

   A property may be green but not have a green third party certification. The green features must be documented and presented to the appraiser. The valuation is of the construction and not the certification; therefore, if the property possesses green features it should be appraised for the features it possesses.

2. **Contact information for details of green,** (LEED consultant, architect(s), builder, charrette member, and engineer)
   Comment: This will help inform the appraiser about the components and makeup of the building. An appraiser should expect to receive all pertinent information from all parties of a transaction.

3. **Energy modeling results (or Third Party Energy Ratings for Residential)**
   Comment: The energy modeling results can be critical in analyzing cost implications due to various green energy strategies or components. The appraiser should verify that the projections used are realistic and that they fit the manner in which the facility will be used. The greatest risk with energy modeling is that the projections employed do not fit actual building use and will result in an under- or overestimate of utility costs. The energy modeling should provide an estimated energy savings. (A cost benefit analysis and/or engineering modeling report may explain the choice and benefit of the systems used.)

4. **Plans and specifications**
   Comment: Even in an existing building, these documents should be made available if possible. Specifications should include product descriptions from manufacturers. This helps inform the appraiser what is actually found at the property. If the property is proposed or new construction, the builder should provide the cost breakdown of the property.

5. **Intended goals of construction or retrofit**
   Comment: If the subject is an existing building that has been upgraded or retrofitted, it is necessary to have basically the same discussions regarding intended goals, projections, etc. Once the validity of the energy modeling projections is established, the appraiser can make projections about projected energy savings.

6. **Commissioning Report (for high performance building systems and/or solar photovoltaic systems)**
   Comment: Commissioning is a third-party verification process used to evaluate whether the systems are designed, installed, functionally tested, and capable of being operated and maintained to perform in conformity with the owner's project requirements. This process is viewed by a number of institutional investors as a prime mechanism of risk mitigation. This factor should be considered when comparing the subject with its competitive set. The nature and extent of the commissioning process should be considered in the risk analysis.

7. **Tenant leases**
   Comment: Among other things, this is important to analyze who benefits from energy efficient improvements – the owner or tenant. It is also helpful to determining whether the leases within the building are similar to and competitive with those signed at the comparable properties. In the area of green strategies, innovations in tenant improvements (TIs) and space design may impact longer-term costs and result in potential savings. There could be reduced downtime between leases and construction and material costs, as well as reduced risk levels associated with space delivery and construction—depending upon the strategies, design, and components used.

8. **Incentives** (such as property tax rebates, utility rebates or incentives: public sector, private sector or utility)
   Comment: Where incentives are substantially monetary in nature or result in monetary, direct, and exclusive benefits to the project or owner, there is a good chance that the market value of the real property may be affected. The appraiser should be prepared to understand and address the contributory value of incentives. The impact of rebates and incentives should be considered in all three approaches to value, as appropriate. The availability and duration of the incentive should be examined and appropriately incorporated into the relevant approaches. Rebates and incentives should not be confused with income tax effects, such as accelerated depreciation, federal Investment Tax Credits (ITC), or Renewable Energy Credits (RECs) which are generally not considered part of the real property for a market value appraisal. Tax effects may have a material influence on the financial feasibility of a project but care should be exercised to separate income tax effects that accrue to the ownership entity from rebates and incentives that accrue to the real property.

9. **Financing Benefits/Burdens**
   Comment: This is important to determining the extent that a discrete loan that stays with the upgrade package may be below or above market and attractive or unattractive to assume. The appraiser should also balance the non-financial attributes of the green project to determine how many, if any, property rights are burdened. Financing products such as PACE (Property Assessed Clean Energy) may reflect a priority lien to the first mortgage, similar to a bond assessment, and typically survive ownership transfers of the property. Appraisers and their clients should consider how to address and report the impact of such financing when developing the Scope of Work.

10. **Operating Expenses.**
    Comment: Operating expenses – both historical and pro-forma – are important to understanding the ongoing operating expense impacts of a green or high performance property. In addition to the typical two or three years of operating expenses, appraisers and their clients may require more detailed reporting of individual expenses.

Client:		Client File #:	
Subject Property:		Appraisal File #:	

Certification or Verification of Green or Energy Efficient Features		
Certification Program and Ratings Attach the rating worksheet that provides the ratings for each element to provide a better understanding of the features. The worksheet will assist in comparing the subject to sales rated by different organizations.	**USGBC LEED®**	**Certifying Organization:** ☐ USGBC (LEED®) ________________*Define rating system http://www.usgbc.org/leed/certification ☐ Core & Shell Only ☐ Interior Design ____________________ ☐ LEED for Existing Buildings: Operations & Maintenance ☐ Other:________________________ Year Certified: _______ ☐ Report Attached or ☐ Certification viewed on site **Rating:** ☐ LEED Certified: ☐ LEED Silver ☐ LEED Gold ☐ LEED Platinum ☐ Describe Score If not listed:________________
	Green Globes®	**Certifying Organization:** ☐ Green Globes® __________________* *Define rating system http://www.greenglobes.com Year Certified: _______ ☐ Report Attached or ☐ Certification viewed on site **Rating:** ____________________
	Energy Star®	☐ **Energy Star®** http://www.energystar.gov/buildings/about-us Year Certified: _______ ☐ Report Attached or ☐ Certification viewed on site **Rating:** ______________________
	Home Innovation Research Labs (NGBS)	☐ **Home Innovation Research Labs (NGBS)*** http://www.homeinnovation.com/green ***Define rating system** NGBS New Construction:______________________________ NGBS Rennovation of Existing Buildings:______________________ Year Certified: _______ ☐ Report Attached or ☐ Certification viewed on site **Version:** ☐ NGBS 2008 ☐ NGBS 2012 ☐ NGBS 2015 ☐ NGBS ________(year) **Rating:** ☐ NGBS Bronze ☐ NGBS Silver ☐ NGBS Gold ☐ NGBS Emerald
	Other Green Certifying Organization	☐ **Name Certifying Organization:**______________________________ Green Certifying Organization URL (website) ______________________ Year Certified: _______ ☐ Report Attached or ☐ Certification viewed on site **Rating:** ______________________
Additions	Explain any additions or changes made to the structure since it was certified:	
	Do changes require recertification to verify rating is still applicable? ☐ Yes ☐ No	
Recycle Programs	☐ Tenant Recycle Program ☐ Green Operations & Management ☐ Composting Program on Site ☐ Other ____________	

*NOTICE: The Appraisal Institute publishes this form for use by appraisers where the appraiser deems use of the form appropriate. Depending on the assignment, the appraiser may need to provide additional data, analysis and work product not called for in this form. The Appraisal Institute makes no representations, warranties or guarantees as to, and assumes no responsibility for, the data, analysis or work product provided by the individual appraiser(s) in the specific contents of the AI Reports®. AI Reports® AI-821 Commercial Green and Energy Efficient Addendum October 2014

Client:		Client File #:	
Subject Property:		Appraisal File #:	

Comments The worksheets will provide a review of all categories and address the six elements of green building identified on the previous page of this Addendum. The worksheet will more specifically identify the green materials included in the property.	If a property is built green but not formally certified, it still deserves proper description and analysis to value the features. The market analysis is of the structure's physical, economic, and locational attributes and not an analysis of its label alone. If no formal certification was obtained but the structure has green attributes, please describe in this area.

Client:		Client File #:	
Subject Property:		Appraisal File #:	

Site Element			
The following items are considered within the appraised value of the subject property:			
Walk Score	Score:_______	http://www.walkscore.com	
Public Transportation	☐ Bus - Distance:______ Blocks Transit Score _____ http://www.walkscore.com	☐ Train - Distance: _______ Blocks	☐ Subway - Distance: _____ Blocks
Site	Orientation - front faces: ☐ East/West ☐ North/South	Landscaping: ☐ Water Efficient ☐ Native ☐ ☐ Built on brownfield ☐ Wetlands - acres:______	
On Site Water Retention	☐ Dry Pond (size) _______ Acres ☐ Wet Pond (size) _______ Acres ☐ Rain Garden ☐ Vegetated Roof	☐ Drip Irrigation ☐ Smart Irrigation Controllers ☐ Irrigation supplied by wet pond or onsite water source	
Parking	☐ On site ____spaces ___ /1,000 SF ☐ Surface material ____________ (pervious concrete, grass, gravel, shell) ☐ Permeable pavement	☐ Parking spaces reduced based on public transportation proximity ☐ Public parking garage or lot _______ blocks from property	
Comments			

Water Element	
☐ Reclaimed Water System (Explain):____________ ☐ Greywater reuse system ☐ WaterSense® fixtures	☐ Waterless urinals ☐ Low flow or sensor water fixtures ☐ Cistern - Size: ______ Gallons for irrigation ☐ Rain Barrels Provide Irrigation ☐ Other: ________________________
Comments: Identify other features that may be included in the element of water that have not been identified under the Site or Water Efficiency Sections.	

Client:		Client File #:	
Subject Property:		Appraisal File #:	

Energy Element

The following items are considered within the appraised value of the subject property:

Insulation	☐ Fiberglass Blown-In ☐ Foam Insulation ☐ Cellulose ☐ Fiberglass Batt Insulation ☐ Other (Describe):________________ R-Value: ☐ Walls _____ ☐ Ceiling _____ ☐ Floor______
Roof	Construction type: ________________ ☐ Vegetated Roof ☐ Reflective Roof ☐ Other:__________
Windows	☐ ENERGY STAR® | ☐ Low E ☐ U-Value ___ | ☐ High Impact | ☐ Storm | ☐ Double Pane ☐ Triple Pane | ☐ Glazed | ☐ Solar Shades
Day Lighting	☐ Skylights #:_____ ☐ Solar Tubes #:_______ ☐ Other (Explain) ________________ ☐ Daylighting ____________________ ☐ Daylighting –optimized fenestration design ☐ Daylight-responsive electric lighting controls ☐ Daylight-optimized interior design (such as furniture design, space planning and room surface finishes) ☐ ENERGY STAR Light Fixtures ☐ LED Lighting ☐ T-8 Florescent Lighting
Mechanicals **HVAC (Describe in Comments Area)**	ENERGY STAR® Appliances: ☐ Dishwasher ☐ Refrigerator ☐ Office Equipment ☐ Other__________ Water Heater: ☐ Solar ☐ Heat Pump ☐ Tankless ☐ Coil Size: ______ Gal. Other features: chillers, boilers, industrial type mechanicals ________________ ________________ ☐ High Efficiency HVAC SEER:______ Efficiency Rating:____% AFUE* ____% *Annual Fuel-Utilization Efficiency ☐ Heat Pump Efficiency Rating: __________ COP:________ HSPF:________ SEER:________ EER: ________ ☐ Thermostat/Controllers ☐ Other:______________ ________________ ☐ Passive Solar Design (Defined in Glossary) ☐ Programmable Thermostat ☐ Radiant Floor Heat ☐ Geothermal
Utility Costs	Average Annual Energy Cost: $ _______ per kWh $____based on:______________(Utility Bills/I&E Statements) Hours of Operation: ________________ ☐ # Employees: _____ After Hours or weekend hours of use: __________ ☐ Daytime cleaning (reduces energy costs) ☐ Dashboards # _____
Energy Audit	☐ Energy Audit attached Has an energy audit/rating been performed on the subject property? ☐ Yes ☐ No ☐ Unknown If yes, comment on work completed as result of audit.
Comments (Include source for information provided in this section) Attach documents or reference source	Information was provided by:

Indoor Air Quality Element

☐ Energy Recovery Ventilator Unit or Whole Building Ventilation System ☐ Other:____________________	☐ Non Toxic Pest Control ☐ Co2 sensors
Comments: Describe additional features implemented that would affect the indoor air quality. Indoor air quality can be affected by building material choices as well as items listed herein. (See Rating Worksheet for items identified in this category)	

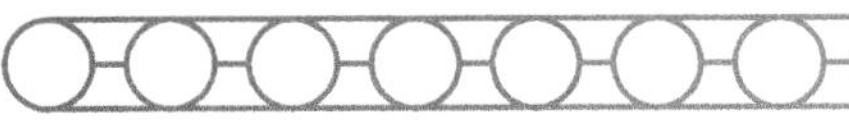

Client:		Client File #:	
Subject Property:		Appraisal File #:	

Maintenance & Operations Element	
☐ Operations & Maintenance Manual ☐ Demountable Walls ☐ Other ___________ ☐ Staff Training Program ☐ Daytime cleaning (reduces energy costs) ☐ Management has Green Training	
Commissioning	☐ Post Occupancy Commissioning ☐ Date of PO Commissioning ________ **Note:** Certifications for certain standards, such as USGBC's LEED EB O&M, are valid for a limited time. In order to maintain that particular certification, the building must be reassessed every five years to determine whether it meets the then-current certification standards. It is essential to verify that a building's certification is valid.
Comments: Note: The information provided on the operations and maintenance reflects details provided by others. Appraisers typically do not have sufficient detail to judge the operations and maintenance of the whole building as a system. Buildings that have been commissioned on a regular basis should have commissioning reports that provide operations and maintenance details by a qualified professional.	

Client:		Client File #:	
Subject Property:		Appraisal File #:	

Commercial/Industrial Solar Worksheet

Property Address or ID:		Date of value:			Appraiser:	
Zip Code:						
The worksheet inputs accommodate the PV Value® tool.		http://pvvalue.com				

Solar Electric (PV)		PV Array #1	PV Array #2	PV Array #3	PV Array #4	PV Array #5	PV Array #6
Leased or owned *							
Years remaining on lease							
Initial net cost if owned		Provide total cost for all arrays					
Current net cost		Provide total cost for all arrays					
RECs (Renewable Energy Credits)	$ per megawatt hr.:						
Real property tax for solar PV system		Solar PV is exempt from real property taxes in some states					
System size in watts (DC watts @STC)							
Array type							
Array tilt							
Array Azimuth							
Azimuth tool can be found at the following link:		http://tools.solmetric.com/Tools/roofazimuthtool					
Age of panels							
Energy production kWh per array or total in first cell	Total production for all arrays kWh						
Source for production							
Location (roof, ground, etc.)							
Type of mount							
Warranty term on PV							
PV panel brand name							
Is PV company still in business?							
Number of inverters							
Age of inverter(s)							
Warranty term on inverter	Years total:			Years remaining:			
Is inverter company still in business?		Company name:					
Utility company name		kWh $/charged by utility company:					$0.00
Evidence of shading							
Evidence of deterioration							
Is there a battery backup system?							
Does the system include lightning protection on both sides of the inverter?							

Documents Reviewed	Reviewed?	In Workfile?
Load analysis		
Shade analysis		
Commissioning form		
Solar installer financial payback analysis		
Warranty terms for inverter		
Warranty terms for solar PV including parts and labor		
Solar PV output monitoring, alert, response, and repair process timing		
If leased, obtain copy of lease and provide terms in comment section below		

Comments:

Roof considerations: Was the roof warranty voided by the PV installation? If the PV installer does not work with the roofing company to ensure that the roof warranty is not voided, additional risk may apply.

Remaining roof life considerations: If the remaining roof life is less than the remaining panel warranty, then an adjustment may need to be made to account for removal and re-installation of the rooftop system.

*NOTICE: The Appraisal Institute publishes this form for use by appraisers where the appraiser deems use of the form appropriate. Depending on the assignment, the appraiser may need to provide additional data, analysis and work product not called for in this form. The Appraisal Institute makes no representations, warranties or guarantees as to, and assumes no responsibility for, the data, analysis or work product provided by the individual appraiser(s) in the specific contents of the AI Reports®. AI Reports® AI-821 Commercial Green and Energy Efficient Addendum October 2014

Client:		Client File #:	
Subject Property:		Appraisal File #:	

Incentives – Amount of Incentive and Terms	
The following items are considered within the appraised value of the subject property:	
Federal	
State	
Local	Note: Tax abatements are available in some areas and make a significant contribution to lower expenses.
Source (For example www.dsireusa.org)	
Comments Incentives offset cost and should be reported in the cost approach section of the report. Incentives	

Completed by:____________________ Title:______________ Date:________

Client:		Client File #:	
Subject Property:		Appraisal File #:	

Commercial Addendum Glossary

Building Envelope: The building envelope is everything that separates the building's interior from the exterior. This includes the foundation, exterior walls, roof, doors and windows.

Energy Recovery Ventilation System: Often called Heat Recovery Ventilators (HRV). These systems replenish the indoor air without wasting all the energy already used to heat the indoor air. In some climates, these systems are also used to handle water vapor in the incoming air.

Earth Advantage Commercial: Earth Advantage Commercial is a green building certification program for small commercial buildings. http://www.earthadvantage.org/commercial/ **Note:** This program does not require energy modeling.

ENERGY STAR®: Energy Star, sponsored by the EPA, rates buildings based on their energy use relative to buildings of similar vintage, design, construction, use and occupancy. Through ENERGY STAR, the nation's most energy efficient buildings can earn ENERGY STAR certification http://www.energystar.gov/buildings/about-us **Note:** The program claims of 35% lower energy costs is not a basis for adjustment in an appraisal. The appraiser must evaluate the efficiency and develop appropriate adjustments using acceptable appraisal methodology.

- **Portfolio Manager:** EPA's online energy management and tracking tool calculates 1 - 100 ENERGY STAR scores for eligible commercial and institutional buildings, such as K-12 schools, office buildings, and many others. Portfolio Manager also allows you to track improvements over time, compare similar buildings within a portfolio, generate reports, and quantify greenhouse gas emissions.
- **Target Finder:** This tool is similar to Portfolio Manager, except it's used to estimate performance. By entering the estimated energy use of a commercial building design or renovation project, you can project its future 1 - 100 ENERGY STAR score.
- **Energy Performance Indicators (EPIs):** Available for 11 different types of industrial or manufacturing plants, EPIs enable energy managers and corporate executives to evaluate the energy efficiency of their plants relative to others in their industry.

National Green Building Standard (NGBS): NGBS is an ANSI-approved green building rating system and part of the International Code Council's (ICC) International Codes (I-Codes). The NGBS provides practices for the design, construction, operation, and certification of new and existing residential buildings, including single family homes and multifamily buildings. Home Innovation Research Labs is the national Adopting Entity and certification agency for the NGBS. www.homeinnovation.com/green

Green Globes®: Green Globes is an online green building rating and certification tool that is primarily used in Canada and the USA. http://www.greenglobes.com

- New Construction/Significant Renovations
- Commercial Interiors (i.e. Office Fit-ups)
- Existing Buildings (offices, multi-residential, retail, health care, light industrial)

Geothermal: A geothermal heat pump uses the constant below ground temperature of soil or water to heat and cool the building. http://energy.gov/energysaver/articles/geothermal-heat-pumps

LEED®: Leadership in Energy and Environmental Design is a green building rating system sponsored by the United States Green Building Council (USGBC). LEED provides building owners and operators with a framework measurable green building design, construction, operations and maintenance solutions. http://www.usgbc.org/DisplayPage.aspx?CMSPageID=1988

- LEED for Building Design and Construction (LEED BD+C) rating systems
- LEED for Interior Design and Construction (LEED ID+C) rating systems
- LEED For Existing Buildings: Operations and Maintenance (LEED EB: O+M) rating systems

Life Cycle Assessment (LCA): LCA is a technique to assess the environmental aspects and potential impacts associated with a product, process, or service, by:

- Compiling an inventory of relevant energy and material inputs and environmental releases
- Evaluating the potential environmental impacts associated with identified inputs and releases
- Interpreting the results to help you make a more informed decision

Source: http://www.epa.gov/nrmrl/std/lca/lca.html

Passive Solar: Passive solar is technology for using sunlight to light and heat buildings with no circulating fluid or energy conversion system. http://rredc.nrel.gov/solar/glossary A complete passive solar building design has the following five elements: (1) aperture (collector) (2) absorber (3) thermal mass (4) distribution (5) control. http://www.nrel.gov/docs/fy01osti/27954.pdf

SEER: Seasonal energy efficiency ratio - The higher the SEER rating, the more energy efficient the equipment is. A higher SEER can result in lower energy costs. http://www.energystar.gov/index.cfm?c=tax_credits.tx_definitions&dts=ssps,mcs,seer,eer .

Water Sense: EPA released its Final Version 1.1 WaterSense New Home Specification. This specification will be effective January 1, 2013 and establishes the criteria for new homes labeled under the WaterSense program and is applicable to newly constructed single-family and multi-family homes. http://www.epa.gov/watersense/new_homes/homes_final.html

Water Heaters: Solar, Heat Pump, Tankless On Demand or Tankless Coil water heaters are described at the following location: http://energy.gov/energysaver/articles/solar-water-heaters.

WaterSense has developed WaterSense at Work, a compilation of water-efficiency best management practices, to help commercial and institutional facilities understand and better manage their water use, help facilities establish an effective water management program and identify projects and practices that can reduce facility water use. http://www.epa.gov/watersense/commercial/bmps.html

Client:		Client File #:	
Subject Property:		Appraisal File #:	

Whole Building Ventilation System: A whole building ventilation system assists in a controlled movement of air in tight envelope construction and may include air-purifying systems. Whole building ventilation equipment is often a part of the forced air heating or cooling systems.

Client:		Client File #:	
Subject Property:		Appraisal File #:	

GREEN PROPERTY VALUATION RESOURCES

Appraisal Institute Introduction to Valuing Commercial Green Buildings
http://www.appraisalinstitute.org/library/bok/IntroGreen.pdf

Appraisal Institute Green Building Education
http://www.appraisalinstitute.org/education/green/default.aspx

Case Studies in Appraising Green Commercial Buildings including functional obsolescence
http://www.appraisalinstitute.org/education/course_descrb/PDFs_for_Web/Course_828/toc-case-studies-green-comm-bldgs.pdf

Capital Markets Briefing Paper green building business case released at the NYSE
http://webstore.ansi.org/FindStandards.aspx?Action=displaydept&DeptID=3144#.UGjO2Y7XfQc

Green Building and Property Value - provides a review of the commercial green building property value identifying the components of green that may materially affect value. This document was developed by the Appraisal Institute and Institute For Market Transformation (IMT)
http://www.imt.org/resources/detail/green-building-and-property-value

Retail Green Lease Primer - This two-page document helps guide retailers and retail owners to improving the efficiency of their facilities. It can be helpful to appraisers in understanding green leases. http://www.imt.org/resources/detail/retail-green-lease-primer

Building Energy Performance Assessment News - This website offers many resources on green mortgage underwriting for commercial and residential properties. Http://www.bepanews.com

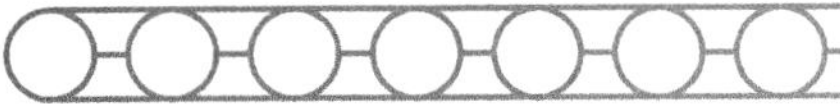

Index